Conflict and Conflict Management

Conflict
and
Conflict Management

by
Joseph S. Himes

The University of Georgia Press
Athens

Copyright © 1980 by the University of Georgia Press
Athens 30602

All rights reserved

Set in 10 on 12 point Times Roman
Printed in the United States of America

Library of Congress Cataloging in Publication Data

Himes, Joseph S
  Conflict and conflict management.

  Bibliography.
  Includes index.

  1. Social conflict. I. Title.

HM136.H48   301.6'3   78-32164
              ISBN 0-8203-0473-5

Grateful acknowledgment is given to Scott, Foresman for permission to reprint material contained in
Fig. 4-3, to the Charles E. Merrill Publishing Co.
for material in Fig. 6-1, and to Macmillan for material in Fig. 6-2.

Contents

PART I. CONFLICT ANALYSIS

1. THE NATURE OF SOCIAL CONFLICT   3
   A Typology of Social Conflicts   6
   The Meaning of Social Conflict   11
   Legitimacy and Nonlegitimacy   17
   Conflict in Contemporary Sociology   22

2. THE EXPLANATION OF SOCIAL CONFLICT   27
   Theories of Conflict   27
   An Explanatory Model of Social Conflict   37

3. SOCIAL STRUCTURE IN SOCIAL CONFLICT   51
   Structural Conditions of Conflict   51
   Conflict in "the Public"   58
   Structural Implementation   60

4. SOCIAL POWER IN SOCIAL CONFLICT   76
   The Meaning and Classification of Power   77
   The Mobilization and Implementation of Power   79
   Black Power:
   Mobilization and Implementation Illustrated   85
   The Organization of Power   91

5. VIOLENCE IN SOCIAL CONFLICT   100
   The Meaning and Explanation of Violence   103
   Theories of Violence   109
   Conditions of Violent Conflict   113
   The Functions of Violence   118

6. THE FUNCTIONS OF SOCIAL CONFLICT   122
   The Manifest Functions of Conflict   124
   The Latent Functions of Conflict   127
   The Dysfunctions of Social Conflict   139

7. THE PREDICTION OF SOCIAL CONFLICT   144
   The Meaning of Prediction   146

Theory and Research in Conflict Prediction   149
A Strategy for Conflict Prediction   154
Predicting Conflict in Soweto   158

PART II. CONFLICT MANAGEMENT

8. INSTRUMENTAL CONFLICT   167
Components and Implementation of Instrumental Conflict 167
Conditions of Nonlegitimate Instrumental Conflict   171
Strategy in Instrumental Conflict   177

9. PREVENTION: ELIMINATING CAUSES   190
The Nature of Conflict Prevention   190
Some Conditions of Conflict Prevention   192
Conflict Prevention: Some Illustrations   198
A Strategy for Conflict Prevention   203

10. PREVENTION: INSTITUTIONALIZING STRUGGLE   212
The Nature of Conflict Institutionalization   212
Some Conditions of Conflict Institutionalization   218
A Strategy for Instrumental Conflict Institutionalization 220
Issues in the Institutionalization of Conflict   231

11. THE RESOLUTION OF SOCIAL CONFLICT   235
The Nature of Conflict Resolution   235
Some Conditions of Conflict Resolution   238
A Strategy for Conflict Resolution   242

12. THE SUPPRESSION OF SOCIAL CONFLICT   257
The Nature of Conflict Suppression   257
Conditions of Conflict Suppression   260
Conflict Suppression Tactics   264
Consequences of Conflict Suppression   274
Continuing Issues in Conflict Suppression   276

REFERENCES   285

INDEX   331

Preface

Until quite recent times most human conflicts have been predatory struggles among relatively small collectivities. The wars of antiquity, the Middle Ages and the early modern era involved small polities and limited numbers of specialized fighters in struggles for territory, populations, plunder, power, and status. The masses of non-elites who were often pawns in these wars engaged typically in such local conflicts as riots, bandit gang-rumbles, and feuds. The expansion of Europe between the fifteenth and nineteenth centuries created a new phase to this small-scale predatory conflict. White Europeans conquered and plundered nonwhites in Africa, the Americas, Asia, Australia–New Zealand and the islands in all the seas.

Thanks to modern industry and technology, in the late modern era international wars typically engaged larger political units and greater numbers of participants. The Napoleonic wars of the late eighteenth and early nineteenth centuries involved most of Western Europe and Western Russia. The Franco-Prussian, the Crimean, and the Russo-Japanese wars were modern binational struggles. It was only in the twentieth century that we could speak of "world wars."

Philosophical innovations of the late eighteenth and early nineteenth centuries generated and justified the claim of the masses of non-elites to the right to help make the decisions which governed their lives. The resulting ferment and tumult produced a new kind of collective struggle called revolution. In the nineteenth century Karl Marx constructed an ideological infrastructure of revolution and packaged it for worldwide dissemination. Revolution swept the Western world and for a time challenged predatory war as the reigning form of human conflict. Between 1775 and 1917 major modern revolutions occurred in North America, France, much of Latin America, and Russia. Internally, in many polities revolution took the form of insurgency and civil war. Following World War II revolution took the form of anticolonial nationalism in much of Asia and Africa. For some contemporary dissidents, e.g., the Moluccans in the Netherlands, the Bader-Meinhoff gang in West Germany, and the Red Brigades in Italy, the distinctive tactic of revolution is terrorism.

Everywhere and at all times some people, perhaps the majority, have longed for peace and security. But it is only in the twentieth century that this longing has been significantly implemented with moral drive, relevant knowledge, and social organization. Revolted by the extravagant death and destruction of World War I, the people of Europe and America came to reject aggressive war as an instrument of national policy and to tolerate the resort to war only in self-defense. Led by President Woodrow Wilson the Allies expressed this moral orientation in the Treaty of Versailles and sought to implement it through the League of Nations. However, hampered by their own mistakes, driven by moral fanaticism, and lacking adequate knowledge, the nations struggled unsuccessfully to maintain international peace.

Following World War II the determination to prevent further war and maintain a structure of peace took a new turn. The victorious countries organized the United Nations and set out, wiser than in 1917, to establish and guarantee a structure of peace. In the late 1940s and early 1950s there was also a flurry of research and experimentation to develop what can be called the science and technology of peace. At the outset this activity was spearheaded by UNESCO. Quickly, though, centers and institutes for research and experimentation to promote peace also sprang up in both Western Europe and North America. Attention focused not only on the problems of international war and peace, but also on local issues of collective conflict as well. Of late, these activities have begun to bear fruit in the limitation of war in the world and in growth of a science and technology of peace. There is increasing willingness on the part of leaders of government and others to apply the growing fund of knowledge and technical skill to real issues of war and conflict.

The lively interest in issues of war and peace that burgeoned following World War II was enhanced in the 1950s and 1960s, particularly in the United States, and applied to the new problems of social movements and riots. The result has been an enormous increase in research and publication on all these issues of conflict and conflict management. These developments are reflected not only in the literature but also in the academic activity of the social sciences, particularly sociology and political science. There is now an important sociology of social conflict. This book seeks to summarize and synthesize some of this accumulated knowledge in both the science of conflict and the technology of conflict management.

Although from the beginning of my professional career in the mid-1930s I have maintained a lively interest in social conflict, I became seriously committed to the study of the subject in the mid-1960s. In 1966, stimulated by Lewis Coser's *The Functions of Social Conflict,* I wrote a paper entitled "The Functions of Racial Conflict" as my presidential address for the Southern Sociological Society. Three years later, when I joined the sociology faculty of the University of North Carolina at Greensboro, I was offered and eagerly accepted the opportunity to teach courses in the sociology of social conflict and social movements. This book summarizes and reports much of what I have learned through these professional experiences. In Part I, I develop a systematic approach to the study of social conflict and apply it in the examination of some leading issues. In Part II, I employ the approach as the basis for investigating leading strategies in conflict management. To assist the reader who may wish to pursue the study of social conflict and conflict management, I have included a list of basic and recent references, as well as a list of bibliographies, at the end of the book.

I am indebted to many people who, over the years, have contributed to the development of this book. Foremost among these are my students who, among other things, for years helped me to review current literature, to clarify and sharpen my ideas, and to edit the manuscript through two revisions. More than that, they encouraged and supported me in those dark days when writing was sheer inspirationless drudgery. Although they were not always aware of it, my colleagues helped me in many important ways. They guided me when I was muddled, drew my attention to important ideas and perspectives, and directed me to significant literature that I had overlooked. While he was still head of the Department of Sociology at the University of North Carolina at Greensboro, Professor Alvin H. Scaff read and commented helpfully on two versions of the manuscript. I am very grateful to these good colleagues. A group of charming young women helped me as research reading assistants. They are Johnna Elliott, Margaret K. Erwin, Betty McVaigh, Marian Neefus, and Mary Rhodes. To each my sincerest thanks. I could not have brought this project to fruition without the patient and loyal help of Mrs. Betty Deskins and Mrs. Helen Taylor, departmental secretaries who uncomplainingly typed and retyped the manuscript. I am also indebted to my devoted wife, Estelle, who put up with me and gave support through the tedious years of authorship. And finally, I owe a great debt of gratitude to the authors of the articles and books that I have used. Some are mentioned in the source notes; others are only listed in the references. To all, however, I speak an enthusiastic word of professional thanks. Although all these persons have made some contribution to this book, I alone am responsible for the ideas and views expressed in it.

JOSEPH S. HIMES

Part I
Conflict Analysis

From the inception of the scientific discipline of sociology, scholars in the field have been interested in the study of social conflict. Late in the nineteenth century two Austrian scholars, Ludwig Gumplowicz and Gustav Ratzenhofer, placed the concept of social conflict at the center of their approach to the study of human society. Writing about the same time, Karl Marx wrote of social conflict as the dynamic force that, in his view, would change the Western world. Social conflict has remained a major issue for sociologists. The result has been a prodigious literature on the subject and a vast range of theories, perspectives, and interpretations. The interest in social conflict was quickened by World War I and intensified as a result of World War II. In the United States further impetus was given to this interest and activity two decades later by the enormities of the social movements that rocked the society. We are now far enough removed in time from these upheavals to survey the field and ask what sociologists have learned about social conflict. Part I of this book makes a modest beginning on that important task.

Conflict analysis is pursued from several different sociological positions. The first task of analysis is to explicate the meaning of social conflict, which is conceptualized by identifying its defining characteristics and described by delineating its most typical manifestations. At the outset it was recognized that the stream of social conflict flows continuously through a field of moral norms which evaluate it and differentiate the permissible forms, the legitimate from the impermissible forms, and the nonlegitimate forms. As conflict develops within this normative field it flares up and subsides intermittently from the level of legitimacy to nonlegitimacy and then back again. The intermittent transformation of legitimate struggle into the nonlegitimate sets the major task of explanation in the study of social conflict. In chapter 2 I examine many different efforts to explain this transformation and seek to synthesize the main ideas in a general conflict-explanatory model. This explanatory paradigm illuminates much of the following analysis and reappears in chapter 7 as the starting point of a strategy of conflict prediction. In chapters 3 and 4 the analysis is advanced from the sociological positions of social structure and social power, both of which are intrinsic in the conception of social conflict. In chapter 5 I examine violence as the leading form of nonlegitimate conflict and turn in chapter 6 to the consequences of conflict. This latter discussion is crucial since it provides a perspective different from the moral norms from which to evaluate social conflict. Part I concludes in chapter 7 with a foray into the fascinating issue of conflict prediction.

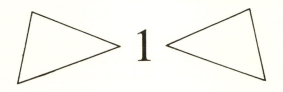

The Nature of Social Conflict

People are aggressive, conflicting creatures. Archaeological and historical records from the earliest times show them engaged in the struggle with their fellows. In ancient times the so-called wars were little more than skirmishes between clans, villages, tribes, or federations of tribes called nations. Alexander's conquest of "the world" was essentially a local fight in the Middle East. The fierce incursion of Genghis Khan and his Tartar hordes across the steppes of Russia into the plains of China and India had few repercussions beyond northeast Asia. The historic struggles among the Greek city-states and the campaigns of Julius Caesar were the only conflicts that left a lasting impression on the course of Western civilization.

Genuine intercontinental wars could occur only after the so-called navigation revolution of the fifteenth and sixteenth centuries in Western Europe. Invention of the sextant and compass, and construction of seaworthy vessels permitted the intrepid sailors of Portugal, Spain, Holland, England, and France to venture beyond the European and North African coastlines. Then began the conquest of the continents and the interminable wars that led to the subjugation of Africa, Australia and New Zealand, Asia, and the Americas. Thus the local feudal wars of Western Europe expanded to continents far beyond the North Sea and the Mediterranean.

Industrialization and the building of nation-states in the eighteenth and nineteenth centuries contributed to the development of modern warfare in the Napoleonic era and its elaboration in the century-and-a-half that followed. These developments pressaged the First World War, which was the prelude to World War II and the dominating threat of a third worldwide war. Meanwhile, the Enlightenment of the eighteenth century and the formulation of the Marxist doctrine of "class struggle" laid the ideological foundations for new types of wars: the national revolution of independence and the interest-group struggle for power, economic advantage, and other secular values. The thirty years following the end of World War II were characterized by a new era of local wars—the first Israeli-Arab war, the Korean conflict, the Algerian affair, the Vietnam

War and scores of lesser wars in Asia, South America, Europe, the Middle East and Africa. In these postwar years, war itself as the dominant form of conflict has been challenged by others—strikes, riots, rebellions, and turmoil of many kinds, both violent and nonviolent.

In the long sweep of history, social attitudes toward conflict as well as its forms have undergone change. Our earliest records, both archaeological and written, reveal few significant or organized oppositions to conflict. War was glorified by the elite classes and endured by the powerless, sometimes enslaved, non-elites. The leaders of the great religions—Confucius, Buddha, Jesus—were voices crying out in a wilderness of bloody conflict for peace and mercy. Throughout the Middle Ages, though, the Roman Catholic Church compiled a tarnished record as the instrument of peace and the agent of mercy and love. The revolutionary changes that destroyed feudalism and ushered in the modern era—the Renaissance, the Reformation, the Enlightenment, the Industrial Revolution—tended to build value-orientations and forces into Western civilization that germinated a new, powerful thrust against conflict. In politics the democratic orientation, as well as the charity movement, the social gospel, and the peace movement, gave momentum to this thrust.

The extravagant brutality and mind-boggling destructiveness of World War I galvanized public opinion to an open opposition to war as a legitimate tool of international relations and social intercourse. Writing of this development, Arendt (1963: 3) asserted that the belief that national aggression is criminal and that war is justifiable only to ward off or prevent aggression, became theoretically and practically significant only after World War I. This seismic shift of world opinion led to important actions reflecting the new view of war and violent conflict. They included, among others, establishment of the World Court, formation of the League of Nations, steady advances in international law, numerous regional agencies for international accord, and the United Nations.

At the same time the conviction spread steadily that social conflict was a proper and important subject of systematic study. From the beginning sociologists recognized conflict as a basic issue of their discipline. Ludwig Gumplowicz (1883) and Gustav Ratzenhofer (1898) in Vienna made conflict the cornerstone of their sociological systems. Georg Simmel (1955), writing in Germany just before World War I, was the first modern sociologist to study conflict systematically. Social conflict, conceptualized as the "class war," became the hypothetical cornerstone of Marx's (1952) politico-sociological schema in the middle of the nineteenth century. The early American sociologists Lester F. Ward (1883), Albion W. Small (1894), Franklin H. Giddings (1896), William Graham

Sumner (1906), and Charles Horton Cooley (1909) saw conflict as a basic and natural process of social interaction. Beginning in the early 1920s, generations of American students learned about conflict from the influential Park and Burgess (1921) text. The current interest in the sociology of conflict dates from the publication of Coser's *The Functions of Social Conflict* in 1956 and Dahrendorf's *Class and Class Conflict in Industrial Society* in 1959.

After World War II the study of conflict burgeoned dramatically. There is now a prodigious literature on the subject, principally from the perspectives of sociology and political science. As revealed by the mass media, social conflict in all its varied manifestations is a leading topic of general interest and attention. Given this growing attention to the issue, we can begin by asking the most basic question, namely, What is social conflict?

One day in the winter of 1976 a radio reporter stopped people on a busy city street and asked them: "Please, will you answer one question? Tell me, what is social conflict?" The first man he stopped was startled and repeated the question in some puzzlement. Then he blurted out: "What is social conflict? Why, it's war like in Vietnam or in Asia, when India attacked Pakistan and set up Bangladesh, or," he hesitated, then added, "like the fighting in Beirut." Reflecting a moment, the next respondent, a middle-aged woman, declared: "Strikes are examples of conflict, teachers in Pittsburgh, doctors in Los Angeles, or airline workers." "The skirmishes over enforced school busing?" the reporter inquired. "Yes," replied several people who had gathered to see what it was all about. At this point a university student interrupted, saying, "Social conflict is the fight for important things, like life, liberty, and the pursuit of happiness, like it says in the Declaration of Independence." "For the Palestinians it's the struggle for turf and independence," a classmate chimed in, and before he was through a freckle-face girl asserted; "Social conflict is the battle for liberation, you know—respect, opportunity, and decency."

These "average citizens" perceived intuitively what social conflict is. They gave the reporter two different kinds of answers to his question. Those who talked about war, strikes, and skirmishes over forced busing defined conflict in terms of what people do. Those who spoke of life and liberty, turf and independence, and liberation and respect conceptualized social conflict in terms of its intended ends. Both definitions are right in part; when put together they produce a more complete definition.

The reporter's question and the people's answers serve to introduce us to the subject-matter of this chapter. The primary task is to present answers to the basic question raised by the radio reporter. Like the people who responded, we will give two different kinds of answers. In the following section we will describe several categories of collective activity that in the aggregate constitute social conflict. In the next major section we will seek to answer the question, What is social conflict?, by dissecting and analyzing the process as an important modal form of social behavior.

A TYPOLOGY OF SOCIAL CONFLICTS

For our first answer to the question, What is social conflict?, we may rephrase the question to read: When social conflict is discussed in this book, what specific forms or patterns of social behavior are envisaged? This section purports to answer that question by presenting a typology of the categories of struggle between collective actors, that may properly be called social conflict. By considering both attacking and defending actors, the forms of struggle can be placed in the typology below. In private conflict and civil strife the attacker is nongovernmental. The defender in private conflict is also nongovernmental, but in civil strife it is a unit of government. The attacker in both social control and war is government; but the defenders are respectively private groups and other governments.

FIGURE 1-1
A TYPOLOGY OF SOCIAL CONFLICTS

Private Conflicts
Civil Strife
Turmoil
Conspiracy
Internal War
Social Control
International War

Private Conflicts

The category *private conflicts* includes struggles between collective actors in which the state or the government is not a primary party to the action. Under this rubric we include feuds, vendettas, gang wars, and gang rumbles. This category also includes that wide range of interreligious, interracial, interethnic, and interclass struggles that characterize most modern societies. In developing societies private conflicts would include interclan and intertribal strife. All modern industrial societies know labor-management conflict and various intrasocietal struggles, such as interregional and rural-urban clashes.

It has been stated that private conflicts do not involve the state or government as a major participant. Sometimes, however, conflicts which in one situation are private, e.g., interreligious, may be international wars in another. Thus in the United States religious struggles are private matters, but in the Middle East or on the Asian subcontinent contending nationality groups also represent different religions. Often also governments enter private conflicts as rule-enforcer or peacemaker.

Private conflicts tend to vary in the degree of organization. Often, though not always, they are well-organized and well-led. Their tactics also vary widely. Sometimes such conflicts are restrained, waged by peaceful methods. At other times, however, they erupt into intense violent struggles.

Civil Strife

We employ Gurr's (1969: 626) term *civil strife* to designate conflicts that involve units and agents of government in some way. Although one collective actor is a private group or organization, the other represents a government, and hence is distinct from private conflict. Gurr (1969: 574) identifies three subtypes of civil strife—turmoil, conspiracy, and internal war.

1. Under the heading *turmoil* Gurr lists such activities as political demonstrations and movements against the government. In this category he also places disturbances and riots, as well as strikes injurious to the public interest. Thus he would categorize as turmoil a rancorous citizens' group at city council that interrupted or prevented the meeting, and a rock-throwing, window-breaking clash with police on a downtown street. Strikes by public school teachers, police, firefighters, railway engineers, and hospital employees are other illustrations. A further instance of turmoil is clashes with the police resulting from confrontations with street crowds.

Often such active conflicts are public expressions of social movements, which view them as tactics in the struggle for "legitimate" rights or ends. Whatever their specific purpose or official role may be, people are involved as "citizens," and so are oriented toward the political organization of the community or society. Gurr's research (1969: Table 17-4, 580) reveals that over half the conflict studied in 114 nations consisted of turmoil.

Although some manifestations of turmoil, e.g., strikes or social-move-ment action, are well-organized and led, others are spontaneous, and poorly organized and led. Because of its very nature turmoil invites pop-ular participation. It is expressed through a wide range of tactics, al-though often these consist of spontaneous improvisations.

American experience in the 1960s familiarized most people with this type of social conflict. People are likely to remember the dramatic events on university campuses, city streets, and Indian reservations. At times turmoil pushed war from the center of attention in the mass media and in popular interest.

2. Gurr uses the term *conspiracy* to refer to limited and secretive plans and actions against a government or its leaders. In these respects it differs from turmoil. Under this rubric are included such actions as secret plots against the government, *coups d'état,* and various kinds of schemes to seize political power. Assassinations of governmental officials as well as plots and plans for assassination are classified as conspiracies. Sometimes these actions are accompanied by small-scale terrorism and guerrilla actions. In every case, whatever their nature, these plans, organizations and actions are aimed against the government and/or some of its offi-cials.

Many events of recent years have familiarized American people with the term *conspiracy*. Numerous earnest, well-meaning spokesmen be-lieved they had evidence of a "communist conspiracy" in the United States. This band of secretive plotters was accused of scheming to take over the government, and so the whole society by a variety of means. The suspicion of conspiracy was so great and so important that a blue-ribbon national commission was appointed to look into the matter in connection with the assassination of President John F. Kennedy. Many people find conspiracy threatening because of the aspect of secrecy. It is believed that the conspirators are planning and plotting against the so-ciety and its well-being while honest citizens are going about their legiti-mate business.

It has been stated that conspiracies are that species of civil strife in-volving secret attacks against the government and/or its leaders. They tend to be well-organized and tightly controlled, since secrecy is essential to their success. Leadership may be good and participants both limited in number and carefully chosen: the theory of conspiracy is built on the notion that too many cooks spoil the broth. Actors in conspiracies tend to use many kinds of tactics, usually chosen rationally for their instrumental value. By the very nature of the organization and action, violence and violence-producing tactics are a common and often favorite tool of conspirators.

3. *Internal war* refers to an organized action of a large sector of a political society in rebellion against and/or withdrawal from a national state. Sometimes internal wars become international when other nations intervene on one side or the other. Greisman and Finsterbush (1974: 38) identified twenty-eight such "international civil wars" in the period 1900 to 1965.

Internal war differs significantly from turmoil and conspiracy. Of the three subtypes of civil strife, this is perhaps the most inclusive. Terms like *insurrection, rebellion, civil war, revolt* and *revolution* refer to various forms of internal war actions. All, however, refer to an organized armed attack against an independent state with the aim of political withdrawal or alteration of the governmental structure.

In some ways the American Civil War of the 1860s is a classic illustration of this subtype. In recent times there have been civil wars or revolutions in Vietnam, Algeria, the Congo, Cuba, Lebanon, and Pakistan. These cases illustrate the essence of the type and suggest the variety of possible outcomes.

This typology of civil strifes—turmoil, conspiracy, and internal war—suggests how one form of conflict may develop into another. The religious struggle between Hindus and Moslems, which had been expressed in part as an internal affair of India or Pakistan, expanded into an international war that later changed into the Pakistani civil war, which produced the nation of Bangladesh. The American Civil War represented the coalition and climax of several streams of internal struggle that had been long in process in the United States.

It has already been stated that civil war and revolution are organized military action of one sector of a polity against the existing government. It therefore is likely to involve the participation in different ways of many individuals and to be rather well-organized and efficiently led. The conflict is always intense and violent. Extensive resort may be made, and especially in recent years has been made, to tactics of terrorism and guerilla action.

Social Control

Social control refers to the actions of governments to resist or counter the conflicts of the collective actors discussed in the foregoing sections.

In many instances governments will be struggling to defend themselves from attacks by hostile groups or organizations. In the case of private conflict, governments will be entering the struggles to enforce the law and reestablish peace. In every case the official authority of the state or some other quasi-official bureaucracy will be engaged in the process of social conflict.

In the case of internal wars, the state is by definition a major participant in the military action. In conspiracies and turmoil the government acts on behalf of itself—and, it may allege, on behalf of the public interest—to suppress, control, or prevent violent or other disapproved conflict acts. With respect to private conflicts, the government plays the role of peace-keeper and guardian of the civic well-being. In the course of fulfilling this role, however, it may be drawn into active conflict.

In this discussion it is neither claimed nor assumed that social control is either inherently legitimate or endowed with a special aura of justification. It is (or appears to be) justified by collective judgments of the community or by self-righteous claims of the control agent. Participants in *all* forms of social conflict claim that their actions are in some way legitimate. However, a judgment of legitimacy is thought to be crucial to the practice of social control. First, the control agent claims that he employs proper forms and amounts of social power to exert control over a conflict actor. Second, he insists that, on the whole, society approves of his tactics. And third, he usually takes it to be true that social control is exercised on behalf of values widely accepted in the community or society. Thus, for example, if the control agent injures or kills people, or damages and destroys property, he claims that such action is justified legally or otherwise, is suitable to the situation, and is in the public interest. As a matter of fact, however, all the conditions of legitimacy are not met in every instance of control action. As a consequence social control itself has become an important issue of controversy in many societies.

International War

The ultimate form of social conflict is international war. Since war has always been among the most disturbing, dramatic, and exciting events in human experience, it has attracted great attention in all ages. An extraordinarily large part of the record of human history is taken up with the accounts of this kind of conflict. Greisman and Finsterbusch (1974: 20–21) identified twenty-five "interstate wars" between 1900 and 1969 that resulted in one thousand or more battle deaths each. They listed an additional nine "imperial or colonial wars" in the period 1900 to 1965.

War is an act or state of military conflict between political units, e.g., nation-states or tribes. The most dramatic recent expressions have been the First and Second World Wars. Wars may be "declared" or "undeclared." That is, one nation may announce formally and publicly that it intends to attack another with military forces, or such announcement may be withheld. In some cases only professional soldiers are involved; in others, though, entire civilian populations are also drawn into military contests.

Of late, since the people of the world have been seriously concerned with avoiding, preventing, or terminating wars, there has been concern with "aggressive" and "defensive" wars. International morality holds that a war of attack, presumably unjustified or poorly justified, is aggressive and thus to some degree reprehensible. On the other hand, the war that defends against such an attack is called defensive and is presumed to enjoy some measure of moral legitimacy. In fact, however, these distinctions are difficult to draw satisfactorily in specific situations. Was the Israeli attack against Jordan and Egypt in 1967 aggressive or defensive? On its surface the war looks clearly aggressive, yet consideration of prior Arab hostility raises some question about this judgment. The fighting in Vietnam has demonstrated that wars may be classified as "formal" or "informal" (or guerilla). This distinction refers to the manner of waging the military action and the traditions of Western warfare.

Since wars are destructive conflicts between whole political organizations, they can exert great influence upon societies. This is doubtless one reason they have fascinated people of all lands and all ages. At times, for example, a vanquished tribe or other group has disappeared. Some members of the defeated group may be taken into slavery and others massacred. Portable property may be taken and all that cannot be taken may be put to the torch, and the place of the vanquished group may be left barren and desolate.

Sometimes a conquering group may invade and occupy the territory of a vanquished group. The defeated group may be reduced to the status of slave or servant, and its property confiscated by the victors. In these cases, victors and vanquished form a new social order in the land.

The Meaning of Social Conflict

We may now revert to the radio reporter's question, "What is social conflict?" That question may best be answered by identifying and delineating the components and characteristics of social conflict as social action.

That is, the question becomes, What do people do when they engage in social conflict? By altering the original question social conflict can be differentiated from other forms of social relations and described in terms of its essential properties.

We begin the task of analysis by sampling some current definitions of social conflict. This exercise will reveal that although these definitions tend to differ in certain respects, all manifest a strong central core of agreement. This core of analytic agreement provides a starting point for reformulating the conceptualization in order to lay the foundation for the subsequent discussion of social conflict in this book.

In 1921 Park and Burgess, heirs to the great sociological tradition, made conflict a central concept in their system of sociology (574–662). They defined conflict as the "conscious, . . . intermittent, . . . personal . . . struggle" for "status." It was understood that this end could be achieved by limiting the opposition. Struggle for status, the central for- mulation in the Park and Burgess study, has remained a central idea, although later scholars have conceptualized the struggle in somewhat different terms. Park and Burgess also specified that conflict was inter- mittent and personal action. These characteristics have sometimes been difficult to demonstrate empirically, and so have tended to disappear from later definitions. The idea that conflict is "conscious" behavior has persisted, but in later discussions has acquired a meaning that Park and Burgess did not perceive.

Mack and Snyder (1957: 218–19) identified the "properties" of social conflict. In the aggregate these properties constitute a definition of the concept and can be listed as follows. (1) Conflict arises from scarcity of positions and resources. (2) It involves at least two parties. (3) The parties are engaged in interaction composed of opposing actions and counteractions. (4) Their behavior is intended to thwart, injure, annihi- late, or otherwise control the opposition, thus enabling the contending parties to gain at each other's expense. (5) Conflict also involves the acquisition or exercise of power, or the attempt at acquisition or exercise. (6) Conflict has important social consequences.

In this analysis Mack and Snyder add several dimensions to the mean- ing of social conflict. They point out that conflict involves the acquisition and use of social power, i.e., the ability to resist or control the opponent. This idea is crucial to the concept and is examined at length in a later chapter. These writers also note that conflict enables actors to gain at each other's expense. This idea is important, for if an actor were not in the way of another actor's acquisition of important values, there would be no occasion for struggle. That social conflict has important social consequences is fundamental to the study of social conflict and constitutes the main premise of the "conflict and change" perspective in sociology. The issue of consequences is examined in a later chapter.

One of the most influential definitions of social conflict was published by Coser in 1968 (232). He wrote: "Social conflict may be defined as a struggle over values or claims to status, power, and scarce resources, in which the aims of the conflicting parties are not only to gain the desired values but also to neutralize, injure, or eliminate their rivals." He goes on to explain that conflict may occur between individuals (e.g., rivals for an academic prize, a business promotion, or a beloved's affections), between groups (e.g., a labor strike, a juvenile gang-rumble, a political insurrection, or an international war), and between an individual and a group (e.g., one policeman vs. a street gang, Joan of Arc against the Church, or a citizen who defies the government by refusing to file an income tax return). Each source quoted either states or implies that there are only two sides to a conflict even though there may be many different participants. Devices like federation, alliance, and coalition permit several actors to struggle together on either side of a conflict.

This definition is consistent with Coser's earlier work (1956: 48–55) in which he differentiated "realistic" and "nonrealistic" conflict. Struggles against collective opponents for the acquisition of scarce values are realistic because they are means toward specific external ends, namely, gaining a scarce value. Thus the strike of a labor union for higher wages and fringe benefits is realistic conflict. In the eyes of an aggressor, a guerrilla or terrorist attack may be seen as realistic insofar as such tactics constitute instruments for the achieving of external goals. Thus, in terms of his definition, when Coser speaks of "social conflict," he is thinking of realistic conflict.

By contrast, nonrealistic conflict was said to be tension-releasing, self-rewarding aggressive action. It serves to express the feelings of a conflict actor rather than to achieve goals external to him. Family feuds and gang rumbles are typical examples of nonrealistic conflict. This kind of conflict is usually not well thought out and often becomes intense and rancorous. Although the purpose of nonrealistic conflict may be self-satisfaction, it always has some unintended consequences for the social system. Sometimes the unplanned effects may be good for the social system, that is, socially constructive. More often, though, the functions of nonrealistic conflict are undesirable or actively harmful. For that reason, this study minimizes the issue of nonrealistic conflict and concentrates on the study of realistic struggle.

The definition of social conflict can now be reformulated to take account of the issues discussed above. Social conflict refers to purposeful struggles between collective actors who use social power to defeat or remove opponents and to gain status, power, resources, and other scarce values. Typical illustrations include international wars, rebellions and revolutions, urban riots and gang wars, labor strikes, religious struggles, protest actions, and social movement struggles.

Social conflict is purposeful behavior. The parties intend to gain scarce values and to overcome obstructing resistance. The actors have usually thought about and talked out what they will do, and so regard their actions as "sensible" or "smart." For example, a labor strike is almost always preceded by some exploration of the situation and planning by the union. Tomlinson (1968: 417–28) and Spillerman (1970: 627–49) have argued that the big-city riots of the mid-1960s expressed purposeful action on the part of the American black community.

But to say that conflict is purposeful is not to claim that it is logical or efficient. Sometimes antagonism, fear, or avarice may distort collective judgment, thus leading to ill-considered plans and actions. Sometimes one or both parties may have inadequate or incorrect information upon which they are basing their plans and decisions. It often happens that the tactics chosen are dictated by a specific ideology and therefore may be inappropriate for the conflict action in hand.

Conflict takes place within a social structure that qualifies it in various ways. For example, racial protest action is likely to occur within local communities. A labor union strike takes place under the aegis of federal and state laws and with oversight of various governmental agencies. The national government and social organization constitute the structural setting of revolutions and many rebellions. The study of these and other conflicts must take account of the relevant units of social structure.

The purpose of conflict is to gain or retain desired values which are usually believed to be in scarce supply because others own or control them. For example, in 1937 the Japanese attacked China to gain territory in Manchuria for the large and rapidly growing Japanese population. Religious groups may fight because each claims to have the ultimate truth, the true faith, or the only correct doctrine. Disadvantaged groups like women, blacks, and youth may struggle against the "establishment" for "liberation" because they feel that they are exploited, oppressed, and treated with disrespect. The values in contest may be tangible (e.g., territory or resources), or intangible (e.g., power, status, or ultimate truth).

An essential element in social conflict is the belief of one collective actor that another is the obstacle to its having the values that it desires.

In order to gain or maintain these desired values—power, status, resources, and other things—the obstructing group must be removed. This requires the use of social power, since the obstructing group will not voluntarily give up the values in contest. Power can be used in many ways to remove the obstructing groups, the resistance, the opponents, the enemies. Power may be used to "neutralize" them, i.e., to make them incapable of obstructing the achievement of the goal. For example, some groups use power in nondestructive ways to make it morally difficult or impossible for their opposition to resist them by violent methods. A powerful authority may neutralize an adversary, a minority group, for example, by dramatically conceding a small point to make the group's larger demands appear unreasonable and the group ungrateful. Power may be used to defeat an opponent, i.e., to make him incapable of resisting further. Defeat may be administered in an election, in a struggle for a single prize, or on a battlefield. However, in order to execute these actions and gain the desired goals, an actor must have techniques for acquiring and manipulating power.

Although the ultimate goal of social conflict may be the acquisition of desired values, an intervening aim must be the removal of those groups that obstruct or limit the achievement of this end. Thus the social operations of conflict are directed against the inhibiting or interfering collective actors. But since the opposing collective actors wish to retain or obtain the same scarce values, they engage in the same kind of social operations. These collective conflict operations are called "tactics."

A conflict tactic may be defined as a specific collective action which mobilizes and applies social power against an opponent in the course of conflict relationship with him in order to initiate a change that will facilitate the attainment or retention of desired values. Thus, as a sociological phenomenon, social conflict is a struggle or contest between collective actors by means of mobilizing and applying social power. The range and variety of specific collective actions that may be conflict tactics are virtually limitless. Concepts like persuasion and propaganda, boycott and strike, blackmail and threat, terrorism and guerrilla operations, demonstrations and siege, civil disobedience and provocation, and military actions suggest some of the kinds and types of tactics that are widely used in social conflict. In sociological literature many of these devices have been examined. For example, recent studies have explored the nature and efficacy of propaganda in war, civil protest in Northern Ireland, land invasion in peasant rebellions, threats in protest situations, and the types and dimensions of nonviolence. In these inquiries many kinds of collective actions are operationalized in analysis to show how power is employed to influence opponents. In social conflict all these are operations of tactics.

However varied or unique, conflict tactics reveal two salient components. First, they are collective actions. They are acted out by labor unions, military units, political cells, or other subdivisions, or by business units, task forces, social movements, and other units of social organization. Often, however, the collective actors are not formally organized. They participate in ad hoc or relatively informal patterns of organized behavior. Typical illustrations include boycotts, demonstrations, bloc votings, civil disobedience and so on almost without end. These modes of ad hoc organization have been called "mass-participation activity patterns" (Himes, 1973: 62–63).

These illustrations serve also to indicate that organization in conflict tactics is highly variable. The groups of actors are sometimes well-organized, sometimes not. In some cases organization is permanent while in others it is transitory. Sometimes it is formal and in other cases rather casual and informal. What is crucial is the fact that variable numbers of individuals pool and systematize their actions in various ways for the purpose of mobilizing and applying social power against an opponent.

The second salient component of conflict tactics is the power operation. Power is mobilized by manipulating a value or a resource of importance to the opponent in a way that he perceives as disadvantageous or threatening. For example, striking workers withhold their labor from employers and boycotting customers withhold their buying power from merchants. Voters withhold votes from certain candidates and concentrate them in support of others. Sometimes collective actors manipulate the sense of safety in the opponent by threatening or actually inflicting injury or destruction. A siege limits the movement and safety of the victim and civil disobedience threatens the sanctity and validity of the law. After examining Gandhi's tactic of "satyagraha," i.e., nonviolent resistance, Tinker (1971: 775–88) concluded that its effectiveness rested upon the fact that the government or other establishment must have the tacit assistance and open cooperation of hundreds and even thousands of persons to maintain its advantageous position.

In the conflict process the tactical operation is aimed and interpreted in such a way that the opponent is made to understand that relief can be purchased only or mainly by the termination or reduction of his resistance to the attacker. The essential relationship thus is one of quid pro quo. Martin Luther King, Jr. (1963: 81) perceived this fact when he explained that by nonviolent direct action blacks aimed to create such a crisis and generate so much tension that whites who had refused to negotiate would be forced to face the issues in contest. Ruf (1971: 201–211) reported that Bourguiba's tactic was to bring so much moral pressure on France by accusing that country of racism, imperialism, and inhumanity, that relief could be gained only by granting independence and freedom to Tunisia. Power (1972: 37–55) examined the tactic of civil disobedience, concluding that the aim was to embarrass, enlighten, and stimulate the opposition, offering relief from this pressure in exchange for modification of the detested legal norms.

Political violence and war use injurious, damaging, and destructive tactics to achieve change. The aim is to weaken the opposition until he is ready to grant demands and access to desired values in exchange for escape from further injury, damage, and destruction. When threats are used the promise of political violence may function to mitigate the quid pro quo exchange and thus preclude actual injury, damage, or destruction.

Although the aim of all tactics is clear—to remove the opposition and gain the desired value—this end is not always the actual outcome. Sometimes the tactic is inappropriate, inadequate, or otherwise ineffective. At other times the tactic employed not only fails to remove the opposition and facilitate gaining the desired value, it provokes unexpected resistance which intensifies the struggle and may, in some situations, lead to defeat. Some of these consequences of conflict tactics will be discussed at greater length below.

LEGITIMACY AND NONLEGITIMACY

Once collective actors have established contact, interaction between them is continuous, revealing a variable mixture of conflict and cooperation. In some situations collective actors may find it gratifying, advantageous, or necessary to collaborate in order to meet certain desires or needs. In others, however, the actors may be divided and set in mutual opposition by the quest for scarce status, power, resources, and other values. Speaking of this matter, Cooley (1918: 39) wrote many years ago that the more one reflects on the matter, the more evident it becomes that conflict and cooperation are not separable processes but really components of the same process, a variable mix of both. These two basic forms of interaction tend to limit each other and to exert both a cohesive and a divisive effect upon the relationship. Instability enters the relationship in part because of the variations of the proportions (or strengths) of the two interactive components.

At the same time every social system tends to establish norms that prescribe the cooperation-conflict mix that is regarded as legitimate. These norms prohibit or limit variations from this acceptable standard and establish sanctions against impermissible deviations. The approved mixture of cooperation and conflict tends to vary from time to time in the same society as well as from one society to another at the same time. For example, in the United States the decade of the 1960s was given to much more social conflict than the preceding ten years. Skolnick (1969: 10–15) has listed periods of intense and violent conflict in American history which were separated by periods of relative calm. Northern Ireland is torn by dissension and violence while the Republic of Ireland appears relatively quiet. Dahrendorf (1959: 239) has observed that conflict tends to vary both in intensity and violence. Such variations tend to increase and decline in a manner that Park and Burgess (1921: 574) called "intermittent."

Since social conflict is continuous and ubiquitous in human society, it is to some degree tolerated. That is, the norms of every society specify or admit that some conflict is permissible. However, no social system tolerates all levels and forms of conflict. Generally, conflict of high intensity and violence is not tolerated because it is perceived as threatening to the well-being or the survival of the system. Coser (1968: 234) distinguishes between "conflicts that exceed the limits imposed by societal consensus and those taking place within the basic consensus."

Conflicts may be defined as legitimate when they are required, endorsed, or permitted by the universalistic norms of an inclusive social system, for instance, that of a society or a community. Terms like nonviolence, protest, struggle, and defensive war reveal popular perception of this fact. The property of legitimacy may be attributed to both the ends and the means of conflict. Turner (1969: 818–19) points out that during the racial struggle of the mid-1960s, violent as well as nonviolent protest under certain conditions was perceived as legitimate. The federal government officially classified the actions of the Indians at Wounded Knee as "protest," even though some groups perceived them as nonlegitimate.

On the other hand, conflicts that are prohibited or disapproved by the universalistic norms of inclusive systems, conflicts "that exceed the limits imposed by societal consensus," as Coser (1968: 234) puts it, are defined as nonlegitimate. Terms like *violence, political conflict, rebellion,* and *aggressive war* reveal collective recognition of this judgment. The management of nonlegitimate conflict is a basic condition of social organization and a necessary activity in all social systems. The conflicts that are defined as nonlegitimate within inclusive systems may at the same time be perceived as legitimate within constituent units of those systems. For example, by reference to the universalistic norms of Northern Ireland and the United Kingdom, terrorism is nonlegitimate. Nevertheless the Irish Republican Army considers these tactics as legitimate means to its collective ends. At the same time it is evident that legitimacy of conflict is defined differently by persons in different locations of the social structure. For example, members of the Protestant community of Northern Ireland consider maintenance of the traditional system to be legitimate, but the Catholics believe violence and terrorism are permissible means of destroying this system. Such divergent perceptions of the legitimacy of conflict reflect the pluralisms and contradictions of inclusive normative systems.

In the history of every inclusive social system the spheres of legitimate and nonlegitimate conflict tend to change in both scope and content. The boundary between the two spheres is therefore marked by a crooked and shifting line. Change in this realm is both uneven in rate and irregular in pattern. These variations issue from the fact that change depends on both time and place. Therefore, in the study of social conflict it is essential to know and to recognize the rules of legitimacy that are in effect in a given place at a given time.

The outcome of conflict as well as its goals and tactics may be differentially perceived as legitimate. For example, Hamilton and Wright (1975: 37) observed that the outcome of World War I was regarded as legitimate by the French. However, the German soldiers who knew they were undefeated in the field saw the outcome as nonlegitimate, and felt no better even though they were told that Germany had lost because of a stab in the back.

Changes in the legitimacy and the perception of legitimacy of conflict are widely reported. As early as 1963, contemplating the nonviolent civil rights movement of blacks in the United States, Vander Zanden (544) asserted that within the inclusive American social system the blacks' tactic of nonviolent resistance, which had been widely regarded as nonlegitimate, had gained a significant degree of legitimacy. By 1969, after observing the big-city riots of blacks, Turner (815–31) could write that under certain conditions even violence was regarded as a protest tactic

and therefore legitimate. The cliché *white backlash* reflects recognition of
the sporadic reversals and rejections of the trend toward the expanding
legitimacy of conflict on the part of blacks.

The tendency to legitimate formerly taboo modes and levels of conflict is illustrated in the experience of many societies. In the long struggle
of the Irish for independence, the spirit of belligerency intensified sharply
in the years around World War I and became institutionalized in the Irish
Republican Army. The militaristic inclination of the Jews was strength-
ened dramatically after the founding of the state of Israel in 1948. Establishment of a Marxist socioeconomic system in Russia launched that
nation on a career of aggressive conflict. Franklin (1956) has explored
the rise of a martial spirit and the legitimation of insurrection prior to
the Civil War in the "Old South." Jablow (1966: 10–12) and Mishkin
(1966: 5–25) revealed how acquisition of the horse complex in combination with pressure from expanding white settlement functioned to
generate ferocious hostility among the Comanches, Apaches, and other
previously peaceful plains Indian tribes.

Until recently in the history of Western civilization, warfare was accepted as a monopoly of the various elites, be they hereditary, political,
or religious. War was not the business of the peasants; it was their fate.
Some peasants fought as soldiers for their masters, but all were pawns in
the game of warfare. The decisions, the strategies, the negotiations of war
remained the exclusive business of the elites. The enlightenment of the
seventeenth and eighteenth centuries and the outbreak of the American
and French revolutions brought this monopoly to an end. The peasants
in France and the settlers in America became prime opponents of the
traditional elites. A new form of collective conflict, the popular revolutionary war, was invented, legitimized, and diffused. In the mid-nine-
teenth century, Marx consolidated the ideological justification of this new
form of war. In the late nineteenth and early twentieth centuries popular
revolutionary warfare emerged as a leading form of collective conflict.
By the middle of the twentieth century the protest and revolutionary
movement had become the primary mode of mass struggle in all modern
societies.

Social systems endow conflict with legitimacy for many different reasons. Some qualify conflict as legitimate in the name of moral and religious values. For example, Mohammed led his Moslem hordes into
endless holy wars. Other societies eschew war and aggression for secular
reasons. After gaining a position of dominance in Western Europe, after
building a powerful navy, and after creating a worldwide empire, the
British took a dim view of war and strove to maintain the *pax Britannica*.

In the Declaration of Independence the American colonists endorsed revolution as a legitimate way for suppressed people to gain their freedom and independence. A century and more later, however, the United States found rebellion and revolution abhorrent. Whatever the justification, it seems evident that the demarcations of legitimate and nonlegitimate conflict reflect self-interests of inclusive social systems.

The definitions of conflict legitimacy issue from three main sources: established tradition, collective policy, and political authority. Tradition, policy, and authority are not discrete sources, but tend to reinforce each other in all systems. For example, the current tendency to denigrate war as a mode of international relations reflects public policy and tradition in the United States; it is also qualified by the authority of the nation.

It seems clear that the bellicose stance of the Soviet Union is established and maintained by authority of the government. However, insofar as a tradition has grown up within the Soviet system, the legitimacy is also sustained by this source. In the Marxist system tradition assumes the form of ideology. But there is no evidence that the orientation toward war has resulted from public debate of the issue. Cantril (1942: 136–50) has shown that the decision of the United States to declare war against Nazi Germany in 1942 came after months of debate. The act of the Congress formalized a collective decision that had been taken by the American people. With this decision and official act the nation had legitimated war against the Nazis. In many societies the relative mixture of legitimacy and nonlegitimacy with regard to conflict arises from a powerful tradition. This fact is illustrated in the pacifism of the Zunis and Hopis and the aggressiveness of the Kwakiutls. The ferocious orientation of the Comanches and Apaches, however, was generated by disadvantageous relations with white settlers. Yet even with such preliterate peoples the orientation toward conflict represents to some degree a collective judgment of each contemporary generation.

The distinction between legitimate and nonlegitimate conflict raises two issues that are basic to the analysis presented in this book. The first is concerned with explanation of the initiation or cause of conflict. The initiation of conflict takes expression in two kinds of situations, although the process of causation is the same in both. It was said above that when collective actors first come into contact an interactive process combining cooperation and conflict is initiated and continues so long as contact is maintained. For example, Europeans and American Indians could engage in conflict only after Europeans had settled in significant numbers on the American continents. Racial conflict in a western city can erupt only after significant numbers of blacks have taken up residence in the city and established continuing relations with whites. Part of the sociological task of causation is to explain the initiation of conflict in this type of situation.

The initiation of social conflict is signaled also by the transformation of legitimate struggle into a nonlegitimate form. This is the situation to which Park and Burgess (1921: 574) referred when they spoke of intermittency. An explanation of the causes of conflict must take this transformation in the form and level of ongoing conflict into account. This double explanatory issue is examined at length in the following chapter.

The second issue raised by the distinction between legitimate and nonlegitimate conflict inheres in the widespread urge to manage nonlegitimate conflict. Since nonlegitimate conflict violates or seems to violate important social norms, many individuals and groups are moved to manage it. Management may be concerned with the techniques and processes of terminating or limiting nonlegitimate conflict, or of restoring the sagging legitimacy of the establishment that is under attack by a dissident group. These issues are examined at greater length in the latter part of this book.

CONFLICT IN CONTEMPORARY SOCIOLOGY

In contemporary sociology social conflict has regained the importance as a theoretical perspective and area of research that it enjoyed at the beginning of the century. Coser (1956: 16) wrote that American sociologists of that time perceived themselves as social reformers. The science of sociology would help them to understand social problems and to devise means of remedy. Conflict was seen to be a creative force that could be harnessed to produce reform and lead to progress. They wrote and spoke for a professional and public audience that was deeply committed to the improvement of society.

Decline of Conflict

However, in the 1940s and 1950s American sociologists lost their interest in the study and utilization of social conflict. Scientific attention was focused on the analysis of social systems, the achievement of consensus and the maintenance of social equilibrium. Conflict not only no longer captivated their attention as a fruitful issue for investigation, it was also perceived as injurious to the consensus of a society and the balance of systems. Speaking of the sociologists of this era, Coser (1956:

20) wrote that they centered attention upon problems of social statics rather than the dynamic aspects of social systems. The older sociologists discussed the need for structural changes; the later generation stressed the need for individual adjustment to existing structures. These latter professionals replaced the study of social conflict with analyses of tension, strain, and psychological malfunction.

As the older conflict sociologists were superseded by the new structural-functionalists interested in structural maintenance, conflict itself came to be viewed more and more negatively. It was seen as having primarily disruptive dissociating and dysfunctional consequences. When these sociologists spoke of conflict, they tended to call it strain, or tension. Such an attitude toward conflict was expressed by calling it "pathological." The result of this radical reversal of interest in conflict was that it virtually disappeared as a topic of serious study and discussion in American sociology. In 1950 Bernard (56: 11–16) asked, "Where is the modern sociology of conflict?" In 1970 Appelbaum (93) lamented that the study of conflict had virtually disappeared from British and American sociology in the twentieth century.

In 1956 Coser (27) suggested some of the reasons for the shift of interest in sociology from the study of social conflict. The most important factors were the rise of applied sociology, the utilization of research personnel and findings by public and private bureaucracies, and the consequent loss of the freedom to choose the problems of research and writing. This shift produced a new audience for sociology and sociologists that was concerned basically with the preservation of the existing order and the prevention of change. Conflict thus appeared as threatening and dysfunctional. The autonomous reform-oriented audience of sociology of an earlier period had largely changed by the time Coser wrote in the 1950s. Politically, this was a time of conservatism and the abhorrence of radicalism. These latter sociologists found the consumers of their theories and findings among such groups as social workers, mental health experts, religious leaders, educators, and public and private administrators who, in the aggregate, were concerned with strengthening common values and minimizing conflict and dissension. Coser (1956: 29) said that the sociologists' images of themselves tended to change from self-conscious advocates of reform to troubleshooting experts in human relations.

The Revival of Interest in Conflict

Even as Coser was writing in the mid-1950s, while most sociologists were still preoccupied with issues of structural maintenance, social consensus, and system equilibrium, a few had rediscovered conflict as a fruitful perspective for research and theorizing. The leaders in this return to the earlier perspective include Bernard, Coser, Dahrendorf, and Gluckman.

Although the single most influential event of this revival was publication of Coser's *The Functions of Social Conflict*, Williams (1972: 12) has shown that significant publications from this new perspective had begun as early as 1947. Coser attacked sterile functionalism by using the functional method to demonstrate that conflict is not always dysfunctional or pathological and to reveal that it has system-adaptive and enhancing consequences. The principal findings of this landmark study are summarized in chapter 6. Here we can illustrate the nature of these findings by citing a few of Coser's propositions. He revealed that instead of being disintegrating, conflict between collective actors often strengthens the internal cohesion and structure of both. It was argued that institutionalization of goal-oriented social conflict, instead of always threatening social systems, often functions as a safety-valve, helping to maintain their integrity and stability. Many limited criss-crossing conflicts, rather than tearing the social order apart, function to sew it together. Coser showed that instead of always being dysfunctional and disruptive, conflict produces social change. For example, goal-oriented "realistic" conflict can revitalize old norms and generate new ones, thus altering the system in important ways.

This change of perspective as well as the new place of conflict in contemporary sociology can be indicated by examining a series of events and developments. In the three decades since 1940 a series of dramatic conflicts forced this issue to the center of world attention. They include, among others, World War II; the Korean, Algerian, and Vietnamese wars; numerous more or less national rebellions and revolutions of independence; and riots of many kinds and in many places, especially in the United States. The impact of these and other conflicts stimulated many kinds of conflict-related activities in many places. These activities included the construction of international agencies to control or prevent war, peace movements in many nations, the establishment of research and planning centers in many countries, and great activity by social scientists everywhere to provide the information and insights required by these applied efforts.

Suddenly there was a great demand for the empirical findings and theoretical insights of social scientists regarding war and peace. To their chagrin, however, it was discovered that they had little reliable theory and few hard empirical findings. In these circumstances the study of social conflict gained the bureaucratic and popular importance that it had been denied for a long time. The resulting burst of activity can be revealed in several ways. The United Nations, through UNESCO, set international teams of social scientists to work on problems of war and peace. Many universities in the United States and abroad established academically based centers and institutes for research and experimentation in this field. American involvement in rebuilding war-torn Europe and Japan and foreign-aid programs in the developing world drew many other social scientists into research and scholarship on war- and peace-related problems. The violent student movement and youthful black and white riots further involved the United States government in research on problems of social conflict. In American colleges and universities social conflict again became a respectable topic of study in the social sciences. Departments of sociology, political science, and history added courses to their curricula on this issue.

These developments indicate the swing of sociological concern from exclusive or major interest in problems of consensus, stability, and equilibrium back to social conflict and social dynamics. They provide ways to suggest the present place of social conflict in sociology. Speaking of the growth of knowledge in the field, Williams (1972: 12) concludes that only a cursory search of the literature on conflict and related issues produced almost five hundred "hypotheses and empirical generalizations." The point may be dramatized by itemizing some of the indicators of this trend.

FIGURE 1-2

SOME INDICATORS OF THE PLACE OF CONFLICT IN
CONTEMPORARY SOCIOLOGY

Government sponsored and funded research.

Research centers or institutes, university-based or otherwise.

Professional associations concerned with issues of war, conflict, and peace.

Professional journals devoted to conflict-related issues.

The volume of book publication on conflict-related topics.

Academic indicators—courses, students, faculties.

Although interest in conflict is again high, the roles, self-images, and audience of the sociologists of conflict today are different from those of the earlier period. At present a growing proportion of sociologists perceive themselves as agents of social reform and societal change. They teach, write, and speak to and for an audience that is committed to peace and dedicated to making far-reaching change in the social order. These new sociologists have produced a staggering volume of empirical research and theoretical generalization on virtually every manifestation of social conflict. But the reform orientation of both sociologists and their audience is different from that of the early part of the century. Today's reformers are not so certain as their predecessors that they can or want to save the traditional system. They want to change it, sometimes in very fundamental ways.

At the same time, the current audience of sociologists is younger and contains more laymen than that of the early reformers. Much of this contemporary audience is nonprofessional, autonomous, and holds no public office. This audience is also to a significant extent drawn from the professional and administrative sectors, but it is motivated more by a sincere desire to understand the society than by a desire to defend the status quo.

The sociology of social conflict today, therefore, is likely to be more scientifically sophisticated and less action-oriented than that of a half century ago. As scientists, today's sociologists are seeking to perform a technical service, that of providing research findings, theoretical perspectives, and realistic insights for agents of change while retaining their investment and concern for the uses and consequence of their contributions. The activist audience can use these products of science for the tasks of reform.

This chapter has examined the meaning of social conflict in two main ways. First, the denotation of the term was given by means of a typology of modes of conflict activity. From another perspective, the chapter has explored the meaning of social conflict in terms of its operational components. The critical issue of legitimacy was discussed and the chapter concluded by considering the study of social conflict in contemporary sociology. In the next chapter we will explore the issue of the causation of social conflict.

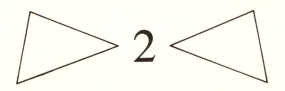

2

The Explanation of Social Conflict

People have always been both fascinated and repelled by the excitement of horror and violence. Some individuals have gone further, seeking to understand and explain these striking phenomena. These are among those thoughtful people who through the ages have pondered the ancient problem of man's inhumanity to man. We can state the question they face this way: Why is there so much war and violence in the world? We can phrase the issue even more sharply: How can we explain the cause of social conflict?

In the effort to answer such questions, thoughtful people have used the resources of knowledge and skill that were available to them. For a long time the data they could draw upon consisted principally of their own personal observations and the accounts (both oral and written) of travelers, old soldiers, and others who had had the opportunity to observe wars and violence. Until recently, also, the scholars' methods of analysis, generalization, and interpretation were limited and sometimes crude. In recent years, however, sophisticated methods of survey research, statistical analysis, and logical interpretation have been applied to the investigation of social conflict.

As suggested in chapter 1, the topic of this chapter is the cause of social conflict, i.e., both the initiation of struggle between collective actors and, especially, the transformation of legitimate into nonlegitimate conflict. Sociological thought on this issue is extensive and varied. Important contributions have been made by scholars throughout the centuries. Here we review many of these contributions and attempt to synthesize and systematize relevant elements of structure, social psychology, and process into a formulation which is both explanatory and predictive.

THEORIES OF CONFLICT

Scholars searched in many places for primary explanations. Some believed they found the key in the individual's heredity. These scholars fashioned the "instinct" theory of conflict. While agreeing that the source of conflict resided within the individual, other scholars formulated the causal force as "tensions" issuing from certain aspects of the social experience. Hegel, Marx, and their followers directed attention to the interactive process itself as the locale of the causal source of conflict. Some other scholars believed that its genesis lay within changes of the social structure. The structural explanation was formulated in various ways. In recent years there is increasing consensus among scholars that some expression of frustration may be the basic causal factor in the explanation of social conflict. The argument is that the frustrations of every social system lead to discontent which under certain circumstances can solidify into social conflict.

Early Theories

In the early years of this century the general instinct theory was the reigning perspective on human social behavior. McDougal (1908), a social psychologist, argued that every individual was born with a full complement of instincts that provided adequate explanations of all his social behavior. Among these instincts were several—pugnacity, acquisitiveness, and self-protection—that were said to function to explain his conflict actions. The explanation of conflict, as of all social behavior, consisted of identifying the proper instinct and indicating how it was triggered and how it operated.

In 1921 Robert E. Park and Ernest W. Burgess (577–78) based their theory of conflict on the idea of instincts. They declared that it was pointless to claim that hostility is not grounded in man's original nature. Speaking of racial conflict they said that there is an instinctive factor in racial prejudice based on the fear of the unknown and unfamiliar. They argued therefore that conflict was universal and natural in human society. In their judgment this instinctive tendency toward conflict was stimulated by racial and cultural differences. While conflict between all kinds of individuals and groups was found, interpersonal antagonism, race prejudice, and international war were identified as the major forms. Finally they argued that, functionally speaking, conflict contributed to the organization, unification, change, and progress of human society.

In 1924 Bernard challenged the instinct theory in a thoroughgoing critique. He pointed out that as analytic tools, instincts provide no way for dealing with exceptions to the rule. For example, the theory cannot explain the absence of conflict between groups that are racially and culturally different even though they may be in constant and provocative contact. Second, Bernard and others point out that instinct theory tends to minimize the nonhereditary elements in social situations, e.g., culture, structure, and interaction. It is implied that such factors exert little or no influence on the causation of conflict, since they constitute nondynamic givens.

Some scholars have found conflict to issue from the release of inner tensions that are built up within individuals by life in modern societies. This "tension theory" of conflict was most prominent in the years just around World War II. In a recent statement Carstairs (1969: 751–64) argues that the rapid population growth that produces human congestion is the root of the social conditions that generate tension. He goes on to declare that, recently, outbreaks of massive violence heightened public attention to these phenomena. The impact of population growth and congestion on social organization led Carstairs to assert that rigid social institutions and traditional value systems can generate a sense of confinement and tension no less frustrating than the bars of a cage. After contemplating these developments he concludes that sometimes following the experience of prolonged tension, collective discontent explodes into conflict and violence that lead to the creation of new social orders.

In general, tension theory argues that typical features of modern urban industrial societies tend to build up tensions in great numbers of individuals. Among the specific conditions often mentioned are congestion and crowding, complexity of social organization, impersonality of relations, and social change and instability. Speaking of these tensions, Bernard (1957: 36) declared that tensions are usually understood to result from experiences of socialization, from structural conditions in modern industrial societies, and from the frustrations of work.

It is claimed that human beings are ill-equipped genetically to cope with such conditions. Lacking inherent mechanisms for reducing their tensions, they look to the social milieu for release. Unfortunately, however, modern societies provide inadequate mechanisms and occasions for socially approved release of tension. Thus Bernard (1957: 36) asserted that tensions and frustrations pile up until in effect groups explode into overt aggression of many kinds and levels of intensity as a method of release.

The tension theory of conflict is difficult to utilize in empirical situations for several reasons. First, it fails to tell us at what level of tension conflict can be expected. Although we may allege that certain conflicts have erupted in response to tensions, we cannot use this knowledge to predict or plan since we do not know what level or degree of tension is likely to produce conflict. And second, both empirical observation and common sense suggest that individuals are capable of enduring high levels of tension for long periods without resorting to conflict. That is, the connection between tension and conflict is neither direct nor inevitable. And finally, as with instincts, tensions are individual states and therefore cannot be employed to explain collective actions. For these reasons, the explanatory value of the tension theory is limited. However, it will be shown below that as an individual socio-psychic state, tension is one correlate of deprivation.

Marx, drawing upon the work of Hegel, utilized a dialectical model to construct a theory of social conflict. In the Marxist view, (Hamilton and Wright, 1975: 6) the development of capitalist society forces the creation of two sharply divided social classes—the bourgeoisie, who own the means of production (land, tools, materials), and the proletariat, who own only their labor. The basic relationship between bourgeoisie and proletariat is one of exploitation and oppression. The historical trend is toward increasing exploitation of the proletariat by the bourgeoisie and polarization of the classes. In the final stages of capitalist development, exploitation produces increasing class consciousness, political maturity, collective action, and finally revolution.

In the construction of his conflict model, Marx (1906) introduced and utilized a number of factors, e.g., structure, deprivation, and interaction, that have figured prominently in later formulations. The dialectical argument postulates that, given the appropriate conditions, conflict is generated within the interactive process itself. If the social structure places two collective actors in positions facing one another and conditions their situations with certain deprivational and motivational factors, then an interactive process of conflict may develop. In this situation the hostile or defensive act of one participant can evoke a magnified response in kind from the other. Caught in this dialectical process, the relationship escalates in intensity and violence to the point of open, destructive struggle. As formulated by Marx and others, the dialectical process leads, somewhat inevitably, to the victory of the initially weaker attacking actor over the initially stronger defending actor.

Scholars like Dahrendorf (1959), Lenski (1966), and Fals-Borda (1969) modified the Marxian formulation. In their hands the dialectical theory postulates that collective adversaries in a conflict influence each other in a way that produces both continuity and modification of the basic social structure. Thus, however stated, the thesis evokes the dialectical conflict response from the antithesis. In the struggle that ensues thesis is defeated by antithesis. In the final phase, i.e., synthesis, certain structural features are absorbed from the traditional system and modified by elements from the antithesis, or novel system. This cyclical process of continuity in change through conflict is as typical a feature of the dialectical model as the idea that conflict is generated within the interactive process itself.

In the dialectical view the inherent materials of the individual were taken as a given, and the social structure, culture, social-psychological elements, and interactive systems were brought into prominent view. Marxist analysts stressed the importance of qualifying preconditions and intervening conditions. In this way the posture of sociological analysis of conflict was advanced. However, the original Marxist view has been criticized and revised to make it more compatible with changing economic conditions and evolving sociological perspectives.

Structure-Frustration Theories

Many students of social conflict sought the keys to its causes in the conditions and changes of the social structure. Marx (1906) made the class structure a central element of his causal model. Parsons (1951) and other American structural-functionalists conceptualized conflict as a pathological byproduct of ongoing social systems. The term *conflict* denoted one situation where interrelated parts of the system failed to fit and function together harmoniously. Conflict was thus seen as "tension" or "strain" within the system (Landsberger, 1961: 219–39).

Dahrendorf (1959) made use of a structural approach to formulate a significantly different kind of conflict theory. Writing in 1958 he asserted (172) that the task of sociological analysis was to associate conflicts with specific social structures, and not to relegate explanation to psychological variables like aggressiveness or hostility, to descriptive-historical factors like mass migrations, or to mere chance. From this perspective the prelude to conflict lies in structural situations in which conflict is potential. Dahrendorf (176) argues that the analytic and explanatory tasks of a sociology of conflict can be phrased in such questions as how conflict groups arise from the structures of society, what forms struggles among such groups may take, and how conflict among such groups affects change of the social structure.

Dahrendorf (1959: 237–39) went on to assert that the initiating structure of conflict is composed of social categories (quasi-groups) of unequal rank and power and divergent interests between which there is an ongoing relationship of cooperation and conflict. The degree of potential for increased conflict implicit in this structural situation is conditioned by such factors as polarization of the categories by status and power disparity; diverse, unmobilized and unfocused interests; and definition of the categories as in- and out-groups. Internal and external forces impinge upon the structure, altering the ranks, power, functions, and relations among constituent categories in the direction of either expanded cooperation or increased conflict. The articulation of manifest interests, the organization of conflict groups, and the increase of conflict are facilitated by the intervention of certain variable technical, political, social, and psychological conditions. Dahrendorf concludes that once this complex process is complete, conflict groups have emerged and stand in a conflict-potential relationship within the associational structure of the social system.

Newman (1973) formulated a structural theory of intergroup conflict. He argued (129–38) that two structural variables, i.e., a vertical factor (stratification and rewards) and a horizontal factor (social status) determine the emergence, frequency, intensity, and violence of intergroup conflicts. His model can be diagrammed in the following way, using illustrations I have supplied:

	Integration	Segregation
Reward Parity	White, middle-class Protestants and Catholics	White, middle-class Natives and Ethnics
Reward Disparity	White, middle-class Men and Women	White, middle-class Americans and Blacks

Using this device, he predicted (157–59) that the greater the extent of reward disparity and social segregation, the less frequent, but more intense and violent, the ensuing conflict. The obverse is correlatively true; i.e., the greater the degree of reward parity and social integration, the more frequent but less intense and violent the resulting conflicts. Newman concluded that pluralistic, structured relationships of dominance and submission, associated with a normative system of competition and achievement, establishes a structural setting for intergroup conflict.

Employing similar structural elements, Williams (1977: 70–73) set forth a theory of intergroup conflict. The components of this model include disparities in the structures of resource capabilities, diversity of articulated group interests, variations in consensus of controls and values, differences of intergroup communication patterns, and decrease of the effectiveness of social controls. Williams used this model to guide his study of intergroup conflict and accommodation in the United States.

In recent years such general theories have been refined and made specific in empirical research. After examining data regarding French populations that experienced hardship after periods of well-being, Snyder and Tilly (1972: 520–32) concluded that power disparity was the prime structural cause of collective violence. Harris (1970: 438–54) explained that the revolution of 1960 in Turkey resulted in large measure from increasing struggle between conflict groups which emerged after a decade of inequality in status and power, and diffuse contention and struggle between two major political categories. Spillerman (1970: 627–49) tested "weak social integration," "alienation from the political system," and "frustrations stemming from deprivation of unattainable aspirations" in the search for the causes of the big-city riots of the 1960s. He concluded that riots were caused by frustrations produced by structural deprivations uniformly felt by blacks in all urban settings. Seeman (1972: 385–402), seeking an explanation of the 1968 riots in France, interviewed 400 employed males in France and a parallel sample in America. He concluded that powerlessness born of structural deprivations was the central explanatory factor.

Without attempting to deny the salience of selected structural factors, another group of scholars have argued that the mechanisms of frustration seem to be the central causal factor in social conflict as found in modern industrial societies. The concept of frustration was introduced to the field of behavioral studies by Sigmund Freud. In 1939 John Dollard (1939: 1–26) and his associates applied the concept to the explanation of collective and societal conflicts. The Dollard theory suggests a direct, somewhat mechanical nexus between socially generated frustrations and widespread aggressive behavior.

Building on the pioneering work of Dollard and his associates, later scholars have made the frustration-aggression hypothesis the central term of an inclusive theory of social conflict. The hypothesis has been refined and reformulated in various ways. Some writers have identified specific structural conditions or relationships that are regarded as significantly frustrating. Other formulations have sought to specify the dynamic elements that lie at the source of frustration. Still other scholars have attempted to isolate the causal nexus between frustration and social con-

flict. The major formulations of the frustration concept are identified in
Figure 2-1.

FIGURE 2-1

FORMULATIONS OF THE FRUSTRATING ELEMENTS IN THE
CAUSATION OF SOCIAL CONFLICTS

Deteriorating material conditions
Rising expectations
Relative deprivation
Rise and drop
Status inconsistency
Cognitive dissonance
Unreciprocity
Reduction of interaction

"Deteriorating material conditions" is the simplistic reading of the
Marxist hypothesis. This is the notion that the poor get poorer and
poorer until in the end they are so frustrated that they revolt. Collective
frustration results from the increasing material deprivation.

The concept of rising expectations states the same argument from the
other side of the coin. It is claimed that frustrations arise because collective expectations increase faster than they can be met. The gap between rising expectations and lagging achievements widens, producing
increasingly intolerable frustrations.

The authors of *The American Soldier* (Stouffer, et al. 1949) formulated the concept of frustration as relative deprivation. This concept
argues that frustration arises from the collective assessment of the group's
situation. The group evaluates its situation by reference to some standard—another comparable group, its own remembered past, some ideal
situation—and judges that it is not as well off as it believes it ought to be,
or as well off as it is entitled to be. This conviction is the source of collective frustration.

The rise and drop hypothesis was developed by Davies (1962: 5–18)
to explain the cause of social conflicts and revolutions. He argued that
intolerable frustration was generated when a group that had experienced
a period of rising material and social conditions suddenly suffered a reversal or drop in circumstances. The frustration thus produced is said
sometimes to be so intense that conflict, even revolution, may ensue.

Lenski (1954: 405–13) drew attention to the frustrating effect of "status inconsistency." He noted that because of achievements or possessions a group may believe that it is entitled to a certain status recognition, but in fact may be accorded a lower or different status. The expected status differs from the accorded status, a condition that may be intensely frustrating, leading under certain circumstances to social conflict.

In a suggestive study Geschwender (1968: 127–35) attempted to synthesize the foregoing frustration hypotheses under the concept of "cognitive dissonance." Geschwender argued that certain experiences and realities generate certain cognitions, i.e., ideas, expectations, perceptions, self-images, notions of rights, etc., within a collectivity. However, the actual experience of the group may force a different cognition upon them. The strain between these dissonant cognitions is frustrating and if not resolved in socially approved ways can lead to conflict.

Palmer (1970: 139–60) perceived the frustrating circumstances in the relations between collective actors. If their mutually oriented actions are harmonious, complementary, and smoothly meshed, i.e., reciprocal, then social relations are themselves harmonious. If, however, such interrelations are not harmonized, fitted, and complementary, i.e., if they are unreciprocal, a state of unreciprocity exists. This unreciprocity is the source of frustration which under certain conditions may eventuate in conflict.

Williams (1972: 11–25) formulated the frustration hypothesis as a "hypothetical law of collective conflict" in which the decrease of interaction in relation to significant interdependences is the crucial motivating factor. The hypothetical law seeks to specify the steps by means of which a decrease of interaction between collective actors leads to conflict. The first step is an interaction within a common culture between two unequal and different collective actors that implements significant interdependence among individual members. If subsequently there occurs a marked and continuing decrease of interaction, while differences and inequalities remain constant and while interdependence remains relatively stable, the result will be: (1) increased cultural difference between the actors; (2) decrease of empathy between the actors; (3) an increase of opposition and conflict over the exercise of authority and distribution of other scarce values, both of which form the basis of interdependence. Williams argues that although his law is generally predictive, under certain circumstances (some of which he mentions) it is more or less inapplicable. For example, reduction of interaction may not lead to conflict when normative controls of duty, loyalty, obligation, or indebtedness have been

internalized. Or again, interruption of interaction may not lead to conflict if the parties are bound together by powerful affective ties.

Runciman (1966: 36–52) has simplified the analysis and discussion
of relative deprivation. He utilized Weber's concepts of *class, status,* and
power to delineate three dimensions typifying relative deprivation. In
terms of the dimension of class, *relative deprivation* was said to refer to
felt disadvantages of income, chances of occupational advancement,
working conditions, and other economic circumstances. The category
status deprivation was used to denote perceived limitations of social
esteem, prestige and honor. In terms of power, relative deprivation was
understood to refer to felt inability to control one's decisions and action,
especially in the face of opposition. All the specific formulations of relative deprivation discussed above can be brought under the three categories of this classification. These dimensions of relative deprivation
have also provided theoretical perspectives for much empirical research
on social conflict.

The relative deprivation theory has been criticized by some scholars.
Gerlach and Hine (1970: xxii) argued that "social disorganization,"
"relative deprivation," and "psychological maladjustment" fail to explain why social movements develop and grow, although they admitted
that all these conditions may motivate individuals to join movements and
struggle for change. To explain the processes of social movements they
assert it is necessary to examine movement dynamics. Snyder and Tilly
(1972: 520–32), after a study of worker violence in France between
1830 and 1960, rejected relative deprivation as a satisfactory explanation and found the cause of collective violence in struggles for political
power. Geschwender and Geschwender (1973: 403–11) identified several types of relative deprivation which were found to be differentially
related to social conflict. They concluded that relative deprivation was
valid as a satisfactory explanation of specific forms of social conflict
under specific circumstances.

Summary

Five theoretical perspectives—instinct, tension, dialectical interaction,
structure, and frustration-aggression—explaining social conflict have
been reviewed briefly. Because they are perspectives on individual behavior, instinct and the tension theory make little contribution to a
sociology of social conflict. The other formulations are not mutually
contradictory, since they approach the explanation of conflict from dif-

ferent social perspectives. In the following section an attempt will be made to synthesize these theoretical perspectives into a single inclusive model for the explanation of social conflict.

AN EXPLANATORY MODEL OF SOCIAL CONFLICT

Thanks to the work of many scholars, there is now a considerable and increasing area of consensus regarding the nature and causes of conflict. Most writers on the subject agree that conflict is generated within the social system itself. As a consequence, such individual factors as instinct and tension are either excluded from serious consideration or minimized as causal elements. Analysis at both the theoretical and empirical levels indicates that the interplay of many factors is involved in explaining social conflict. However, it seems evident that the relevant factors stand in different positions and play different roles in the causal process. These considerations permit us to identify four classes of causal or explanatory conditions which are differentiated by their positions and roles in the causal process. The first class of conditions is called *basic categories* because they constitute or decisively influence the setting of conflict. The second set of factors is called *structural preconditions* because they precede or undergird the causal process. A third group of factors called *motivations* inject a dynamic dimension into the causal process. The fourth cluster of factors, called the *catalyzing situation,* qualifies the causal process, releasing accumulated conflict potential and actualizing the potential for nonlegitimate conflict. In the remainder of this section types of factors in each class are examined, set in the causal system, and linked to preceding and succeeding classes of factors in a way that will explain why social conflict is the expected outcome. The explanatory model is outlined in the interrelated propositions of Figure 2-2.

Basic Categories

The collective components of an established social order (e.g., groups, social categories, associations, organizations) engage in relations composed of mixtures of cooperation and conflict. As Park and Burgess (1921: 559) have shown, these processes sift and sort the societal components into two broad categories that differ in rank, power, interests, and functions. This two-category structural framework is expressed in many ways. Dahrendorf (1959) conceptualized the structure in indus-

FIGURE 2-2

OUTLINE OF EXPLANATORY MODEL

I. The structural framework of social conflict is a social order composed of two broad categories
   A. which are differentiated in status, power and functions,
   B. between which there is a continuous pattern of cooperation and conflict,
   C. in which a potential for heightened conflict is intrinsic and increasing.

II. The following types of factors, called preconditions, are intrinsic in the basic conflict structure:
   A. functional failures of the social institutions;
   B. imperfect integrations of the inclusive and constituent social systems;
   C. disjunctions, incompatibilities, and clashes of correlated cultural elements;
   D. unreciprocity of social relations;
   E. weaknesses, inadequacies, and disjunctions of the control and policy systems.

III. A series of consequent deprivations, frustrations, and dissatisfactions
   A. function to inject a dynamic property into the causal process,
   B. thereby significantly enhancing the probability that potential conflict will be transformed into active conflict.

IV. A syndrome of interconnected structural, ideological, power, leadership, and other factors thereby significantly enhances the probability that ongoing legitimate conflict will be transformed into nonlegitimate conflict.

V. A collective cognitive-affective situation
   A. is qualified by actual awareness of the conflict structure, background conditions, and motivations;
   B. is intensified and ignited by a precipitating event;
   C. transforms legitimate into nonlegitimate conflict.

trial societies as a class pattern. Students of community conflict (Coleman, 1957; Gamson, 1966: 71–81; and Spillerman, 1970: 627–49) identified different pairs of categories for different conflict incidents. In feudal systems the interacting categories were called peasants and gentry. In ancient Greece they were called citizen and barbarian; in Rome, patrician and pleb, and in contemporary India high caste and low caste.

Two sets of external and internal factors fix these categories in the social structure and maintain interaction and stability. Factors like the power of the general establishment, interdependence, and unpreparedness of the social categories (especially the inferior and weaker) for struggle tend to maintain stability in the structure. On the other hand, polarization of the social categories by status disparity; by diverse, unmobilized, or unfocused interests; and by their definition in the conflict roles as in- and out-groups along with other circumstances produces instability in the structure. With change, conflict groups and associations emerge in each of the interacting and opposed categories to implement and execute social conflict.

By its very nature such a structural arrangement contains a built-in potential for social conflict. Some of the intrinsic forces are revealed as pre- or infraconditions. Such systematic and structural stresses produce states of deprivation and discontent which enhance the inclination for conflict. In time and after change this built-in potential tends to be realized in expressions of social conflict that sometimes exceed the prevailing boundaries of legitimacy. In the following section we will examine some main types of structural preconditions which constitute the first step in the causal process.

Structural Preconditions

In conflict the contending parties struggle for status, power, scarce resources, and other values. Structurally inherent potential for conflict is heightened when one party believes that access to such values is blocked by the other party. This structural arrangement is perceived to be deprivational and constitutes one prior or underlying condition of conflict. Such structural preconditions are evident in many conflicts. For example, in Northern Ireland the Roman Catholics, and in Lebanon the native Moslems, believed that they were in an inferior position, excluded from the government, exploited and impoverished and otherwise deprived. In Northern Ireland they blamed the Protestant majority and in Lebanon the Christian minority.

The structural preconditions of social conflict vary in both time and place and in terms of how they are perceived. For example, fluctuations of the economic cycle from boom to depression reflect variable functional adequacies of the economic system and the increase and decrease of such depriving conditions as unemployment, inflation, and commodity scarcity. Often groups have initiated conflict because their perception of structural malfunction and sense of deprivation increased even though actual conditions had improved. Gurr (1969: 580) reported that variations of the magnitude of civil strife in geocultural regions were associated with structural differences. In order to examine the relation between magnitude of strife and social structure he computed the following scores by weighting and combining the number of participants, the duration of incidents, and the number of casualties in relation to population size:

Europe	Latin America	Islam	Asia	Africa
4.6	9.6	9.7	10.7	11.7

These differentials of conflict magnitude were attributed mainly to variable structural conditions in the several regions.

Let us examine five of these variable structural preconditions: institutional failure, relatively imperfect integration of social systems, cultural disjunctions and clashes, unreciprocity of social relations, and inadequacy of control and policy systems.

1. The failure of institutions to function as expected and to produce promised rewards is seriously frustrating. In the case of the economy such failure is indicated by increasing inflation, unemployment, exploitation, or the abuse and pollution of natural resources. Failure of the government is revealed as an inability to maintain social order, high taxes, inequities, and injustices perpetrated by the legal system, or unreasonable restrictions of the actions and movements of people. Denial of expected educational opportunities to some groups, training that fails to equip people for the life they must lead, and use of schools to support other failing institutions are among indicators of educational failure. Ryan (1969: 118–20) says that failure of "accommodative mechanisms" or institutions is a further precondition of conflict. Instances of such failure would be the absence or breakdown of grievance machinery, recreational programs, recognition rituals, agencies of planned change and the like. For example, lack of recreational programs was part of the background of the Soweto riot of 16 June 1976.

The research on social conflict has produced numerous instances of institutional failure as part of the background of greater or lesser episodes of conflict. After a study of four modern revolutions—the British, the American, the French, and the Russian—Brinton (1965: 28–71) named institutional shortcomings of the *anciens régimes* as important preconditions to revolution. The National Advisory Commission on Civil Disorders (1968: 203–74) cited long-standing institutional and structural malfunctions as background factors in the street riots of 1967 and before in the United States. Horowitz (1972: 294–312) cited economic and political decay of inner cities as structural correlates of urban riots. Baul and Slaughter (1971: 475–87), using data from a 1969 sample of 69 and a 1970 sample of 120 academic institutions, concluded that institutional impersonality constituted a central structural basis of student demonstrations.

2. Relatively imperfect integration of social systems constitutes a further precondition of social conflict. Failure of institutions is conditioned in part by states of imperfect internal integration. The working parts of such systems fail to operate harmoniously, thus reducing their efficiency. One consequence is the failure to produce generally expected results. Another is the state of structural strain, i.e., personal discomfort and discontent, that is associated with frustration and the drive to remedial struggle. When these conditions of imperfect integration, operational failure, and strain become widespread, an important potential for conflict has been generated.

In his discussion of imperfect integration of social systems, Ryan (1969: 52–56) draws attention to "the internal system," "the external system" and "the ecological system." He notes, for example, that exhaustion of natural resources, damage or destruction of the physical environment, and pollution of streams and the air produce a loss of integration within the ecological system of modern societies. Klitgaard (1972: 41–49) cited racial polarization, and Luterbacher (1975: 129–38) identified international bipolarity and generational separation as disintegrative conditions that contribute to conflict. The divergence of interests between owners and workers to which Marx drew attention has been reformulated by Rostow (1952) and Dahrendorf (1959). Smelser (1963), Gamson (1966), and Coleman (1957), among others, have examined this precondition of conflict at the community level.

3. Cultural dissent and conflict is a further dimension of structural stress in the background of social conflict. Various concepts have been developed to capture specific aspects of this phenomenon. Ogburn (1922) invented the term *cultural lag* to designate the condition when seen in terms of relative rates of cultural change. Looking at the front of the process, other writers have spoken of "cultural leads." The divergence and clashing of different culture complexes or systems is captured by the concept *cultural pluralism*. The juxtaposition of rural and urban, immigrant and native-born, or lower- and middle-class groups produces the phenomenon of cultural pluralism. When a variety of cultural systems exists within a restricted locale where no one is dominant, the result is cultural disunity and nonintegration akin to normlessness. It is seen that in a restricted locale, where a variety of cultures exist with none dominant, all these conceptual formulations provide ways to state the conflicts between divergent and inharmonious values and norms. This is relatively imperfect integration of the normative system. Cultural condi-

tions like these impede communication, accentuate ethnocentrism, and facilitate the formation of those hostilities that often precede social conflict. Sometimes culture conflicts accompany institutional failure and imperfect system integration.

The classic contemporary instances of social conflict that are grounded in and facilitated in part by culture conflict are the Catholic-Protestant struggle in Northern Ireland, the Hebrew-Moslem clash in the Middle East, the ancient conflict between Hindus and Moslems in the Indian subcontinent, and the Moslem-Christian strife in Lebanon. Marx argued that one dimension of the class war as he conceptualized it was value and norm differentials between proletariat and bourgeoisie. Degler (1972: 68–72) argues that basic cultural differences underlie conflicts between American Indians and the rest of the society. The investigations of intertribal conflicts in Latin America, Africa, and Asia all refer to cultural conflicts as one component of the prelude to open struggle.

4. Another aspect of the structural background of conflict is revealed in social interaction. Institutional failure, imperfect system integration, and culture conflict produce "unreciprocity" (Palmer, 1970: 139–60) in social relations. With the increase of population, growth of size, and increase of specialization, the individual experiences what Wilson and Wilson (1961: 24–44) have called change of "scale." This process refers to the number, diversity, and specialization of services required to meet the individual's "dependencies" in modern society. Under conditions of tribal society or life in small rural localities, all his dependencies can be fulfilled by a limited number of individuals through numerous multipurpose, intimate contacts. In urban industrial society, however, the same core of dependencies requires the services of numerous dispersed, specialized contacts. The decisive condition of social interaction resulting from change of scale has been expressed in such concepts as impersonality and individuation.

This interactional condition of conflict has been observed in many types of social situations. Much of the research identifying withdrawal from the surrounding society as well as the experiences of disenchantment and dissatisfaction has been organized by means of the concept of alienation. Marx early identified alienation with work in industrial societies. Studies of conflict among blacks, workers, youth, the poor, Indians, and other groups (Degler, 1972: 68–72; Seeman, 1972: 385–402; Baldassare, 1975: 815–25; and Martin et al., 1974: 266–74) recognized alienation as part of the structural background of these struggles. Some students of aging (Cummings and Henry, 1961) have called that process "disengagement," to designate withdrawal of older people from the relationships that were typical of their working years.

5. Variable states and processes of collective policy and social control may function to enhance the probability that conflict will erupt. Intergroup policies that are repressive, unclear, and inconsistent tend to be frustrating and push dissatisfied groups toward social conflict. Empirical research (Johnson, et al., 1973: 698–721; National Advisory Commission on Civil Disorders, 1968: 299–318) reports that harsh and unsympathetic policies serve to incite low-status and dependent community groups to aggressive conflict.

At the same time, inconsistent social policies are often equally inflammatory. In a study of anti-European violence in Africa, LeVine (1959: 422) found that inconsistent intergroup policies were strongly related to violent outbreaks of Africans against white settlers; the inconsistency and unpredictability were the frustrating elements. By the same token, LeVine reported that clear and consistent policies, even though repressive, tended to inhibit the resort to aggressive and violent tactics.

Much research (Cochran, 1971: 232–37; Smelser, 1963: 261–69; Dahrendorf, 1959: 239; National Advisory Commission on Civil Disorders, 1968: 323–36; Janowitz, 1968) indicates the variable influence of social control and social control agencies on the initiation and development of social conflict. Social control that is weak or ineffective has been shown to invite or permit dissatisfied groups to resort to conflict as the instrument of goal achievement. On the other hand, control that is excessive, harsh, or inept may provoke such groups to retaliate with coercive actions. Social control that is adequate in amount and judicious in application tends to have a stabilizing effect. Deprived and discontented groups may be deterred from engaging in extreme struggle to attain their goals. However, research has revealed that the kind and type of control that is optimal varies from situation to situation. There is also some evidence that, for a time at least, massive, overwhelming repressive control will prevent the outbreak of aggressive struggle by deprived and dissatisfied groups.

Motivations: The Prime Cause

Structural preconditions contribute to the causation of social conflict when they generate motivating attitudes and feelings. An impressive consensus in the social sciences identifies some form of the frustration mechanism as the prime motivation in social conflict. This motivational hypothesis has been substantiated in empirical research. For example, Tomlinson (1968: 417–28) and Spillerman (1970: 627–49), among others, have explained the big-city riots of the 1960s by intense relative deprivation and discontent which became endemic and surfaced in the black community in the 1950s and 1960s. After a review of the research literature on civil rights protest and violence, Geschwender and Geschwender (1973: 403–11) concluded that the relative deprivation hypothesis was confirmed as the prime motivational force. A voluminous literature points to frustration, discontent, and accumulated grievances as motivating forces in such conflicts as those in Northern Ireland, the Middle East, and the Indian subcontinent.

The frustration concept has been formulated in different ways. An examination of the relevant literature suggests that, however formulated, the mechanism contains three operating components. The first is a state of denial, withholding, withdrawal or loss of substantive rewards. The frustrated actor cannot achieve a value that he desires and is striving to gain. Geschwender (1968: 127–35) noted that the state of deprivation is expressed as incongruity, i.e., "dissonance," between perceived desires and perceived achievements. A group can increase the perception of deprivation by comparing itself unfavorably with another group in a similar situation. Such a perception is called relative deprivation. The deteriorating material conditions, the rising expectations, the rise-and-drop, and the status inconsistency hypotheses stress this component of the mechanism.

The second component of the mechanism, here called frustration, is blockage of interactive behavior. Such behavior is the goal-oriented action of a contending party that fails to gain the desired values because of the interference of another party. In the literature such blockages are called "frustration," "unreciprocity," and "decrease of interaction."

The third component of the mechanism, which we call discontent, consists of collective feeling, states, and images that accompany deprivation and frustration. These affective and cognitive states inject a dynamic property into the causal process and increase the likelihood that non-legitimate conflict will take place. In the literature this component is referred to as "structural strain," "dissatisfaction," and "discontent." Under much motivation a group may be moved to reject its unsatisfactory situation and to seek improvement through overt struggle against the frustrating object.

Although the deprivation-frustration-discontent mechanism functions as the prime motivation in most situations, in some cases other motives appear to be operative. For example, it seems doubtful that the Soviet

Union was motivated by a sense of relative deprivation and discontent in 1956 when Hungary was invaded and the liberal rebellion was crushed. It appears more likely that the invasion was motivated by Soviet ideology that demanded suppressive action in case of rebellion in a satellite country. Turner and Killian (1972: 291–97) have argued that militant movements are constrained by their ideologies to employ coercive and violent methods and to avoid conciliatory tactics, which can be interpreted as evidence of weakness.

Sometimes the motivation for conflict seems to be embedded within the dialectical process. Aggressive action motivates responding aggressive action. Lambelet (1975: 123–28) points out that "armamentism," or the dialectics of the arms race, functions as a strong motivation to international armed conflict. It seems likely also that some conflicts are motivated by avarice, i.e., the struggle for values without the sense of their being scarce or blocked. Such a motive seems to have been operating when Mussolini invaded Ethiopia in 1935 and when the Soviet Union annexed the Baltic states just after World War II. The study of social conflict requires the search for the motivation that is predictive of empirical outcomes.

Catalyzing Situation

Over time, a series of variable conditions converge in the casual process at a point and in a way that is decisive in initiating conflict. This cluster of factors qualifies the collective action so that it functions to release the accumulated conflict potential and to transform it into nonlegitimate conflict (Cochran, 1971: 232–37). The components of the situation include conditions not hitherto significantly evident in the process as well as those that have already surfaced. The authors of the Report of the National Advisory Commission on Civil Disorders (1968: 118) present a graphic description of this typical, catalyzing situation.

> We found that violence was generated by an increasingly disturbed social atmosphere, in which typically not one, but a series of incidents occurred over a period of weeks or months prior to the outbreak of disorders. Most cities had three or more such incidents; Houston had 10 over a five-month period. These earlier or prior incidents were linked in the minds of many Negroes to the pre-existing reservoir of underlying grievances. With each such incident, frustration and tension grew until at some point a final incident, often similar to the incidents preceding it, occurred and was followed almost immediately by violence.

The two-party categorical framework of conflict is the setting of the situation. Thus, for example, as a labor union moves forward through the causal process to the initiation of a strike, thought and action take place against the backdrop of management and labor and the class system. The tense cabinet meeting where the decision is taken to strike first with devastating air power and armor never loses sight of the enemy and the whole binational situation. The sense of the structural framework is brought vibrantly into consciousness so that, in fact, it is no longer background, but instead is part of the tense present situation.

Preconditions and infraconditions are brought into the stream of consciousness in the present moment. All the frustrating circumstances— unemployment and poverty, constitutional and legal exclusions from power, denial of a homeland turf, cavalier withholding of respect and recognition—come to life in the tense executive meeting, the street experiences, the quick angry confrontation with police, the fury of the propaganda blast, in all those moments of thought and experience when the potential and readiness of conflict are quickened into active struggle.

Images of the detested enemy, the steady mood of anger, the slogans that embody hopes unfulfilled, the intense urge to struggle, the justifications of present attitudes and intended actions—these and other cognitive and affective elements are captured in the ideology that, as Gerlach and Hine (1970: 159–82) have asserted, constitute the "basis of decisive action." The present situation makes sense, is in fact real because it is illuminated and justified by a set of premises and doctrines. Ideology is not (not at least in the catalyzing situation) an abstraction, a set of impersonal ideas. It is rather the pulsing stuff of which life is made, and the intense motivation to struggle for change and advantage.

This galvanizing situation also includes some sense of power. Such a sense may emerge from the feeling of the righteousness of the cause, the temporary escape from the constraints of reality, the euphoria of crowd excitement, the perception of the strength to be found in numbers, and the ephemeral intoxication of slogans and myths. Such a heady sense of power can sweep the group across the line that separates the potentiality of conflict from the actuality expressed in open struggle. This transitory sense of power is mixed with the nagging sense of powerlessness to produce a confused judgment regarding the group's power potential and the appropriate action to be taken.

The situation that links motivations to conflict is further intensified by the actions of leaders. Agitators, activists, provocateurs, and others who arouse participants to actions manipulate accumulated potential and generate active conflict in the situation. Sometimes such leaders operate on the grand scale, moving from one location to another. Many others

The Explanation of Social Conflict

are local, limiting their leadership to a single community or group. In
both cases their role may be decisive in precipitating active conflict.

The final and decisive ingredient in such conflict-potential situations
is a catalytic agent, or "precipitant" as MacIver (1942: 163–78) called
it. Any phenomenon, individual, or event may become a triggering agent.
It is virtually impossible to predict that a certain event or person will be
a conflict catalyst. It is easier to identify the catalytic agent in retrospect.
In every case, though, when a catalyst has ignited the fire of conflict,
releasing its potential, the causal process is complete. The National Advisory Commission on Civil Disorders delineated the nature and role of
"precipitating incidents" in their report (1968: 117–18).

> In virtually every case a single "triggering" or "precipitating" incident
> can be identified as having immediately preceded—within a few hours
> and in generally the same location—the outbreak of disorder. But this
> incident was usually relatively minor, even trivial, by itself substantially
> disproportionate to the scale of violence that followed. Often it was an
> incident of a type which had occurred frequently in the same commu-
> nity in the past without provoking violence.

A Note on Research

When used in research this theoretical model suggests the major related
operations. First, at a predetermined starting point in the causal process
quantitative and/or descriptive assessments can be made of such background factors as (a) structural potential for conflict, e.g., stratification,
rigidity, complexity, and impersonality; (b) the state of the conflict
actors, i.e., social movements and establishments, or the situation of in-
and out-groups; and (c) the condition of the conflict groups themselves,
i.e., nature of organization, manifest interests, belief systems, and level
of discontent. These data can be combined into indexes of conflict potential at the beginning of the causal process.

Next, quantitative and/or descriptive readings can be made of such
structural conflict-causing changes as increasing institutional failure, system disintegration, cultural incongruence, interactional unreciprocity,
and growth of anomie, alienation, and disengagement. The data can be
subjected to analysis to determine major causal factors, or conflict indicators. In another research context, these factors can serve as conflict
predictors.

Third, various steps can be taken to estimate the resultant increase of
the level of structural strain, i.e., the frustration-deprivation-discontent
motivation to resort to nonlegitimate conflict. And finally, the researcher

could characterize the catalyzing situation and process, placing all the previously mentioned factors within an ongoing, conscious, collective process of intense interaction in which a precipitating event is injected. By analysis these factors could produce another variable index.

The explanatory model predicts that *typically* when social conflict between collective actors for important scarce values escalates, it will have been preceded by the causal process delineated above. Geschwender (1968: 133–35), Gurr (1970: 22–58), and Newman (1973: 97–190) have argued that the more intense the motivation the more certain it is that the outcome will be heightened conflict, and the more intense and/or violent the ensuing struggle is likely to be. However, the model cannot predict that escalated conflict will ensue every time from the developed causal process. In the short run and under specific conditions, the causal process may not lead to escalated nonlegitimate conflict. In the period prior to the onset of conflict, when all the causal factors are present, the participants may accept the situation or seek to withdraw from it. Later, however, with continued causal pressure and triggered by a catalytic agent, they may resort to increased conflict. At the same time, when responding to the same causal situation, some individuals and groups may engage in violent struggle while others may reveal limited, legitimate protest only. Faced with the pressure of conflict-causatory conditions, some individuals and groups may temporize, practicing alternative strategies of adjustment, and putting off the day of direct open attack against the frustrating object. For present illustrative purposes such alternative strategies may be classified as:

1. Innovation—The improvisation of novel, approved means to achieve desired ends when socially approved means are inaccessible.

2. Escape—Action that intentionally avoids facing the frustrating conditions or factors.

3. Self-manipulation—Changing self to harmonize with the problematical situation rather than attempting to modify it.

4. Scapegoating—Displacing aggression and conflict against a substitute noncausatory and safe object, individual, or group.

Some years ago Merton (1957: 131–60) pointed out that when the social structure prevents social categories from attaining approved ends by approved means, they may create alternative approved means to these ends rather than resorting to conflict. The frustrated group may seek to win approval and success by exploiting or maximizing some approved characteristic or resource within its control. For example, in many societies suppressed categories strive for recognition, wealth, and power by excelling in athletics, music, or some other field that removes them from competing with or attacking the frustrating agent. Jews in the Middle Ages and blacks in recent America are cases in point. Significant for the present discussion is the fact that motivating energies are drained off into activities that impede or prevent the actualization of conflict potential. Thus an innovating group in the Mertonian sense does not become a conflict group, at least not for a while.

Merton (1957: 140–55) cited "ritualism" and "retreatism" as mechanisms for escaping from remedial conflict action. The ritualist avoids struggle by accepting goals that are respectable but less worthy than those favored by prevailing values, while the retreatist withdraws from participation in the general social system. Neither of these categories attacks the frustrating, depriving condition by means of social conflict. The retreatist may escape by resorting to drugs, alcohol, or sex. In many societies deprived groups and categories have ritually escaped from struggle against elites by glorifying inferior and achievable goals. Some individuals (Crouch, 1968: 7) escape the threat of conflict by immersing themselves in the busywork that manipulates the symptoms of their frustration and deprivation without facing it in direct struggle. These are the busybodies who flit from committee to committee, talking about the problem, lamenting it, viewing it with alarm, and assuaging their frustrations by their words and gestures. Millennial and revivalistic ideologies and schemes are still other devices of escape. In this situation the group creates a nonrealistic world to which it adjusts. In all such cases groups are distracted from social conflict. The force of motivation that could power social conflict is diverted into alternative lines of collective action.

In still other instances, groups may refrain from engaging in social conflict by manipulating themselves. Self-manipulation is implicit in some of the escape techniques mentioned in the foregoing paragraph. Sometimes groups manage a potentially conflict-laden situation by acting out submission to the frustrating and presumably dominant group. For example, an etiquette of submission functioned for centuries to prevent open clashes between elites and inferiors in societies like India, England, and the United States. At other times, such groups may construct ideological systems which define the frustration/deprivation relationship in different terms. "Chosen people" doctrines perform this function. The frustration and deprivation are defined as tests of the inherent worth of the suffering people. The group socializes itself to belief that, as sufferers, they are chosen people with demonstrated virtues, who will in time receive their just rewards while their oppressors are doomed to everlasting punishment for their wickedness.

Scapegoating is an ancient and well-known device for managing the pressure to attack a powerful frustrating object. A group may perceive that it is deprived and may recognize the source of its suffering. But if it understands that direct conflict against the oppressor is strategically ill-advised in present circumstances, the discontent, hostility, and aggression built up in past experiences can be safely displaced against a defenseless substitute object. Such exercise may be psychologically and emotionally therapeutic and strategically safe at the same time. The group engages in conflict, or a reasonable conflict substitute, but does not risk struggle against the powerful frustrating object. The classic example of scapegoating in recent history is the Nazis' oppression of the Jews in the 1930s and 1940s. In the United States, oppressive and exploitive white plantation and mill owners in the South encouraged poor whites to make scapegoats of poor blacks. In this way poor whites were prevented from uniting against the plantation and mill owners, who were abusing poor whites as well as poor blacks.

As predicted, conflict will occur when the causal process is fulfilled, when escapist alternatives are rejected, and the frustrated group opts for struggle as the means to remove opposition and to gain desired values. Conflict, as the instrument of collective action for relieving deprivation and making change, is likely to be legitimized by calling it protest, struggle, liberation, or the like. The use of social power to damage, injure, or destroy the opponent is fused with communication to stipulate the change sought and the scarce value desired.

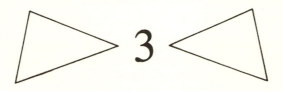

3

Social Structure in Social Conflict

When the early European and American social scholars talked about social conflict, they were usually thinking about a process of social relations. Their focus was the interlocking series of actions and reactions of adversaries or contending parties. The rise to prominence of the structural-functional perspective in the 1940s and 1950s directed the attention of sociologists away from social processes toward social structures. It was the pioneer modern sociologists of social conflict—Jessie Bernard, Lewis Coser, and Ralf Dahrendorf—who made social structure the analytic perspective for the study of social conflict. Writing in 1958, Dahrendorf (171–73) asserted that the analytic journey toward a sociology of social conflict must begin with consideration of the social structure.

Blau (1975), however, has shown that social structure has at least three different meanings. Coleman, Homans, and Merton (Blau, 10–11) conceptualize social structure as a "configuration" of stable social relations among persons. Blau (11–13) concluded that Parsons, Lipset, and Bottomore perceive social structure as a fundamental substratum, conceptualized by abstraction from people's conduct and relations, that molds social life and history. According to Coser, Lenski, and Blau, (14–15) social structure is a multidimensional space of differentiated social positions of the people in some collectivity.

In this chapter these conceptualizations have been employed to provide different perspectives from which to approach and examine the relationship of social structure to social conflict. These relations are examined under two main rubrics, structural conditions of conflict and structural implementation of conflict. The issue of the structural consequences of conflict is reserved for chapter 6, where the functions of social conflict are explored.

STRUCTURAL CONDITIONS OF CONFLICT

Social conflict takes place within structural contexts of many kinds. The nature and orientation of a structural setting in many cases may influence the outbreak and development of an episode of conflict. For example, as Paton (1976: 18–19, 88–89) has shown, extreme structural rigidity and exaggerated stratification functioned over time to facilitate the severe Soweto riot of 16 June 1976. In the present section we examine some structural conditions that research has shown to be conducive to the outbreak of nonlegitimate conflict. The aim is to bring into view the variety and overlap of structural conditions that serve to facilitate social conflict. The conditions discussed here are illustrative of the range and variety of structural circumstances that, in some situations, tend to facilitate social conflict.

Some of the norms, traditions, and customs in a society may establish a normative framework for conflict. The pattern tends to vary from society to society. Sometimes this normative context may be actively expressed as a Martian heritage, the Roman god of war symbolizing the stance, or as a tradition of manly aggressiveness. In other circumstances, the context may be formalized in a revolutionary or coercive ideology. The law of war and customs of struggle have often been crystallized into a normative context that operates to facilitate the recourse to nonlegitimate conflict.

The Martian orientation of Napoleonic France was generated in the long smouldering struggles between peasants and nobles and the endless violence of the French Revolution. The Prussian orientation toward war emerged from the endless struggles among quasi-independent principalities that in the nineteenth century were fused together to form modern Germany. Graham (1970: 74–82) has argued that the value thrust of the American tradition constituted a fertile setting for the violence that has been so characteristic of the society. In many other nations, e.g., ancient Rome, pre–World War II Japan, the Soviet Union, or Cuba, a Martian tradition has constituted a durable context facilitating the recourse to war.

The ideologies of some organizations and movements commit participants and followers to a norm of violence or other nonlegitimate tactics as the proper or permitted mode of struggle. As Turner and Killian (1972: 291) note, under the control of a militant ideology recourse to any other form of action "will be met by considerable cost or punishment." In such situations, the ideology consists of formulations of the justifications as well as the patterns of conflict behavior. Beit-Hallakmi (1972: 19–26) has argued that "rigidity" of personality has been fused with other social and cultural elements to form an Arab ideology in their war with the Jews.

In all societies, customs are found that function to justify conflict in one set of circumstances while forbidding it under other conditions. Sometimes such customs have been formalized into law, e.g., treaties, conventions, or contracts. For example, custom in international relations tends to permit warlike action in self-defense. Teutonic common law permits a man to kill or injure another in defense of his home, his family, or himself. The customs of the feud approve killing a member of the enemy clan, but injury of a fellow clansman is prohibited. The customs that have been formalized in the laws of states and international codes were once quite informal in character. In many situations they establish a framework for the facilitation of conflict.

The conflict-facilitating normative structure may in some situations take the form of cultural pluralism. Diversity and looseness is formalized, thus enhancing both the motivation and the freedom to engage in conflict. Morrison and Stevenson (1972: 82–103) argued that cultural pluralism contributes to political instability in developing societies, thus increasing the chances of social conflict. The clash of divergent norms and the resultant collective frustration operate to magnify the disposition to resort to conflict to achieve desired ends.

In virtually all contemporary theories of conflict, stratification is regarded as one contributory factor. The role and significance of stratification varies from one system to another. In some explanatory systems, e.g., the Marxian formulation, stratification is conceptualized as the central causal factor. In others, e.g., the frustration theory, social stratification is seen as a secondary or contributory condition. However formulated, these theories agree that social stratification positions actors in ways that are conducive to social conflict.

Marx argued that modern industry enabled one category or "class," the bourgeoisie, to control the means of production and thereby to gain great wealth, vast power, and high social status. The other "class," the proletariat, owning only their labor which they must sell to the bourgeoisie, was relegated to increasing economic poverty, status inferiority, and relative powerlessness. In Marx's view, this inequitable relationship cast the classes in the roles of natural enemies. In time, the situation would deteriorate until it would explode into violent revolution.

Dahrendorf (1959: 237–40) conceptualized the stratification structure as composed of two "quasi-groups" of unequal rank and power and revealing dissimilar latent interests. With change, latent interests become manifest and each category generates interest groups that become "conflict groups of the class type."

By inequitably allocating status, power, resources, and other values, the stratification structure creates the value scarcities that constitute the goals of social conflict. As Hoivik (1971: 2) has shown, this structure thus functions to ensure that certain categories and groups experience deprivation, frustration, and dissatisfaction. Thus it is possible to assert that inequitable distribution of power and status in a structure functions to determine the nature and level of collective conflict.

Two other circumstances of stratification serve to exacerbate these conflict-prone experiences. First, stratification systems and their inclusive social structures often lack the social mechanisms for reducing or off-setting these experiences of structural strain. Barber (1957: 482–85) illustrated this relationship by showing how rebellion in modern Europe was prevented when the social strata were open. And second, prevailing ideologies may also work to intensify further the shared feelings of discontent and resentment. The pressure to struggle for relief sometimes becomes unbearable, and conflict may explode violently.

Rigidity and instability are other structural conditions which have been found to be conducive to conflict. Although both conditions are widespread in complex social systems, they occur also in less highly developed societies. Gurr (1969: 614–15) found lack of "institutional strength," i.e., rigidity, to be one underlying condition of civil violence. Rigid institutions could not "absorb" or "deflect" ordinary collective conflict. The result was the buildup of tensions and the escalation of struggle. According to Dahrendorf (1959: 239) the intensity of conflict or the level of violence is conditioned by changing the rigidity of surrounding social structures. When the higher ranks in a stratification structure are closed to individuals from the underclasses, for example, structural rigidity is present.

Structural rigidity functions in at least two ways to increase the chances of nonlegitimate struggle. First, it tends to support and exacerbate inequalities in the allocation of power, status, resources, and other important values. In this way rigidity contributes to value scarcity and to the perception of it. For example, much research has demonstrated the fact of sexual stratification in the United States. Acker (1973: 936–44) complains about the rigidity of the American sex structure in the light of these data. Second, structural rigidity also enhances the psychosocial correlates of nonlegitimate conflict. We noted this condition in the discussion of the background of social conflict. The lack of change, unavailability of acceptable compensations, and sense of alienation all intensify the feelings of discontent and anger. The formal and detailed account of the background of the riot in Cincinnati in the summer of 1967 included in the Report of the National Advisory Commission on Civil Disorders (1968: 47) contains the following statements showing how structural rigidity fed into the development of social conflict: "Without the city's realizing what was occurring, over the years protest through political and non-violent channels had become increasingly difficult for Negroes. To young, militant Negroes, especially, such protest appeared to have become almost futile."

On the other hand, structural instability resulting from rapid, uncontrolled change may also be conducive of conflict. Gamson (1966: 73) stated that "structural strain" resulted from such change as "rapid economic growth or decline, heavy in-migration and out-migration, or shifts in the distribution of power in the community." Basic structural connections are either broken or loosened and the whole system seems in danger of collapse. People may experience intense anxiety, frustration, and discontent. Competition for scarce resources and for positions of safety and security is intensified. Kelidar (1975) has shown that endemic structural instability in Iraq has long been associated with internal and external conflict and tensions. The conflict situation may be exacerbated by the circulation of rumors or the operation of ideologies propagated by various interest groups. Smelser (1959) showed how social instability produced by rapid change in the early years of the British industrial revolution functioned to facilitate intense conflict and violence on the part of the textile workers in the English midlands. Their destruction of the new machines and factories was their way of recovering the security and predictability in life that they enjoyed in the era of cottage industries.

Structural stress, or malintegration, constitutes another condition of conflict. Structures in which the working parts fail to fit and function together harmoniously and efficiently may lead to conflict. Although this condition is typical of both stratification and rigid or unstable structures, it is also present in other situations. For example, uneven change rates and trends in sectors of social systems that are interrelated lead to malintegration of the total system. In a study of developing societies, Melson and Wolpe (1970: 1112–30) observed that in the process of modernization unequal rates of change within communal systems produced structural stress. These differential rates of mobilization exacerbated communal conflict by multiplying internal social cleavages. The same effect often results from remedial change or social reform. The change that seems to solve a social problem in one social sector may produce disharmonies in other sectors of the system. For example, President Nixon's plan of "revenue sharing" to reduce the domination of the federal government has been shown to be related to inefficiencies, corruption, and other malfunctions of participating state and local agencies. In a study of collective efforts to install fluoridation systems in a group of New England communities, Gamson (1966: 71–81) showed how this remedial program functioned to facilitate internal community conflict. The advocates of fluoridation found themselves engaged in struggle against conservative municipal administrations as well as those interests which regarded any change as undesirable.

The development of industry in traditional societies tends to produce structural stress. Writing of this process, Broom and Selznick (1968: 472) pointed out that all societies do not experience the same degree of stress in the process of change. In some the transition is fairly smooth, while in others disorganization and stress are serious and prolonged. Within advanced industrial societies, incompatible patterns of organization within a single industry may generate structural stress. For example, some years ago the ladies' garment industry consisted of hundreds of small independent firms. Then the workers in this industry organized within a single inclusive union. The union encountered difficulty in dealing systematically with so many different firms, and the industry was torn with labor-management strain until, in self-defense, it formed an inclusive organization to manage relations with the union.

Structural stress is disturbing and frustrating for individuals who must live and act within the disorganized system. There is a tendency to tug and haul, to bicker and blame, and to take mutually incompatible defensive and face-saving actions. This structural condition functions in at least two ways to intensify the possibility of conflict. With a concern for the adjustment of the system, some individuals and groups may define the stressful condition as a social problem. Their laudable efforts to solve the problem may embroil them in conflict with others who are pursuing different remedial courses as well as with those who wish to defend the status quo. On the other hand, some other individuals and groups may perceive the situation as personally deprivational and frustrating. They will be moved to struggle for security and the scarce values that have personal importance for them.

Complexity and impersonality of structures are a further conflict-facilitating condition. The structures of many societies are typically complex and impersonal; they often appear to be incomprehensible and overwhelming. The experience and perception of complexity and impersonality, whether real or imagined, are threatening and frustrating for many people.

The responses to complexity and impersonality have been conceptualized in several ways. Marx employed the term *alienation* to characterize the dehumanizing effect of modern industry and the estrangement of workers from their jobs. Under factory conditions work lost its creative character in the impersonal relations with machines and in the repetitive, segmented activities of the job. The capitalistic industrial structure had assumed a degree of complexity that appeared incomprehensible and threatening.

Seeman (1959: 783–91) identified isolation, powerlessness, meaninglessness, and self-estrangement as the core components of alienation. These are ways in which the individual has been excommunicated or has withdrawn from his complex, impersonal world. Feeling isolated and powerless to control the experiences of his life, the alienated individual becomes estranged from himself as well as from his meaningless world.

Many writers such as Clarke (1972: 400–523) and Baul and Slaughter (1971: 475–87) have stressed the impersonality of complex social structures as one condition of conflict. Complex and specialized groups and situations engage individuals not as whole people but in terms of their segmental roles as workers, passengers, shoppers, voters, viewers, etc., almost without end. Relations under such circumstances tend to be casual and impersonal. The studies of university conflict and violence in the 1960s frequently referred to the impersonality of large campuses as an underlying factor. In a study of the decline of political homogeneity in modernizing India, Somyee (1973: 799–816) reported that political parties tended to build patchwork structures of segmented support for candidates and issues on multi-caste lines rather than to rely on the traditional castes. This condition tended to exacerbate political conflict. Impersonality is also related to rigidity of structure and instability of organization resulting from rapid change.

Sometimes a longstanding low-level controversy between traditional adversaries may be intensified, expanded, or prolonged by sponsorship from the outside. For example, by sponsoring both sides, the Soviet Union and China transformed an ancient animosity into a full-scale grudge war between Cambodia and Thailand. Other illustrations of sponsored conflicts include the Zimbabwean guerrilla struggle in Rhodesia and the Ethiopian-Somalian war in the Horn of Africa. In these situations, the external sponsor adds a new structural dimension to an existing internal conflict. It has been suggested that the revolutionary terrorism of the Red Brigades in Italy is Soviet-sponsored.

Another aspect of complexity and impersonality is captured in one version of the conception of mass society. This view of the matter has been expressed by Bell (1960: 21–22), Riesman (1950), and Bensman and Rosenberg (1963), who insist that modern man wanders lost in the impersonal jungle of his social world. It is implied that masses of people are alienated and dehumanized in the vast, complex, and impersonal world. Such interpretations contend that structural complexity is pervasively conducive of strain, tension, and conflict. Anxiety, frustration, and dissatisfaction are widespread. The search for a way out of this insupportable dilemma gets fused to struggles for important scarce values such as security, response, and a sense of belonging. Alienated and anomic individuals are apt to foment social conflict.

CONFLICT IN "THE PUBLIC"

Social conflict takes place within a social system which in a general way can be thought of as its public. Although it is theoretically possible that some members of a social system may remain totally unaware of and unresponsive to a significant conflict, it seems more likely that all or at least a very large proportion of the members would be conscious of the struggle. By considering the actions and reactions of individuals toward conflict, it is possible to place the members of a social system into categories. In this way we can account for virtually all members of the social system. Such a series of categories is shown in the items of Figure 3-1. Although all the roles identified fall into patterns of awareness, responsiveness, and action, they designate different kinds of action.

Participant roles are those of attacker and defender. Within each of these categories, degrees and modes of involvement are indicated according to whether the participation is that of an organization member, a nonmember ("regulars" and "ad hocs") or a member of a coalition. Another significant group is involved in the conflict, not as attacker or defender, but as conflict manager. Managers seek to control the conflict on the basis of their judgments of what is legitimate. This topic is explored at some length in chapters 9 to 12 in Part II below. Here we simply point out that an important category of system members is involved in the conflict without actually participating in it.

The neutrals are portrayed as a series of "publics." This term acknowledges that they are not participants, while stressing the fact that they are aware of and responsive to the struggle. Many members of the community express their interest in and response to the conflict in audiencelike behavior. This large category of neutrals applauds or disapproves what they see and hear and thus helps to validate or veto the conflict action. At another time the same and other individuals may form a bystander public. They are affected by the inconveniences, disruptions, or even injuries of conflict. They respond in self-defense. For example, the Rhodesian Africans who remain in tribes are not directly involved in

FIGURE 3-1

PARTICIPANTS, MANAGERS, NEUTRALS

I. The Participants: Attackers, Defenders
    A. Organizational participants (officers and members)
    B. Nonmember participants
        1. The "regulars" (volunteers, supporters, etc.)
        2. The "ad hocs" (those who rally for special occasions)
    C. Coalitional participants (members and constituents of allied organizations)

II. The Establishments: Conflict Managers
    A. Governments (official control agents)
    B. Bureaucratic institutions (universities, industries, ecumenical organizations)
    C. Associations (American Friends Service Committee, American Arbitration Association)

III. The Neutrals
    A. Neutrals as audience, interested, watching, responding to conflict and validating or vetoing the conflict
    B. Neutrals as "bystander public"
        1. Affected by conflict, victimized, inconvenienced
        2. Responding and acting in self-defense
    C. Neutrals as "mediating public"
        1. Interested, responding, interpreting
        2. Explaining, clarifying, influencing
        3. Acting as a link in communication between the conflict and the community
    D. Neutrals as "fair-play public"
        1. Watching for fair-play violations
        2. Sympathetic to underdog or victims of "dirty politics"
    E. Neutrals as "public-interest public"
        1. Concerned with due process, general welfare, larger community
        2. Possibly acting to influence public policy and action

the guerrilla fighting. Nevertheless, both guerrillas and security forces abuse and attack them for helping the other side. Thus stimulated, these bystander neutrals react, sometimes calling down a plague on both participants' houses, sometimes taking one side or the other. Turner and Killian (1972: 294) have observed that at times some neutrals may be drawn into concern over conflict through humanitarian sympathy for the underdog or through condemnation of "dirty politics." They demand fair play and if pushed hard enough may desert the position of neutrality for direct involvement. In another hypothesis, Turner and Killian (224) note that some neutrals respond as a "mediating public." In this role they seek to understand, explain, or interpret the conflict to others, sometimes for clarification, sometimes in order to influence their listeners. Some of these same neutrals, together with others, may become concerned with the "public-interest" implications of the conflict. These neutrals form a "public-interest public" which may push for due process, ethical behavior, or the like.

This line of discussion brings us around to Spencer's (1971: 219–31) conclusion about the neutrals, that in fact they are not neutral at all. These members of the social system are socially effective even though they are not directly engaged in the conflict itself. When organized and acting in the various roles of neutrals, they are drawn into interest in and concern with the conflict. Thus without fully intending to do so, they manage to influence the course of the conflict in some way.

STRUCTURAL IMPLEMENTATION

Dahrendorf (1958: 175) suggested that the genesis of conflict is to be found in aspects and changes of social structure. However, specialized forms of social structure are required if the conflict is to take place. The ordinary arrangements of civilian life or day-to-day activities may function to generate collective struggle, but in order to actively engage in struggle new and different modes of organization are needed. For example, a Plains Indian war band differed significantly in structure from a hunting party, even though both may have included the same braves. In preparation for a strike, a labor union organizes its members for the encounter, deploys pickets at the company's factories or mines, and initiates a boycott of its products. We recognize the distinction between ordinary structures and those needed in times of conflict by such expressions as "going on the warpath," "mobilization for defense," and "deploying forces." Although specialized forms are required for the mounting of conflict, such organizations differ in degree of formality, inclusiveness, and relative permanence. For example, in the United States "the military" constitutes a formal, restricted, and permanent form of conflict organization. A protesting, confronting, or rioting minority group will be much less formally, technically, and permanently organized.

In the present section we examine three aspects of the specialized mode of conflict structure. First we investigate what Rummel (1976: 253–55) called the "conflict structure." Next, we discuss the more or less commonplace forms of social organization—associations, movements, and organizations—that execute conflict as a part of "business as usual." And third, we consider the organizational devices that permit pluralities of collective actors to cooperate within the two basic conflict roles of attacker and defender.

Conflict Structure

Social conflict refers to struggle between collective actors. Whatever the general social setting—international war, street riot, labor strike, legal contest—the structure of conflict is basically the same. It is composed of two actors, facing each other and positioned in such a way as to invite struggle. Referring to the dynamic component of this arrangement, Rummel (1976: 253) declared that the conflict structure is "the *tendency* of interests to oppose each other." In this struggle of actors and opposition of interests, the participants play two roles, attacker and defender. One actor attacks the other because the other is known or believed to obstruct the achievement of desired scarce values. The actor under attack is likely to defend himself, to return the fight. Thus, as Mack and Snyder (1957: 218) and Williams (1972: 18) have suggested, from the outset and by the very nature of conflict, the actors play both the roles of attacker and of defender simultaneously. These two roles, positioned to ensure confrontation, and bound together by an interactive process of struggle, constitute the key components of the conflict structure, whose working parts include: (a) two social roles, each of which may include one or more collective actors; (b) two social positions that place the roles (and the occupying actors) in the posture of confrontation; (c) a set of scarce values (e.g., power, status, or resources) that are the goals of struggle, and ancillary values that condition the conflict in various ways; (d) a set of norms that embody the social values and pattern and systematize the conflict relationship; (e) a relationship characterized by a series of struggles between the actors that is more or less patterned by traditional and emergent norms.

The fact of a basic conflict structure has been recognized by most students of social conflict. Marx saw major conflict as emanating from the inevitable revolutionary struggle of the proletariat against the bourgeoisie. All sectors of the industrial society would feed into one or another of these inclusive camps confronting each other in the posture of escalating struggle. Employing a cyclical model, Lenski (1966: 1–23) saw the two actors as "thesis" being attacked by "antithesis," while Fals-Borda (1970: 1–9) called the establishment "topia," being attacked by "subversion." Brinton (1965: 28–133) wrote of "revolutionists" and "old regimes," and Gamson (1966: 71–81) saw the struggle of com-

munity adversaries as a conflict between "partisans" and "authorities."
Of late, scholars have conceptualized the attacking actor as a kind of
social movement. The defender is envisaged as the "establishment," the
"social order," or "the power structure." Referring to the social movement's opposition to the social order structure, Turner and Killian (1972:
159) wrote that an inherent tension qualifies relations between collective
behavior and any established social order. The literature on social movements, e.g., Blumer (1951: 99–120), Lang and Lang (1964: 489–542),
Turner and Killian (1972: 245–405), Ash (1972: 1–28), and Wilson
(1973: 300–331) envisaged this actor as a large, complex collectivity including an indefinite number of subordinate groups and associations.
Under the aegis of the structure and ideology of the social movement,
all these collective units can find positions on one or the other side of a
conflict enterprise.

In a conflict the actors play two roles. Israel attacked Jordan in the
1967 war and Jordan defended herself as best she could. The White Cap
Boys challenge the Northside Gang and the rumble is on. Usually these
two roles have other dimensions. Each side is likely to view the opposition as an out-group, but often one group is treated like a social inferior
and perceives itself as such. In this case, the other group is cast in the
role of social superior. The social act of conflict is the interlocking and
reciprocation of these two roles. The answer to attack is defense.

The actors who perform these roles occupy positions that place them
in confrontation and ready them for struggle. They face each other in
suspicion, mutual alertness, and growing readiness for overt struggle.
The level of tension and strain is heightened dangerously. One actor, the
potential attacker, perceives the other as obstructing the achievement of
desired ends. In return, this actor is seen by the other as challenging and
threatening. In this situation, conflict is the outcome to be expected.
Conflict position and confrontation can take the form of a hostile crowd
encountering the police on a city street. They are what a government is
concerned about when it accuses a neighbor of mobilizing troops along
its frontier. When the neighbor's forces are dispersed and no longer in
combat readiness, then attack is not expected.

The existence of scarce values, or at least the assumption that certain
values are in scarce supply, is a working part of the conflict structure.
For example, it may be believed that there is not enough water in the
river that separates two nations to provide adequate irrigation for both.
Competitors may be convinced that the market that they share is not
large enough to consume the full product of both national industries.
White workers may fear that blacks can be hired only by the white

workers' losing their jobs. If a company management thought that gross income was adequate to retire outstanding bonds, pay satisfactory dividends, provide for replacement and expansion, cover obsolescence, and all the rest, it might not refuse the pay raise and fringe benefits that the union is demanding. Acquisition of scarce values is the ultimate goal of conflict. Removal of a competing or interfering collective actor is the immediate end of conflict. Without the existence both of a valued goal and an interfering opponent, social conflict is not possible.

Social conflict is also qualified by a series of ancillary values. Conflict may be important to save face, enhance in-group solidarity, improve a public image or bolster self-respect. Even in realistic conflict, the struggle itself is sometimes also a value. Such ancillary values are built into the total conflict structure.

The interactive process of social conflict is more or less confined to the patterns of social norms. For example, the legal norms of the Taft-Hartley Act and the several state codes of industrial relations establish a normative framework for labor-management conflict. The loosely codified conventions of international law establish such a framework for international war. The unofficial norms of morality, and community patterns of fair play, set metes and bounds to other conflicts. However, the normative framework of some conflicts is vague and ambiguous. For example, lacking clear normative controls and guides, the nation panicked in the 1960s when racial conflict, student violence, city riots, and massive demonstrations erupted. There are rules to govern labor-management strife, but criminal gang-wars and youthful gang-rumbles take place in a no-man's land of normative ambiguity and ambivalence. In such situations, ad hoc norms tend to emerge to govern and pattern conflict relations.

Finally, the continuous interactive flow of attack and defense, thrust and parry, advance and retreat constitute an essential part of the conflict structure. The interactive parts are complementary, interlocked, fused together, and continuously active. They create a stream of interaction that flows through the channels of the norms. Thus, for example, in a strike the union gives a story to the press and places an advertisement in the morning paper. The company replies with a news conference and feature story. The union establishes a picket line and the company either locks the workers out or seeks to penetrate the picket line. In this way the skirmishing may go on for days. Each act is both initiation and response. Each actor seeks to remove the other from the struggle or to defend itself from being removed. It takes two to make a conflict.

This system of working parts constitutes a series of heuristic perspec-

tives from which to investigate and interpret social conflict. Each may be
a point of focus for analysis. At the same time, each may provide a perspective from which to approach the study of the other parts. Thus, for
example, a researcher might investigate the normative aspects of riot behavior or of international war. Such an approach could result in delinea-
tion of a relatively durable arrangement of social norms that constitutes
the structure of riot or war. At the same time, focus on the normative
aspect of the generic structure provides insights into the nature of the
conflict roles, the conflict positions, and the conflict process.

Further, the conflict structure is supported by certain properties or
intrinsic characteristics of the opposing roles of attacker and defender.
Rummel (1976: 253–54) argued that "attitudes," or action orientations,
are generated by groups and "the more distant such groups are in status
and in meanings, values and norms, the more different their attitudes."
Such attitudes or orientations reinforce the conflict-prone tendencies of
the basic roles. We can identify and examine three such conflict-oriented
attitudes or role dimensions: the ethnocentric, the power-status, and the
change-oriented. Each role characteristic is associated with a typical
structural pattern.

The ethnocentric role dimension is identified with structural positions
of in-group and out-group. When the in-group position is taken as the
point of reference, then the groups are native or foreign, friend or foe,
we or they. That is, when a group becomes a collective conflict actor,
then in relation to a prospective opponent it perceives itself as in-group,
native, friend, or "we." A proclivity to oppose the other group is built
into the collective role. For example, in a study of church-state relations
in Zaire, Adelman (1975: 102–15) found that conflict between the two
actors was grounded in differences of "identity" and "allegiance." Each
side took itself as the in-group reference point from which to see and
respond to the other.

The nature of this built-in proclivity to oppose the other group is captured in the concept of ethnocentrism. The in-group's members, characteristics, possessions, history, and so on are the bases for disparaging the
out-group. The result is a predisposition to glorify one's own and to
denigrate the other group. As Sumner (1940: 27–28) noted, this ethnocentric sense of difference from the putative enemy—the force of internal
group cohesion, the opposition to the out-group foe, the sense of rivalry,
hostility, and threat in the interactive situation—all are aspects of the
in-group–out-group structure. Such a judgment and evaluation leads to
the tendency to avoid or oppose the other group. Withdrawal is usually

in a self-flattering, upward direction, since the other group is perceived as low in relation to one's own group. Disparagement and avoidance of the other group is accompanied by feelings of disgust and abhorrence. Such feelings reflect a willingness or readiness to attack the rejected group, and a limited sense of compassion. The out-group is perceived as harboring ill-will against the in-group and thus constitutes a potential foe. Under such circumstances, to attack is to defend oneself. The function of ethnocentrism in the conflict roles is illustrated in the black-white conflict in Rhodesia. From the beginning of settled contact in the 1880s (Davies, 1975), the white "Europeans" and the black Africans have regarded themselves as in-group and out-group. Although struggle has not always been violent, it has been qualified by intense ethnocentrism, especially on the part of the "Europeans." This fact was clearly manifest in the intransigence of the Ian Smith government in 1975 and 1976 during negotiations over black-majority rule.

Another dimension of the attacker-defender role structure is some expression of the rank/power differential. This dimension is captured in such paired concepts as elite and non-elite, dominant and minority, bourgeoisie and proletariat, and high and low caste. These concepts indicate that power and rank vary; high rank is associated with great power and low rank with limited power. At the same time, role tags are associated with corresponding structural settings. That is, elite, dominant, bourgeois, and high-caste groups always occupy high status in social structures, and the opposite is true of the lesser rank in each pair.

Perceptions of difference in rank and power generate self-conceptions that correlate with the ethnocentrism discussed above. Invidious contrasts function to isolate the groups. Differences in power tend to generate reciprocal feelings of insecurity and threat. Members of each category look at those in the other with some distaste and suspicion. The categories are tied together by a relationship of interdependence and tension.

As Marx and other observers have reported, such paired and differentiated categories tend to see each other as natural enemies. Negative evaluations, feelings, and attitudes that constitute a potential for struggle are built into the rank/power role dimension. In this situation of inequality, different traditions tend to impose different rules for struggle. In one tradition, the advantage of power and status constitutes the invitation and justification to attack and conquer. Thus, for example, because Mussolini believed that Italy was superior to Ethiopia in the mid-1930s, he did not hesitate to lead Italian forces into an invasion of the weaker nation. However, another tradition dictates *noblesse oblige* and restrains the powerful from taking full advantage of its position. Thus in recent years the United States has often refrained from attacking weaker nations even though provoked.

The core conflict roles also contain a built-in ingredient that orients collective actors for or against social change. This change-orientation is captured in such paired concepts as thesis and antithesis, boundary-maintaining and boundary-extending, topia and subversion, ideologic and utopian, and status-quo and reformist. These terms also suggest positions within the social structure. Thus, a boundary-maintaining, status-quo ideologist would take his position on the side of the social order. He is socially identified with the present and is oriented to resist rapid or inclusive modifications of the social order. A boundary-extending, reformist subversive would either favor or tolerate radical change. He tends to identify with the future. Thus Gerlach and Hine (1970: xiii) observe that what may seem to be slow or normal change to one group may be experienced as radical or revolutionary change by the other. For example, in the decade after the 1954 Supreme Court decision outlawing school desegregation, many conservative Southerners regarded the beginning of desegregation of public schools as runaway integration of the races. But the NAACP lawyers who had argued and won the case, and others, believed that their hard-won victory was being frustrated and nullified.

It is evident that the change-orientation dimension is also associated with the ethnocentric and rank/power dimensions discussed above. Any actor who espouses change, therefore, may be seen as an alien and suspect because he also differs in rank and power. The opposed orientations to change build a potential for conflict into the paired roles and so undergird the disposition to attack or defend.

Role Reversal

In the course of continuous conflict, actors may switch roles. The defender goes on the attack, reducing the former attacker to self-defense. For example, in 1967 Israel attacked two Arab neighbors in the so-called Six Day War, but in 1973 two of her Arab neighbors attacked Israel. Moreover, in the course of this latter conflict, Israel went from defense to attack, forcing both opponents to defend themselves. In the United States, for the last quarter of a century the opponents of school desegregation have been on the attack against the supporters of this practice. In the mid 1970s, however, use of the tactic of inclusive, court-enforced busing of school children to achieve "racial balance" generated widespread resentment and resistance. Under the banner of the "anti-busing movement," the former defenders have gone on the attack, altering the conflict structure and situation.

The illustrations sketched above suggest some of the conditions that influence the switch of conflict roles. In the school situation, change of tactics by advocates of desegregation altered the legitimacy pattern and incensed defenders who, therefore, gained new public approval. In the brief Yom Kippur War of 1973, Israel recovered from the shock of surprise, regrouped her forces, brought up reinforcements, and went on the offensive. That is, time and opportunity for such tactical adjustments functioned to influence the switch of conflict roles.

The will to attack may arise within a defending conflict actor from the sense of desperation. Hard-pressed and faced with apparent certain defeat, a conflict defender may see attack as the only possibility left to him. Such an actor may marshal his small resources and attack with a vigor that shocks the more powerful and advantaged opponent. A last-ditch attack of this kind may stave off defeat and in some instances has led to surprise victories. This seems to have been the case in the so-called Winter War when little Finland turned the tables on big, powerful Russia and held her at bay.

The switch of conflict roles may have consequences not only for the collective actors but for the outcome of the conflict itself. Such a switch can affect public judgments of legitimacy in such a way as to influence the outcome of the struggle and the status of the conflict actors. The defending party that enjoys widespread sympathy may, when going on the attack, alienate internal supporters and outside allies. For example, it was noted above that adoption of the court-enforced busing tactic generated widespread public disapproval. In the case of school desegregation, it seems likely that this disapproval may affect the course of the long-time struggle for desegregation. On the other hand, when the aggressor is forced onto the defensive, he may acquire an aura of legitimacy that was impossible so long as he was the aggressor.

If a hard-pressed defender suddenly acquires new resources, it may become possible to go on the offensive. New resources may come in various forms and from several directions. A tactic of one actor may generate a sense of outrage in the community. A weak party, struggling to defend itself from an attacking bully, may suddenly acquire the aura of legitimacy because it finds itself in the role of underdog. New allies for either actor may arise from unexpected directions and for reasons often best known to themselves. For example, a powerful actor may discover that a hard-pressed defending group is politically or strategically important and therefore must be aided. The strong actor may intervene or threaten to intervene on behalf of the weak party. In the midst of a discouraging struggle, a hard-pressed actor may discover manpower and natural resources that had been overlooked in calmer times. For example, it may be recognized that marginal population categories—the old, the disabled, and the mentally retarded—can be put to important use. Armed with such new-found resources, a conflict defender may think it is possible to go on the offensive.

Finally, the switch of conflict roles may reflect prior structural changes within one or both actors. A shift of ideology or the drift of public opinion may lead the members of a social movement or the citizens of a nation to withdraw support from the incumbent leadership. The conflict can no longer be prosecuted successfully under these circumstances. A switch of role and strategy is indicated, if not obligatory. The leaders may find it expedient to search for ways to terminate the conflict. Sometimes in mid-conflict collective actors may redefine the terms of the conflict. Turner and Killian (1972: 310) point out that social movements undergo internal shifts of ideology and therefore corresponding shifts of strategic approaches. In this case, the movement may switch conflict roles.

The switch of conflict roles clearly has important consequences for each actor. In both cases internal organization, strategic considerations, the mobilization and commitment of resources, states of public opinion, sense of the legitimacy of the conflict, relations with other social units, and the like, will be affected to a greater or lesser extent by the reversal of conflict roles. Some of these consequences may turn out to be crucial for the outcome of the struggle. They must certainly be taken into account by both sets of conflict managers.

Organizations, Movements, Associations

Social conflict is implemented by the ordinary structures of society. This is managed in two ways. First, entire societies, organizations, or associations may play the roles of attacker and defender. At the same time, constituent units (groups, associations, or communities) of inclusive societies may act out the twin roles of a restricted conflict. On the other hand, specialized conflict structures (the military, the vigilante organization, the warrior band) may play the roles of attacker and defender for a larger, more inclusive social unit. For example, one business firm may struggle against others for control of a limited market. The blacks, women, or ethnic groups of a multi-group society may engage in conflict against other such groups or against the Establishment for first-class citizenship or for "liberation." A modern nation uses its military force to fight a war and the Ku Klux Klan may don its hoods and become a vigilante organization. In this section we illustrate the implementation of conflict on the part of ordinary social structures by examining the actions of organizations, movements, and associations.

The most inclusive conflicts, e.g., international wars and revolutions, are implemented by the principal institutional structures of societies. In developing societies, this organizational framework of wars and warlike conflict is likely to be the tribe or the tribal federation. The structural agent of war in the peasant societies of both medieval and modern times is the principality, the shiekdom, or the major agrarian unit. In other societies, the church has been the structural agency for war. For example, in the Middle Ages the Roman Catholic Church was the attacker in the Crusades, and Islam waged the endless wars of Moslem proselytism. Although modern wars and revolutions generally issue from secular deprivations and controversies, religious organizations sometimes set the structural stage for such conflicts. This is the case of the Hindu-Moslem feuds of India, the Protestant-Catholic internal strife of Northern Ireland, and the civil war of Christians and Muslims in Lebanon. In the modern world the typical structural apparatus for international war is the military arm of the nation-state. Biderman (1967: 122–37) called the military a special kind of institution designed to guard and maintain the ultimate values of a society. In this way, societies arm themselves with specialized personnel, organization, and equipment for the inter-societal business of conflict. Often also, as is shown below, nation-states clustered under alliances or coalitions to prosecute the great wars of the nineteenth and twentieth centuries. Within such great modern societies as the United States, West Germany, or Japan, major conflict takes place between the gigantic intrasocietal bureaucratic structures: labor and management, minorities and dominants, political parties of the right and left, and so on. As shown above, these units enter into conflict action by fulfilling the roles of attacker and defender.

In the modern world, much conflict action is expressed as dissent from or opposition to established social orders. Struggle is aimed as much at change of the social order as at achievement of cherished values brought about by that change. Social movements consist of social units, either already established or improvised for the purpose of struggle, acting to promote or prevent social change, often through conflict. Thus Turner and Killian (1972: 246) refer to a social movement as a "collectivity" acting continuously to affect the course of social change. There is much evidence to suggest that at present a very substantial proportion of all collective conflict issues from the action of social movements. For example, Europe's part in World War II resulted from the efforts of the Nazi movement to change the political and social order of Western Europe. The contemporary intranational and international wars, e.g., the Vietnam War, the endless Northern Irish civil strife, the devastating Lebanese civil war, and the struggle of blacks in southern Africa for majority rule and the abolition of apartheid, are all manifestations of conflicts brought about by social movements. At the same time, much of the warp and woof of ordinary continuous struggle within all modern societies is the product of social movements. The labor movement gives battle for the legitimate rights of workers and the minority movements fight for liberation. Recent American history is replete with such movements as anti-pollution, peace, women's liberation, antiabortion, population control—the list is virtually endless.

Social movements function in various ways to organize individuals and groups along lines of social conflict. In this respect, Ryan (1969: 172–212) called attention to such organizational types as "general" and "specific," "active" and "expressive," and "reform" and "revolutionary." Social movements also structure the beliefs, thoughts, and feelings of participants and followers. These sociopsychological elements are arranged in ideologies that affect the motivation and commitment of members, the goals that are sought, the targets that are attacked and the strategies and tactics of conflict that are adopted. Often social movements lead their participants into various forms of nonlegitimate struggle. For example, guerrilla tactics and terrorism are common practices of revolutionary movements. Such movements also organize some of their members and followers into military and quasi-military structures which specialize in violent conflict action.

The term *social movement*, as customarily used, has at least three distinguishable referents. In its basic sense a social movement is conceptualized as an inclusive organization of an indefinite number of individuals and groups engaged in advancing or preventing social change. This is the conceptualization that is denoted in such names as the peace movement, the women's liberation movement or the black civil rights movement. Basic constituents are indefinite numbers of groups and associations of various kinds and sizes. Some observers, e.g., Turner and Killian (1972: 245–348 passim) also use the term *social movement* to refer to a specific organization or association that is engaged consciously in the business of affecting social change. Thus they would consider the National Organization of Women, the American Civil Liberties Union,

or the African National Council as social movements. Thus conceptualized, all such organizations or associations are understood to be acting to affect the course of some social change. Other scholars tend to use
the term to designate broad trends or drifts within an inclusive society.
They speak of the liberal or conservative movements. Such a social
movement's operations consist of programs and enterprises of the organizations and associations which espouse the ideological orientation
that is said to characterize the movement. Bell (1960: 100–112) wrote
about the so-called McCarthy movement. This was the diffuse, amor-
phous, reactionary orientation of American life that was symbolized by
the late Senator Joseph McCarthy. In such usage, basic reference is to
the direction of action that is revealed by many individuals and groups,
among which there is no inclusive organization nor clear sense of cor-
porate existence. The movement in this sense nevertheless affects the
course of social change and often provides a structural framework for
social conflict.

Clustering Mechanisms

Although the contending parties can play only two basic roles in a conflict, it is nevertheless possible for many different groups to participate
directly in the action. For example, in the Middle East most of the Arab
states participate in one way or another in the inclusive role of enemy
to Israel. Joint participation of a plurality of collective actors in each of
the basic conflict roles is made possible by means of clustering devices.
Although the variety of such devices is almost limitless, most can be
subsumed under the four following generic types:
    1—*Council:* a unifying and coordinating agency composed of the
heads or other representatives of a series of autonomous groups, who act
in cooperation in a conflict enterprise.
    2—*Coalition:* a temporary arrangement for joint conflict action made
by a number of groups that wish to retain their separate identities.
    3—*Alliance:* a contractual arrangement for joint action by a group of
independent collective actors who establish a specialized apparatus for
their joint conflict action.
    4—*Federation:* the political union of a series of groups under which
the management of external relations, especially relations of conflict, is
monopolized by the inclusive organization.
    Groups of all types use these collective devices in various ways and
and in various combinations to cluster and collaborate for the conduct of
social conflict. In these ways they can play the roles of attacker and de-

fender. For example, the American peace movement of the early 1970s was composed of a loose coalition of hundreds of national, state, and local organizations, all joined together to oppose the United States' military involvement in Vietnam. NATO, in addition to being an acronym for the North Atlantic Treaty Organization, is also the title of that body's specialized military apparatus. A score or more of nations, large and small, cluster under this alliance to defend against what is perceived as the threat of Soviet aggression. At the same time, the NATO foreign ministers use the council device for periodic consultations and policy coordinations. The coal miners' strike of 1977 and 1978 was possible because the labor union functioned as a federating agency for the local unions at a number of mines scattered among several states. Although most of the mines were struck, there was in fact only one strike, that of the United Mine Workers against the coal mine operators. Institutionally speaking, there was only one strike, although it took place on a number of widely dispersed locations.

Collective actors may cluster for attack or defense by means of some kind of council. For example, heads of state may gather in a widely heralded consultation at a summit conference to bolster determination to act in a certain way and to coordinate collective strategy. Such a council of heads of state is a temporary device, but sometimes councils are more durable mechanisms of clustering and coordination. In both cases the council is composed of official representatives of autonomous groups who need or wish to cooperate for conflict, but prefer to retain their independent identities.

Councils differ in both the formality of their organization and the permanence of their existence. The Nordic Council linking Denmark, Finland, Iceland, Norway, and Sweden is a durable, significant organization of states. In periodic meetings, prime ministers and their aides develop and coordinate various policies and strategies. Considerations of conflict constitute only one class of problems taken up by this council. Sometimes the council is an adjunct of a permanent political organization. For example, NATO supports a council of foreign ministers who meet periodically to consult on matters of common defense and security. At other times, the council is a fragile, one-time mechanism required for action in an extraordinary situation. Writing about black conflict leaders, Himes (1973: 101) reported that in 1962 and 1963 they joined in a council to promote the "March on Washington." This ad hoc group included James Farmer of CORE, James Foreman of SNCC, Martin Luther King, Jr., of the SCLC, A. Phillip Randolph of the BSCP, Roy

Wilkins of the NAACP, and Whitney M. Young of the Urban League, with Bayard Rustin as administrator.

Another means for clustering separate collective actors in a single conflict action is by coalition. A coalition is a device for temporary joint action by collective actors who wish to retain their separate identities. The cooperating parties come to an agreement on the extent and manner of involvement in the joint conflict action. They pool some of their resources to develop an organizational apparatus to administer the conflict operation. Sometimes the coalition, a species of council, may be informal. Leaders agree to confer from time to time about programs and activities and to brief one another on important developments or actions. Sometimes, however, the coalition is more formal and may be specified in some kind of document. The effect in both cases is to merge the separate units temporarily into a single organization for the purpose of waging conflict.

The coalition device has been employed by collective actors in many kinds of struggles. For example, Atkinson (1968: 48–52) reported that in the "war against poverty" in the 1960s, numerous organizations joined in the tactic of coalition building to gain strength for the main assault. Terrill (1972: 220) reported that the Chinese government, guided by Mao, clustered its allies in an arrangement called a "united front" to form an overarching coalition. Odegard (1928) reported that during the great struggle against beverage alcohol, the Anti-Saloon League had tied some sixty thousand national, state, and local organizations into a grand coalition. In such instances, when the struggle has ended, the coalition tends to dissolve and the various independent organizations resume their separate and relatively unconnected identities. As treated by Wood (1972: 512–21) the National Council of Churches is an example of a much more durable coalition.

The alliance is even more durable a clustering of collective actors. Each actor makes commitments of a contractual nature to the alliance. Thus the actors are clustered under treaties and conventions that may commit them to mutual support in case either an attack or a defense seems warranted. At the same time, each collective actor retains its autonomy with reference to issues and actions not specified in the agreement. The alliance mechanism is used to put together clusters of collective actors, often called leagues, organizations, or pacts. For example, in medieval times a cluster of towns in northern Germany and its environs formed the Hanseatic League for the promotion and protection of commerce.

Modern alliances also sponsor activities in addition to conflict. Such activities are justified as being supportive of the principal purpose of military defense. For example, the Organization of American States promotes free trade and cultural exchanges among the nations of South and North America. NATO sponsors research, academic and cultural exchanges, and similar activities among member nations that are seen as contributing to the organization's basic defensive purpose. Collective actors (nations) of the North Atlantic region are joined by alliances to work to develop joint plans and facilities for managing the issues of potential military aggression and conflict with outsiders. Thus the NATO apparatus manages the "Cold War" (in part at least) while maintaining a posture of impregnable defense against the possibility of "hot war" with the Soviet Union. The answer to NATO is the Warsaw Pact, through which the Soviet Union, according to Terrill (1972: 219–20), has clustered members of the "socialist community" into a "defensive bloc." Such leagues, organizations, pacts, and blocs function to cluster independent polities by agreements for the purposes of implementing aggressive or defensive conflict.

The federation is the most formal clustering device. In the basic sense, the word means either total or partial political union of entities that were formerly fully autonomous politically. For example, after the United States Constitution was ratified, the thirteen original quasi-independent colonies lost their political independence within the national union. But even before this event, the colonies had clustered and collaborated under the aegis of the "confederation" in order to wage the Revolutionary War. Following the successful revolution and under the new federal constitution, the former colonies relinquished to the new central government the right to conduct foreign relations and wage international war. The thirteen identifiable political entities were fused into the federation, and declaring war became the monopoly of the national state. In time, they lost the sense of political independence and gained a new awareness of historical and cultural identity.

The organized units called federations differ significantly in the degree to which dealing with conflict is centralized, since the constituent units have relinquished this right. In the United States, as well as in the German Federal Republic, this centralization is almost complete. Only the federal governments may engage in international war, although the several states conduct lesser forms of struggle among themselves and with other social units such as industrial corporations or crime syndicates. Sometimes a so-called political federation, e.g., the short-lived, fragile, and improvised United Arab Republic, is little more than a loose league or coalition within which each state retains most of its autonomy. The Republic was a temporary conflict-coordinating device intended to facilitate the struggle against Israel. Still other kinds of federations, such as the American Federation of Labor, handle the matter of conflict in other ways. Within the AFL and by the nature of industrial relations, each international and national union retains the responsibility for struggle with its industry or industry-group. Automobile- or steelworkers conduct contract negotiations and, if need be, organize and promote strikes against the industrial giants. The AFL supports such labor union conflicts, but does not participate directly, functioning instead more like a social movement engaged in struggle for social change, principally in labor legislation and the rights and perquisites of workers. This type of federation produces a division of labor in the conflict activities of the clustered conflict actors.

It can be said in summary that any given conflict enterprise may engage a plurality of conflict actors as participants in the two basic conflict roles. Collaboration is made possible by the act of clustering and numerous devices of clustering are in general use. This section has examined four such devices—the council, the coalition, the alliance, and the federation. In actual practice, however, these clustering devices seldom appear in pure form and often overlap.

4

Social Power in Social Conflict

Etzioni (1968: 313–14) has observed that the realization of most societal goals, especially when they are sought by opposing actors, requires the application of social power. This observation implies that in the enterprise of social conflict, one important activity is the search for and use of power. Almost any manifestation of struggle or contest will illustrate this fact. Although the Third World nations have outnumbered the United States and her allies in the United Nations for some years, American influence has tended to dominate the policy of the United Nations from the beginning. The economic counterpart to this activity may be illustrated by a labor union's approaching contract negotiations with the employer, taking a strike vote, raising a "war chest," and making other preparations to exert "pressure" on management. Virtually every description of the black minority in the United States has characterized it as relatively powerless, yet in the 1950s and 1960s blacks mobilized enough power to conduct moderately successful struggles on several fronts. The importance of power was anticipated in the definition of conflict presented above, where power was made an essential component of the concept. It is important, therefore, that we examine the relationship of power and conflict before proceeding further with the discussion.

In this chapter we explore the relationship of power to conflict by considering three main issues: the nature and types of social power, the mobilization and implementation of power, and the distribution of social power in social organization insofar as that distribution affects conflict. Initially, we examine the meaning of social power as revealed in the literature and discuss the confusion of terminology that accompanies the attempt to classify power. The second issue taken up is the mobilization and implementation of power. This issue is critical since many conflict groups are inherently weak and therefore must exert ingenuity and effort to locate the power they need to gain the ends they desire. We conclude the chapter by reviewing patterns of power organization in various kinds of societies and observing how various patterns of power distribution affect the enterprise of social conflict.

THE MEANING AND CLASSIFICATION OF POWER

In the literature two principal perspectives on social power have emerged. From one, social power is viewed as potential, i.e., an available capability of a social actor; and from the other, as active, i.e., a dynamic property of social relationships. The perspective of potential power is captured in Weber's (1958: 180) classic definition. He stated that power is "the chance of a man or a number of men to realize their own will in a communal action even against the resistance of others who are participating in the action." When Weber spoke of a "number of men," he envisaged a collective actor in the "communal action." Power was perceived as the probability that these men command enough potential capability to gain their way if they were to mobilize this potential. If they decided to take this "chance" and exercise their capability, overt struggle would take place. However, Weber seemed to imply that under certain circumstances the men might not take the chance and exercise their potential power.

In this potential form power is not only the capability of controlling decisions and actions, even against opposition; it is also the capability of preventing such decisions or actions from being made. Bachrach and Baratz (1962 and 1963) explored the latter aspect of the concept and called it "undecision." Thus they observed that social power has "two faces." In a study of black power in community decision-making, Banner (1975) showed that white community leaders in Knoxville, Tennessee, not only controlled important decisions of the black subcommittee, but also prevented certain issues from coming to public attention and being decided and acted upon.

The other perspective on social power portrays it as an active aspect of dynamic social life, a property of social relations. Rossi (1957: 425) perceived power as a relationship between social actors. Olsen (1970: 2) envisaged power as "a process in social life." This perspective of the power relationship is implicit in Tinker's (1971: 775–88) observation that the chief wielders of power must have the tacit assistance and co-operation of hundreds and even thousands of persons in order to exercise their power. Coleman (1973: 1–17) put the matter this way: actors are related to events in two ways—control of actors over events and consequences of events for actors.

From this perspective power may be conceptualized as a property or component of a social relationship. Simon (1953: 500) defined power as an "asymmetrical relation" between an "influencer" and an "influencee" that causes "some change of behavior." Eckstein and Gurr (1975: 15–18) note that such relations can occur between different social units, among members of a unit, or between hierarchical elements of a unit. In the relationship, initially the influencer exercises more power than the influencee. Thus power in the relationship flows predominantly in one direction, although a power relationship is reciprocal. This view of the matter is consistent with the fact noted in the foregoing chapter that actors, i.e., influencer or attacker and influencee or defender may switch roles in the course of the conflict relationship. Finally, the application of power in a relationship produces some change of behavior through a "feedback" process. That is, the influencee is forced to make adjustment to the influencer's initially greater power. But the influencee's adjustive change of behavior forces the influencer to change his behavior in some measure. And so it goes; win or lose, the exercise of power in a conflict relationship always produces some behavioral change.

The foregoing discussion has indicated that social power has at least five salient characteristics. First, from one perspective power is seen to be potential—the capability of actors to overcome resistance and achieve ends. Second, such power involves chances or probabilities; on the one hand there is a chance that the potential may or may not be mobilized and, on the other, that when mobilized it may or may not achieve the end sought. Third, social power is socially significant in two ways—when it is mobilized, active, and existing within a relationship, and when it produces a threat effect, by anticipation of its active application. Fourth, power is exercised in a relationship as push and resistance. Actors play the roles of attacker and defender, of influencer and influencee, in relationship to one another. Even though they may switch roles, the relationship unfolds as challenge and response, thrust and parry. And finally, some change of behavior always ensues from the commitment of power to social relations. The changes are sometimes manifest, i.e., intended and recognized, and sometimes latent, i.e., unintended and unrecognized. Often also they may be dysfunctional, i.e., maladaptive to the relevant social systems.

By differentiating and emphasizing different dimensions of the generic concept, four main types of social power have been identified. They are authority, force, dominance, and influence. Authority is the power vested in organizations. In his classic study, Weber (1958: 297) differentiated the subtype "charismatic authority," issuing from belief in the sanctity of the extraordinary, from the "traditionalist (patriarchal) domination," emanating from belief in the sanctity of everyday routines. With increasing complexity and formality of organization a new type, bureaucratic authority, tended to emerge, be absorbed into the social structure, and become hedged about by rational constraints.

Force, unlike authority, refers to power in the command of an individual. It is said to constitute an actor's unique coercive power as derived from sources in his control. Reflecting a common value-judgment, Goode (1972: 507–19) complained that power is a loose concept that is used to avoid recognizing the category of force. An actor's rank and role in an organization give him power over those beneath him who are subject to his official control. This is called dominance and is distinguished from authority, which is the power vested in the official roles and controlled by the official rules of the organization. By reference to various dimensions, Rummel (1976: 175–88) differentiated "coercive," "bargaining," "intellectual," "authoritative," "altruistic," and "manipulative" power. Lasswell and Kaplan (1950: 55–102), d'Antonio and Form (1967: 11–12), Dahl (1963: 40), Rossi (1957: 425), Miller (1961: 47–49), Gamson (1968: 59), and others have differentiated "influence" from "authority" as types or components of power. Although there are differences of detail, these formulations tend to agree that influence refers to personal and informal expressions of power. Authority, on the other hand, is seen as the formal and official power lodged in the offices of an organization, especially the government, and hedged about by official rules. Although the terminology in the sociology of social power constitutes a jungle of jargon, we will take the four types—force, authority, dominance, and influence—as basic.

Scholars regularly differentiate and recognize various degrees or amounts of social power. These differentials are verbalized in such terms as powerful and powerless, strong and weak. Alcock and Newcombe (1970: 336–43), Simon (1953: 500–512, 514–16), and others have experimented with the quantification and measurement of power. As yet no altogether satisfactory method for quantifying social power has been formulated. We continue to rely on "accurate" descriptions to indicate differentials of social power. These descriptive measures are probably more reliable and accurate when the referent is potential power than when we are talking about active power.

THE MOBILIZATION AND IMPLEMENTATION OF POWER

Social power does not exist in a vacuum. Potential power exists as a property of a social phenomenon called a power resource. Potential power must be extracted from the power resource and thus converted into active power before it can be used. This operation is called power mobilization and includes a series of related steps. Active power must be delivered and injected into a social relationship in order to achieve the ends of conflict. The delivery, injection, and manipulation of social power within social relations is called implementation and includes several related operations.

The range of phenomena that constitute power resources is great. Many students of the subject, e.g., Bierstedt (1950: 730–38), Blalock (1950: 53–59), Etzioni (1968: 131–349), Olsen (1970: 67), and Coleman (1973: 1–17) have developed lists of power resources. Olsen (4) stated that these resources may include "tangible" goods, e.g., money, buildings and land, organizational members, and equipment, as well as "relatively intangible" assets such as knowledge, legitimacy, values, skill, and organizational entity. Coleman (1973: 1–17) sees "control of events" as an important power resource. The wide range of particular resources can be summarized into the following five broad categories: (a) natural resources, including a society's territory; (b) numbers of people, especially adults; (c) the economy, especially technology and material equipment and tools; (d) the inclusive social organization; and (e) the inclusive cultural system, including material as well as nonmaterial items.

The phenomena that have value and therefore constitute power resources vary with both time and place. For example, in modern urban industrial societies, technology, heavy equipment, and financial credit are important power resources. In ancient societies with little technology and equipment, power was more likely to be derived from intangible social or supernatural sources. In 1850 a cotton planter in an East Coast state might have regarded his slaves as an important power resource. The abolition of slavery abolished this power resource. Under the apartheid system of South Africa the black population (numbering some 20 millions and several times larger than the white sector) as presently treated constitutes a source of only limited social power vis-à-vis the white establishment.

The power options and possibilities of action on the part of social actors vary with both the kind and amount of their resources. Thus Etzioni (1968: 327) asserted that collective actors with more resources, particularly economic and coercive, are likely to command more options to use, save, invest, or produce power than weaker actors. Minority groups who control few and limited resources have access to little power and few power options.

In spite of its promise, potential social power resides, dormant and inactive, within a resource much like physical power within plutonium. Once it is released from imprisonment within a host resource, social power becomes active and capable of performing tasks. It is active power that gains one's will, overcomes resistance, influences people, and causes change of behavior. But active power cannot exist in a social vacuum. Once it is released from its host in a resource, it must find another residence. This new host is a social relationship. Once active power becomes part of a relationship it qualifies that relationship dynamically and consumes itself in social action.

The mobilization of potential power takes place in a two-step process including (1) the identification, discovery and control of accessible resources; and (2) the transformation of potential into active power, i.e., extracting potential power from power resources. These operations are shown in the first part of Figure 4-1. Search for power resources is un-

FIGURE 4-1

DIAGRAMMATIC REPRESENTATION OF THE FOUR-STAGE MODEL
OF POWER MOBILIZATION AND IMPLEMENTATION

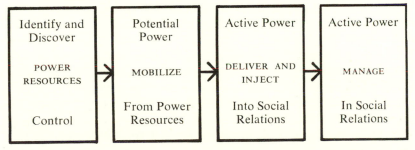

complicated in some situations since some actors command large reserves of power resources. Other actors may have access to few resources and must identify and claim new ones. The search includes three related operations: identification of valued phenomena as possible power resources, locating accessible supplies of such phenomena, and establishment of control over these reserves of resources. The search is evident in wealthy, advanced societies. For example, when a modern nation prepares for defense against a possible attacker, it must first "mobilize." That is, the government must have access to readily accessible and useable reserves of manpower, raw materials, military and industrial equipment, appropriate modes of organization, trained leadership, and the like. Since these resources exist, are well-known, and easily accessible, there is virtually no search. All such power resources must be readied for immediate use, i.e., transformed into active power in military fighting.

Sometimes societies or groups have access to power resources of which they are not aware. For them the problem is failure to recognize available resources as such. It was in this connection that Karl Marx made a substantial contribution to our understanding of the phenomenon of power in modern industrial societies. He drew the attention of the proletariat to the fact that their numbers, and the labor that these numbers represented, constituted a power resource of great importance in the struggle with the bourgeoisie. Schechter (1963: 49–57) explained how Mohandus Ghandi used the Indian minority population in South Africa in the years before and after World War I as the resource to mobilize countervailing political and economic power against the colonial regime of Jan Christian Smuts. This account is particularly instructive as regards the tactics of organization, control, and collective action required for mobilizing the power potential of a population.

In World War II when full military mobilization and high-level industrial production exhausted the traditional reserves of manpower in the United States, various marginal and dependent population sectors were perceived as sources of potential manpower. Thus women found important work roles in all branches of the armed forces. The elderly, the disabled, and the racial and ethnic minorities were redefined as potential industrial and service workers. Shortages of metals, rubber, and the like led to redefinition of used and scrap material as important. It seems likely also that the developing societies will continue to recognize human and natural resources, traditionally beyond their control, as power resources in the growing struggles against the advanced Western societies for liberation and self-determination. Thus oil in the Middle East, the black populations in Rhodesia and South Africa, rubber and tin in Southeast Asia, and indigenous raw materials in many other places are now being perceived as resources and brought under the control of rebellious peoples in the increasing struggle against external domination. In a later section of this chapter we will see how American blacks have mobilized their people to produce active power in their struggle against the white establishment.

Collective actors develop and apply tactics for converting potential into active power. For example, in the military field, troops, armaments, equipment, ammunition, and the like constitute potential power resources. The resources must be deployed in appropriate ways and activated—moving troops, firing artillery, operating equipment, flying planes, etc. In this way military power is made active and applied to the relationship with the enemy. A union may organize the workers in a certain industry. In preparing for the negotiation of a labor contract, the union may take a strike vote, organize a war chest of contributions from its members, and formulate plans for a strike. The union membership, the strike vote, the war chest, and the labor of the workers constitute potential power. If the negotiations break down, the union may then activate this potential power by calling its members off the job, picketing the struck plants, soliciting public support, and using the war chest to support striking workers. The organized and protesting farmers establish a lobby in Washington and harass congressmen and senators on behalf of desired agricultural legislation. The embattled women pressure national professional associations to refuse to hold annual meetings in states which have failed to ratify the Equal Rights Amendment. All such actions are power mobilizing tactics.

An influencing actor can exert power against a defender by means of threats. First demands for concession or compliance must be issued to the defender. He is warned that if he does not agree, he will be injured in specific ways. To back up the threat and to show that the attacking actor can indeed inflict the promised damage, his power resources are brought forward, arranged, and displayed in full view of the opponent. The opponent is expected to be frightened and to recognize that in his disadvantageous power position, concession and/or compliance is the better part of wisdom. In ancient times conflict actors were wont to frighten their enemies by marching round and round their walls, rattling their sabres and shouting ferociously. For the same purpose the police of a big city may seek to quell a potential riot by deploying large numbers of officers in a show of strength. A massive imposition of force to crush one conflict is often used to deter other possible conflicts. Modern nations often use "war games" for the same purpose. In such tactics power is mobilized without committing resources.

In conflict, active power must be managed in order to overcome resistance, change behavior, and achieve desired scarce values. As noted, these management activities are called power implementation and consist of two related operations: delivery and injection of active power into a relationship, and manipulation of the power within that relationship to achieve maximum effect. Although, as shown in Figure 4-1, power implementation is connected operationally to power mobilization, analytically the two processes are distinct. For example, the angry, disillusioned American farmers may organize, refuse to plant crops, demonstrate, and try to exert pressure on the government by a march on Washington. The power mobilized in these activities is implemented by publicly announced demands, lobbying sessions with members of the Congress, and confrontations with the secretary of agriculture and the president.

Power implementation is carried out by conflict groups such as social movements, interest groups, associations, and organizations through a series of power-implementing tactics. Such groups, organizations, and structures devise and execute the activities that inject power into relations with opponents and focus and manipulate it for the best effect. For example, one nation may send its troops into attack against another, and thus mobilize violent military power. However, it is the declaration of war, the propaganda blast, or the diplomatic representation that focuses this act of power on the issues at contest in the relations between the two polities. Without such communications that focus, explain, and demand the defending nation might not know why it was being invaded. When the hordes of peace people gathered in Washington in the early 1970s and obstructed traffic, interfered with governmental operations, and harassed administrative personnel, they had to use other tactics to make it clear that their thrust of struggle was against the administration for its war policy and against the Congress for retaining the Selective Service Act. Thus delivered, focused, and managed, the active power of the peace movement could operate to overcome resistance, initiate significant change, and achieve the ends of peace. Although all collective conflict actors execute the twin operations of power mobilization and implementation, their tactical skills may vary significantly. In a struggle over farm legislation the embattled farmers may be much less skilled and adroit in the power-manipulation game than the opposing party machines, the business lobbies, or the government administration. In South Africa, the Soweto Africans, with their overwhelming numbers and almost total control of the industrial labor resource of Johannesburg, found it almost impossible to mobilize and implement this massive power resource.

Power is mobilized and implemented by both governmental (official) organizations and groups and by nongovernmental (civil) groups and organizations. The official agencies that mobilize and implement power often maintain a specialized collective apparatus for this task, e.g., judicial institutions, police organizations of various kinds, and military structures. The official and quasi-official agencies of government mobilize and implement power for three purposes. First is social control or conflict activity that responds to the nonlegitimate struggle of citizens, constituents, and private groups. For example, official power is mobilized and implemented to quell a street riot or subdue a gang-rumble. Social control also responds to the threat of violent actions for conspiracy or incipient rebellion. The second occasion for the use of official power is the response to internal war, i.e., revolution, civil war, or insurrection. In these situations the government must mobilize appropriate power and implement it in order to quell the uprising and restore order. The third form of official conflict action is international war. The inclusive society, the nation-state, attacks another polity either in aggressive action or in self-defense. Violent military power must be mobilized and implemented to achieve the official purposes of the society.

Conflict groups employ a wide range of implementing tactics to deliver, inject, and manipulate active power in relations with opponents. The essential function of such tactics is to qualify the exercise of power with the meanings and purposes of struggle. For example, Martin Luther King, Jr., explained in "Letter from a Birmingham Jail" that the aim of his power operations in Birmingham was to create so much "crisis" and "tension," i.e., power effect, that the white leaders who refused to talk with him and his associates would be forced to negotiate the issues in contest. When the Red Brigades of Italy kidnap a leader after assassinating his guards, they always follow this power act with a message to explain its purpose and introduce the raw active power into relations with the government. Usually, as noted above, the tactics that serve to mobilize active power work also to deliver and manage that power within the relevant social relations. Thus, for example, the Japanese employed the attack on Pearl Harbor in 1941 to strike a devastating blow against the American navy and to notify the United States that war had started between the two nations.

BLACK POWER: MOBILIZATION AND IMPLEMENTATION ILLUSTRATED

The mobilization and implementation of social power for social conflict can be illustrated in many ways. There are, however, certain analytic advantages to be gained from examining the process in the experiences of the social movements that represent weak social sectors. Typically, such movements start from a minimal power position with access to limited power resources and imperfect mobilization tactics. In the experiences of these movements the steps of the power mobilization-implementation process are revealed and brought into play. The literature permits us to examine this process with some clarity in the case of the black protest movement of the 1950s and 1960s.

Typically, the black category was fixed in the American social structure at an inferior and ancillary position. Legal sanctions, powerful customs, and entrenched habits perpetuated this arrangement. In time the structure became rigid, and changed only little with the passing of the generations. In addition to status inferiority, the objective consequences of this structure included relative powerlessness, material deprivation, and sociopsychological resentment. The production and maintenance of inferiority and powerlessness were central functions of the racial structure. The most evident effects of inferiority and impotence were low income and economic poverty, educational limitations and occupational unpreparedness, poor housing and neighborhood deterioration, and poor physical and mental health. This structural arrangement and its consequences were produced by the twin mechanisms of prejudice and discrimination.

This racial structure was the setting of frustration and aggression. Years of life under these conditions generated intense feelings of frustration, resentment, and hostility. Perceptive students of the black experience (Grier and Cobbs, 1968; and Hendin, 1969) report that inability to rectify these deprivations and frustrations tended to produce a state of "black rage." The overwhelming power advantage of whites issued from their near-monopolistic control of the major power resources—natural resources, the geographic territory, the population as a whole, the economy, the inclusive social organization, and the cultural system.

Traditionally, the leading black conflict organizations (the NAACP and the National Urban League, among others) depended on technical representatives and coalition building to mobilize and implement the social power they needed. Lawyers, social workers, and public-relations experts sought to generate and manipulate the law, human relations, moral guilt, and similar forms of secondary potential power. At the same time, these organizations undertook to build power-producing coalitions with white middle-class liberal organizations. However, the leaders of the new civil rights protest organizations recognized that they must have access to new and additional sources of social power. Martin Luther King, Jr., James Farmer, James Foreman, Stokely Carmichael and other leaders deliberately undertook the search for new power resources. They experimented with various forms of power-releasing and delivery tactics, and, as King (1963: 81) reported of the experience in Montgomery with the bus boycott, they were sometimes surprised by the effects of their efforts. As Aberbach and Walker (1970: 367ff.), Benson (1971: 328–39), McCormack (1973: 356–409), Gelb and Sardell (1974: 507–30), and others have reported, this process of search and experimentation included the invention and diffusion of the concept and slogan "black power."

These experiences confirmed the conclusion that the power resource most immediately accessible to blacks was the black population itself, some 20 millions in a population ten times as large. It was discovered that by mobilizing this power resource they could release six kinds of active power, or "influence" as Williams (1977: 147–68) called it. These included political, economic, and legal power, public opinion, moral guilt, and coercive power. This view of the active components of black influence is summarized schematically in Figure 4-2. The various black social movement organizations wielded these forms of influence in a running power duel with the authority of the political and bureaucratic establishment.

In order to mobilize the potential power inherent in the black population it was first necessary to organize and control that population. Himes (1973: 18) said that organization for mobilization of black power required: (1) inspiring and galvanizing those who are sacrificing their individual power; (2) fitting them into a division of labor by assigning to each a standardized role he could understand and perform; (3) imposing control over relevant behavior and generating self-discipline as soon as possible; and (4) sustaining the morale and enthusiasm of the individual actors who possess the power and make the sacrifices.

The organization of blacks took two main expressions, formal organization and patterns of activity involving mass participation. Some blacks were organized as members of formal associations like the NAACP, CORE, and SNCC. Others were affiliated with formal nonmembership organizations like the National Urban League and the SCLC. Typical illustrations of the second expression of organization, patterns of activity involving mass participation, include boycotts, demonstrations, bloc voting, and civil disobedience. These were indefinitely expansible patterns of action providing standardized places for participants. Many participants entered at the announced starting time and left when the activity was terminated. Others came and went as they pleased.

The organized masses were employed to mobilize and deploy the types of potential power listed in the figure. In a boycott purchasers were asked to withhold their business from offending merchants, bus companies, or the like. In the relationship between boycotting blacks and the company, active power is used to overcome the resistance to discussing the contested issue and to work for a mutually satisfactory solution. A sit-in interferes with business as usual and so functions to activate potential power and inject it into a social relationship with the same effect. Organized registered voters can dominate or decisively influence elections

FIGURE 4-2

ORGANIZATION AND RELEASE OPERATIONS IN THE
MOBILIZATION OF BLACK POWER

I. Levels of Black Power Resources
    A. Numbers of people (the primary level)
    B. Residual economic, political, legal power, public-opinion, moral
       and coercive power (the secondary level)
II. Power Release Operations
    A. Organizing black people
       1. Formal organizations
       2. Activity patterns involving mass participation
    B. Power release operations
       1. Release of economic power
          a. withholding (boycott and its variants)
          b. obstruction (sit-in, preventing ticket sales, obstructing
             construction)
          c. support (reverse boycott, concentrating in support of
             friends)
          d. accumulation (savings in banks, savings and loans, insur-
             ance companies, etc.)
       2. Release of political power
          a. elections (registration campaigns, bloc voting, coalitions)
          b. organization (standard parties, new forms, caucuses,
             conventions, etc.)
          c. influence (lobby and pressure techniques)
       3. Release of legal and court power
          a. influence (law, administration, and enforcement)
          b. civil suit and injunctive relief
          c. civil disobedience
       4. Release of the power of public opinion
          a. present the merits of the cause to the nation
          b. stimulate and encourage favorable attention of the media
          c. release information (statements, press conferences, pub-
             lications, etc.)
       5. Release of moral force
          a. image (the posture of moral worthiness)
          b. public display of unjust abuse by whites accepted or in-
             vited
          c. platform (the core values and moral ground)
          d. guilt feelings generated among whites
       6. Release of power of violence or threats of violence
          a. as coercive force
          b. as catalytic of remedial action

that are closely contested. Recognition of this potential can affect relations between blacks and whites in the direction of facing issues and solving problems. Blacks organized in demonstrations—silent marches, public petition meetings, or civil disobedience—can act out a good news story for the media. Such public relations are used in several ways to mobilize power. On the one hand, such symbolic and dramatic communications win friends for the cause and help to build coalitions with liberal white groups. On the other, they function to trigger embarrassment and guilt feelings among morally sensitive whites. In another tactical action poor blacks can accumulate their small savings in a building and loan company and thus create the capital that can be manipulated to overcome the white lending agencies' refusal to serve black citizens. Each of these tactics functions in two ways in the process of mobilizing power. First, it activates potential power and injects it into the black-white relationship, and second, it manipulates the active power in the relationship in such a way as to facilitate discussion of and solution of the problems at issue.

The tactics of the release of power tended to function as tactics of power delivery. Perception of this fact prompted Martin Luther King, Jr., to speak of "direct action." The black masses who produced the social power also acted to inject it into critical relations with whites; the power activators were those who delivered the power. In some other cases, viz. the legal staffs of the NAACP, specialists performed the task of delivering the power.

By means of different albeit related tactical mechanisms, power was manipulated in the relationship with whites. In this way the "influencer" could create an "asymmetrical" relationship with the "influencee" which resulted in some change of behavior. The change of behavior was the concession sought as the objective of conflict. Power was manipulated in this black-white relationship not only to force the community that refused to negotiate to confront the issue in contest, but to change its behavior in some respect as regards that issue.

Communication tactics accompanied by power injection caused the public to direct its attention to the account of deprivations and discontents that blacks wanted whites to recognize and understand. The other side of the account of wrongs was the catalogue of goals and objectives that blacks sought from change. These goals and objectives were packaged in specific requests and/or demands, usually presented as negotiable. A series of justifications accompanied requests and demands to make them appear fair and reasonable. Power was managed in the relationship to gain attention for these messages, and it was hoped a favorable hearing for them would be won, as well.

For example, a silent march and demonstration in any community might end at city hall, where the leaders presented the mayor with a list of grievances and demands. The celebrated March on Washington of 1963 ended at the Lincoln Memorial where in public orations all the participating leaders stated the aims and hopes of the tactical exercise.

Other tactical mechanisms, supported by active power, sought to initiate a process of negotiation. Within the socially approved tradition requests and demands were presented as pleas and petitions for consideration. The aim was to initiate a process of discussion for negotiation that would end in concession or compromise. Blacks offered racial peace, support of the basic values, and active participation in the general racial system, in a tradeoff for the goals and objectives they had set out. This process of negotiation, qualified by a show of power, was cast in a rhetoric of reasonableness, compromise, and peacefulness. The King technique required all these power operations to be conducted in the posture of "nonviolence."

Under other circumstances, the power operation was combined with the tactic of confrontation. Communication was clothed in a rhetoric of defiance and threats. The posture of request and demand was rigid. Demands were declared to be "nonnegotiable." The white establishment was offered the option of conceding to the demands set forth or suffering the threatened consequences. Early on in the movement, confrontation was seen as a tactic of last resort, after less militant and more traditional mechanisms had been exhausted. Later, though, when the ideology of "black power" had become widely accepted, confrontation acquired a standing and justification of its own. It sometimes was the tactic of first resort, chosen in place of the traditional tactics, which were denigrated or rejected. Confrontation became a favorite tactic of black university students in their struggles with putatively discriminating officials. An important building or sensitive facility would be occupied. The students' representatives faced the administration with a set of "nonnegotiable" demands with the insistence that they be acceded to by a certain deadline or the students would inflict certain nonspecific damages. The aim was to produce specified changes without negotiation, since, in unhappy past experiences, they had learned that the university officials could out-talk them.

The ultimate tactical accompaniment of active power in social relations was violence. The relationship was accompanied by and qualified by intentional acts of injury. In these situations violence was a communication mechanism, designed to initiate a substantive exchange of ideas. Himes (1973: 23) points out that violence is not itself the change-producing tactic. It is rather an intermediary, attention-gaining, communication-mobilizing device. Substantive change issues from the more ordinary processes of negotiation, persuasion, and compromise that are set in motion by violence. The function of violence in the power-change nexus is illustrated in Rustin's (1966: 29–35) account of a conversation with a black youth following the Watts riot of 1965. The boy exclaimed, "we won!" The astonished Rustin pointed to the death and destruction in the area and demanded to know what they had won, and how. In reply the youth explained that they won because they had made the mayor, the chief of police, and the whole world pay attention to them and their plight.

It has been difficult, if not impossible, to measure the relative power mobilized by blacks in support of their struggles for change. A few studies have reported plausible estimates of the effect of black power on selected urban communities. Baron (1968) attempted to estimate the effect of black power in Chicago and concluded that it was only marginal, becoming really significant in influencing important community decisions only when augmented through coalitions with various white organizations. After a study of the Welfare Rights Organization in New York, Gelb and Sardell (1974: 507–30) concluded that poor black organizations could influence decision-making only when supported by coalitions and when "key actors in the political system are sympathetic." From a study of decision-making in Knoxville, Tennessee, Banner (1975) found that unaided efforts of black organizations would not insure that their concerns would get on the community agenda for discussion and decision, nor that, once on the agenda, they would win a favorable decision. To guarantee such outcomes, Banner concluded that blacks needed the support of local coalitions and the intervention of federal agencies and finances. After a study of political power in poor neighborhoods, Lamb (1975: 3–27) reported that although increasing numbers of poor people participate in protest activities, community political leaders still believe that control over services should reside exclusively with those who finance them, with the "able-bodied taxpayers."

The Organization of Power

In every social system, resources of power are unevenly distributed. As a consequence, some categories control or have access to more potential power than others. The inequitable distribution of potential power is conditioned by features of the social structure. For example, social stratification everywhere insures the inequitable distribution of potential power among the constituent social ranks. The poor, although usually more numerous than the wealthy, are also less powerful than the advantaged groups. This inequitable distribution of potential power exerts a significant effect upon the pattern and nature of social conflict. For example, it was shown that blacks in the United States were at a severe disadvantage in terms of power when they faced the decision to struggle for "legitimate" rights and opportunities against the dominant white category in American society. In this chapter we will examine the distribution of power and its effect upon social control in different types of societies, within national social systems, and within communities of modern societies.

Power is organized differently in feudal societies from the way it is in tribal systems. Ryan (1969: 411) notes that in the former, major power resources and actual power are concentrated in the hands of a hereditary landed class that usually controls the government. The feudal chiefs administer this power through subordinates and aides, some of whom are blood relatives. Power ties between hereditary chiefs and the peasants are conditioned by dependency, fealty, and force. Although the feudal chiefs are independent rulers, they often participate in loose federations. The chief is only slightly accountable to his peasant constituents for the exercise of his hereditary powers under the power system.

In tribal societies, on the other hand, major power is more widely distributed than in feudal systems. Chiefs are titular heads of tribes or extended clans. Sometimes they gain their positions by heredity; sometimes they are chosen by the people in some form of election. The chief's power therefore is not absolute and he is accountable to the members of the tribe or clan. Often tribes or extended clans reveal hierarchical prestige systems within which power is organized and exercised. The residual power left in the hands of the tribe members is organized on the basis of sex, age, class status, and smaller kinship units. The result is a diffuse pattern of power organization which permits dissenting clans and aspiring leaders to mobilize counter-power and instigate conspiracies and other kinds of struggles of rebellion.

In the advanced urban industrial societies the major units of social organization and power control are the functional, interest-centered bureaucracies—government, economy, education, the military, welfare, law, and so on—which MacIver and Page (1955: 229–37) called "the great associations." In such modern societies the economy may be subservient to the state, and the family, though often called the most essential institution, is dominated by the power of the others. Yet the power of these great associations or bureaucratic institutions may be organized in different ways. For example, one crucial difference between so-called democratic and so-called authoritarian systems is the degree of concentration of the power of the great associations. Figure 4-3 suggests that al-

FIGURE 4-3

ANALYTIC CONTRASTS OF DEMOCRATIC AND
AUTHORITARIAN POLITICAL ORGANIZATIONS

Democratic	Authoritarian
Functions	
Maintain internal order	Maintain internal order
Manage relations with others	Manage relations with others
Supervise the economy	
Execute limited economic activities	Operate total economy
Conduct essential planning and development	Conduct inclusive planning for development
Provide services for citizens	Use citizens rationally for benefit of the state
Act principally for the individual	Act principally for the inclusive society
Norms	
Explicit codified legal	Explicit codified legal
Limited technical	Extensive technical
Voluntary citizen action	Citizen regimentation
Roles-Statuses	
Ranked cadres of explicit governmental	Ranked cadres of explicit governmental
Limited cadres of technical	Extensive cadres of technical
Many voluntary citizen	Few voluntary citizen
Citizen and alien (open categories)	Citizen and alien (closed categories)
Implementing Groups	
Government as core group	Government as core group
Numerous secondary associations	Few secondary associations
Many interinstitutional associations	Few interinstitutional associations

Taken from Joseph S. Himes, *The Study of Sociology* (Glenview, Ill.: Scott, Foresman, 1968), p. 193.

though in both kinds of states power is concentrated, the manner of concentration differs significantly.

The distribution of power among the great associations is adjusted roughly to the problems served and relative need of each. In spite of this fact, power is inequitably and nonrationally distributed among these associations. For example, military organizations sometimes retain great power far beyond the time when they serve a major function in the life of a society. As a consequence other associations such as education or welfare tend to be neglected for lack of the power required to execute needed changes and mount significant programs.

This mode of organizing power in the modern urban-industrial societies significantly conditions the distribution of power among the several constituent categories and the patterning of social conflict. For example, Ploss (1967) pointed out that power in the Soviet Union is so concentrated and monolithic that the exercise of countervailing influence by social movements, minority political parties, and independent trade unions is virtually impossible. Civil strife of the kind that Gurr (1970: 572–631) described is largely unknown in the Soviet Union today. On the other hand, relatively open bureaucratic societies like the United States and the United Kingdom tend to invite the mobilization and utilization of countervailing power on the part of dissident groups against domination of the great associations. Ideological systems of both kinds are prone to take advantage of their great concentrated power through political ventures and sponsorships outside their boundaries.

It is an arresting fact that in most social systems social power is concentrated in the hands of an elitist or ruling category. In these societies the bulk of the population occupies inferior ranks and is relatively weak. Such an image of the power of human societies is so common and so visible that it almost seems to be natural; systems with more equitable distribution of social power among the various social categories are less commonplace. Elitist concentration of social power can develop in several ways.

In some societies major social power is controlled by a category of hereditary elites and transmitted by the rules of inheritance. Such power is an inalienable possession of certain members of the society. The most familiar type of hereditary concentration of power is the monarchy. By the same token, relative powerlessness is a hereditary state of the numerous inferior poor of such societies. In addition to monarchy, other common types of hereditary, elitist systems of power include imperial systems, feudal arrangements, some tribal systems, and caste structures. This mode of power concentration and control tends to discourage political dissent and the exercise of countervailing power. Major manifestations of conflict take the form of inter-society wars and skirmishes.

Hawley and Wirt (1968: 37–87) point out that power elites can gain dominance also by conquest, revolution, and election. Establishment of new power elites has been a common occurrence in the modern world as one aspect of the expansion of Europe. In this way the Spanish gained dominance in South America and the English speaking peoples became power elites in North America, South Africa, and Australia, to mention a few instances. Lenski (1966) has shown that power is transmitted, and new elite categories come into being in societies, by the revolt of the powerless masses and their establishing themselves in the position of dominance. In the Soviet Union, for example, the Communist revolution abolished the hereditary system and created a new elite caste from the ranks of peasant and workers. In some cases, a political party of non-elites such as a socialist-labor party or an agrarian party may win an election and, through its leadership cadre, replace the traditional party of aristocrats, industrial tycoons, and upperclass families. If this party is politically astute, it may stay in power for a generation or more. This pattern of elite success is illustrated in the replacement of the Tory Party by the Labor Party several times in modern England. Occasionally, a worker-peasant political coalition in a South American country may, by election, replace the machine run by the aristocracy and the Church. Sometimes, however, such transitions result from revolutionary coups.

Within elite systems, however derived, power tends to be concentrated and organized by the hierarchy wielding the power. At the top will be found that cadre of individuals who control and wield major social power. Below them and subject to them are located other cadres of administrators and sub-administrators. The leaders at the top typically control major decisions and make basic policies. The sub-categories of wielders of power are charged with executing these decisions and policies. The whole power system rests upon the large base of the relatively powerless under-classes of peasants, lower classes, workers, outcastes, and the like. This numerous category of individuals wields little power and neither makes nor executes basic collective decisions. Their main function is to comply with the power. The system continued in operation not only because the power elites enforce it, but also because the relatively impotent categories do not fully withhold supportive compliance. As Tinker observed of India, the chief wielders of power must have the assistance and cooperation of hundreds and even thousands of individuals in order to retain and wield their power. As a consequence, the ruling elites seldom have to mobilize the full measure of the potential power in their command in order to retain their advantageous position and to fend off dissenters or attackers.

Many scholars have described elitist power arrangements in the organization of social power in modern societies. Some years ago, Michels (1915) argued that in contemporary societies power tended to gravitate toward the control of certain classes and roles which emerged in time as a powerful elite. Mosca (1938) explored the idea of a universal ruling class in modern societies. Ploss (1965) studied the issue of revolt and reform in the Soviet Union and concluded that the Communist elite and the totalitarian system precluded the possibility of significant opposition emerging and expressing itself. The political system institutionalized a power elite whose members were always drawn from the closed Communist Party. Keller (1963) amends the concept of a ruling class by proposing the experience of "strategic elites" who stand behind and, in some measures at least, dominate and control this so-called ruling class.

Several scholars have reported the existence of an American power elite. Mills (1956) argued that an alliance of the leaders of big government, big industry, and big military constituted the American power elite. This elite consisted of a circulating class of people of power, constantly renewed from the general ranks of the society, and maintained by the nature and needs of the nation's gigantic bureaucratic structures. Hunter (1959) confirmed this image of the American power elite with his concept of "top leadership" in the United States. He envisaged a loose category of individuals of power and decision at the highest echelon, loosely held together by informal social ties, but capable of functioning as a controlling unit. Domhoff (1974) in *The Bohemian Grove and Other Retreats,* also contends that there is an American power elite. He envisages the elite as fundamentally an interlocking system of powerful leaders focusing in on a series of centers of convergence and interaction.

The issue of an American power structure or power elite has been the topic of a lively debate. The primary opposing view is contained in the concepts of "countervailing power" and pluralist power organization." Responding to the idea of a national power elite, Galbraith (1952) argued that the control of the elites is limited by the "countervailing power" of subordinate and secondary groups such as organized labor, the religious establishment, the farm bloc, and scores of other dissenting interests and organizations. The encounters between these two centers of power set the stage for some of the major conflicts in modern societies like the United States. The concepts of countervailing power and pluralist power envisage not only the traditional dissenting sectors, e.g., organized labor, agriculture, religious denominations, and professional associations, but also the series of social movements that represent still other subordinate and relatively impotent categories in the nation such as the poor, blacks, youth, women, and the aged.

The elitist-pluralist power argument has been most fully explored in reference to the organization of power at the community level. Hunter's *Community Power Structure* (1953) picked up the challenge and stated the elitist position in terms of communities, thereby initiating a long and vociferous debate. This theme was argued later by Rossi (1957: 415–43), D'Antonio and Form (1965), and many others. In 1967 Gilbert (373–83) could summarize the empirical findings and theoretical derivations from community power studies in 166 localities. In that same year, Pellegrin (451–56) reviewed other articles on the same topic. In 1970 Miller published a comparative study of community power structures in four different countries. Most of these studies reported some manifestation of elitist concentration of power in modern urban communities.

In 1958 Dahl (463–69) criticized the elite power model and initiated another line of inquiry. Others joined this trend, which took the form of what is called a pluralist model of countervailing power. In addition to Dahl, this theme was argued by Agger and Goldrich (1958: 383–92), Polsby (1959: 232–36) and Danzger (1964: 707–17). One result of this decades-long debate was to leave the issue of power organization open, but to draw attention to the role of power in societal and community conflicts. Domhoff (1978) reinvestigated power structure in New Haven and took exception to Dahl, arguing that community power structure is really elitist, but dominated by the national power elite.

The pluralist argument admits that a modified elitist power structure may be found in most modern social systems, but maintains that this elitist structure is limited to varying degrees by countervailing centers of dissenting power. Perrucci and Pilisuk (1970: 1040–57) formulated the model as a series of "resource networks" resulting from "inter-organizationalities" which surround and offset modest but effective elite structures. Such offsetting subordinate power centers may be organized around common interests such as schools, fluoridation, taxes, pollution, land use, and the like. Concerned people whose interests differ from those of the elites join together to express their views and mobilize power in social movements. Sometimes the countervailing power structures are organized within such social categories as the aged, ethnic groups, working classes, or religious bodies. Categoric similarities become the basis of mutual identification, and internal association functions to generate common interests around which power is mobilized.

Such subordinate power groups may operate in various ways to influence decision-making and collective action in the social system. In the larger American society, groups like organized labor, religious bodies, professional associations, and women's organizations mobilize the power resources at their command to affect the decision-making of the President, the Congress, administrative and regulatory agencies, and sometimes the courts. After a study of New York City, Bell and Held (1969: 142–77) reported that power in metropolitan areas is organized and expressed through a multiplicity of small interest groups. A common practice among such countervailing groups is to maximize power by building coalitions with other dissenting bodies. There may be times when, because of current opinion, the subordinate power groups may join with the elitist organization in support of a policy or program which they favor. In this instance, the power effect of the system is maximized and action has the aura of unanimity. Reflecting on this condition Aiken and Mott (1970: 361) conclude that, although many different community power patterns of a pluralistic nature have been revealed, the significant issues emerge at the "interfaces" where these various lines of interest and power intersect and where conflicts are generated.

Writing in 1970, Miller (228–31) employed these power model formulations as the heuristic tools to investigate the power structures of Seattle, Washington; Bristol, England; Cordoba, Argentina; and Lima, Peru. One leading finding was that differences in the structuring of power were correlated with differences in the nature and patterning of community conflict.

In Seattle, where the business ethic prevailed, economic interests exercised dominant power under the guise of "community action" to manipulate collective decisions to their advantage. The other power sectors—government, education, church, labor—sometimes acting alone, sometimes in coalition, opposed the economic interests on behalf of change around specific community issues. Though often spirited and vigorous, these community conflicts were generally nonviolent and conventional in method. As a consequence, Miller could show that conflict for control of collective decisions could be predicted as a measurable outcome of the opposition generated by the several power sectors.

Although the value base of Bristol was essentially similar to that of Seattle, the power-conflict model differed in several respects. First, the business and industrial occupations commanded less prestige and power than those in the United States. At the same time, labor wielded relatively more power than in the United States, because it was implemented by a political party and because of its socialist ideology. Other sectors—the law, education, and government—exerted more power than was customary in American communities. Power being rather more equally distributed, conflict tended to be more balanced, compromise more characteristic, and relations less qualified by tension than elsewhere.

In Cordoba and Lima, relations among the various power sectors were tense, threatening constantly to erupt into violence. Deep cleavages between the hereditary organizational elites and the other power sectors were reinforced by the private-public split of the economy. The powerful and unstable vested interests were opposed by pressure for change from both the ideological right and left. In periods of crisis the landed aristocracy, the Church, the military, industrial leaders, and the middle classes could form shaky coalitions to defend the society. The threat of violence and pressure for change were kept alive by widespread deprivation, rapid social change, and radical ideologies of the right and the left.

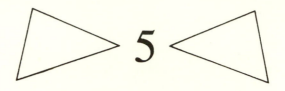

5

Violence in Social Conflict

Violent conflict is both widespread and commonplace in modern and modernizing societies. In such societies, the use of social power by some collective actors against others in the struggle for scarce values often leads to injury or death of persons and damage or destruction of property. This fact is supported by reports of the mass media. For example, although the belligerents changed from time to time, war was continuous in Vietnam for twenty years. For six years between 1964 and 1969, riots erupted each summer in the ghetto districts of big American cities. In Northern Ireland guerrilla and terrorist violence has characterized the struggle between Catholics and Protestants for years. In 1975 and 1976 Lebanon was harassed by a deadly though informal struggle between the Christian phalangists and the Moslem radicals. Violence has also earned brief attention from the press for making an appearance in many other societies—Algeria and Cyprus, Kenya and the Philippines, French Canada and Chile, the Middle East, and the Indian subcontinent, to name only a few.

The prevalence of violent conflict in societies is also substantiated by empirical research. After a study of conflict during several centuries of Western European history, Tilly (1969: 4–45) concluded that violence erupted frequently and in many places. Although the eruptions varied from time to time and shifted from place to place, the pattern was continuous. Many scholars (e.g., Walker, 1968; Grimshaw, 1969; Skolnick, 1969; Graham and Gurr, 1969; and Crotty, 1972: 26–27) have documented the prevalence of violence in American society. Although many readers may be familiar with the violence on campuses and in ghettoes during the 1960s, the research reveals that violent episodes have characterized American history since the beginning of white settlement on the continent. Skolnick (1969: 10–15) identified a series of periods of violence in American society from its earliest settlement to the twentieth century. These periods and patterns, together with main patterns and periods of the twentieth century, are shown in Figure 5-1. This exhibit is remarkable not only because it shows that American life has always

FIGURE 5-1

PERIODS AND TYPES OF POLITICAL VIOLENCE IN HISTORICAL AND CONTEMPORARY AMERICAN SOCIETY

The Skolnick List

The Indian wars, seventeenth to nineteenth centuries

The "Whiskey Rebellion" and other early Appalachian fights, seventeenth to nineteenth centuries

The Revolutionary War, late eighteenth century

Slave rebellions and post–Civil War anti-black violences, nineteenth and twentieth centuries

Anti-slave struggles and Civil War, nineteenth century

Anti-immigration violence, nineteenth and twentieth centuries

Violence surrounding the organization of labor, nineteenth and twentieth centuries

Violence accompanying struggle for women's suffrage, nineteenth and twentieth centuries

Contemporary Violence

Student violence on university campuses

Black ghetto riots and disturbances

Indians fighting in symbolic locations

Middle-class youths committing violence in the interest of international peace

Lawless violence on the part of the police, the national guard, and other agents of the law

Vietnam, an extravaganza of violence and brutality

been characterized by violent conflict, but also because it demonstrates that virtually every sector and group in the nation has been caught up in violence at some time. These authors conclude that violence in American life should not be seen as unexpected and that it results from a cluster of factors, including the psychological hangovers of slavery; the side-by-side existence of mass consumption with pockets and strata of poverty; the clash of inconsistent ethics that leaves many people without clear guides to social action; the practice of violence for good causes by our revolutionary fighters, frontiersmen, and vigilantes; dashing of immigrant dreams of an earthly paradise; and the accumulating tensions resulting from rapid industrial and urban growth.

It was said above that violence is generally regarded as a form of nonlegitimate conflict. It is said to fall outside the normative core of the social system. This view is expressed in various ways when people respond to violent acts of conflict. Sometimes the press and leaders of a community blame riot violence on "outside agitators." Revolutionary criticism and violence are said to be the expression of "alien spirits" and "foreign radicals." Skolnick reported (1969: 9) that some whites found the cause of violence in the ghetto riots of the mid-1960s in a "racial characteristic" peculiar to blacks. Such people refused to recognize the tendency toward violence as intrinsic to the American cultural heritage and conditioned by factors unique to the American social scene.

The tendency to regard violence as alien and nonlegitimate is consistent with the long-standing American ideology of assimilation. From the beginning of the country's settlement, it was recognized that the new population was both culturally and racially mixed. However, as Gordon (1964: 40) noted, the heritage of democracy and freedom supported the notion that these diversities, especially cultural diversities, could be harmonized through a process of assimilation. It seemed only natural that assimilation would issue from the fundamental processes of freedom, conscious choice, enthusiastic competition, and necessary cooperation. All the divergent peoples in the growing population would surely win their place in the societal mainstream by "peaceful progress" which would result from enlightened competition. Under these benign conditions, populations would be assimilated, progress would continue, and violence would be unnecessary. This point of view led some people to believe that conflict could be eliminated and the ideal of a harmonious society could be achieved.

On the other hand, some members of the community regard violence as legitimate and necessary. Established authorities, when challenged by rebellious organizations, insurgents, and revolutionaries, or confronted by terrorists and conspiratorial cabals, employ violence as the legitimate tactic to meet this threat and to maintain order. At the same time, many observers have shown that important sectors of the American public perceive riot violence as legitimate if it occurs under certain conditions. For example, Turner (1969: 818–19) reported that the violence of blacks rioting in large cities was perceived as legitimate when, among other things, it was preceded by nonviolence, seen as spontaneous, naive, and unplanned outbursts, interpreted as limited protest that got out of hand, or constituted nonviolent action turned violent under the stimulus of rumor and crowd excitement. In this situation, violence gained legitimacy and has popularly been regarded as protest action.

The Meaning and Explanation of Violence

Although quantitatively speaking, violence is only a minor part of the whole corpus of social conflict, it is nevertheless arresting and significant by its very nature. For this reason violence has occupied the time and attention of many scholars. Violence is important in the social sciences and in the study of social conflict not only because of its inherent nature and social consequences, but also because people in all kinds of societies have defined it as being socially important. In the present section, we begin the study of violence in social conflict both by examining its nature and by offering an explanation of it.

The Definition of Violence

In ordinary usage, the meaning of the term *violence* would seem to be self-evident. However, close inspection of the ways in which the term is used reveals ambiguity of meaning and disagreement about usage. For example, some writers restrict *violence* to mean the infliction of "physical" injury, while others speak of "psychological" violence. *Violence* is an important term in the vocabulary of crime, but by and large, crime is not a concern of the study of social conflict.

Writing about the disturbances and riots of the mid-1960s in the United States, Skolnick (1969: 5–6) defines violence as the "intentional use of force to injure, to kill, or to destroy property." In the introduction to their symposium on violence in America, Graham and Gurr (1969: xxx) declare that violence is defined as "behavior designed to inflict physical injury or damage to property." Grimshaw (1970: 9–20) defines "social violence" as assault upon individuals or their property because of their membership in a social category. Thus when blacks living in big cities destroy the ghetto stores of white merchants who reside in middle-class suburbs, or when Christian phalangists kill Moslem radicals in Beirut, these acts are seen as "social" violence. Neiberg (1969: 13) defined "political violence" as "acts of disruption, destruction, injury" whose underlying conditions "have political significance." He explains *political significance* as meaning modification of the behavior of others in a bargaining situation that has consequences for the social system. Rittberger (1973: 217–25) differentiated "direct" or "personal" violence from "indirect" or "structural" violence. Kabwegyere (1972: 303–24) distinguished "physical" violence, which hurts humans, "psychological" violence, which hurts the human psyche, and "structural" violence, which is abuse of the have-nots by the haves.

The foregoing discussion suggests that when violence is considered as a form of social conflict, it contains at least three salient elements: a social relationship, the application of social power, and a specific set of consequences. A relationship between collective actors who play the roles of attacker and defender is essential to the conception of violence as social conflict. The infliction of injury, disruption, or destruction outside such a relationship is not violent conflict. For example, the injuries and deaths resulting from automobile accidents are not connected with social conflict.

Violent conflict can occur when enough power is applied by one actor against another to produce injury, disruption, or destruction. If, as King (1963: 81) said, a social movement generated great "tension" and "crisis," but left no permanent or significant damage, the struggle could be called "nonviolent." If, however, in the conflict relationship property were damaged, the social structure significantly disintegrated, or people were injured or killed, the process would be violent conflict.

Most writers agree that violent conflict always leads to the injury or death of persons, the injury or destruction of human psyches, the disruption or destruction of social organization, and/or the damage or destruction of material property. A conflict is violent only when it leads to one or more of these consequences. Violence is thus inherent as much in the consequences of action as in the nature of action. We may now conclude this discussion by reformulating the definition of violent conflict. Violent conflict refers to intentional struggle between collective actors that involve the application of significant social power for the purpose of injuring, disrupting, or destroying human beings, human psyches, material property, and/or sociocultural structures.

It may help to clarify the definition of violence to cite some typical examples. For this purpose a series of categories and specific manifestations is presented in Figure 5-2. The items in this list have been drawn in part from the entries in Figure 5-1 above and in part from the typology constructed by Brown (1969: 45–84). It is not claimed that the list is either all-inclusive or that the items are mutually exclusive. Doubtless some important types of violence have been omitted, and the categories presented reveal considerable overlapping. Nevertheless, the types and specific manifestations serve as a definitive referent for the concept.

The phrase *violent political actions* covers a wide range of intentional violence inflicted on governments and quasi-governmental organizations. Sometimes, as with assassinations and terrorism, these actions are also

FIGURE 5-2

A TYPOLOGY OF VIOLENCE

Violent Political Actions
        Conspiracy and assassination
        Terrorism and guerrilla attacks
        Indian wars, civil wars, rebellions, revolutions
        International wars

Riots
        Maritime, labor, revolutionary riots
        Economic and political riots
        Urban race riots
        Urban ghetto riots
        Agrarian riots

Violence for Purposes of Social Control
        Police (federal, state, local)
        Nongovernmental (industries, universities, etc.)
        Vigilantism
        Lynching—Western frontier, Southern racial

Racial-ethnic-religious violence
        Slave and anti-slave riots
        Nativist activities (Klan, "Know-Nothing," etc.)
        Anti-Catholic, anti-Chinese

Other Violent Crimes
        Interstate gangs
        Horse theft and counterfeiting
        Train and bank robbery, hijacking
        Big-city organized crime
        Freelance multiple murder
        Family feuds (Southern mountain and Southwestern)

Adapted in part from Richard Maxwell Brown, "Historical Patterns of Violence in America," in Hugh Davis Graham and Ted Robert Gurr, eds., *The History of Violence in America* (New York: Bantam, 1969), pp. 45–84.

referred to as crimes. Civil rebellions, revolutions, and international conflicts are called wars. The next category, riots, is listed separately, not because it differs intrinsically from violent political actions, but because it comprises a large and identifiable category of violent actions. Riots generally involve violent struggle of one social category against another, e.g., whites against blacks, Protestants against Roman Catholics, or labor against management. Although riots tend to violate political norms and so trigger the intervention of governments, they are often less well-planned or openly intentional than wars or revolutions. Riots are widely reported in the modern world; nevertheless, Hobsbaum (1959), Rudé

(1964) and others show that they have been commonplace in most eras. It is evident that such manifestations of political violence are usually regarded as nonlegitimate by established institutions and norms, and so are defined as either crimes or wars. However, from the perspective of the perpetrators, such forms of political violence are seen as legitimate.

The term *social control* refers to forms of violent behavior enacted by governments and authoritative institutional organizations in the course of maintaining order and preventing change. For these purposes police, parapolice, and military forces are maintained. Governments and such authoritative institutional organizations as universities, industries, and business firms make a heavy appeal to legitimacy to justify their violent actions. As Chalmers (1965) has shown, vigilante organizations like the Ku Klux Klan justified their floggings and lynchings by insisting they were maintaining moral probity and community order. However, we have noted above that such claims of legitimacy are moot and constitute a topic of continuing controversy.

Racial, ethnic, and religious violence is revealed ordinarily in riot, vigilante, and lynch behavior. In the present discussion these manifestations of violence are placed in a separate category because they are so typical and widespread in American society. Many observers have noted that the extreme racial, ethnic, and cultural diversity of American society constitutes one condition for violent conflict. The last category contains a mixed bag of violent behaviors that are only tangentially related to social conflict. Some of the specific manifestations, e.g., horse theft or train robbery, are no longer generally practiced, while others are quite recent, e.g., plane hijacking. Occasionally, one or another of these forms of violent crime may be associated with collective conflict.

Two Unsettled Issues of Violence

It seems fairly evident that the injurious and damaging consequences of violent action are clear. For example, tossing a hand grenade through an open pub door or launching a revolutionary attack are intentional acts. However, some other aspects of violence are ambiguous and unsettled. Does damaging action in a nonviolent effort make the whole activity violent? Is violent conflict always nonlegitimate? Such considerations as these make it clear that issues like the legitimacy of struggle and the tactics of nonviolence remain unsettled questions in the study of social conflict.

At first blush, it would seem that violence is categorically nonlegitimate. Both the motivation to commit violence as well as the violent act itself would seem to violate the moral norms. Thus it would appear that the matter is settled and beyond reasonable discussion.

However, as shown in chapter 1 above, it is evident that certain kinds of violence and (under certain circumstances) violent acts enjoy varying degrees of approval in every society. For example, the authority of the state and the force of law legitimize injuries to persons, damage to property, and destruction of both in the name of social order and the general welfare. A robber or rapist may be shot on the spot and, armed with appropriate papers, the police may break one's door down and effect forceable entry. The norms of high castes, hereditary aristocracies, or conquering groups render exploitation and suffering of inferior, weak, or subjugated peoples fully legitimate. The spoils of war belong to the victor. It was mentioned above that violence committed in the course of "protest action" is sometimes defined as legitimate. At the same time, a single act of violence, the American Indian Movement's occupation of Wounded Knee, South Dakota, in 1974, was simultaneously defined by different publics as both legitimate "protest" and nonlegitimate "crime" and "rebellion." When the same injurious and damaging act can be defined as both legitimate and nonlegitimate, meaning is mixed and people are likely to be confused.

Within limited circumstances, it may be possible to generalize that some violent acts, e.g., the execution of murderers or the smashing of revolutionary organizations, are legitimate, but such judgments are likely to be challenged by dissenting groups or sectors. Though unsettled, the issue of the legitimacy of violent conflict has considerable heuristic and practical importance. For example, in the discussion of the management of conflict, and especially violent conflict, in Part II of this book, this issue continues to arise. The question constantly facing the analyst and activist is "whose conflict and violence shall be managed in behalf of whose interests?" Should social movements be controlled because they seek to make social change, or should they be encouraged for that reason? This issue is at the heart of the research on war and the international efforts to prevent and control war. The issue of the legitimacy of violent conflict constitutes one of the continuing frontiers of research in the sociology of social conflict.

The dramatic activities of Gandhi and King gave great prominence to the term *nonviolence*. The research and discussion that followed these activities tended to confuse nonviolence as a tactic of social conflict and nonviolence as a heuristic concept of sociological analysis. This confusion remains one component of the issue of nonviolence. As an analytic concept, the meaning of nonviolence derives from definitions of violence like those quoted above. If violence is conceptualized as the intentional use of social power in a conflict relationship to injure, disrupt, or destroy the opponent, then nonviolence is evidently the intentional avoidance of producing such consequences in the conflict relationship. In nonviolent conflict, people are expected to act intentionally in ways that will prevent their actions from producing any of these harmful consequences.

Chatterjee and Bhattacharjee (1971: 155–61) report that, in analysis, nonviolence has been practiced in various ways. Writing in 1970, Sharp identified the following nine operations: nonresistance, active reconciliation, moral resistance, nonviolent direct action, selective nonviolence, passive resistance, peaceful resistance, "satyagrha," and nonviolent revolution. Later, these nine components were reduced to four basic elements of nonviolent action. Other writers (Klitgaard, 1971: 143–53) characterized nonviolence as a "tactic."

The difficulty with this interpretation of nonviolence is the fact that the collective conflict act that is intended to produce no harmful effect may, and in fact often does, produce all the harmful consequences mentioned. This fact has been reported often in the investigations of nonviolent conflict actions. Writing of streetcar boycotts by blacks in southern cities in the late 1890s and early 1900s, Meier and Rudwick 1970: 9–24) reported that some of the target companies were bankrupted as a consequence. As conceived and launched, the boycotts were intended to be nonviolent struggles. Participating blacks were required to refrain from injuring or damaging any person or property connected in any way with the streetcar companies or local citizens. Refusal to ride the streetcars temporarily dislocated some social patterns, e.g., segregated riding patterns, customary family relations of blacks, and ordinary shopping, working, worshiping, and visiting activities of blacks. Insofar as this collective conflict behavior failed to produce personal injury, permanent structural disruption, or property damage, it was in fact nonviolent.

In some other cities and at other times, streetcar or bus boycotts did involve intentionally harmful behavior. Participants attacked persons and property as a part of the total boycott effort. Such attacks were used to press the effort of the boycott. The injuries and damages were expected to coerce the target group into negotiating and settling the issues in contest. When the boycott effort was reinforced by intentional violence, the total conflict episode was called violent. In common usage the term *violence* tends to subsume in one term both harmful and nonharmful tactical activities.

Although Meier and Rudwick did not report it, the nonviolent streetcar boycott of the southern blacks may have become violent in at least two inadvertent ways. First, on being called names, pushed around, having smoke blown in their faces, or being struck by provocateur whites, the nonviolent blacks may have fought back. The boycotting participants may also have been carried away by the excitement of the crowd at a rally. The resulting injurious behavior could not be called "intentional." Nonetheless, by focusing on the violent acts and their harmful consequences, some members of the public would perceive this violence as "criminal," i.e., nonlegitimate. Some other persons, by considering the background experiences of blacks, the legitimacy of their cause, the provocations they endured, the effects of excitement in the crowd, and other factors, may perceive the violence as part of the "protest," i.e., legitimate.

Second, as Meier and Rudwick reported, some of the boycotts lasted for years. As a consequence, some of the streetcar companies were bankrupted. Workers lost their jobs. Stockholders failed to receive dividends and saw their shares become virtually worthless. Important social structures—the business firms, the segregation patterns of public transportation—were either destroyed or severely disrupted. In other secondary and subtle ways the boycott had harmful consequences for persons and property.

For our purposes, three usable propositions can be derived from the foregoing discussion. First, on theoretical grounds it is possible to differentiate violent from nonviolent conflict. For this end, the intention, not the consequences of conflict action, must be stressed. Second, it is recognized that nonviolent as well as violent conflict action is capable of producing harmful consequences. And third, nonviolence is probably more correctly and usefully perceived as a conflict tactic. To call conflict nonviolent is to direct attention away from the functions of action and enlist the judgment of legitimacy in its support. These are strategic assets in the enterprise of social conflict.

THEORIES OF VIOLENCE

Continuing interest in violence has stimulated the formulation of theoretical explanations. Some of these are common-sense formulations, of only slight heuristic value, even though they may have received wide popular acclaim. Others represent serious attempts to explain the burgeoning of violent behavior in recent years.

Alienation has been cited frequently as the leading cause of collective violence. Kornhauser (1959) saw alienation as a central feature of mass society and the major contributor to mass violence. Nieberg (1969: 20) reported that one popular explanation of collective violence is found in the activities of Communists, psychopaths, the downtrodden and other alienated persons. He says this formulation is often referred to as "the riffraff theory." This notion holds that "riffraff" types exercise a kind of spontaneous and mysterious charisma over communities, thus initiating and escalating violent activity. In further analysis, Nieberg finds three faults with this theory: (a) it fails to explain how the "riffraff" achieves leadership, (b) it overlooks the fact that social contagion is not an automatic and independent process, and (c) it does not see that extremist and violent acts are not idiosyncratic.

The "frontier theory" holds that violence has been built into the American tradition, which continues to exert strong control over contemporary people. Elliott (1952: 273) suggests that as the frontier closed, people migrated to cities, bringing with them the culture of Dodge City shootouts, gunslinging, gangsterism, and vigilantism. Graham (1970: 74–82) found the frontier tradition of violence to be important in contemporary American life. One variant of the frontier theory is the "gun theory" that holds that the widespread ownership of guns functions to support the tendency toward violence. While both these formulations are attractive and seem to have some validity, they fall short of an adequate explanation of modern widespread violence.

McLuhan (1968) advanced the notion that electronic mass communication creates situations that generate violence. He argued that these modern communications are transforming and retribalizing society, creating an intense immediacy of human contact and experience, a strong tendency toward violent action. In one form or another this electronic tribalizing theory has been adduced to explain many violent events of recent years. Because of the traumatic and intense experience, the electronic media are held to be directly responsible for personal violence, quite apart from the operation of all other variables. Although the McLuhan thesis has been persuasive and seductive, it contributes little that is new to the explanation of modern violence. Many young people who have experienced electronic communication have committed acts of violence, but it is also true that many others come through the same experience without resort to violence. The research (Turner and Killian, 1972: 199–222) has demonstrated persuasively that the impact of mass communication is filtered through and conditioned by interpersonal contacts.

The writings of people like Lorenz (1966) and Ardrey (1966) revived the Freudian notion of a so-called "killer instinct." This theory argues that each person possesses a hereditary destructive drive which, if the social controls relent for a moment, breaks out and goes on the rampage. The recent surge of violence is explained by widespread release of this ordinarily pent-up instinct to kill and destroy. Skolnick (1969: 9) reported that the notion of a killer instinct was often voiced in popular explanations of the riots and violence in the big-city black ghettoes. This theory need not detain us since it is an attempt to revive and resuscitate the instinct theory that was exploded many years ago.

Graham (1970: 74–82) reported that historians often sought to explain collective violence in terms of economic factors and processes. Scholars on the moral left, in the tradition of Marx and Beard, have argued that elites have conspired repressively to defend privilege and exploit the weak and the poor. Violence results from the protest of the have-nots against this repression. Such a view of the causation of collective violence is widely held and repeated. Although a correlation between economic factors and collective violence can often be demonstrated, these factors are only one component in a causal syndrome.

Grimshaw (1969: 2) points out that psychologists and psychoanalysts tend to look for proneness to violence in the individual personality, especially traumatic experiences of very early life which are often associated with sexual insecurities. For example, Hersey (1968) and earlier Sterba (1947: 411–27) pointed to sexual competition and fears as causes of the two Detroit riots.

Grimshaw (1969: 3) adds that psychologists have stressed the dynamic interplay between the individual and his environment. This line of theorizing has taken several forms, e.g., the frustration-aggression hypothesis, the authoritarian personality thesis, prejudice, and other learned attitudes. For example, Clark (1944: 319–37) and Clark and Barker (1945: 143–48) pointed to individual attitudes to explain violence, and Ransford (1968) found its explanation in group attitudes.

Graham and Gurr (1969: xxvi) note that sociologists and political scientists have generally stressed the tension-generating aspects of incompatible social values and maladaptive institutions as the source of violent conflicts among groups. Writing in 1939, Dollard and his associates formulated the sociopolitical hypothesis of frustration and aggression. Over time, the hypothesis has been reformulated in many ways, mainly by specifying the source and nature of frustration. These formulations of the basic sociocultural hypothesis were examined in chapter 2, where an inclusive theory of social conflict was constructed. The reader is referred to that statement, which is understood to provide an adequate explanation of violent conflict.

The explanation of violent conflict in some situations is fairly straight-forward. For example, a terrorist attack, an assassination or an aggres-sive war is likely to follow conscious decision and careful planning. The explanation is to be found in the processes of individual or collective thinking, decision, and planning that preceded the violent act. In some other situations, however, explanation is more complex and obscure. For example, the reason for the violence of riots or the shift of a social move-ment from nonviolent to violent tactics is not so straightforward nor self-evident. What is required, as Firestone (1974: 116–42) suggests is a theory that emphasizes the interdependence of causal factors. We can illustrate this mode of explaining collective violence by examining a situ-ation that occurred in Chicago a few years ago.

Collective Violence at the Bandshell

One afternoon during the 1968 Democratic Party nominating conven-tion, a crowd gathered at the bandshell in Lincoln Park to stage a protest rally. Though not yet violent, the crowd was excited and animated. Some participants were angry at being denied access to the convention floor. Others came out of curiosity, to see and to hear. From the outset the crowd displayed the major ingredients of a violent outburst—a pervasive feeling of relative deprivation, sharp polarization of the crowd and the police, a high level of crowd excitement, the acceptance of violence as a legitimate alternative to other courses of action, intention and readiness on both sides to commit violence, a haunting sense of expectancy. At first, both the crowd and the police were raising the level of excitement and shifting toward violence. In time, the shift seemed to generate its own momentum. The lowering of the flag was the catalyst unleashing the unstable potential for violence that was building in both polarized camps.

According to Walker (1968: 215–30) the crowd numbered about one thousand by 2:15 P.M. but later it was estimated to be from eight to ten thousand. There were all types—hippies, students, curious onlookers, provocateurs, and police, both uniformed and in plain clothing. Some persons on each side were armed. It was reported that literature was passed out urging all kinds of action from passive resistance to violent overthrow. Leaflets were handed out by police declaring that the rally at the bandshell was legal but that no permit for a rally at the amphi-theater, where the convention was taking place, had been issued. Speak-ers urged the crowd to protest their treatment at the convention and to march. Lively jeering, namecalling, and heckling took place between po-lice and protestors. The crowd became so large, dispersed, and inclusive that no single focus of interest could be maintained. It split into a series of divergent and relatively independent clusters. Meanwhile, the police had gathered in strength, waiting, alert around the perimeters of the crowd.

The report stated that at about 3:30 or 4:00 P.M. the first violence erupted near the bandshell. While someone was giving a speech against the draft, a young man in an army helmet climbed up the pole and began lowering the flag. This symbolic act set off a frenzy of confused and clashing actions. People began shouting and dashing about. It was reported that the police pushed forward through the crust of the crowd to arrest the man. This action set off the violence. Reports of who struck first are mixed, but presently participants and police were locked in a frightening, violent melee.

CONDITIONS OF VIOLENT CONFLICT

It has been said that collective conflict is a struggle for valued ends in which actors use social power against each other. Often, although the resistance of the opponent may be overcome, injury or destruction does not result. In other cases, however, it is, or seems to be, necessary to harm the opposition in order to achieve the end of social conflict. It is important to know under what conditions an actor will turn intentionally to violent tactics in order to achieve his ends. In this section, we will examine some of the conditions that tend to enhance the chances that collective actors will resort intentionally to tactics that harm opponents in the course of struggling for valued ends. Our aim here is to advance the understanding of the nature and causes of social conflict. We will refer to this same issue in Part II of this book, where we discuss the management of social conflict. At that point, we will wish to know the conditions that must be managed in order to prevent or reduce the possibility of violent conflict.

In some societies, the orientation of the tradition is an important condition of violent conflict. Certain societies, e.g., the Apache and Comanche Indian tribes, Napoleonic France and the Soviet Union have a reputation of belligerence and aggressiveness in international relations. The feudal era of Western Europe was notorious for the almost continuous struggles among the quasi-independent duchies. Graham and Gurr (1969: xxv–xxvi) note that the United States has a long history of internal violence. The American tradition is said to support violence as a legitimate tactic of conflict. The orientation toward violence was enhanced by conditions on the frontier, the extravagant diversity of nationalities and cultures, the absence or inadequacy of established social controls, and the historic role of firearms. The result, as Graham and Gurr conclude, is that although the verbal tradition seems to stress peace, order, and regulated competition, the active tradition is strongly oriented toward violence.

In some systems the tradition is formalized in a national or group ideology. For example, Communist ideology in Cuba supports the exportation of revolution to other developing societies. The Marxist-Leninist ideology of the Soviet Union legitimizes the resort to political and military violence of many kinds to advance the cause of Communism in the world. Turner and Killian (1972: 291–93) observe that coercive strategies of some social movements require them to perceive violent tactics as legitimate and intrinsically preferable to persuasion or bargaining. Grundy (1973: 1–27) showed that after 1950 the ideological thrust of black African leaders in South Africa swung perceptibly from Gandhian nonviolence toward pragmatic violence. In situations like those cited above, the traditional orientation favoring violence is rationalized, systematized, and installed in the idea system of the nation or group.

In some other societies, the orientation toward violence is established in a military tradition. If the military is dominant, many spheres of life aside from the military, e.g., the administration of criminal justice, extralegal social control, management-labor relations, and superior-inferior relations, may be qualified by extensive violence. Dornbusch (1955: 316–21), Blake (1970: 331–50), and others have shown that legitimization and acceptance of violence are intrinsic to socialization within the military. Learning to inflict and accept injury or death becomes one of the trained capacities of the military person. The pervasive involvement of the United States in the Vietnam War illustrates how the military tradition supported the orientation toward violence in American society. In the jungle, fighting where ally and enemy were not separated and often difficult to distinguish, American soldiers developed the capacity to accept widespread human suffering as an aspect of the military way of life. After discharge from military service, many men brought these attitudes and habits and the custom of possessing and using firearms back into civilian life. Studies of the street riots of the mid-1960s (Report of the National Advisory Commission on Civil Disorders, 1969; Walker, 1968; Skolnick, 1969) showed how many of those men, both participants and police, took to riot violence with the aptitude and enthusiasm that they had perfected in the jungles of Vietnam.

Many scholars have reported that the adequacy and nature of social control also function to condition the resort to violence. Gurr (1969: 581–82) showed that inadequate control in developing societies facilitated violence in collective conflict. He found that the rate and amount of violence was greater in those nations than in the advanced societies which not only had well-established agencies of social control, but also possessed strong traditions of collective self-discipline. After a longitudinal study of urbanization and collective violence in nineteenth-century France, Lodhi and Tilly (1973: 296–318) found that "normlessness was intrinsic to the urban organization." As a consequence, social control was relatively lax and collective violence tended to be widespread.

Excessive use of force or repression often functions to escalate conflict and lead to the resort to violence. The effects of excessive and inept social control were illustrated in the account of violence at the bandshell that was described above. In this connection, Adamek and Lewis (1963: 342–47) examined the consequences on social behavior of the police violence at Kent State University in the spring of 1970. During April and May 1971, 233 students, 64 of whom had previously participated in violent confrontations, were asked about their reaction, actual or imagined, to a violent encounter with the police. Adamek and Lewis report that two-thirds of those who had participated in the student rally said the violent confrontation left their political attitudes unchanged or intensified. Only a third admitted that their attitudes may have become more liberal.

LeVine (1959: 420–29) reported that inconsistency of intergroup and public policies tends to facilitate the resort to violent action. In a study of black-white relations in Africa, he found that inconsistent policies, even when permissive, served to aggravate the tendency toward violence. Such policies tended to frustrate people, making them uncertain and insecure. The effect of inconsistent social policy is illustrated in the case of court-enforced school busing in Boston in 1975 and 1976. The federal court ordered busing of students to achieve racial balance in Boston's South High School. However, the Board of Education opposed the order and failed to support it fully. This inconsistency of policy frustrated some citizens and appeared to be an indication of inadequate control to others. One consequence was the tendency of many individuals to resort to disorderly and violent behavior.

Inadequate or apparently inadequate social control permits and encourages groups to take the chance of violent means to achieve their ends. Johnson (1977: 48–52) cites "toleration" as one of the causes of the widespread resort to terrorism in recent years. In some societies, the government and societal establishment perceive the use of terror as consistent with general policy. In other cases terrorism is tolerated because nations have not developed methods for coping with the terrorists. International organizations like the United Nations cannot formulate consistent policy and take strong action, because member nations are in disagreement over the issue. The result is, as Johnson has written, a state of toleration of terrorist activity.

Lack of nonviolent alternatives of action constitute still another condition of violence. When conflict actors are unacquainted with nonviolent means, or if they do not have access to such alternatives, they may resort to violence, believing it to be the "only" way to get the ends they seek. This condition may be seen in the history of American labor relations. Taft and Ross (1969: 281–395) showed that labor-management violence was rife in the United States before the New Deal years largely because neither side knew about or could make use of the nonviolent means of struggle. Once the Wagner Act had been passed in 1935 and the new labor-relations system became available and understood, violence in industry declined sharply. Both sides now had access to a nonviolent method of struggle.

Nonviolent alternatives to struggle require leadership, special organizations, tactics, and similar resources. Thus, if there are no mediators, conflict adjudicating agencies, or established patterns of compromise, negotiation, and exchange, contending parties may see violent struggle as their only resort. Ignorance of existing resources has the same practical effect as their nonexistence. For example, once the United Nations was invented and established, it required some years to develop the specialized resources of skilled leadership, specialized organization, and appropriate procedures for handling the traffic of international conflict in nonviolent ways. As suggested, pacific and nonviolent traditions are another device for avoiding violence. However, as we have learned from watching the United Nations, it requires time and practice to distill and establish a body of nonviolent traditions.

Sometimes, nonviolent means to desired ends are not used because there is a perception that no known legitimate and nonviolent techniques are successful. This conviction is a common experience of groups that find themselves in a revolution against an established political authority. As mentioned above, Grundy (1973: 1–27) argued that the black leaders of southern Africa turned from Gandhian nonviolent tactics to organized revolutionary violence because they were convinced that the traditional nonviolent tactics no longer worked. If they were to be free and independent, they had no alternative save violence and coercion. Under such circumstances, violence is believed to acquire the aura of legitimacy.

Finally, it was said in an earlier chapter that selected structural conditions function to facilitate the resort to violence. Here we limit our attention to three such conditions: prolonged and pervasive tension, anomic conditions, and alienation. Each is a background factor which, among other things, either permits or encourages the resort to violent conflict action.

The phrase *prolonged and pervasive tension* refers to a state of defensiveness and readiness resulting from perceived hostility or threat. The sociopsychological state has been triggered by a threatening, ill-defined, and unsettled collective experience. As a consequence, groups have been polarized and the sense of danger persists. For example, as mentioned above, the crowd gathered at the bandshell in Lincoln Park during such a period of tension. The disturbance the previous evening at the amphitheater polarized participants and police, left the issue unsettled, and heightened the sense of continuing danger of confrontation. Other well-documented illustrations include the experiences on the West Coast just following the attack at Pearl Harbor and riot-prone cities such as Newark and Detroit, as described in the Report of the National Advisory Commission on Civil Disorders (1968: 56–68, 84–107) in the summers of 1967 and 1968. Prolonged and pervasive tension had three salient characteristics: polarization of relatively intransigent opposing groups, an ill-defined but palpable sense of menace, and the expectation that violence may erupt at any time. Turner and Killian (1972: 111–31) conceptualized prolonged and pervasive states of heightened readiness for action as "diffuse crowd behavior." Interaction tends to generate "emergent" norms which legitimize violent action in the situation. The mass media disseminate and sustain the collective tension throughout the larger community.

Alienation and anomie also facilitate the resort to violence by releasing some individuals from the ordinary normative controls. This sociopsychological condition of violence has been reported repeatedly in the studies of disturbances and riots. Students, blacks, and other young persons are portrayed as alienated and detached from community norms. It seems likely also that the persons who commit acts of terrorism have become detached from moral norms and established social systems. This condition also functioned to support the radical ideologies that foster and legitimize terrorism, street violence, and similar extreme forms of conflict.

It was said earlier that structural anomie and alienation emerge in situations of widespread and basic social change. Lodhi and Tilly (1974: 296–318) pointed to "normlessness" as one characteristic of urbanization in nineteenth-century France that conditioned widespread collective violence. The campus and ghetto riots in the United States were associated with basic transformations of the inclusive social system. Turner and Killian (1972: 269–88) conceptualize this inclusive liberalizing trend as a "general social movement." In those dislocations, young people of all classes and categories were severely detached and liberated from the constraints of traditional norms and values. In the nonindustrial world the process of modernization exerts a similar dislocating effect upon what were formerly tribal and peasant peoples. The literature suggests that where anomie and alienation are rife, deep-seated, and persistent, individuals and groups tend to become increasingly violence-prone. However, they may live for a long time in this state of readiness without becoming overtly violent in their behavior.

The Functions of Violence

The most obvious consequences of violent conflict are the injuries and destruction that are intended. These effects are self-evident, often dramatic, and lead to the disapproval that is the general response to violence. Yet a moment's reflection will suggest that violence has other consequences, some of which are beneficial both to individuals and to social systems.

The achievement of intended ends is one manifest function of violent conflict. This is so because violence is undertaken by design or intention as a tactical device to achieve certain stated or generally perceived ends. As one instrument of collective struggle, violence seeks to manipulate power and scarce values in order to bring about social change, to gain calculated advantages, to relieve social problems, or to achieve other intended ends. For example, it is evident that among other things the acts of violence perpetrated in Northern Ireland, Lebanon, or Rhodesia by revolutionaries, guerrillas, and terrorists are designed to gain political and economic advantages, to win liberation or to defeat detested "establishments." Insofar as any of these ends may be actually achieved, they constitute manifest functions of violent actions.

Tomlinson (1968: 417–28) illustrates this instrumental function of violence from a study of responses of blacks who were interviewed just after the Watts riot of 1965. Of the 56 percent of the respondents who claimed that the riot had a purpose in their view, each cited one or more of the following "goals" of the riot: (a) to call attention to problems of Negroes in the area; (b) to express the hostilities of Negroes to whites;

(c) to initiate action to improve conditions, to end discrimination, or to communicate to the power structure.

Some years ago, Merton (1957: 131–94) showed that some individuals and groups are so located in the social structure as to be effectively barred from achievement by legitimate means. Later, Cloward and Ohlin (1960: 175) pointed out that some groups are even barred from ordinary nonlegitimate means. In these situations violence becomes an accessible means to achievement. Coser (1967: 79) argues that for many revolutionaries, violence offers a means for "affirming identity and for claiming full manhood hitherto denied to them" by the established power structure. At the same time, the commitment of violent acts may offer downtrodden and despised persons the opportunity to achieve status, prestige, and recognition in the conflict group.

Fanon (1963: 73 and passim), Freire (1970), and others have argued that at the sociopsychological level, violence can achieve other consequences. It is asserted that in some circumstances a violent act may constitute an achievement in itself and, as such, is intrinsically satisfying. Fanon saw the destructive violence in Algeria as the neocolonialist effort of the oppressor to introject his consciousness into the oppressed. He reasoned that therapeutic violence must be exercised by the oppressed, not only for the sake of the revolution, but also to cleanse the oppressor's destructive consciousness from the self of the oppressed. These writers contend also that violence has a significant unifying effect among the weak, deprived, and oppressed groups of a social system. Nieberg (1969: 4) has argued that violence performs a "regenerative" function for social systems. He points out that within the context of the system where it occurs, widespread violence represents a "strain toward social reintegration and legitimacy." Nieberg thus sees disturbances and riots in systems like the United States as serving to regenerate, reintegrate, and increase flexibility in the social system.

Coser (1967: 82–87) reports that violence functions as a "danger signal" for the social body. Sometimes this is intended, or at least perceived as significant in retrospect. Tomlinson (1968: 417–28) revealed that blacks in Watts recognized after the fact that they used their violence to call attention to unacceptable conditions in their neighborhood. They were saying that the legitimate means of petition for redress of wrongs had been used without success. Violence was, if not the last, the best resort. It seems evident that much of the civil and revolutionary violence of modern times has been used either deliberately or unconsciously to mount a danger signal. The limited violent acts are employed to warn the community of even greater dangers ahead. Coser stresses the fact that for weak and inarticulate groups and categories violence is a peculiarly important device of communication. The danger can be averted and the problem remedied only if it becomes evident to sensitive and perceptive members. But often the sensitive members are powerless and the powerful are insensitive.

Coser (1967: 87–92) states that violence serves a catalytic function. That is, violent acts may initiate significant social change. For example, nonlegitimate acts of violence committed by police or public officials to maintain "law and order" may outrage an entire community. Southern sheriffs and other law officers had used extralegal violence for a long time against blacks without any marked public reaction. However, as Coser (1967: 88) has shown, such control methods "became suicidal" when mass communication brought them into general view. These violent practices ignited a vehement nationwide revulsion. The classic instance of the catalyzing effect of nonlegitimate police violence (see Adamek and Lewis, 1973: 342–47) is the Kent State University case.

Violence may also stimulate remedial social reaction. Tomlinson (1968: 417–28) reported that participants in the Watts riot believed they had intended to generate this kind of collective reaction. Stimulated by a violent episode, established authorities may set out, often in haste, to initiate remedial and palliative programs. Often the violently protesting rebels are invited to participate in the processes of change and remedy. Nieberg (1969: 4) saw this reaction as a "regenerative," "integrative," or "flexibility" enhancing function of violent conflict.

The dysfunctions of violence are self-evident. Violence injures and/or destroys. Each of these consequences is maladaptive for one or all of the social systems involved in any episode of violent conflict. For example, the capacity of an army to carry out its intended objectives is diminished to some extent when soldiers are injured or killed. The damage or destruction of military equipment and material is also dysfunctional for the military system. Violent conflict interferes with the efficiency and operations of social systems whether or not injuries or destruction are perpetrated. In violence, actors and resources are diverted from basic ends of the system to the purposes of violent action. Consumable resources are diverted to the needs of violence and there used up. The focus and thrust of ongoing systems are directed away from established goals to the ends of violent conflict. At the same time, in most systems, violent conflict deviates from, challenges, or violates established values and norms. Thus, while unity and cohesion within conflict actor systems may be enhanced, within inclusive systems violence tends to be dysfunctional.

The dysfunctions of violence are usually visible, dramatic, and threatening. Norms exist to control this form of nonlegitimate collective action. A considerable amount of the time and attention of the system may be directed to evaluating and sanctioning nonlegitimate forms of conflict action. As a result, violence receives a great deal of attention in most systems and draws strong condemnation upon itself.

The dysfunctional consequences of violent conflict are easy to illustrate. In the prolonged struggles in Northern Ireland and Lebanon, thousands of individuals have been injured and killed. The functioning of many families, communities, and formal associations has been hampered by the loss of these members and participants. At the same time, violent conflict has severely disrupted the former social organization in both these countries. Life is more difficult than formerly. Equally significant is the fact that valuable, sometimes irreplaceable, resources have been consumed in the fighting.

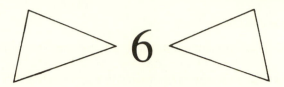

6

The Functions of Social Conflict

As shown in the foregoing chapter, it was widely believed for a long time that conflict, especially nonlegitimate conflict, is both undesirable and harmful. This popular view of the matter had two limiting effects for systematic investigation. First, it tended to foreclose inquiry into the nature and functions of conflict; since such information was already available, this kind of activity could only confirm the obvious. And second, the consequences of conflict were generally viewed in moral terms. This perspective further impeded scientific inquiry. As a result, although many observers had recognized that conflict often had desirable effects, the systematic study of the subject has been undertaken only recently.

These limitations of traditionalism have been substantially rectified by the functional perspective in sociological analysis. First, as Davis (1957: 767) suggests, the search for the consequences of social action has been elevated to a major position in the enterprise of scientific social inquiry. The consequences of conflict therefore could no longer be taken as "givens," but become instead the objects of systematic research. It was at first suspected, and then soon confirmed, that the consequences of conflict are not necessarily always undesirable or harmful. The effects of violence and other expressions of nonlegitimate conflict became dissociated from automatic moral condemnation. It was also possible to recognize that the consequences of an episode of conflict were often given opposite evaluations by different groups. Thus, the desegregation of public schools that was the result of a long process of legitimate and nonlegitimate struggle was judged as desirable by reference to the norms of the larger community, but considered as undesirable by the defenders of the structure of racial segregation.

This perspective on the consequences of social action is contained in the concept *function*. The concept has been developed and refined by Parsons (1951), Merton (1957: 19–84), and Levy (1952). The salient ideas of the concept can be summarized in the following propositions:

1—Functions are the objective consequences of social action.

2—Social action is the dynamic aspect of social systems for which functions have relevance.

3—Functions reveal three principal variable characteristics: level of intention, level of recognition, and degree of relevance for involved social systems.

Using these three variables, Merton (1957: 51) delineated three basic types: manifest functions, latent functions, and dysfunctions. He wrote that manifest functions are the intended and recognized "objective consequences" of social action that contribute to the adaptation or adjustment of a social system. This relationship is illustrated in American industries. The struggles of labor unions, including many strikes, led to the higher wages, shorter hours, and improved working conditions which were the objective ends of effort.

Latent functions, on the other hand, are the unintended and often unrecognized objective consequences of organized social activity. For example, Lodgaard (1977: 2–22) observed that although the SALT talks failed to achieve all the intended aims, the superpowers probably saw long-term benefits from talking to each other, from clarifying common interests, and from reducing international tensions. As a more negative instance of a latent function, it can be argued that the extreme mechanization of mining in the United States coal fields is explained, in part at least, by militant unionism in the coal industry. Himes (1968: 50) pointed out that international wars have created or abolished nations, shifted populations, improved the social positions of minority groups, and otherwise modified the face of the map and the course of history in unintended and unanticipated ways.

Dysfunctions are the objective consequences of social action that militate against the adjustment or adaptation of a system. Dysfunctions are unintended and often, though not always, unrecognized. They limit the efficiency of the system and thus reduce its capacity to attain its manifest functions. The dysfunctions of international wars are often more visible and insistent than their latent functions. Wars have decimated populations, destroyed natural resources, and disintegrated political organizations.

The conflicts in Western Europe that ushered in the modern era also generated structural rigidity which was dysfunctional for the social system. When the traditional modes of unitary integration within the feudal system broke down, the clash of conflicting values and interests, constrained by the rigidity of medieval structure, required new forms of unification and integration. New bureaucratic modes of organization, with emphasis on calculable, methodical, and disciplined behavior emerged at roughly the same time in which the monolithic medieval structure broke down. Gradually, though, these patterns also became rigid and exhibited the blight of ritualism.

This threefold classification of social functions provides a model for the organization of the present chapter. The first part contains a discussion of the manifest functions of social conflict. The main section of the chapter will be concerned with examining latent functions of conflict as these have been reported in the literature. A shorter, final section will review the main dysfunctions of conflict that have been reported.

THE MANIFEST FUNCTIONS OF CONFLICT

The students of social conflict have sought to identify and conceptualize the intended, or manifest, functions of conflict. Coser (1968: 232) states the aims of struggle as "values or claims to status, power and scarce resources." Park and Burgess (1921: 574) list status as the central aim of social conflict. In chapter 1 it was stated that the aims of conflict include "status, power, resources, and other scarce values." The fact that these are manifest functions is affirmed in the assertion that conflict consists of "purposeful struggles between collective actors." Bernard (1957: 38) reported the aims of social conflict as "scarce or incompatible values." Such values may include all the specific phenomena named above as well as many others not listed there.

These typical definitions reveal a significant scholarly consensus regarding the manifest aims of conflict. They declare that groups engage in struggle for the express purpose of gaining values that either are in fact or are believed to be in scarce supply, or that are incompatible. Further, there is impressive agreement that power, status, and resources are the leading categories of scarce values for which people engage in conflict. Also, it appears that the definitions imply that change is a manifest aim of social conflict. The status, power, resources, and other values to which the scholars allude can be gained only at the price of change. Feierabend and Feierabend (1972: 911–28) found from a study of 84 polities that a high level of "regime coerciveness" in conflict was correlated positively (.47) with rapid rate of socioeconomic change. Thus, it seems clear that struggle for change, which permits or facilitates the acquisition of specific values, is an intended end of social struggle. Social change is also an important latent function of conflict and will be discussed in this context in a later section of this chapter.

The sociologists may agree that the manifest aims of conflict include status, power, scarce resources, and other values. The participants in actual conflict enterprises, however, seldom state their aims in such categoric or general terms. The intended goals of struggle are much more likely to be formulated in terms of an actual political situation. For example, Lodhi and Tilly (1973: 296–318) in a study of collective violence in nineteenth-century France found that collective violence reflected variable struggles for "national power." In the continuing struggles between labor union and industrial management, the manifest goals of struggle are likely to be stated as higher wages, shorter hours, safety equipment and conditions, and packages of fringe benefits including pensions, vacations, retirement, health and welfare services, and so on. The goals of the struggles between Jews and Arabs or between Hindus and Moslems may be stated as territorial integrity, national security and boundaries, political independence of displaced persons, noninterference in internal affairs, and so on. The manifest goals of the struggle against various establishments waged by disadvantaged groups within a single society, such as blacks and women in the United States, may be stated in terms of civil rights, collective recognition, improvement of competitive opportunities, and such vaguer concepts as "liberation." The Africans in Rhodesia and Southwest Africa struggled for "majority rule." Analytically, all such specific aims of conflict can be conceptualized as status, power, scarce resources, and other values.

The manifest aims of collective conflict are matters of policy and public relations. They represent some measure of consensus and collective representation by the conflicting groups. Thus formulated, such aims are often embodied in polemical documents such as manifestoes and political proposals. They also form an important part of the public-relations posture of the respective groups. The statements of leaders and reports in the news media concern these stated aims of struggle. In time, these stated aims become elements of group ideology. In this way they become institutionalized within the group.

Since manifest functions are both intended and recognized, they have an existence both before and after the conflict act. Prior to conflict, functions are articulated and formalized in the rational considerations and prevision of the conflict group. In this form they are embodied in its ideology and strategy. They are put into practice in the form of aims, goals, plans, or programs of conflict action. Afterwards some of them occupy an important place in the lists of the group's accomplishments. Manifest functions constitute the fulfillment or realization of at least some of the plans and aims of the conflict group. What was intended beforehand is recognized as a *fait accompli* in the end.

But such achieved goals and fulfilled plans are manifest functions only if they contribute to the adjustment or adaptation of the social system. That is, such accomplishments tend to facilitate communication, increase efficiency, enhance integration of parts and operations, and in other ways contribute to the improvement or efficacy of the system. At the same time, such accomplishments of conflict may reduce discontent and enhance the sense of well-being of participants in the system, but this is incidental to their character as manifest functions.

This way of formulating the matter recognizes that manifest functions contribute to the adjustment or adaptation of the system of the conflict actor that intended and recognized the aims achieved. This fact is important since several systems are involved in any conflict act, namely, the systems of the attacking actor, of the defending actor, and of the inclusive community. Accomplishments that constitute manifest functions for the attacker may also be manifest functions for the inclusive community. For example, school desegregation may be seen as an intended and desirable accomplishment by both the NAACP and the general community. Equally relevant, however, is the fact that one actor's manifest functions may be dysfunctional for another. School desegregation may be functional for the attacking actor, i.e., the NAACP and its allies, but that goal may be catastrophic for the social system of the hard-core segregationists.

All the stated goals of an organization do not become manifest functions; first stated goals must be achieved. Nevertheless, even the effort at goal-achievement that fails may produce unintended consequences of either a functional or dysfunctional character. Thus for example, failure in a conflict enterprise may lead to increased internal group cohesion, more efficient organization, and other structural changes undertaken as preparation for a second try.

Manifest Functions of Racial Conflict

In 1973 Himes (150–56) attempted to identify the manifest functions of "racial conflict," i.e., the conscious struggles of American blacks in the decade and a half between 1954 and 1970. The analysis began by identifying the reduction of prejudice, alteration of the racial structure and reconstruction of the American order as the principal objectives of struggle. It was recognized that these are not mutually exclusive aims. Achievements on any of these fronts thus constitute gains on the others. Although Himes admitted that racial conflict failed to accomplish all its objectives, there was evidence to indicate that the racial conflict had had objective consequences.

After examining available evidence, Himes concluded that from the perspective of the general societal system, racial conflict produced modifications of the legal rules, alterations of sublegal institutional structures, and some diffuse reduction of racial prejudice. From the point of view of the attacking black minority, there was a significant enhancement of group solidarity and self-esteem, advancement in collective status, improvement of the power situation of blacks, and betterment of the substantive conditions of life.

The nature and extent of these manifest functions of racial conflict can be illustrated by citing the evidence presented by Himes of changes of the legal rules governing race relations in the nation. In this arena the subjective aims of blacks were listed as freedom and dignity of the individual, equality before the law, the right to life, liberty, and the pursuit of happiness, equality of opportunity, basic human respect, and growth of the free personality. Continuous efforts to achieve these aims led to modifications of the legal basis of the racial structure through legislative enactment, court decisions, and administrative regulations and enforcement. Although such actions were taken one at a time, in the aggregate they produced far-reaching objective modifications of the racial structure. Figure 6-1 presents an inventory of the major categories of legal changes that were associated with the racial conflict of the time. Each category refers to a relatively uncodified cluster of legislative enactments, court decisions, and administrative operations at all levels of government that tended to affect almost every aspect of the general social structure and the traditional racial system.

THE LATENT FUNCTIONS OF CONFLICT

Like manifest functions, latent functions are objective consequences of social conflict. However, they are unintended and sometimes also unrecognized. Thus latent functions are not built into the aims, plans, and programs of conflict groups. They are not articulated in the rhetoric of conflict and formalized in ideology and strategy. Latent functions are adventitious consequences of conflict. They are the unexpected developments, occurrences, or changes that arise in the course of conflict action. They result from resistance or yielding, connection or separation, reaction or insensitivity for which there is no plan or preparation. For example, Grundy (1973: 1–27) showed how the swing toward violence within the black societies of southern Africa resulted from prior struggles with intransigent whites in South Africa and Rhodesia. As noted earlier, the militancy of labor unions in American industries produced higher wages, which led to increased mechanization.

Such unintended and unanticipated consequences may be functional,

FIGURE 6-1

MAJOR CATEGORIES OF
CONFLICT-INDUCED LEGAL CHANGE IN THE
RACIAL STRUCTURE

VOTING RIGHTS: Abolition of white primary, removal of registration restriction, federal supervision of registration procedure.

MILITARY SERVICE: Prohibition of segregation and discrimination in all branches of the armed services.

TRAVEL: Prohibition of segregation and discrimination on public carriers, in stations, and other related facilities.

EDUCATION: Prohibition of segregation and discrimination in both public and private lower and higher education.

EMPLOYMENT: Prohibition of discrimination in employment in government, government-contracted activity, and in all employment subjected to the interstate authority of the federal government.

PUBLIC ACCOMMODATIONS: Prohibition by law and court decision of segregation and discrimination in places of public accommodation, e.g., hotels, restaurants, movies.

PUBLIC SERVICES: Prohibition of discrimination in public services such as health and welfare.

HOUSING: Action against segregation and discrimination in public housing, publicly financed housing, and in general housing situations and accommodations.

SUPPORT SERVICES: Anti-poverty programs, Job Corps.

Taken from Joseph S. Himes, *Racial Conflict in American Society* (Columbus, Ohio: Merrill, 1973), p. 152.

i.e., adjustive or adaptive for the social systems involved. Coser (1956: 80) wrote that this was true of only those conflicts that do not threaten basic goals, values, and interests. They tend to enhance integration, improve communication, clarify operations, sharpen group boundaries and in other ways increase the efficiency and economy of a system. In such instances latent functions constitute a kind of system-relevant bonus of conflict. It must be remembered, however, that consequences that are functional for the system of one conflict actor may be dysfunctional for the other.

The latent functions of conflict can be recognized and investigated only after the fact. They have no prior existence in the form of aims, goals, or plans that can direct the observer in his search. They must be sorted out from among the residue of struggle. The observer is guided to them by their characteristics of lack of prior intention and adaptive enhancement of the conflict system. Scholars have long recognized the existence and importance of latent functions. However, systematic investigation of the topic has developed only recently.

The latent functions of social conflict have been reported in various ways. Some scholars (Coser and Himes) have produced inventories of typical latent functions of conflict. Other students of social phenomena (Durkheim and Dahrendorf) have examined the latent functions of conflict within the context of changing social organization.

Inventories of Latent Functions

When Coser (1956: 29–31) set out to revive interest in the study of social conflict and to begin developing a sociology of social conflict, he commenced by examining its latent functions. This action both expressed his judgment and emphasized the importance of latent functions in a systematic study of conflict. For this purpose Coser inventoried the leading functional propositions contained in Georg Simmel's essay *Conflict*. Coser analyzed, critiqued, and reformulated sixteen of Simmel's major functional propositions in *The Functions of Social Conflict*. This little book not only constitutes the most impressive inventory of the latent functions of social conflict, it also established the baseline from which the modern sociology of conflict has developed. Later, in 1957, Coser delineated two additional functional propositions. These eighteen propositions formulated by Coser are summarized in Figure 6-2.

This remarkable list identifies many, but by no means all the latent functions of social conflict. Perhaps most of the unintended consequences of social struggle are specific to conflict situations. That is, although a specific latent function may be categorized within a type, it is nevertheless uniquely shaped by the specific circumstances of the conflict enterprise in question. Moreover, it will be seen that each function identified and examined by Coser is in fact a cluster or family of related propositions. For example, realistic conflict may serve to enhance in-group solidarity. At the same time, the realistic conflict that attacks or threatens basic consensus and core values is likely to reduce the cohesion and integration of the group. If, on the other hand, the conflict group is a rigid system, then conflict with an out-group may have still other kinds of

FIGURE 6-2

COSER'S LATENT FUNCTIONS OF CONFLICT

PROPOSITION 1. The Group-Binding Functions of Conflict.
Conflict maintains a sense of identity and boundary lines of groups by (1) continuing social divisions and stratification systems and (2) facilitating attraction between higher and lower classes.

PROPOSITION 2. The Group-Preserving Functions and Significance of Safety-Valve Institutions.
Conflict is often required to maintain a relationship. At a cost, systems maintain institutions to manage hostile sentiments and to preserve integrity.

PROPOSITION 3. Realistic and Nonrealistic Conflict.
Realistic conflict is instrumental, external, goal-seeking struggle. Nonrealistic conflict is tension-releasing, self-rewarding action.

PROPOSITION 4. Social Conflict and Hostile Impulses.
Conflict is interaction between subject and object. Hostile impulses are states of feeling and/or motivations which may have utility for conflict.

PROPOSITION 5. Hostility in a Close Social Relationship.
Relations within intimate systems reveal a unitary quality characterized by positive and negative cathexes in ambivalence.

PROPOSITION 6. The Closer the Relationship the More Intense the Conflict.
When one actor feels that the other is a threat to group identity and unity, the struggle between them will be intense. Although such conflicts are more intense, they are not more frequent than in distant relationships.

PROPOSITION 7. The Impact and Function of Conflicts in Group Structures.
Conflicts that do not contradict the basic and core values are functional by eliminating dissociating elements. Loosely structured groups and open societies use realistic conflict to weld the constituent units together.

PROPOSITION 8. Conflict as an Index of Stability of Relationships.
Stable relationships may be characterized by realistic conflict, provided it does not affect basic consensus and core values. Conflict in secondary relationships indicates the operation of a protective balancing mechanism.

PROPOSITION 9. Conflict With Out-Groups Increases Internal Cohesion.
Realistic conflict mobilizes energies and increases cohesion in solidarist groups. In nonsolidarist groups these conditions may lead to despotism and/or centralization.

PROPOSITION 10. Conflict With Another Group Defines Group Structure and Consequent Reaction to Internal Conflict.
Groups faced with continued struggle tend to be intolerant, assuming a sect-like character, remaining limited in size, and tightly cohesive. Ideologically tolerant groups are likely to be large and to manage internal differences by flexibility of structure.

PROPOSITION 11. The Search for Enemies.
Rigidly structured groups in conflict may search for or conjure up enemies to maintain internal unity and cohesion.

PROPOSITION 12. Ideology and Conflict.
Rigid collective actors fighting for ideological goals may be more radical and intense than when struggling for personal ends. However, objectification of a conflict in an ideology may be unifying when both parties seek the same goal, e.g., the establishment of truth by contending scholars.

PROPOSITION 13. Conflict Binds Antagonists.
Conflict may bind opponents by initiating new forms of interaction, by imposing a single universal norm, by promoting new norms, by reaffirming dormant norms, and by increased intensity of participation. Thus conflict facilitates change and readjustment by innovating norms.

PROPOSITION 14. Interest in the Unity of the Enemy.
If the two parties to a conflict are relatively balanced, a unified attacker prefers a unified opponent. A common organizational structure of conflict facilitates common rules of struggle.

PROPOSITION 15. Conflict Establishes and Maintains Balance of Power.
Conflict may enable groups to avoid disequilibrium by modifying the basis of power relations, thus balancing and maintaining the social system. In this way conflict creates and modifies norms, leads to matching of modes of opposition organization, and establishes a balancing mechanism by adjusting relative power.

PROPOSITION 16. Conflict Creates Associations and Coalitions.
Conflict promotes organization by bringing unrelated groups together into temporary coalitions and associations around pragmatic interests within flexible inclusive systems.

PROPOSITION 17. Change within Social Systems.
Conflict prevents rigidity and facilitates internal system reorganization by facilitating the innovation of elements.

PROPOSITION 18. Change of Social Systems.
Conflict promotes transformation of social systems by altering all major structural relations, basic institutions, and prevailing values.

Taken from Lewis A. Coser, *The Functions of Social Conflict* (New York: Free Press, 1956), pp. 33–149; Lewis A. Coser, "Social Conflict and the Theory of Social Change," *British Journal of Sociology* 8 (1957): 190–297.

social consequences. While Coser has identified and examined eighteen key latent functions of conflict, he has actually done much more. He has given us an important and fruitful way of studying social conflict.

This study of social functions makes it clear that both nonlegitimate and legitimate conflict may be adaptive and adjustive for social systems. It is implied, for example, that under specific conditions violence may be functional for certain social systems. Thus, writing in 1967 (73–93),

Coser identified three latent functions of violence which he called "achievement," "danger signal," and "catalyst." These findings were discussed in the preceding chapter and will not be examined further here. Suffice it to say merely that all forms of social conflict, realistic and nonrealistic, legitimate and nonlegitimate, may under some conditions be functional.

Some of the functions examined by Coser are consequences of struggle between collective actors. Propositions 14, 15, and 16 illustrate this type. At the same time, some other propositions may apply to interpersonal conflicts as well. The group of propositions focusing on the role of hostility, i.e., numbers 4, 5, and 6, reveal this dual applicability.

This inventory of social functions of conflict provides a perspective from which to evaluate social conflict. The whole list of propositions argues cogently that social conflict is not intrinsically either good or bad. Each conflict act produces consequences that are system-enhancing as well as some that are system-detracting. Conflict is strain-reducing for some individuals, and strain-intensifying for others. The functional perspective provides a mechanism for evaluating conflict while retaining attitudinal objectivity. To say that under certain circumstances conflict reduces the integration of a certain social system is to evaluate the conflict without moralizing about it. In the sociology of social conflict this evaluative capacity is an achievement of importance.

Finally, an examination of Coser's work on functions leads us to recognize that this book contributes other important ideas to the sociology of conflict. It introduced the definition of social conflict that has now come to be standard in the field. The differentiation of realistic and nonrealistic conflict defines types and establishes a perspective that is important. The analysis of functions led Coser to examine the conditions of conflict. These and other contributions not only illuminate the functions of social conflict; they also fill in important parts of the foundation of a sociology of social conflict.

Social Conflict and Social Change

It was said above that the intended consequences of social conflict include a wide range of specific goals. These goals were conceptualized categorically as status, power, scarce resources, and other values. In the course of struggling for these ends, collective actors may alter the integration of social systems, modify ecological patterns, create new social institutions, rearrange hierarchies, change power structures, alter effort-reward patterns and create new value systems.

All social systems have built-in, more or less effective mechanisms for managing and resolving the internal conflict that tends to threaten their integration. In the course of working out these conflicts through such mechanisms, accommodative novelty is generated, causing the social systems to change and persist. Eisenstadt (1963 and 1964) has illustrated this process of accommodative response to conflict in the experiences of the so-called "early empires." He found that the process of institutionalizing political systems tended to build in mechanisms of change which in the end could lead to reorganization of the political systems. Cohen (1964: 495–521) reported that under other circumstances the process of accommodative change was gradual and developmental. From a study of the Kanuri of Nigeria he discovered that conflict was built into the political organization in such a way as to produce a pattern of continuous, long-range change of the modernization type. He found that conflicting standards of behavior of the various sectors tended to generate innovations, some of which were tolerated through established patterns of selective enforcement. Commenting on this pattern of change within social systems, Ryan (1969: 119) asserted that internal conflict, rather than being universally disintegrative, actually serves to maintain equilibrium in flexible and changing systems. This viewpoint implies that accommodative mechanisms exist and operate within such systems. Typically, Ryan concludes, this process of conflict accommodation leads to social change.

On the other hand, sometimes social conflict eventuates in change, not within social systems, but rather affecting the entire system. Change of this kind is ordinarily called revolution and involves resort to widescale violence. Coser (1968: 235) points out that rigid social systems that refuse to tolerate accommodative changes and that permit unresolved latent conflicts to accumulate may therefore enhance the chances of violent attacks against the consensual structure leading to changes of societal systems. Change of social systems refers to drastic alteration of all major structural relations, basic institutions, and prevailing core values. Change of this order of magnitude and depth is generally analyzed under the rubric of revolution. Such change typically leads to destruction or decay of old structures and emergence of new ones.

Conflict Theories of Social Organization

Some scholars have argued that social conflict is the major source of organization in society. That is, the pattern or form of organization in social systems issues from the influence of social struggle. However, although such theories agree regarding the source of social organization, they differ as to how conflict operates in the organizing process. In this section we will demonstrate this difference by examining conflict theories of social organization as formulated by Durkheim, Burgess, and Dahrendorf.

Durkheim believed that conflict played a crucial role as a source of initial specialization in the early stages of the development of society. Alpert (1939: 93–94) reported that he put the central question in the following way: why does an increase of interaction necessitate a growth of the division of labor? In Durkheim's (1933, 1938) view the main intermediary "factor," i.e., condition, is the increase of the intensity and severity of the struggle for existence, resulting from an increase in the degree of interaction. As the starting point, Durkheim said, any society, i.e., an on-going social system that is in some measure an established organization in equilibrium, is postulated. One important value for the members is the desire that the society should both exist at the moment and persist into the future. At the same time, each member of the society also wishes to survive. He further postulates that whether because of increase of population, from new modes of communication, or from some other reason, the intensity of social interaction were to increase, in such an event, an increase in the intensity and severity of competition and conflict must also result. This is true because there are more persons to be taken care of in the same environment; there has been an increase of social demand coupled with a constancy of social resources. Meanwhile it is also assumed that the individuals wish neither to perish, nor to leave their society, nor for the society itself to perish. Under these circumstances, and assuming that conditions remain the same, the only alternative outcome is division of labor, that is, increase of the intensity of social interaction through increase of specialization in the division of labor. In this way struggle for survival and well-being is made less severe while the intensity of interaction, as it must under such circumstances, remains high or goes even higher. The result is a form and pattern of mechanical organization adjusted to the available resource base and the level of struggle produced by the intensity of interaction.

Writing more than half a century ago, Burgess (1925) formulated a theory of urban organization that was persuasive for a number of years. He believed that social struggle constituted the main social force holding social systems together and producing order and structure in human affairs. After studying the urban Chicago community for a number of years from this perspective, he concluded that struggle tended to assign individuals, groups, and institutions to ranked positions and specialized geographical locations. The successful ones were separated from the failures. Conflict also sifted and assigned social units, i.e., groups and institutions, by cultural, ethnic, and racial characteristics.

Each type of social unit found a place in the ecological structure. Burgess pointed out that commercial and light manufacturing enterprises took up positions in the central part of the city, while heavy industry was relegated to the periphery. The most successful families established residences in the suburban commuter zone, and the others were located by degree of success in zones extending outward from the center of the city. Thus an ecological structure emerged that reflected the social and economic pattern of the city.

This status-geographical system was portrayed in the celebrated "concentric zone" model of the city. The ecological zones were called central business zone, slum zone in transition, working-men's zone, residential or middle-class zone, and upper-class area or commuter zone. As one moved outward along a horizontal axis from the center to the periphery, one passed through these ecological zones. As one moved upward along the vertical axis from lowest to highest rank, one passed through the status gradations that corresponded to this ecological organization.

Burgess claimed that each separated and positioned social unit tended to acquire a role and function in the social whole commensurate with its social-geographical location. Thus a slum of servants was found close by the "gold coast" which it served and which supported it. The "gold coast" was located in the suburban periphery far from the deterioration, congestion, noise, and pollution of the old city. Working-class homes were close to the places where their inhabitants worked, or at least close to easy transportation. The central shopping area was, by reason of its location, accessible to all members of the community.

The whole complex structure, argued Burgess, was tied together by meaningful systems of communication and interaction. Integration was achieved through interdependence of the specialized parts and by social control exercised by the inclusive governmental system. Burgess concluded that the process of struggle that produced the system in the beginning was the leading force making for its modification or decay.

This theory has been critiqued and confirmed by two later scholars. In 1938 Hoyt formulated the ecological pattern in terms of "quadrants" or "sectors." However, he found that although the ecological pattern differed from the concentric zone model, his findings tended to confirm the general status-geographical pattern and the central role of conflict in generating social organization within urban communities. Writing in 1945, Harris and Ullman (14–16) delineated the pattern as "multiple nuclei." They argued that the spatial pattern of cities was built around several distinct nuclei, each forming the focus of a subordinate structure. However, this formulation tended also to confirm Burgess' thesis of spatial-social organization resulting from struggle within the urban community. In recent years this whole theory of urban social organization has been seriously challenged. It is said to be simplistic, designed to fit mainly the unique Chicago community and unsuited to the emerging evidence of changing urban organization.

In a remarkable discussion of the source of cohesion and integration in society, Dahrendorf (1959: 157–65) identified the "two faces of society" which he called "integration and values" and "coercion and interests." He concluded that the coercion model was basic, while the integration mechanism played a secondary and supportive role. In a later section of his book, he undertakes to show how conflict produces social organization. The variable organization of societies that emerges from this conflict is a latent function of collective struggles for various specific goals. Dahrendorf began by arguing that stability and organization in industrial societies initially was maintained by the control of the major bureaucratic centers of power, the "authoritative associations." However, from the outset, the system included important sources of instability and potential change. The population was divided into two unorganized and opposing categories, "quasigroups," that differed in rank and authority and that were distinguished by divergent "latent interests."

Dahrendorf argued that this unstable pattern of organization was the function of prior class conflict and that it would be altered by the renewal of that conflict. He identified certain "conditions," i.e., "technical conditions [personnel, charter], political conditions [freedom of coalition], and social conditions [communication, patterned recruitment]," in the societal situation that he believed tended to lead to conflict and change. Initially, these factors generated conflict groups within the quasigroups. Some individuals within the weak and subordinate category began to reveal the traits of personality and character that pressaged the emergence of organizational leadership. Within the unorganized category the political conditions of organization appeared when individuals coalesced into groups and when marginal power and novel ideas emerged. Improvement of communication established the social conditions of organization. Intensification of the sense of deprivation and rising level of expectations, when combined with internalization of organizational roles, established the psychological basis of organization.

In Dahrendorf's view, these factors in combination led to several significant changes. Latent interests of the quasigroups became manifest and were expressed as organizational goals. With leadership, motivation, and increasing power, specific organizations called conflict groups emerged within the quasigroups to seek the manifest interests through collective struggle. The "class conflict" that issued from this situation tended to produce changes in the initial social organization. A new pattern of quasigroups, interests, status, and power was produced, which in time became crystallized into a class system in an industrial society.

Some Latent Functions of the Social Movements

A remarkable series of social movements burgeoned in the United States during the decade of the 1960s. The most notable include: (1) The black civil rights movement; (2) The youth-student movement; (3) The poor people's movement; (4) The women's liberation movement; (5) The peace movement; (6) The population control movement; (7) The anti-pollution movement; (8) The Indian rights movement. Although the stated goals of these movements differed in specifics, they tended to converge in general aim and to reinforce one another in several ways in pursuit of improvements in the quality of American life.

It is evident that the movements achieved some of their stated goals. In an earlier section of the present chapter we have illustrated the achievements of the black civil rights movement. Two of the major goals of the peace movement were achieved, repeal of the Selective Service Act and withdrawal of American military forces from Vietnam. Goal achievement on behalf of the poor and underprivileged is revealed in the social legislation enacted in the 1960s. The various programs for control of population growth and improvement of the environment indicate still other manifest functions of the social movements. At the same time the cumulative impact of these movements generated some significant unintended social consequences for American society. As illustration, three will be examined briefly. They include the extension of the boundaries of popular participation, the increase of institutional flexibility, and the regeneration of public morality.

The social movements served to extend popular participation in at least two ways. First, the movements won new power for the youth, students, minority groups, the poor, women, and other traditionally weak sectors. As a result, the power differential between these groups and the dominant sectors of the society was reduced. All these groups thus participated more widely and significantly in the power relations of the society than had been the case previously.

The diffusion of social power is related to the other way that participation patterns changed. In generating and exercising power, groups and individuals whose social actions were traditionally marginal to somewhat significant found themselves drawn more fully into the mainstream. Armed with their new sense of power and stimulated by both rising expectations and exciting examples, they took to the streets and besieged the institutions to press for changes. In this way they participated more widely and more significantly in the affairs of the society than had been their wont. For example, thousands of rural and small-town blacks registered and voted for the first time. Students participated in collective actions that won for them serious hearing by university trustees and administrations. Poor people erupted from the anonymity of big-city ghettos, and Indians streamed out of the invisibility of reservations to participate in the news, the debates, and the actions of the times. Such extended boundaries and altered patterns of participation have contributed significantly to the adaptation and vitality of the inclusive social system.

Simpson (1972: 1–6) has conceptualized the process of institutional change as infusing elements of nonrationality into the structure of bureaucratic organization. The derationalizing of the bureaucracies is said to occur in several ways. Hard-pressed from all sides by the embattled movements, the formal institutions searched for help with their problems. Some found the assistance they needed in the concepts, proposals, and programs of the movements that were pressing them to change and adapt. Such new ideas and formulations introduced elements of flexibility and nonrationality into the institutional structures. Thus Simpson wrote (1972: 2), "But more and more, bureaucracies are becoming less and less rational, and rational values are in retreat." The growing nonrationality, informality, and flexibility were unintended consequences of the conflict actions of the social movements. Activism was institutionalized as the former elites of the movements were drawn into the bureaucracies. The unmeasurable values and qualitative contributions of these new officials tended to transform bureaucratic decision making into a nonrational political process. The bureaucracies were forced to appeal to outside publics for bargaining power and validation. Westhues (1972: 81–89) confirmed this effect when he reported that the hippie alumni tended to abandon the extreme versions of their values and focus on achievement of the basic humanitarian goals. These consequences worked to bring the public bureaucracies into adjustment with the temper of the times.

A third latent function of the social movements was the regeneration of public morality. This fact was revealed in both a new thrust and a new seriousness of moral considerations in public affairs. Many of the dramatic events of the 1960s and 1970s indicate the potency of the new public morality. These events include, among others, the passage of civil rights legislation, the termination of United States military involvement in Vietnam, and the traumatic Watergate affair.

It was said above that although the movements differed as regards specific goals and tactics, they all tended to converge around certain central aims. These aims can be phrased in several ways. We can speak of the convergence around humanistic ends in contrast to materialistic ends. The central thrust of the movements may be said to be the improvement of the quality of life for all Americans. However different the movements may appear to be, they all agreed that moral values and moral considerations must be the touchstone and measuring stick of social action. The basic question raised by all the movements and on every hand was, Is it right?

The unrelenting and ubiquitous pressure of the movements tended to turn the face of the total society slowly toward such considerations of public morality. Without formal action, indeed even without recognizing it, the level and vitality of public morality altered. In the end, by the mid-1970s the society and its agents, government, economy, education, etc., could take dramatic actions in the name of the regenerated public morality that only a few years earlier would have been thought virtually impossible.

THE DYSFUNCTIONS OF SOCIAL CONFLICT

Social conflicts that attack or threaten core values and basic concerns may be dysfunctional for social systems. The consequences of such conflict tend to be maladjustment and disintegration. Such outcomes of conflict are not intended and may also go unrecognized. When recognized they may be given negative evaluations and decried as problematical. What is important in this connection is the fact that the same conflict act that produces manifest functions and latent consequences also causes dysfunctional results. The nature and range of these phenomena can be revealed by examining four classes of facts, including the nonproductive consumption of resources, the maladaptation or disintegration of social systems, the production and maintenance of dissociative sentiments, and the development of social and individual problems.

It is evident that function and dysfunction are not dissociated. A dysfunctional limitation or maladaptation may be the price that a social system has to pay for a functional gain. For example, in time of war the nation may lose governmental and economic efficiency, but the war may also generate enhanced integration and heightened capacity for concerted and rapid action. In a school district embattled over racial desegregation, effort and resources may be diverted from education, yet at the same time concern over the quality of education may be intensified. Also, a functional gain in one system may be balanced by a dysfunction in a related system. For example, it was said above that racial conflict functioned to enhance societal integration within the United States. However, this gain could be accomplished only at the price of reducing the efficiency of the previously segregated racial system.

One dysfunction of social conflict is the nonproductive consumption of resources. In the course of collective struggle human and material resources, both tangible and intangible, are transformed into social power and then consumed in the act of conflict. Resource consumption is built into the conflict act itself. Yet in the process of consumption part of such resources are transformed and reappear, as it were, in the form of social change. Some part of the resources are transformed into unuseable form, and may be thought of as social waste.

The waste of resources in conflict can be illustrated in various ways. Etzioni (1968: 325) points out that some resources are lost in the process of mobilization. The amount of resource waste in power mobilization varies with the relative efficiency of the process. Thus, resource waste would be higher in a riot than in a strike. The evidence also suggests that excessive or prolonged resource waste may be maladaptive or disintegrative for a social system.

Violence, because it is defined as intentional damage or destruction of property or people, often represents another instance of resource waste. Such damage or destruction constitutes the price paid by a conflict group for the ends sought. Perceived in these terms the price paid may be wasteful in terms of the gain achieved. Tropper (1972: 97–98) estimated the resource investments of actors in experimental conflict situations. He concluded that sometimes more resources may be consumed in pursuing victory than it is worth.

Resource waste in conflict may appear as personality maladaptation. If the struggle is prolonged, making great demands upon participants, the individual's resulting habitual adjustments may turn out to have trained him to be incapable of functioning properly in the inclusive social system. For example, the patterns of hostilities that emerge in all great wars serve afterwards to divide the world and make harmonious international relations difficult if not impossible. Blake (1970: 331–50) examined this issue in connection with military socialization. He found that training men for military service enhanced their efficiency in this area, but reduced their fitness for normal and useful functioning in civilian society.

From the perspective of specific social systems, conflict may waste resources in other ways. When resources are diverted from socially approved uses to conflict (whether approved or not) they become unavailable for the manifest aims of the system. For example, school districts may utilize tax funds to oppose court-ordered busing of children instead of supporting or improving the quality of instruction. The individuals who are killed or injured in the course of conflict represent resources that have been consumed. Sometimes the individuals thus consumed (say, the general of an army or the executive of a corporation) may be crucial to the social system. In the event such leaders cannot be replaced, their loss may be catastrophic for the system. Similarly the damage or destruction of certain material resources may severely handicap social systems. This is why in war each side seeks to destroy the military industries, communication systems, and agriculture of the enemy.

Several intervening variables may condition the waste of social resources in the process of social conflict. If the efficiency of the mobilization of resources and the execution of conflict is high, then resource consumption may be minimized. Inefficiency in either or both these spheres will contribute to high consumption of resources. If conflict tactics make the most of action that is low in intensity and violence, then resource consumption will be minimized. The opposite characteristics of tactics may lead to an increase in the use of resources. If nonproductively consumed resources are replaceable, then the effect on social waste may be mitigated to some extent. In this connection, Coser (1956: 48–55) has stated that by definition realistic conflict is likely to be more resource-economical than nonrealistic conflict.

Under some conditions social conflict may contribute to the maladaptation and disintegration of social systems. Initially, conflict reduces internal cohesion, impedes clear and effective communication, limits harmony among complimentary working parts, and intereferes with the exercise of control over the ongoing system. At the same time, the capacity of systems to perform manifest operations can be limited by the dysfunctional effects of conflict. For example, countries like the United States, the Soviet Union, and the People's Republic of China neglect the historical purposes for their existence by diverting enormous resources to preparation for war. Ryan (1969: 120) pointed out that when a conflict reaches stalemate, disorganization of the contending parties is a possibility.

This dysfunctional effect of conflict is also revealed by internal cleavages and clashes. For example, Burrowes and Muzzio (1972: 211–26) reported that the Arab League was torn by squabbles and bickering among its members while they strove to unite in the fight against Israel. The result was that the League was ineffective as a conflict structure. Social conflict with an out-group may also generate internal conflicts. The norms of jungle fighting may be injected into the routines of daily life, creating a world peopled with hunters and the hunted. "Doves" and "hawks" develop different argots to contain and manipulate their differences of value, understanding, and feeling. Conflict-based subcultures and ethnic groups may arise to plague the inclusive group that is already absorbed in fending off an out-group enemy. In time, the superimposed splits may become deep, even threatening the integrity and survival of the social system itself.

The maladaptive and disintegrative tendencies issuing from social conflict may be revealed in still other ways and along other dimensions. The anomie that has crept into the crumbling system may be matched by increasing alienation of individuals from the split and clashing value system. Alienation may be revealed in various kinds of erratic behavior and personality maladjustments. In the United States during the protracted Vietnam War, these reactions to anomie and alienation took the form of the increase of drug use and addiction, rebelliousness of youth, unorthodox religious activities, and other forms of deviant behavior. At the same time alienation expressed itself in reaction against military service, the rejection of established authority, normative and value deviations called the "youth culture," and the like. Initially these novel and deviant forms of individual and social behavior appeared as deviations. In time some of them were institutionalized into forms of social change.

A further dysfunctional consequence of social conflict may be the emergence and crystallization of dissociative social sentiments. We noted above that conflict may function to increase internal group cohesion and heighten morale. At the same time, conflict with an out-group may generate or intensify sentiments of ethnocentrism and out-group hostility. Such sentiments serve to support or intensify the conflict. Raab (1974: 53–55) examined both the Arab and the worldwide attitude toward Jews following the Six Day War of 1967. He found that a new anti-Semitism had developed that was relatively impersonal and directed against Israel as a nation. At the same time, the heightened ethnocentric attitudes of the Arabs as reported by Burrowes and Muzzio (1972: 221–26) tended to be inconsistent and politically ineffective because of internal cleavages. Nevertheless, these and similar nonrational sentiments have limited utility in the conflict situation. They gain a residual usefulness in the parochial way of life.

Ethnocentrism and rejection are by definition accompanied by reduction of the capacity to empathize with the adversary. The conflict takes on an implacable dimension and the chances of managing it are reduced. The enemy is a nonhuman, an animal, a thing, undeserving of sympathy and consideration. The lines of conflict have further hardened and the possibilities of withdrawal or termination have been made even more difficult. No longer an object of empathy, the enemy is now not an end, but rather a means to some different and external end. He is to be used, and when no longer usable, to be removed. Finally, and sometimes initially, the response to the conflict adversary may be cast in terms of antagonism or hostility. For genuine reasons or by means of propaganda and brainwashing, the group learns to hate or scorn the enemy, "the barbarian," the "savage Indian," "the *Boche*," "the Japs," and so on. Such epithets serve to capture and concentrate the antagonism and to keep it active and mobile.

Because the dysfunctions of conflict always exist within a medium of active moral values, they tend to be defined as social or personal problems. The maladaptive and disintegrative consequences of conflict insure that some needs and desires will not be fulfilled. The social apparatus for the satisfaction of needs and desires breaks down or is rendered relatively inefficient.

The widespread existence of unfulfilled needs and desires leads to feelings and perceptions of frustrations and deprivation. People recognize or believe they recognize that they are not receiving the gratifications and experiences to which they have become accustomed, or to which they believe they are legitimately entitled. They grow restless and look around for relief.

States of frustration and deprivation lead directly into sensations of discontent and unhappiness. And, as we saw in chapter 2, widespread, unrelieved sensations of discontent grounded in the sense of deprivation are the "prime cause" or basic motivation in the causal syndrome of social conflict. Thus, as Dahrendorf has suggested, one of the consequences of social conflict is further conflict.

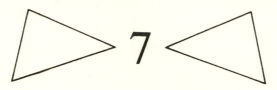

7

The Prediction of Social Conflict

In this chapter we will examine the possibility and role of prediction in the study of social conflict. Drawing upon a growing body of literature on the subject, we will first undertake to define what is meant by prediction. Such a definition will provide a perspective from which to explore the relation of conflict prediction to conflict theory. To show how social scientists have approached the task of prediction, a number of studies will be summarized and evaluated. With this material in hand, we will then undertake to develop a strategy for conflict prediction. The chapter will conclude with a description of the background and prediction of conflict in Soweto, South Africa, in June of 1976.

On the face of it, it may seem evident that, no matter how imperfect our social-science technology, the effort to predict the onset of nonlegitimate conflict would be an altogether praiseworthy activity. Unfortunately, however, this is not necessarily the case. In many societies, efforts to foretell the possible outbreak of nonlegitimate conflict are qualified by crisscrossing value-judgments. As a consequence, conflict prediction tends to stimulate lively controversy in many places. Two of these controversies can be mentioned.

This chapter will argue that the social sciences have a long and impressive (though not perfect) record in social prediction, including the prediction of the onset and termination of nonlegitimate conflict. A number of studies will be cited and evaluated to indicate the techniques of conflict prediction and the nature of predictive strategy. A research strategy will be outlined to show how scientific investigation can be used in the process of conflict prediction. But even as this side of the argument is being advanced, it is recognized that some social scientists contend that social science is not yet capable of making reliable and useful predictions of the onset of nonlegitimate conflict. Wiles (1971: 32–39) presented this side of the argument. He believed that the analytic capacity of the social-science tools of prediction has been exaggerated. In support of this contention he cited the inaccuracies of predictions in a number of recent sociopolitical crises. He concluded that the advent and immense development of social science in recent years have had only little significant impact upon the practical alleviation of crisis-generated conflict. Although, it is hoped that we may be sobered by this caveat, we should not be deterred from continuing the search for ways of bringing social science to the service of conflict prediction.

The clash of value-judgments bears upon the issue of the uses of increased knowledge of the techniques of conflict prediction. If improved skill in conflict prediction can inform social policy and public action, who really benefits from this gain? The social traditionalist would answer that the general community is the gainer, for it is evident that nonlegitimate conflict is basically disruptive and destructive. The community is better off when such conflicts can be anticipated, and either hedged off before they develop, or resolved once they start. But this argument either denies or ignores the fact that some actors in the social system stand to benefit from nonlegitimate social conflict. According to Grady (1976: 277–92) this is the issue that was raised many years ago by Locke's declaration of the "right to disobey and to revolt." Now as then, the argument gets entangled in the question of who is to judge. Now as then, also, this judgment is made by the "establishment" and is perceived by the discontented as denial of justice and oppression. Disenchanted, discontented, and dissident groups and sectors of the community may see nonlegitimate conflict as their only or last resort in the unequal struggle to gain scarce or denied social values. For example, Grundy (1973: 1–27) reported that the African groups and leaders in southern Africa felt themselves ineluctably forced to violence as the only way to gain freedom and independence. The Red Brigades and other Communist groups in Italy regard terrorist violence as the proper way to advance the cause of revolution in that country. Prediction of their planned actions, such groups contend, would give the corrupt and unjust establishment an unfair advantage in the unequal struggle. With prediction, they would be forewarned and could take steps to prevent liberating action.

This discussion does not seek to settle these issues. Perhaps they cannot be settled to the satisfaction of all parties. Our purpose is to inform readers of this book that the academic and applied activity of conflict prediction takes place within a field of opposing value-judgments. Understanding this fact may be as useful in informing social policy and public action as the advances in the technology and sophistication of prediction. The scholars who contribute to improvements of social science in this field are thus warned that their scientific actions have social consequences for which they are, in part at least, accountable. Perhaps in the end this is really the purpose of the caveats.

THE MEANING OF PREDICTION

Himes (1964: 525) wrote that the term *prediction* in social science refers to the act of stating beforehand the outcome of a course of social
change that must or may occur in the future. Several basic elements are
involved in the predictive operation: knowledge of the outcome under
previous similar conditions; understanding of the critical factors that controlled the previous outcome; knowledge of present conditions, especially
the state of the critical indicator factors; and an estimate of the probability of various possible outcomes under various sets of conditions. Parsons
(1937: 612) argued that the predictive act can be thought of as a "mental experiment." He goes on to point out that when difficulties make it
impossible to control or reproduce the actual situation and to manipulate
the indicator factors to see what would happen, the scholar must resort
to the mental experiment. That is, he translates present data into a model
or equation based on previously known situations in order to estimate
the possibilities of various outcomes. This perspective on prediction is
supported by many scholars. For example, Clendinnen (1966: 215–29)
has argued that prediction is an inductive process of thinking. Writing in
1964, Bell (845) stressed "method" and "data" as essential elements in
the predictive operation. However, Bell noted that the actual operations
of prediction may vary significantly along several dimensions. By emphasizing such variable dimensions, he was able to identify and characterize
the following twelve methods of social prediction.

Social physics: Prediction by emphasizing impersonal forces such as
competition or technology rather than willed or planned efforts. Example: Marx's "laws of motion" of capitalism.

Trends and forecasts: Prediction by extrapolation from a time series,
in linear, cyclical, or alternative models based on the definition of upper
and lower limits. Examples: economic forecasting, demographic trends,
and technological change.

Structural certainties: Prediction based on custom and law, analogous
to institutionalized behavior. Example: the modernization line in a developing society.

Operational code: Prediction utilizing a leadership pattern, guide to
political action. Examples: "the American style" and societal optimism.

Operational system: Prediction by specifying the underlying source of
"renewable power" which ensures continuity in a system. The coexistence
of many competing operational systems is a problem.

Structural requisites: Prediction based on the use of typologies of functions, structures, and styles to estimate the capacity of governments to meet minimal concerns and avoid strains and problems.

The overriding problem: Prediction based on governments' ability to solve overriding problems as a prelude to dealing with others, e.g., solidarity must be attained before identity can be sought.

The prime mover: Prediction made by searching for the effects of a major determinant or independent variable. Example: the functions of military technology.

Sequential development: Prediction relies on projections from sequential phases of social systems. Examples: predictive capacity of Parsons' western institutional development scheme.

Accounting schemes: Prediction by summing up all major forces operating within a social unit and projecting expected developments as controlled by these.

Alternative futures: Prediction by creating a paradigm of organization and development and estimating chances of alternative lines of development under variable sets of conditions.

Decision theory: Prediction by specifying probable outcomes if one or another choice is made. Examples: linear programming, game theory, simulation.

This list suggests several aspects of social prediction that are important. In the first place, through this array of twelve predictive methods Bell draws attention to the variety of factors that have been employed as predictors. The predictive factors that have been used include, among others, processes, trends, structures, leadership, national style, system power, and developmental stages. Bell also makes it clear that social prediction is a common practice in social, economic, and political affairs. For example, most people are acquainted with and depend upon predictions of economic changes, the outcomes of elections, potential performances of students entering colleges and universities, future developments in many areas of human relations such as marriage, interracial and interethnic relations, and demographic trends.

This material also illustrates the main features of the technique of scientific social prediction. First, research has indicated that a certain factor or group of factors has carried the major causal force behind certain social, political, or economic outcomes of development. Second, it is reasoned that, if conditions remain the same, the factor or factors can be expected to produce changes of the same type, magnitude, and direction as those observed in the past. However, it is recognized that under altered collateral conditions, the outcome produced by the factor may differ in ways that can be estimated or specified. This logic of analysis provides a basis for making predictions of developments in the social, economic, or political spheres.

These considerations make it evident that the act of social prediction requires various kinds of information, or "data," as Bell has called it. The researcher or administrator who sets out to make a prediction must have knowledge of the predictive factor being used. It is imperative to know about the past performance of the factor. The more exhaustive and accurate these data, the greater the reliability of the prediction. For example, time series of economic factors covering a significant period of time in the past are essential for economic prediction. The prediction of the outbreak of violence in an urban community requires empirical data on the "prime mover," or some cluster of independent variables. These data should show how the predictive factors behaved in past situations of change under specifiable sets of collateral conditions. The process of prediction will ask how these factors will behave in the future under conditions that are assumed.

Knowledge of the conditions surrounding the past performance of the predictive factors must also be known. These conditions are qualifying elements of action and function to limit or enhance the causal capacity of the factor or factors in question. For example, The Report of the National Advisory Commission on Civil Disorders (1968: 203–74) identified and assessed a wide range of social, economic, cultural, and political conditions that both contributed to and qualified the outbreak of violence in American cities during the mid-1960s. Bell has suggested also that by identifying alternative conditions it is possible to make alternative estimates of the outcomes of processes of change.

Under the terms of the theory of conflict that was presented in chapter 2, it is possible to identify both long-range and short-run predictors. Long-term predictive factors can be located among the cluster of items classified as "societal preconditions." From a large number of items, it is possible to factor out those that carry the major burden of causal force. This limited number of major conflict causes can be employed to predict long-run developments that may lead to the outbreak of serious conflict. For example, if structural conditions like institutional failure, system malintegration, or cultural incongruity continue to develop, it can be predicted that in the long run, major conflict will erupt. On the other hand, short-run predictors of conflict can be found in the strength of "motivation" in the "catalyzing process." The immediate intensifying of cognitive and affective aspects of the interactive process is indicative of the danger of immediate conflict. For example, researchers for the National Advisory Commission on Civil Disorders (1968: 35–108) reported finding conflict-predictive factors in the immediate prelude to every riot studied. Increasing tension, growing excitement, magnified edginess and touchiness of local residents, and heightened sense of unrelieved frustration warned of the immediate danger of violence. Both long-run and short-range predictors are illustrated in the case of Soweto described below.

THEORY AND RESEARCH IN CONFLICT PREDICTION

Scientific approaches to conflict prediction reveal a controlled interplay between theory and research. Employing available conflict theories, some social scientists investigate the possibilities of predicting conflict as the outcome of ongoing processes of change. Other scholars utilize the findings of such empirical studies to build conflict-prediction theories. In the following paragraphs we will review several examples of the relationship of theory and empiricism in the effort to predict the onset of conflict. Even though scientific work in this field is increasing, we need to be reminded of Professor Wiles's caveat regarding the present limitations of the science of conflict prediction.

Studies in the field of conflict prediction tend to focus on two main issues, the initiation and the termination of conflict. As noted earlier, since conflict is continuous, initiation refers in reality to the escalation of legitimate struggles into nonlegitimate levels or forms. For example, the eruption of a riot or the outbreak of a war represents the transformation of previous struggles into nonlegitimate forms. However, the central issue in such research is not really the escalation or transformation of conflict, but rather the calculation beforehand of the possibilities that a given course of social change will eventuate into struggle rather than some other outcome. Studies in predicting the termination of conflict are, by the same logic, attempts to predict scientifically the deescalation of nonlegitimate conflict. That is, they seek to calculate the possibilities of reducing nonlegitimate conflict to permissible forms of struggle.

In 1959, Dahrendorf constructed theoretical models for the prediction of the escalation or deescalation of both the violence and the intensity of conflict. He wrote (212) that the level of violence, which constitutes a "manifestation" of conflict determined by the "weapons . . . chosen by conflict groups," varies on a scale from zero to one. Dahrendorf's model permits prediction of the escalation or deescalation of violence by assess-

ing the variable effects of five structural factors. The predictive model
can be summarized as follows. The increase or decrease of violence is
predictively linked to variations of selected, empirically observable elements of the social structure, including: (1) Relative effectiveness of
internal organization and control of conflict groups; (2) Relative superimposition of separate conflicts; (3) Relative level of real or imagined
deprivation; (4) Relative openness to outsiders of the status rank system; (5) Relative adequacy and appropriateness of social control. Predictions of increase or decrease of violence along the 0–1 scale depend
upon reading or estimating variations of the cluster of five empirically
observable structural elements.

Dahrendorf also constructed a model for predicting the variations of
conflict intensity, which was defined (211) as "energy expenditure and
degree of involvement" by the parties to a conflict. Variations of the following empirically observable structural factors were said to control increase or decrease of conflict intensity: (1) Relative conditions of class
organization; (2) Relative separation or superimposition of class conflicts within different associations; (3) Relative dissociation or superimposition of group conflicts in the same society; (4) Relative dissociation
within an association of the distribution of authority from the distribution of rewards and facilities; (5) Relative openness of classes.

In 1954 Dubin (527) formulated a "stability prediction" of labor-
management relations for several decades in American industry. Writing
a decade later (1965: 352–63), he delineated the theoretical model
upon which this prediction was based. Speaking of this matter, Dubin
(1965: 352) asserted that prediction was based on the model of a social
"system" and the "links" between it and the industrial institution. He
argued (359) that these links were produced by two related "laws" of
social systems. The first law reflects the stabilization of group behavior
through institutionalization and routinization. That is, habituation and
sanction of group behavior generate the momentum that perpetuates societal and industrial structures. The other law recognizes that individuals
and groups whose behavior has been so institutionalized or routinized
develop a sense of commitment to the action and generate an investment
in the institution. In other words, management, union, and worker receive payoffs from the institutionalized patterns and therefore prefer
existing arrangements to possible alternatives. The prediction, that of industrial stability in this instance, represented an estimate by Dubin of
the degree to which union-management relations and collective bargaining had, in fact, become institutionalized, and the extent of the participants' individual and collective investment in the ongoing system. When

Dubin (1965: 359) formulated this stability prediction, he assumed that existing conditions (as of 1953) would continue basically the same for the prediction period. This assumption implied that changes like increased automation that did occur would be in line with the trend of institutionalization, and that radical changes like extensive and severely frustrating unemployment would not occur. Dubin concludes (359) that the key variable in the predictive process was the judgment that "persistence of the system state seemed highly likely."

In 1963, Dubin (1965: 353–59) tested the prediction made a decade earlier by analyzing data on actual labor-management strife. These data were manipulated to test the prediction in two ways. In one, time series were extrapolated beyond 1953 to see whether this mode of prediction proved as accurate as projection from the theoretical model. The other test involved examination of the "slope of the trend line" (353) of actual work stoppages for the decade from 1954 to 1963 to see whether it conformed to or deviated from the stability prediction curve. The data used constituted measures of both the intensity and the length of strikes.

This evaluation of the stability prediction by means of "crude measures of reality" (359) permitted Dubin to conclude that the prediction was "reasonably accurate" for the period under study. That statement summarized actual findings from analyses of prediction along two dimensions: (1) intensity as measured by number of industrial disputes, number of workers involved, and proportion of work days lost by strikes; and (2) length as indicated by annual number of work days lost by strike and the average number of work man-days lost per striker. The stability prediction, based on the theoretical model, equaled, or exceeded actual performance as revealed by all the indicators except "number of workers involved in work stoppages."

Klingberg (1966: 129–71) undertook to develop and apply a method of predicting the termination of wars. Some previous experience had suggested that the end of a war might be predicted by an analysis of the casualties and population losses sustained by the belligerents. In the study summarized here, Klingberg tested two hypotheses. First he reasoned that for certain types of wars there might be a constant ratio (for defeated nations) between battle casualties and population losses. That is, this "constant ratio" might serve as one predictor of the termination of war. The second hypothesis stated that certain trends in battle casualties throughout a specific war might serve as predictors to indicate the end of that war. Statistical data from wars between 1618 and 1918 were used in this study to test the hypotheses.

Klingberg's findings were relatively inconclusive. His data failed to show that there was a general ratio between casualties and population losses. However, investigation of statistically revealed trends during long wars indicated that certain shifts in these trends might be used to help predict the approaching surrender of one belligerent. Klingberg identified six indicators that proved significant in predicting the end of wars. The six indicators include: (1) Casualty percentage ratios between the opposing belligerents; (2) Army-size ratios; (3) Proportion of battle defeats; (4) Intensity of fighting; (5) Abnormal increase in the number of prisoners or sick; (6) An increase in the rate of relative casualties for the defeated nation (as compared to the victor).

Klingberg concluded that probably the most important single indicator of war termination by surrender is the relative decrease in the size of armies associated with decline of materiel. Under these conditions, one belligerent finds it increasingly difficult to continue the struggle. However, Klingberg cautions that all the indicators listed above must be kept in mind and introduced into the analysis when prediction of the progress and possible termination of a war is being made. With this kind of multi-factor method, using data from past experiences, it is possible to predict the length of a war and the approach of termination. However, it is difficult, if not impossible, to predict accurately during a war how long it will last because it is impossible to secure all the data required at the time. Klingberg holds out hope that further research and refinement of techniques may lead to more comprehensive and reliable predictions.

A theory for predicting the outcome of controversies over community issues was constructed by Miller and Form (1957: 137–47) and later subjected to test by Hansen (1959: 662–71) in Denver, Colorado. The controversies in Denver developed around proposed amendments dealing with the right to work and civil service issues. Hansen undertook to predict the outcome of the Denver election on these two controversial issues by an application of the Miller-Form prediction method. He postulated theoretically (662) that the outcome of a civil controversy would be controlled by the "combined force of three factors." The first factor was said to be critical "high intensity" activation of those parts of the "institutional power structure" whose interests are affected by the issues. The institutional power structure was said to include such sectors as business, labor, religion, education, political parties, government, and so on.

The second factor used was the disposition, both for and against the issue, of the "community power complex," i.e., the "most influential organizations" in the community. The crucial operation here was to estimate the relative weight of community power exerted for or against the issues by these organizations. The third factor was the relative solidarity, activity, and interest-spread of the "top influentials," i.e., the most powerful and prestigious leaders in the community. Again, it was considered to be crucial to estimate how strongly these leaders would come down on the two sides of the issues. The assumption in this predictive methodology was that the political expressions of the community would either be funneled through or manipulated by the major institutional structures, social organizations, and individual leaders.

Hansen (666) made both a "stringent" and a "liberal" interpretation of his findings. On the first issue, the right-to-work amendment, the stringent interpretations produced a negative vote of 59 percent. The liberal interpretation yielded a negative vote prediction of 69 percent. Hansen reported that the actual negative vote was 65.8 percent. Thus on this issue the Miller-Form predictive model was validated. Prediction on the civil service amendment was also correct, but somewhat less exact. The stringent-to-liberal prediction spread was from 50 to 100 percent in favor of the amendment. Hansen (688) noted that although the amendment failed to pass in the state as a whole, it did pass in Denver by a 54 percent majority.

The literature includes many other studies in which testing a predictive model is not the central issue. They focus on a search for the prime causal factors in a variety of conflict situations. In each case, however, the researchers note that the prime cause is by that very fact a predictor. That is, it is recognized that the explanation of past conflict provides a theoretical basis for predicting the possibility of future struggle, other things remaining equal. This literature is important for our present purposes because it directs attention to the range and variety of factors that have been recognized as conflict-predictive. These findings also reflect the range of social predictors that Bell enumerated in the article cited above.

Cole (1969: 506–20) investigated the relative impact of a cluster of factors as causal influences for teachers' participation in union strikes. It was evident that by virtue of membership in the union the teachers viewed striking as an acceptable option. Moreover, Cole reported that the strike action of individual teachers who were aware of the participation of colleagues could be predicted since these colleagues formed a reference group. Green (1975: 69–77) studied the relation of modernization to civil strife with data drawn from 103 societies with populations of one million and more. Green analyzed his data by means of six predictive models. The results showed that a political organization model was superior for two types of prediction. First, political organization proved predictive of the relationship between modernization and civil strife. And second, the factor of political organization also made predictions of the magnitude of civil strife possible.

Portes and Ross (1974: 33–56) examined the relationship between two basic factors and the leftist-radical orientation of peripheral low-class settlements in Santiago, Chile. The authors reported that the literature cited two factors as theoretically most predictive of this orientation: frustration and anger, and political socialization and the cognitive framework of experience. Portes and Ross found that both factors functioned to generate the leftist-radical political orientation. However, they suggest that frustration and anger operated as an indirect determinant, while political socialization exercised a more direct influence. Thus it can be concluded that political socialization can serve as a strong predictor of the leftist-radical political orientation among lower-class, peripheral groups. This discussion of the nature of prediction and examination of some theory and research on conflict prediction permit us to attempt the construction of a predictive strategy.

A STRATEGY FOR CONFLICT PREDICTION

The scientific study of conflict prediction involves the following related components. (1) A problem of study which can be stated as a question: In a dynamic, changing social system with ascertainable structural and motivational conditions and with an escalating pattern of conflict causation, what are the possibilities that nonlegitimate conflict will be the actual outcome? (2) A method of study which Parsons (1937: 612) has characterized as mental experimentation. That is, being unable to perform an actual experiment in a laboratory, the predictor executes a logical experiment, manipulating factors and estimating possible outcomes. And (3) A strategy of experimental analysis which employs a general theory of conflict as the formula or equation within which to substitute and manipulate actual values of the predictive variables while estimating possible outcomes.

The essential elements of such a predictive strategy were suggested in the research reported above. The search for critical causal factors has been going on in many places and for a long time. Many scholars sought to find the one most reliable predictor of conflict in specific situations. Dahrendorf identified a cluster of general conflict causal variables and suggested that they could be used as predictors operating within a definitive scale. Dubin and Hansen began with conflict-causal models which they treated as predictive instruments. They tested these predictive models against actual outcomes of conflict. Klingberg employed the predictive strategy to anticipate the termination of war as the outcome of an ongoing conflict development process. It is possible to synthesize these and other ideas into a general strategy for the prediction of the onset of non-legitimate conflict. In each case, application of the strategy requires the use of current data for the specific situation under investigation.

The logic of a strategy for prediction can be summarized in the following functionally related steps:

1—Begin with the general explanatory model that was developed in chapter 2. The major items of this explanatory model are set out in Figure 7-1. The major causal indicators and their values will already have been ascertained.

2—Calculate present values of the prime causal indicators or predictors and identify and evaluate any new factors that may have emerged since the original research was carried out.

3—Introduce the current values of these causal variables, or predictors, into the predictive model.

4—Manipulate these variable predictors one at a time, and then in combination, to see what will happen, i.e., to ascertain the possible alternative outcomes.

The predictive model set out in Figure 7-1 includes the categories of variables that research has shown to be conflict-causal. We noted in chapter 2 that these clusters of variables can be combined into a small number of causal indexes or conflict predictors. The figure indicates that the "societal preconditions" can produce up to four such predictors. Earlier, these were called long-term predictors because they reflect trends of basic societal change. Motivational and catalytic factors can be combined into another predictor of short-run changes. This indicator reflects short-term rises and falls of collective motivation, mood, attitude, and feeling. As Dahrendorf has shown, such factors fluctuate along a scale that reflects variable degrees of intensity and increasing or decreasing likelihood of conflict outbreak. The logic of the predictive experiment postulates that the process of causation that operated in past situations will unfold the same way in future situations provided correlated conditions are the same. If it is known that certain conditions are different now from what they were earlier, the researcher must take account of this fact and make the appropriate adjustments.

The first step in the process of conflict prediction is ascertaining the relative values of the predictive factors. If appropriate research facilities and records are available, the values of some of the factors can be cal-

Figure 7-1

A Predictive Model

I. Societal Preconditions
  A. Structural maladjustments
      1. institutional failures
      2. malfunction of accommodative mechanisms
      3. malintegration of social systems
  B. Cultural inconsistency
      1. cultural lags or leads
      2. cultural pluralism
      3. normative inconsistency, normlessness, i.e., anomie
      4. value conflicts
  C. Interactional unreciprocity
      1. of content: cognitive and affective sterility
      2. of directionality: condescension and deference
      3. of power: coercion and compliance
      4. of instrumentalism: exploitation or fulfillment
  D. Alienation
      1. sense of isolation
      2. sense of powerlessness
      3. sense of meaninglessness
      4. sense of self-estrangement
II. Collective Motivation
  A. Sense of deprivation
      1. absolute
      2. relative
      3. drop following rise
      4. in status
      5. cognitive
      6. in interaction
  B. Sense of discontent
      1. rejection of situation as unacceptable
      2. unpleasant feelings, i.e., strain
      3. belief that one deserves better
      4. conviction that change is possible
      5. determination to strive for improvement
III. Catalyzing Process
  A. a stream of interaction and self-consciousness,
  B. in which societal and motivational elements are fused
  C. in the course of mass, public, and crowd behavior
  D. and expressed as grievance, criticism, hope, threats, and proposals,
     i.e., "agitation,"
  E. qualified by anxiety, resentment, excitement, and anticipation,
  F. which could eventuate in reform or explode in conflict,
  G. and which can be detonated by a commonplace incident.

culated quantitatively. For example, the existing records may include rates of unemployment, measures of school dropout, data on political or economic attitudes, and indexes of political or social alienation. In some cases, it may be necessary to collect and compute these quantitative indexes. Often, however, it may be mandatory to rely on precise description and careful estimates of the values of the variables under consideration. For example, it may not be possible to measure system malintegration, cultural pluralism and normlessness, interactional unreciprocity, and the existing level of collective discontent. Nevertheless, these factors can be scaled from careful description and then quantified for measurement. All of these operations are illustrated in the causation of any conflict process. For example, The Report of the National Advisory Commission on Civil Disorders presented a mixture of quantitative data and precise descriptions of the background factors and prime causes of the big-city riots of the 1960s. From these data it was possible to explain causes of the riots, construct "patterns of disorder," and attempt limited prediction of future developments. And finally, once the values of current predictors have been calculated, they can be compared with values of the causal indicators from earlier actual conflict situations. Thus it is possible to make a judgment of their relative intensity as conflict predictors.

Armed with these data, the researcher can now initiate the second step of the predictive process. Based on the explanatory theory, a predictive equation can be formulated as follows: $X+Y+Z\cdot M=NLC$. In this equation, X, Y, and Z are the values of the prime societal predictors. M is the motivational predictor produced by calculating the drive effect of deprivation and discontent as exacerbated by the catalyzing process. Thus, the sum of X, Y, and Z times M equals the predicted level of likelihood of nonlegitimate conflict, NLC in the equation. Such an operation permits one to handle a variety of possible situations. In one, the sum of X, Y, and Z may reveal high intensity, while M may be low or only moderate in intensity. Such an equation might produce a prediction of limited likelihood of conflict in the immediate future but strong possibilities for a later time. On the other hand, if the values of X, Y, and Z show low intensity while M is of high intensity, there is little likelihood of conflict in the immediate future. Under such circumstances, the societal agencies are capable of handling collective discontent in alternative ways. If all the factors reveal high intensity, the prospects of nonlegitimate conflict are high for the short run.

These variable predictive alternatives have been revealed in many actual conflict situations. As will be shown below, for many years the racial situation in Soweto (Johannesburg, South Africa) has led thoughtful people to predict the possibility of violent conflict. All such predictions tended to maximize the estimates of intensity of the long-range basic societal predictors. Beginning early in 1976, the M variables began to intensify dangerously. By late May and early June of that year, these predictors had become so high and intense that immediate violence was predicted in several quarters. In all of the big cities where riots erupted, background conditions had reached the point where prime societal predictors indicated the almost certain likelihood of violence. However, the actual eruption of violence did not follow in every case. In some cities, e.g., Watts, Detroit, or Newark, all factors converged in high intensity and riots erupted. In some other cities, e.g., Houston, the black community seemed ready for explosion months before the riot actually erupted. In still other cities, e.g., Syracuse, Denver, and New Orleans, even though some predictors were at high intensity, no riots developed. Two explanations of the failure of riots to develop in these cities can be cited. It may have been that all the factors had not yet reached the required level of intensity to produce the explosion. On the other hand, either by deliberate action or by adventitious circumstance, the buildup of causes of conflict took another turn and produced an outcome different from conflict.

This discussion of the process of scientific prediction of social conflict has great practical reference. Situations like the Middle East, Rhodesia, South Africa, and Iran are distinguished by the constant threat of major nonlegitimate conflict. The actions of international and national leaders are conditioned very much by their estimates of the likelihood or the possibilities of maintaining a low profile of nonlegitimate struggle. On the other hand, nations and communities risk or court conflict because they cannot or will not use existing capabilities and facilities of conflict prediction.

PREDICTING CONFLICT IN SOWETO

The relevance of the predictive model and operation of the prediction process can be illustrated by the outbreak of riot in Soweto, South Africa, on 16 June 1976. In spite of a dearth of quantifiable data, the example of Soweto has been chosen for several reasons. First, the conflict in Soweto was publicized all over the world. Second, significantly, the imminent outbreak of violence in that Johannesburg township was predicted by responsible authorities of the community several days before the fighting actually began, and it is possible to describe how that prediction was arrived at. Finally, heavy predictive reliance was placed on new motivational factors and rapid intensification of the catalyzing process.

On 11 June 1976, the Director of the South African Institute of Race Relations, in a strongly worded message to a member of the South African Parliament, warned of the possibility of violence in Soweto. The Soweto *World* reported on 15 June 1976 that on the previous day Councillor Leonard Mosala declared at a meeting of the Urban Bantu Council that "enforcing Afrikaans in the schools might result in another Sharpeville shooting incident if the matter is not dealt with immediately." These predictions were grounded in a reading of the societal preconditions and estimates of the possible impact of new factors and increased intensity of motivation.

Preconditions of high intensity in Soweto had been reported for a long time. Over time these conditions tended to worsen gradually. Under the structure of apartheid the Africans in Soweto, as Himes (1968: 290, 292) showed, like forced laborers in the Soviet Union and the outcastes of India, were "in fact not really members of the society." Law and custom relegated them to the lowest-ranked, most dangerous, lowest-paid, and most unrewarding jobs. Exclusion from political power, denial of major educational opportunities, and elaboration of a rigid occupational hierarchy left the Africans no chance for upward mobility. Unemployment, though high in Soweto, was officially nonexistent since no adult African could be unemployed and remain legally in the township. Although incomes had been increasing recently, the Soweto Africans remained very poor, able to afford only the most meager necessities. All housing in the township, except that of a few lucky individuals, belonged to the West Rand Administrative Board, the city agency that controlled all townships. Dwellings were small, devoid of amenities, and uncomfortable. According to the New York *Times* (17 June 1976), rents, averaging about $11.50 per month, absorbed a quarter or more of family incomes. The "community" of Soweto (Imrie, 1976) was a vast field of little boxlike houses, beer halls, and bottle stores, stretching endlessly in all directions, all looking very much alike, lined up on unpaved streets and punctuated at every fourth or fifth building by an outside water tap.

Being politically subjugated, the people of Soweto had no voice in making the rules by which they were forced to live. Paton (1976: 18) wrote that for the last twenty-eight years, ever since the establishment of apartheid in 1948, the people of Soweto had been treated as "persons of no account" with no control over their affairs. They were forbidden

to buy houses or land "in the towns and cities," and indeed forever forbidden to reside inside South African urban places. The Soweto Africans
were excluded from any part in the government and repressed by the
laws which they could not influence. In fact, the laws, the courts, and the
police were major agents of their exclusion, repression, and exploitation.
Moreover, the institutions that contribute to the quality of life—education, welfare, health, recreation and entertainment, and so on—were
either inadequate and inept or lacking altogether.

The potential for conflict was not relieved by accommodative mechanisms. Few recreational facilities, places of entertainment, or sports fields
existed to permit children and youths to sublimate aggressive frustrations
in socially approved activity. According to Wolfson the West Rand Administrative Board "provided . . . beer halls (and bottle stores or liquor
shops)" as well, which produced a major part of its income. Imrie (*Rand
Daily Mail,* 12 May 1976) sharply criticized the practice of making the
township administration dependent upon profits from the sale of liquor
and beer. As a consequence many adult Africans were kept distracted,
impoverished, and servile by excessive use of alcohol. On June 11, it was
announced in Soweto (South African Institute of Race Relations, RR.
119/76: p. 9) that a residents association would be organized to represent parents in matters regarding the school dispute. This was an unusual
step, for ordinarily, few organizations, mechanisms, or procedures existed
through which residents could air their grievances and gain serious hearing. To organize and complain was to invite attention from the police
and run the risk of "detention," or some other repressive reaction. In the
human jungle of Soweto there was virtually no way to recognize and
reward the praiseworthy achievements and earnest efforts of township
residents. The apartheid policy neither envisaged nor provided any way
or program to implement progressive change. The aim was to keep the
segregated structure fixed, unchanging, and unyielding.

As a social system, Soweto was split and divided along several sub-
system lines. Writing in late summer, Paton (1976: 18) showed how
desperate the split had become between parents and their children "who
won't go to school, who burn down their classrooms, who terrorize their
own parents, who threaten their own fathers if they go in the morning to
their work in the cities, who warn them not to come back at the risk of
their lives." The government settled African people by tribal groups
within the townships. For example, the Zulus, Bosotho, the Xhosas, and
other tribes were housed in separate though contiguous subareas of
Soweto and the other townships. Cultural differences, ancient enmities,
and divergent interests among these tribes were fomented. Government

policy and practice operated to separate the relatively well-off Africans from the hordes of poor, ill-educated and maladjusted persons, thus generating suspicion and antagonism between African classes. In the African world of Soweto, the white community of Johannesburg, the West Rand Administrative Board, the field administrators who man the offices within Soweto, the police and military, educational officials, all were seen as "the enemy." The white and black worlds of South Africa were separated and opposed by deep-seated hatred.

The cultures of Soweto formed a crazy quilt of pluralisms. The African cultures differ from those of the "Europeans," or whites. For example, a striking picture on a glossy tour book issued by the South African Tourist Board shows an African woman garbed in indigenous costume and carrying a bundle on her head, crossing a busy street in Johannesburg while the traffic waits for the light and modern business buildings frame the whole scene. It was noted above that Soweto included many divergent and competing tribal cultures. *Afrikaaner* and *English* are labels of different and incompatible culture systems. Within the "European" community, immigrant and native, rural and urban, and nationality denote still other cultural diversities. In the spheres of politics, economics, religion, and family, words like radical, liberal, conservative, and reactionary refer to still other significant cultural cleavages. The June 16 riot dramatized the age-based cultural split that was described above. Such cultural cleavages both undergird and reveal the tensions and strains of the South African racial system.

Informed observers had recognized and reported these structural potentials for conflict in the African racial situation for a long time. At the same time, relations between Africans and "Europeans" were cast by apartheid in a sterile etiquette that forbade Africans to express genuine ideas and feelings that the "Europeans" did not wish to hear or know. The status structure produced an exaggerated gulf between the groups and demanded that "Europeans" *must* condescend (often contemptuously) toward Africans who, in return, *must* defer. The etiquette permitted few variations from this manner of interaction. The power differential of the racial structure was overwhelmingly in favor of the "Europeans." As a consequence, "Europeans" coerced and Africans complied. Life for Africans was an endless experience of frustration, abuse, and exploitation. Everywhere Africans are perceived by "Europeans" as objects to be used. Speaking of the mood and tone of life in Soweto, Paton (1976: 18–19, 88–89) said the African community was pervaded by a deep and ineluctable sense of alienation. People felt inexpressibly isolated, powerless, and estranged from themselves and from the world around.

This gradually worsening pattern of high-level societal neglect, institutional failure, and general mistreatment produced a pervasive and nagging sense of deprivation, frustration, and discontent among the people of Soweto. Discontent, the longing for liberation, and the orientation toward rebellion were further intensified by developments both outside and inside South Africa. For many years the United Nations had tried to persuade South Africa to modify or withdraw its rigid policy of apartheid. The governments of some Western nations joined in this growing pressure. Many private organizations in the West kept up a continuous barrage against South Africa for the repeal of apartheid. After 1974 the so-called Front Line black nations of southern Africa, especially Botswana, Zambia, and Tanzania, began to pressure South Africa in opposition to apartheid and in support of independence for Southwest Africa (Namibia).

All through the 1970s, the Zimbabwe guerrilla fighting intensified and seemed to be making real progress. In 1975 Angola and Mozambique won their independence from Portugal by military action. In that same year negotiations between the Rhodesian Africans and the white regime, which had been going on for years, broke down in a hopeless squabble at the Victoria Falls meeting. The situation in Rhodesia looked bleak. Meanwhile, the United States and the United Kingdom intervened in a final effort to renew negotiations between black and white Rhodesians and to forge a peace. In this effort, Secretary of State Kissinger visited southern Africa and supported the United Kingdom in convening the Geneva Peace Conference. The Front Line black African nations increased their pressure on South Africa and supported the Rhodesian peace efforts. These developments tended to increase restlessness and excitement among the African people of South Africa.

Contemporaneous with these events, several developments within South Africa operated to further intensify the excitement of the African people. For several years agitation and controversy had been increasing around two issues, independence for the "homelands" and the struggle over nationhood for Southwest Africa. The South African government had set aside special territories as homelands for the African tribes. In order to legalize the fiction that Africans are visitors in the Republic of South Africa, it was decided to make the Africans citizens of the homelands, which would be granted independence. This action would legalize the claim that all Africans outside the homelands and inside the Republic of South Africa were visiting aliens. On 25 October 1976, the first of the homelands to be given its independence was the Transkei. It was planned to prepare the others for independence as rapidly as possible. Excitement was further intensified by the decision of the Department of Bantu Education to require most African public schools to use Afrikaans instead of English as the official language for certain subjects. The Africans, parents and children, hated Afrikaans and saw this action as the latest and most intolerable indignity perpetrated against them by the government. Without the chance to learn English, they would be locked linguistically into South Africa with no link of communication to the rest of the world. Resistance, protest and opposition against this policy had been going on in many parts of the country for months. The protests and excitement escalated and resentment increased ominously, especially within Soweto.

All these factors gained dynamic reality in the self-conscious interactive process of life in Soweto. The history of maltreatment and the structure of suppression and degradation became tormenting, demeaning experiences of the moment. The sense of deprivation, frustration, and discontent deepened and intensified, becoming a palpable driving force. The life of African people in Soweto was quickened by a desperate longing for liberation, a deep yearning for a better life, and a rejection of the unbearable conditions they were forced to accept. All the sociopsychological forces converged in an almost irresistible determination to act, to try to do something about their intolerable situation. Apparently without plan or signal, a spontaneous, catalyzing event was injected into this volatile and explosive situation. The children of Soweto gathered in front of a school on 16 June 1976. Ten thousand of them began marching in protest against the hated language policy and on behalf of their schools. They were confronted by the police. Tension increased on account of the confrontation and exploded into riot action when the police fired tear gas into the crowd.

The elements of the predictive process are now all clear and in place. The X, Y, and Z of societal conditions are evident, and by comparison with any earlier date, at their highest level of intensity. Progressively and relentlessly, ever since the installation of apartheid in 1948, the whites had been tightening the structural control over the Africans. Everyone who observed South Africa from the perspective of these basic societal predictors concluded that, unless basic changes were initiated soon, violent conflict between the two racial groups was inevitable. But it was difficult if not impossible to put an exact date on this prediction. However, the date of that predicted outcome was moved closer to the present by a series of recent events. Within a year and a half developments both inside and outside South Africa had heightened the sense of deprivation, frustration and discontent alarmingly. The catalyzing process had intensified and accelerated ominously. The sudden, unexpected issue of the Afrikaans language was the last factor required to bring the causal process to a climax. It was now possible for the Director of the South African Institute of Race Relations and the African Councillor to predict immediate outbreak of violence in Soweto. Both believed the only hope of escaping violence was certain immediate changes. However, even if they had wished to prevent the eruption of violence, the white officials and leaders could not have headed off the riot. By 15 June 1976, it was too late. At this time and point in the process, violence had become the only conceivable outcome of the conflict-causal process.

Part II
Conflict Management

Speaking of the changed orientation toward conflict that followed the end of World War II, Smith (1971: xv) asserted that traditional attitudes of pessimism and hopelessness are being replaced by feelings of ambivalence and even of hope. One evidence of this changed orientation is the growing application of research and scientific method to the problems of war and conflict. In the late 1940s and early 1950s the United Nations sponsored a variety of research and planning activities related to war and peace. At the same time, public and private agencies devoted to research and action on these issues proliferated. This new activity is focused in and led by such organizations as The Center for Conflict Resolution (University of Michigan); The Peace Research Institute of Norway; Studies of International Conflict and Integration (Stanford University); The Center for Policy Research (Columbia University); The United States Arms Control Disarmament Agency; The Center for Policy Study (University of Chicago); the Consortium on Peace Research, Education and Development (University of Colorado); The Center for the Study of Democratic Institutions (Santa Barbara); as well as the United Nations. These and other institutions have advanced the view that prevention and control of war and other collective conflicts is a proper issue of collective decision and action. As Likert and Likert (1976) have suggested, this growth in knowledge and sophistication would seem to justify a shift from the idea of "conflict control" to "conflict *management.*"

Following the Likert lead, this part of this book will examine the modes and techniques of conflict management. It has been suggested above that in many situations groups manage conflict, even nonlegitimate conflict, in order to use it as an instrument of collective policy in the quest of power, status, and other scarce values. We call this mode of management "instrumental conflict," and explore this strategy in the first chapter of this part of the book. On the other hand, it has also been pointed out that the dominant norms of every social system classify certain manifestations of conflict, including some expressions of instrumental struggle, as nonlegitimate. This judgment commits the dominants of the social system to act to manage such nonlegitimate expressions of conflict. In this context *manage* means both collective effort to prevent nonlegitimate conflict from developing, and, once developed, to intervene to return it to the level of legitimacy. Social systems that opt to manage conflict in this way typically utilize four management strategies here called: (1) prevention by institutional facilitation of legitimate conflict; (2) prevention by removal of the causes of nonlegitimate conflict; (3) resolution or termination of nonlegitimate conflict; and (4) suppression, or crushing of nonlegitimate conflict. Each of these strategies is examined in a chapter of this part of the book.   .

Instrumental Conflict

In the era of nonviolent mass action, blacks struggled against discrimination and abuse by means of sit-in demonstrations, mass marches, boycotts, and other action patterns. Students, teachers, hospital workers and factory employees organize and go out on strikes for the same kind of ends. These workers use the tactic of work stoppage to gain ends that they regard as important. In 1965, believing that all other tactics had failed, the Africans of Rhodesia launched a guerrilla attack against the white government and social regime of that society. For all these groups social conflict was the social instrument for the achievement of social ends. But, the reader might protest, is this not realistic conflict? Why introduce another term to talk about this phenomenon? Intrinsically, realistic conflict and instrumental conflict are similar. But in terms of the characteristic of conflict to be stressed, the two are different. In applying the concept *realistic* to conflict, Coser (1956: 48–55) stressed the location of the ends of struggle. But by the term *instrumental* the intention of conflict is emphasized. The goal of realistic conflict is some value that lies outside the conflict relationship. Writing two years earlier, Guetzkow and Gyr (1954: 367–82) employed the term "substantive" to designate this form of conflict. In the present context, the term *instrumental* is used to direct attention to the deliberate, purposeful, tool-like character of realistic or substantive conflict. In chapter 1 all conflict was said to be "purposeful" and directed to the acquisition of power and other values, all of which lie outside the conflict relationship. But in order to stress the fact that conflict is the social tool for attaining these values it is called instrumental.

COMPONENTS AND IMPLEMENTATION OF INSTRUMENTAL CONFLICT

All manifestations of instrumental conflict are characterized by four essential components. Instrumental conflict is (1) grounded in group policy, (2) directed to external goals, (3) based on calculation of means and ends, and (4) collectively controlled. Thus, it is suggested that the collective actor that opts to resort to deliberate struggle as the way of solving a problem or achieving a goal has already engaged in an interactive process that includes, among other elements, the acquisition of necessary information, the dissemination and interpretation of this information, the definition of goals and problems, and the acknowledgment of a variety of alternative proposals for remedial action. In some situations, these interrelated processes may have been precisely defined and formally executed. More often, however, they are analytic aspects of a unitary and continuous process of interaction. For example, the American Civil Liberties Union or the Legal Defense Fund of the NAACP may engage in meticulous investigation, lengthy and explicit discussion of the issue before it, and careful identification of viable alternatives before taking any action. On the other hand, a rebel mass of migratory farm workers, Rhodesian African peasants, or dissident Argentine cowboys may perform all these interactive functions in a single tumultuous participatory meeting. In both cases, however, these communicative processes may result in a collective decision or policy to initiate a course of instrumental conflict such as launching a legal battle or perpetrating a guerrilla war.

The decision to resort to instrumental nonlegitimate conflict may develop through a gradual process. In a study of the process involved in the decision of the United States to enter World War II against Hitler, Cantril (1942: 136–50) showed that sentiment and opinion favoring declaration of war developed step by step over the two-and-one-half years between the Nazi attack against Poland in September 1939 and America's formal entry into the war in 1942. By examining public opinion polls of the time, Cantril identified the progressive issues of the growth of the decision by means of a series of questions: "Sell war supplies to democracies?" "Relinquish neutrality to help Britain?" "Resist Nazis by aid short of war?" "Resist Nazis at any cost?" "When do we fight?" In the spring of 1942 President Roosevelt recommended and the Congress formalized the collective decision in a declaration of war. Sometimes the decision to engage in conflict is diffuse, not marked by any ceremonial act. Speaking of the initiation of riot action in the 1960s, the National Advisory Commission on Civil Disorders (1968: 118) asserted: "As we see it, the prior incidents and the reservoir of underlying grievances contributed through a cumulative process of mounting tension that spilled over into violence when the final incident occurred." When it came, the decision to riot had not been taken definitively or formally. Indeed, it was hardly recognized as a collective decision. People just began acting out riot behavior as if by a common and unspoken understanding.

Second, instrumental conflict is directed toward the achievement of goals that lie outside the struggle experience itself. In this respect, instrumental conflict is realistic conflict. While each struggle may function to release tensions and ventilate feelings, these are incidental aspects of the process. Conflict is perceived as the collective instrument for gaining status, power, resources, and other scarce values. This is task-oriented collective action. For example, as Josephy (1973: 18–19 and passim) reported, when the members of the American Indian Movement invaded the village of Wounded Knee and prepared for battle, they were seeking to achieve a series of specific external goals. Their objectives had been set forth in manifestoes and other public statements. These objectives were related to changes of the sociopolitical structure and constituted achievement of certain specific rights, opportunities, and experiences. Violent, nonlegitimate conflict was the chosen social instrument for seeking these goals.

Sometimes the line connecting instrumental conflict and the stated goals of an embattled group may seem unclear, ambiguous, or nonexistent. Many people could see no connection between the street riots of the 1960s and the goals of urban blacks. They viewed the riots as wanton and pointless destruction. Moreover, the participants in the conflict often found it difficult to articulate the instrumental connection of their struggle and their collective aims. Nevertheless, the connection existed and thoughtful observers have revealed it. For example Tomlinson (1968: 417–28), from a study of 585 informants in the Watts area, concluded that what seemed to produce riots was "the shared agreement" by blacks "that their lot in life is unacceptable." This almost universal judgment was coupled with the view of a significant minority of blacks that "riots are a legitimate and productive mode of protest." That is, upon reflection, after the fact, these blacks perceive nonlegitimate violent riot action as an appropriate and legitimate instrument of achieving important collective goals.

The third component of instrumental conflict is rationality. The reason for struggle and the tactics of action have been thought about. There has been some calculation of means and ends and a conscious effort to fit the former to the latter. The conflict participants engage in the struggle because they think it is the way, perhaps even the best way, to solve their problems and gain the values they are seeking. Turner and Killian (1972: 9) assert that in terms of "external criteria," social action is

called "rational when it is an efficient way of achieving some goal."
When we use the term *rational* in the present context, we claim only that
the conflict actor regards instrumental conflict tactics as efficient. His
thinking about the issue and calculating of means and ends is, he hopes,
designed to assure efficiency of his goal-linked collective action.

This conscious effort to think through the operation of conflict and to
match means to ends can be illustrated in various ways. Himes (1961:
99–100) showed how black students in southern American colleges re-
hearsed and sharpened protest tactics for action in the demonstrations,
sit-ins and marches of the early 1960s. Under supervision of experienced
black leaders, they practiced actions in sociodrama, searching for faulty
representations, schooling themselves for the discipline required, and
striving to understand the feelings and interpretations of whites by taking
their roles. It seems evident that the Irish Republican Army continues to
utilize terrorism as a prime conflict tactic because it has judged that this
is the best, i.e., most efficient, way to bring the British to heel and gain
their goals.

Finally, instrumental conflict is controlled. That is, conflict action is
constrained by the needs of the conflict enterprise. Feelings are kept (in
some measure) under check. Specific actions are made to conform to the
demands of the conflict plan and the needs of the ongoing situation. The
regulars in battle situations, whether military forces or party members,
present the best example of control. Long training has generated internal
discipline that minimizes impulsive, extraneous, or inefficient actions.
Volunteers in the excitement of the fray illustrate the situation of least
control. However, if the conflict is planned and deliberate, precautions
must be taken to achieve control of these participants. Without such control the chances of success are reduced. In the early civil protest, control
over youthful black college and high school students was achieved by
rehearsing for action and by careful monitoring of participants in the
throes of action. In the case of rebellious groups and revolutionary movements, the ideology often performs the same function.

Control is also produced by regulation and coordination of actors
within the collective enterprise. This end is achieved by the actions of
leaders, the enforcement of a division of labor, and collective understanding of the goals of the entire action. In this way, the efforts of the participating individuals are standardized, coordinated, and focused in terms
of the nature and aims of conflict. It is through control in both these
senses that conflict can function as a social instrument for a collective
actor.

CONDITIONS OF NONLEGITIMATE INSTRUMENTAL CONFLICT

Legitimate struggle to achieve valued social ends is a normal aspect of life in all societies. Thus, Democrats and Republicans struggle in the political arena for control of the government, and groups of citizens band together in social movements to bring pressure on the administration to alter its policies or to enforce existing laws. Labor and management struggle within the confines of the law for the ends that each regards as important. Almost every conceivable form of social structure is engaged at some time to implement this struggle. The conditions that help instrumental conflict to attain its goals, both legitimate and nonlegitimate, are numerous and variable. In the present context we ask about the circumstances that orient actors toward nonlegitimate rather than legitimate means. The research has identified many conditions that support the resort to nonlegitimate instrumental means. For present purposes, they are grouped as failure of legitimate means, relative strength of conflict actors, inadequacy of social control, ideological orientation, and shift of group orientation. The logic of conflict causation suggests that when a collective actor experiences one or more of these conditions, he may resort to nonlegitimate means to attain valued goals.

Under ordinary circumstances an actor will try traditional legitimate means to achieve his ends. Thus, for example, the Rhodesian Africans sought through legitimate means of persuasion, petition, and exchange to gain their ends of freedom and political participation. They were tempted or forced to resort to guerrilla war and acts of sporadic terrorism only when they believed the old legitimate means had failed. Thus it appears that groups are inclined to resort to nonlegitimate tactics when the legitimate means of relief or satisfaction have been tried and have failed. The group may feel trapped by the system and its sense of deprivation may become intolerable. Nonlegitimate conflict appears to be the only acceptable recourse under existing circumstances.

For example, it was reported that many urban blacks turned to rioting because they were convinced that traditional, legitimate means had all been tried to no avail. Discussing the riot in Cincinnati in 1967, the National Advisory Commission on Civil Disorders (1968: 47–48) wrote: "Without the city's realizing what was occurring, over the years protest through political and nonviolent channels had become increasingly difficult for Negroes. To young, militant Negroes, especially, such protest appeared to have become almost futile."

Abandonment of legitimate means may result not only from their failure, but also from their inaccessibility. Merton (1957: 131–60) has noted that when legitimate means to esteemed ends are inaccessible, groups may turn to nonlegitimate means. In this situation, groups and individuals may experience the sense of intolerable frustration and impatience. Merton notes that while exclusion from legitimate means may lead to deviance, it does not necessarily nor always produce this outcome. The groups have options other than nonlegitimate behavior.

Gamson (1966: 71–81) has observed the same relationship between the failure of legitimate means and the resort to nonlegitimate struggle. He reports that when citizens petition the city government again and again for change or relief, and receive only delays, broken promises, or outright rejections, the result may be "rancorous" conflict. Gamson understands rancorous conflict to refer to nonlegitimate but not violent tactics of struggle. When legitimate means fail or are inaccessible, nonlegitimate tactics tend to acquire some measure of legitimacy. They may become acceptable to individuals and groups who traditionally had rejected them. The situation seems to accord nonlegitimate means a measure of justification that they never had before. The injustice of the denials, failures, and rejections the group has experienced is balanced by the apparent justice of the nonlegitimate means. That is, if the rules of the game are redefined in such a way that unfair and unjust official conduct is perceived as permissible, then the conflict actor may feel justified in regarding nonlegitimate tactics of defense and struggle as also legitimate.

The relative strength of a conflict group may operate as a further condition tending to facilitate the resort to nonlegitimate tactics. If the group feels itself strong in the face of the opposition, it may reckon that there is little to lose by taking the chance. There is the possibility of winning. The strong group may assess its strength in relation to that of the opposition and calculate that it has a good chance of winning in a nonlegitimate struggle. It sees little risk of losing by attacking another group. This judgment may be reinforced if at the same time social control is weak or ineffective. For example, it seems clear that India was confident that she could defeat Pakistan in the war for the establishment of Bangladesh. The greatest risk was the influence of unfavorable world opinion, and India decided that she could live with this. It now seems clear also that after the Americans withdrew military forces from Vietnam, the North Vietnamese and Viet Cong were certain they could vanquish the South Vietnamese almost at will. In spite of the peace agreement, the International Commission, and the burden of world opinion, they saw little risk in pushing forward to total victory. Brinton (1965: 27–66) has observed that weakness of the opposition may be revealed as indecisive and insecure leadership.

If, on the other hand, the conflict group perceives itself as very weak in the face of the opposition, it may be tempted for different reasons to risk nonlegitimate conflict. The prize of struggle as defined in its objectives may be great. At the same time, the group is so badly off and weak that it calculates it has little to lose by the possibility of failure. As a matter of fact, its very weakness and deprivation may operate to press the sense of frustration beyond the limits of endurance and induce the group to become "reckless." In any case, it may seem better to have tried and failed than to continue in an insufferable situation. In this event, weakness rather than strength may operate as a condition promoting resort to nonlegitimate conflict.

Violent and terrorist activities of small and weak groups like the American Indians, the French Canadians, and the Irish Republican Army illustrate this risk-taking motivation to nonlegitimate means. Such conflict actors calculate that the rules of fair play and the burden of public opinion will help deter the retaliation by their stronger opponents. Meanwhile, by their audacity and intimidation, they may gain some, at least, of their objectives.

In contrast to these conditions, the resort to nonlegitimate tactics may be impeded by the perception that the actors on both sides of the conflict enjoy relative equality of strength and vigor and adequacy of social control. The evidence seems to suggest that actors who see themselves as relative equals in strength are not likely to attack each other. This fact is illustrated by the absence of overt struggle between the United States and the Soviet Union, who face one another in a "balance of power" or a "balance of terror." The so-called *pax Brittanica* of the late nineteenth century was a similar expression of parity of strength among several groups of Euro-American polities.

Inadequate or inappropriate social control often functions to invite nonlegitimate conflict as an instrument of group policy. Collective actors suspect or believe that they can get away with actions under these conditions that would be penalized were the control agencies strong and skilled. The violence and terrorism in Beirut during 1975 and 1976 resulted in substantial measure from the breakdown of police and military control. In Italy, the leaders of the Red Brigades continue to flaunt its terrorism because its members are contemptuous of the inadequate and inept agencies and programs of law and order.

It has often been observed that "inadequate" social control does not necessarily result from weakness of forces. Frequently adequately staffed and equipped control agents are prevented from using their forces or hesitate to do so; the Italian government and police, for instance, are morally prevented from meeting the Red Brigades' terrorism with naked force. In this connection Smelser (1963: 261) observed that if it were only a matter of force, most episodes of violence or terrorism could be put down easily. However, Smelser goes on to note that these control agencies do not always employ the full force at their command adequately or effectively, which permits or invites conflict actors to engage in nonlegitimate struggle to secure their objectives. Vattachi (1958: 104) showed how the failure to use available control resources in Ceylon led to widespread and untrammeled nonlegitimate actions. He reported that a wave of illegal strikes erupted and spread all over the country within two years. The police were said to be under orders not to interfere with the strikers and demonstrators, even when they damaged people and property.

It has been revealed that inappropriateness of social control may also serve to provoke nonlegitimate action. Worchel et al. (1974: 37–54) report that if struggling groups believe that public agencies and authorities are unfair, dishonest, or untrustworthy in responding to their demands, they may feel justified in resorting to nonlegitimate means. Violent or coercive tactics may be used to stimulate quick and realistic action. Disenchanted conflict actors may resort to violent tactics to signal the possibility of greater danger to indifferent or intransigent authorities. For example, from a study of a sample of 5,545 junior and senior high school students in Western Contra Costa County, California, Elder (1970: 445–61) found that among the black students (approximately 75 percent of the sample) willingness to resort to violence was associated with the decline in expectation of change. It is perceived, or at least believed, that the public authorities will respond only to dramatic, nonlegitimate actions. On the other hand, excessive or brutal control actions may function to escalate the conflict. The attacking conflict group's nonlegitimate action is invited, permitted, or provoked by the excesses of the police or other control agents. For example, the National Advisory Commission on Civil Disorders (1968: 3–4) showed how police actions in Newark functioned to escalate violence in the disastrous riot. Conant (1968: 420–33) reveals in some detail how nonlegitimate control actions operate to stimulate conflict action in kind. After an instigating incident, a crowd gathers and a process of "keynoting" begins. Leaders tempted to violence articulate the anger of the group and suggest possible violent courses of action. At this juncture, the police appear and try to disrupt the keynoting and disperse the crowd. Their tactics—ordering, forcing, sometimes "roughing up"—not only fail to control the crowd; they actually push some of the keynoters and followers rapidly into the direction of violent action. The result may be that kind of crowd action that is called a riot.

It has been shown that in many situations the tenets of social and political systems tend to commit followers to nonlegitimate conflict as the approved or preferred mode of struggle. Thus the crucial variable is internal commitment rather than external circumstances. Many years ago Coser (1956: 111–19) pointed out that, if a collective actor fights for an ideological, superpersonal aim, action is more likely to be intense or violent than if the aim is a specific or personal value. Thus, the requirements of Marxian ideology function to commit the dedicated followers to "the revolution," and Mao's "little red book" is full of exhortations to the faithful not to stick at any means to achieve the glorious ends of the revolution. The requirements of a revolutionary or militant ideology can restrict the tactical alternatives of social movements and other collective actors. Nonviolent means may be defined as both ineffectual and impermissible, or at least suspect. Members and followers are forbidden to resort to such tactics. At the same time, coercion, violence, and terrorism are legitimated and given collective sanction by the norms of the conflict group. Thus, for example, Rhodesian African guerrillas are constrained by ideological commitments to attack white plantation owners and their subservient black farm workers. Such action is perceived as a positive contribution to the ends of the struggle. In such an ideological situation, nonlegitimate tactics are not perceived as the last resort; they are defined as the first and proper resort.

Turner and Killian (1972: 293) examine the power and process of ideology as a determinant of conflict approach. They point out that participants in social movements committed to "coercion" strategy are effectively prevented from resorting to "persuasion" or "bargaining" strategies. Such a shift opens them to the risk of being regarded as cowardly or untrustworthy; they are suspected of being soft or of selling out to the opposition. Only the hard line of coercion can be trusted as the sign of orthodoxy on the part of members and followers. The dynamic of ideological commitment is also illustrated in the case of conflict groups that undergo a shift of orientation. Groups that start out with nonviolent ideologies of persuasion or bargaining may in time and with disappointing experience tend to swing around toward increased militance as their basic ideas and perspectives change. This condition of nonlegitimacy of instrumental conflict is examined in the next section.

Sometimes group orientations toward problems and experiences shift in midstream. Such shifts of group orientations may lead to nonlegitimate action. After observing crowd behavior in the 1960s, Johnson (1973: 1–17) examined this process there and in other collective behavior as an instance of "risky shift." A group or association that at one time was committed to nonviolence and traditional tactics may at a later time risk engagement in instrumental nonlegitimate conflict. The remarkable career of SNCC, the Student Nonviolent Coordinating Committee, is a case in point. Organized in the spring of 1960 under the tutelage of Martin Luther King, Jr., the black intercollegiate student group was committed to nonviolence. A few years later, however, it took a dramatic turn toward violence with leaders like Stokely Carmichael, H. "Rap" Brown, and Floyd McKissick. The same switch from legitimate to nonlegitimate conflict tactics was revealed in the career of the SDS, Students for a Democratic Society.

Such a shift of group orientation may result from several factors. It has been suggested above that a group committed to instrumental conflict by legitimate means may encounter continual failure. This experience may drive the group to nonlegitimate tactics for the achievement of its socially approved ends. Such a shift of means may reflect modification of the group's ideology. For example, Grundy (1973: 1–27) reported that for many years prior to the end of World War II the ideological orientation of black Africa was grounded in the Gandhian nonviolent tradition. During and just after the war, however, black leaders found it increasingly difficult to deal meaningfully with white colonials and leaders in these terms. After World War II, the ideological lines hardened on both sides. As a result, the grounds for negotiation diminished and the space for compromise narrowed. Grundy reported that in consequence after 1950 the ideological thrust of black African leaders and organizations swung perceptibly away from Gandhian nonviolence toward pragmatic violence.

A change of the composition of conflict group membership may be another source of shift in group orientation. If a stable, old-line protest organization acquires a large youthful or radical membership, it may experience significant change of group policies. The new youthful or radical members may be impatient with the conventional conflict methods, and begin to press for more militant tactics. Such a shift of group membership and consequent conflict orientation has been revealed in many protest organizations, political parties, labor unions, religious bodies, and other typical social movements. After a time, they may be perceived as typically extremist or radical in contrast to their earlier image.

Sometimes the shift of policy orientation may result from a change of group leadership. Occasionally the leadership of a traditional organization is radicalized due to infiltration by an already radical organization. Record (1964) has shown how the Communist Party of America sought with varying success to infiltrate and radicalize the NAACP. Occasionally, the radicalizing of the leadership of a traditional conflict group is the result of a shift in ideology. Killian (1972: 41–49) explains that the ideological shift toward "extremism" in the "black revolution" led to radicalizing of leaders and members and increased polarization of relations with the opposition. Nelson (1971: 353–71) argued that ideological shift in the "southern civil rights movement" issued from radicalization of the black leadership.

The shift of orientation may take a group from compliance and accommodation toward instrumental conflict. More often, however, it signals the transition from legitimacy to nonlegitimacy in the method of conflict action. In every case, though, such an orientation shift will exert some significant effect on the form and pattern of instrumental conflict.

Strategy in Instrumental Conflict

Because instrumental conflict arises from collective decision, it is controlled to some extent by collective planning. Some thought has gone into the means to be employed to achieve the ends that are desired. The result of this collective thinking is a series of intervening decisions that constitute what is called a "strategy." In the aggregate, these decisions constitute a model for conflict action. This model is correctly called strategy because it embodies the calculations of ends and means, the judgments of appropriateness and efficacy of action, and the considerations of initiative and management underlying execution of the scheme. The model is a social organization that links attacker and defender in a system of social relations with reference to the values that are the objective of struggle.

Some conflict organizations articulate their strategies in formal statements. For example, Martin Luther King, Jr., (1967: 144–46), speaking for his various social movement organizations, delineated a strategic model for increasing the employment of blacks in big cities, which he called "operation breadbasket." The model involved four operational steps. First, a team of black ministers would call upon the managers of a business or industrial firm requesting information on the total number of employees, the number of black employees, job classifications of all workers by race, and pay scales by race and job classification. These data would be analyzed as the basis for determining the number of new and upgraded jobs for blacks to be demanded. Next, the team of clergy-men would return to negotiate with management their demands for increased and upgraded employment of black workers. Third, they simul-taneously initiated the "pacification" process. They would seek to bring the black community under the control of the principle of nonviolence; at the same time, they would strive to engender awareness among mana-gers of the devastating problems of the black ghetto and how the business and industrial leaders contributed to these conditions. The aim at this point was to stimulate a sense of moral shame which would arouse feel-ings of guilt, sympathy, and personal responsibility in the managers. It was hoped that the managers, thus "pacified," i.e., burdened, would voluntarily alter their hiring practices. Finally, if these negotiations and pacification activities failed, then the ministers would lead a boycott of the companies' products in the black community. The boycott and picketing was the power operation used to enforce the demands of the black community.

In other situations, the strategy is implicit in the conflict action and must be deduced by examining the pattern of activities. For example, it was widely alleged in 1975 and 1976 that the Rhodesian guerrillas who were attacking the Europeans from Mozambique and Zambia were guided by a grand strategy. This scheme was not set out in any docu-ment, nor, for that matter, had it been delineated formally in the speeches of political or guerrilla leaders. Yet, as reported, the strategy outlined a series of action steps and the rationale for each. Guerrilla leaders in Mozambique and Zambia would continue to recruit, train, and arm youthful fighters from Rhodesia. In the winter, during the dry season, when the "security forces" could operate with facility, small bands of ten to twelve men would be sent across the Zambezi River into Rho-desia. Military operations would be kept to a limited scale until the be-ginning of the rainy season in October. At that time, the guerrillas would have the advantage of short, cloudy days, muddy roads, and the cover of the bush. After the beginning of the "spring rains" the pace and intensity of the attack would be increased until, it was believed, the Smith regime would be "toppled" by the weight of the guerrilla attack.

The reader must be cautioned that in common usage the terms *strategy* and *tactic* are often not well differentiated. Often both terms seem to have the same referent in meaning. The term *strategy* is employed to designate both a plan or program of conflict as well as the specific types of techniques or actions to be used. For example, the term *nonviolence* is frequently used in this way. A reader or listener cannot know whether an inclusive plan of attack or a specific type of conflict action is meant. In the present discussion, the two terms will be given distinct referents. *Strategy* will refer to the plan, program, or model of social conflict, while *tactic* will be reserved for specific techniques or types of techniques. Thus tactics are components of strategies. For example, protesting blacks in the United States undertook to struggle against the traditional segregated and discriminatory racial structure. In this struggle, many different techniques and actions, i.e., tactics, were employed. Some of these were calculated to avoid the inflicting of injury or damage upon the opposition. These were nonviolent. In the remainder of this section strategy in social conflict will be examined in two ways. First, some of the literature will be reviewed to illustrate what the referent of strategy is in social-science usage. This material will demonstrate that strategy, whether explicit or only implied, is an essential aspect of instrumental conflict. This case material will later be used to generalize about the concept of strategy. At that point, we will undertake to define conflict strategy and to delineate its salient components.

Some Strategic Models

As reported in the literature, most strategic models are tailored to meet the perceived needs of specific groups and categories, and to fit their unique situations. For example, after a study of the "welfare rights movement" of New York, Gelb and Sardell (1974: 507–31) proposed a strategic model "for the powerless." Drawing upon his experience as a social action technician in poor rural communities, especially in the South, Kahn (1970: 105–13) formulated the operations and steps of a strategic model to demonstrate how these people can get power. From a study of black and white junior and senior high school students in California, Elder (1970: 445–61) identified appropriate strategies for groups struggling for racial change. Till (1970: 313–23) was concerned with the problems of citizen groups which sought to influence public policy in the city, the state, and the nation. He explored some of the issues of strategy construction for these groups. In the remainder of this section we will examine four strategic models in some detail. This and other case material may enable us in the following section to generalize about the concept of conflict strategy.

From a review of a wide range of social movement materials, Turner and Killian (1972: 291–93) could identify three basic strategic models which they called "bargaining," "coercion," and "persuasion." They assert that these types are differentiated by the way in which conflict groups attempt to influence target groups. That is, strategy is the approach to conflict that determines the choice of tactics. In bargaining, the conflict group seeks to control the target group by managing an exchange relationship. Turner and Killian (291) explain that bargaining occurs when the conflict actor controls some exchangeable value that the target group wants. For example, a labor union agrees to exchange regularity of work and increased productivity for higher wages and job security. Control is exercised by offering the value (or some of it) for compliance. That is, by such an offer the conflict group persuades the target group to act in a desired way. Bargaining characterizes the strategic situation of groups whose ideologies permit flexibility and adaptability in conflict and which at the same time possess exchangeable resources. This strategic model is typical of such groups as organized labor, minority-group movements, agricultural groups, political associations, and occupational organizations. Bargaining also fits the strategic situation of groups operating in open systems with free-enterprise economies and a tradition of competitive struggle.

In coercion, the conflict actor uses power to restrict the options of the opponent. Pursuit of a course of action other than that demanded by the conflict group, according to Turner and Killian (291), "will be met . . . by cost or punishment." In coercion, the tactics employed are often non-legitimate and morally off-limits. Frazier (1968: 27–40) showed that coercion is sometimes fused with alleged nonviolent conflict actions. He examined the phenomenon of "nonviolent coercion" in the early sit-in movement. Turner and Killian (291–92) cluster a range of tactical actions under the rubric of coercion. These include, among others, the threat of total destruction; weakening, inconveniencing, or embarrassing the opposition; terrorism; civil disobedience, and so on. Coercion is a form of "negative bargaining" in which the target group escapes cost or punishment and the conflict group gains compliance with its demands. This strategic model is typical of ideological groups, revolutionary and rebellious organizations, and groups that believe all other noncoercive methods have failed. Coercion represents the strategic style of ideologic groups operating within authoritarian systems or subsystems where exchangeable resources are scarce and free exchange is not typical of the way of life. The coercive strategic model of ideologic groups commits, or at least orients, participants to nonlegitimate modes of struggle. While coercive groups may feel that they control few exchangeable resources, they believe they have the power required to enforce compliance of target actors. For these reasons, bargaining and persuasion are eschewed. They are often regarded as indicative of weakness or untrustworthiness.

Persuasion as a strategy is a relationship of communication, not one of either exchange or compliance. It consists of the use of symbolic manipulation to achieve desired ends. Turner and Killian (292) explain that the core operation is to identify the action proposed to the target group with values that are held by that group and which are endorsed by the larger community. This operation is expected to stimulate feelings of guilt and responsibility within members of the target group. The strategic aim is to induce the target group to make concessions because such action will both relieve the sense of guilt and accord with established community expectations. Persuasion strategy is characteristic of poor groups with inferior status and limited power. They have few recognized exchangeable resources, and so cannot bargain successfully for desired values. At the same time, such groups feel themselves to be threatened by more powerful target groups. Coercion is therefore too risky. The appeal for concessions through moving representations seems to be their only or best strategic approach. King's "operation breadbasket," described above, illustrates the fusion of these three strategies into a single model.

Gurr (1970: 352–57) developed a model with strategies for "incumbents," "revolutionaries," and "the discontented." The strategies suggest different approaches of conflict to achieve the different objectives of the three categories. In this formulation, stress is upon differences and desires of the conflict actor groups. Gurr shows how the characteristics of conflict actors, the nature of their objectives and the features of the conflict situation operate to qualify the strategies to be used. Gurr declares that the objective of typical incumbent groups is to maintain stability in the social system. Their first option is to prevent change and to maintain the existing distribution of advantages. However, he goes on to say, if change or progress is permitted, all sectors should gain at the same rate, even if the rate is slow. If discontent is active and widespread, incumbents should seek to reinforce their legitimacy while censoring criticism, providing diversions, and making equitable self-help concessions. If discontent is politicized, control policies and sanctions must be applied firmly, equitably, and consistently. Another control tactic is removal of sources of discontent.

The strategy for revolutionaries includes four related steps. Gurr (353) asserts that ideological appeals constitute the first step toward revolutionary success provided they define new aspirations and specify means for their attainment. These appeals should be directed toward the more susceptible sectors of the society—subordinated urban classes, new city migrants, and people on the margins of expanding economies. In the second step, the revolutionary ideologies should offer means and justifications that are compatible with the discontents and cultural experiences of the audience. These appeals can demonstrate the weakness or selfishness of the incumbent regime, induce extremist responses, put the establishment in a bad light and at a disadvantage, and therefore suggest that revolutionary violence is a real possibility. Third, the revolutionaries must organize for defense and expect eventual attack. Such organization should be revolutionary in character (not self-helping), rewarding for its members and protective of them, and able to generate supportive resources and facilities. Finally, the strategy for revolutionaries requires open violence against the hated and oppressive regime. However, such violence must be controlled and kept within the resource capabilities of the revolutionary participants.

Gurr (355–57) states that the discontented prefer peaceful means to attain their goal of increased well-being. He went on to say that dissident groups should make two kinds of appeals—one intended to mobilize potential followers and the other intended to justify their claims. The tactics of limited violence can dramatize claims, ventilate hostility, and signal the possibility of more violence if concessions are not granted. However, the most essential task is to organize: to expand the organization, to improve its internal structure, to enhance the common purpose, and to maximize the use of resources. Such organizations can function best through persuasion and political bargaining with establishments.

Himes (1974: 43–45) outlined three "strategic styles" of American minority groups. He declared that they struggle for full societal membership by three basic approaches, called "institutional integration," "secession," and "social assimilation." Analytic models of the strategic styles were constructed of the following four components: (1) A collective judgment of "legitimate rights" as the appropriate goals of endeavor; (2) An assessment of the nature, location, and strength of the opposition; (3) An assessment of the chance of success and therefore of the kind and amount of effort required; (4) A choice, more or less rational and explicit, of the tactics required for this effort.

Institutional integration defines collective goals as the legitimate right to participate in all sectors and every rank of the bureaucracies, i.e., economy, government, education, housing, military, religion, etc. The main obstacles are legal and quasi-legal rules of the powerful bureaucratic institutions. Institutional integration calls for power-wielding tactics ranging from the nonviolence of marches and demonstrations to the violence of disturbances and riots, from the sentimentalities of kneelings and children's marches to the instrumentality of power politics and consumer pressure. Institutional integration was said to be typical of the strategic approaches of blacks, Mexicans, Puerto Ricans, and perhaps the Chinese.

Secession refers to collective struggle for geographical separation and local political autonomy. The society is perceived as oppressive and the minority group estimates that its legitimate aims cannot be achieved within the social system. This approach to struggle envisages resort to a wide range of tactics, some legitimate, some not. Secession is the typical strategy of the American Indians, although for a long time some blacks have also espoused this approach.

Social assimilation refers to collective struggle for total acceptance into all aspects and levels of the society. This approach is consistent with the democratic tradition and the national ethos. If the minority group is white, it may calculate that its chances of success are good, provided it covers up cultural differences and strives for integration into the informal and intimate life of the dominant society. The strategy of social assimilation is most typical of advantaged Jews and small numbers of Japanese, Chinese, and Puerto Ricans.

Gamson (1975) examined the nature and role of strategy in the careers of fifty-three organizations, called "challenge groups," that attacked the status quo between 1800 and 1945. The fifty-three organizations fell into twenty-one categories and include such diverse groups as: (1) American Association of University Professors; (2) American Committee for the Outlawry of War; (3) National Brotherhood of Baseball Players; (4) Brotherhood of the Kingdom; (5) National Urban League; (6) National Student League; (7) German-American Bund; (9) International Association of Machinists; (9) Bull Moose Party (Progressive Party); (10) Federal Suffrage Association. Data about the groups and their strategies were drawn from published historical sources and entered upon questionnaires that made the information comparable and available for quantitative analysis. The research focused upon two central issues. One was concern for the strategic models and methods of the various challenge groups; and the other was the search for the variable conditions that affected the nature of the strategy employed. In this study, Gamson has demonstrated the crucial role of social strategy in the process of instrumental conflict.

Structurally, the strategies were shown to include four components which were called "challenge group," "antagonist," "target" and "tactics." Gamson (14) asserted that the nature of challenging groups is indicated by differences among the targets for these groups. He identified three such targets, which were called "influence," "mobilization" and "benefits." The defining characteristics of challenge groups were revealed in other ways. Although the challenge groups were diverse in many ways, all were similar in their social protest against the American status quo. Since they were locked with the established social order in struggle for change, they belong to that category of organizations that have been called social movements. Gamson (14, 16) conceptualized the intervening objective as the quest for conflict resources which he perceived as the power of decision-making groups and "the mobilization of an unmobilized constituency." These resources facilitated and empowered the struggle for structural change which it was believed would eventuate in achievement of the variegated desires of the challenge groups. Gamson saw a challenge group as an organization that initiated its protest against the status quo by the quest for these interconnected objectives. He also perceived that the very nature of challenge groups, even their orientation toward challenge, was conditioned by a number of factors including, among others, "internal organization" as well as the nature of the target of struggle. Thus, while all fifty-three organizations were challenge groups, they were unique in their character as challenge groups.

Antagonists were sectors or agents of the status quo "lying outside of [the] constituency" (17) of challenge groups and against which the brunt of the struggle was directed. As a matter of fact, antagonists were identified in advance by particular challenge groups as the actual or symbolic opponents. They were treated as the resistance, the opposition, the enemy, whether or not they were in fact. This definition issued in part from the fact that antagonists were representatives of the established social order, and in part from the fact that they were believed to be the reason why the challenge group was deprived and discontent. With an antagonist in hand, conflict was possible. That sector or agent of the establishment that was perceived as antagonist was believed to obstruct the aims and desires of the challenge group. It was understood to be opposing the challenge group because it controlled or appeared to control, values that the challenge group desired. As suggested, targets, which must be distinguished from antagonists, were the intervening objectives of challenge groups. Gamson recognized that certain preliminary goals must be achieved before significant social change could be effected. These ends of struggle were called targets. However, it was suggested that targets, though different from antagonists, were controlled by antagonists. As shown, there were three categories of targets which he called "influence," "mobilization," and "benefits." Gamson (14, 15) stated that influence as a target is that "set of individuals, groups, or social institutions" whose decisions or policies prevent a challenging group from attaining the change it seeks. Such a target becomes the object of attack by a challenge group and in defending itself becomes an antagonist as well as a target. For example, the International Association of Machinists might have challenged the establishment to change existing labor laws. However, the influence required to bring this change about resided in political parties, Congressional committees, and the legislative and executive branches of government, which were also antagonists in the struggle. Challenge required managing or at least manipulating the influence of these groups in such a way that it could be used to secure the change of existing labor legislation.

The individuals and groups whose "resources and energy" the challenging group requires to implement its program of change are called targets of mobilization. Thus a challenge group might seek to recruit a population sector or to draw another group into membership or coalition in the course of mobilization. Relationships between challenging groups and the objects of mobilization are different from those involved in influence. To achieve influence, the challenging group must attack the object which is perceived as antagonist. The relationship of mobilization leads the challenging group to persuade and cooperate with the groups in question since they are, in themselves, the resource that is sought. Gamson (15) differentiated "creation" and "activation" as types of mobilization. In his analysis, he stressed creation, e.g., recruiting new previously uncommitted members. Once such resources had been mobilized, the challenging group could use them to move the status quo and thus to effect social change. Gamson (16) asserts that benefits accrue to the groups and individuals who will be "affected positively" by the changes resulting from the challenging group's efforts. Gamson called these groups "beneficiaries," and defines the relationship between challenging and beneficiary groups as one of providing and receiving. Beneficiaries may be the constituencies of challenging groups, although this is not necessarily the case. A challenging group's strategy may involve simultaneously all three of these patterns of social relations—struggle with an antagonist for influence, persuasion of groups or resources, or disbursing to beneficiaries the rewards of the societal challenge. However, the patterns will be uniquely stressed and variably interrelated in the strategy of each challenging group.

Tactics are seen as the style and the specific instruments of challenge. In the course of mounting an attack pressing a struggle, challenging groups resorted to a full range of possible tactical styles and instruments. Styles varied from legitimate to nonlegitimate modes of protest, from traditional to guerrilla patterns of warfare, or from the blitz attack to the prolonged siege. Specific tactics are limited in variety only by the ingenuity of the challenging group. For example, Gamson (41–44) cites "displacement" of the antagonist as one common strategic style of the fifty-three challenging groups that he studied. Within this style, the groups made use of a wide range of specific tactics varying from the implausible to the efficient, from violence to nonviolence. For example, (42) Gamson reported that the Brotherhood of the Cooperative Commonwealth advocated an "implausible colonization scheme" to displace the government of the State of Washington while the American Party of the 1880s wanted to dislodge the government by a straight electoral challenge. In the structure of strategy as conceptualized by Gamson, tactics establish the specific interaction between challenge groups and their antagonists. The determination of style and choice of specific tactical instruments was conditioned by a variety of intervening factors. Gamson (41) notes that the "magnitude of goals" is one such conditioning factor. This magnitude is recognized as the difference between one-issue demands and multiple demands, between extremist demands and those that do not challenge the legitimacy of the system, and between influencing, infiltrating, or replacing elites. In addition, it was perceived that many other conditions would, under certain circumstances, influence the choice of style and specific instruments. These factors include, among others, the size and strength of the challenge group, its ideology and tradition, the resources at its command, the state of internal organization, the nature, size, and strength of antagonists, the quality of judgments that can be made with available information, the rationality and detail of inclusive and contingency plans, environing conditions, and the force of collective determination and commitment.

A General Strategic Model

With the foregoing illustrative material before us, it is possible to make some general comments about the nature of conflict strategy. It has been said that much social conflict is instrumental, i.e., it is the social instrument chosen by collective decision as the collective means to the attainment of important social values such as status, power, resources, and the like. Collective planning, which is the essence of strategy, is a necessary condition for the execution of instrumental conflict. Although strategic prescriptions and requirements are not always logically organized and clearly articulated, they are necessary elements of instrumental conflict. Drawing upon a wide range of materials, it is possible to construct a generalized model of conflict strategy. The components of this model are set out in Figure 8-1.

FIGURE 8-1

A MODEL OF SOCIAL CONFLICT STRATEGY

I. Collective actor, attacker, or challenge group
    A. Motivation
        1. Deprivation and discontent
        2. Belief that change is possible
        3. Desired collective satisfaction
    B. Goal Levels
        1. Conflict resources (power, personnel, etc.)
        2. Structural changes (arrangements of status and power)
        3. Desired collective satisfaction

II. Strategy: social means
    A. Components of strategic plan
        1. Successive action steps
        2. Appropriate conflict tactics
        3. Contingency plans for unanticipated developments, for victory, for defeat
    B. Conditions of strategy
        1. Characteristics of the conflict actors
        2. Potential third party intervention
        3. Relevant information
        4. Host social organization and culture
        5. Internal organization and psychological state of the challenge group

III. Resistance, obstruction, defender, antagonist
    A. Controller of required resources (material, personnel, etc.)
    B. Obstruction in path of conflict goals
    C. Counterattacker

Attacking and challenging groups are pushed into strategizing by the motivations that were shown in chapter 2 to cause conflict, and guided in this planning enterprise by the nature of the goals they seek. Such collective actors are strategy-consuming social entities just because they are engaged in calculated social struggle. Garner (1977: 157–62) and Gamson (1975: 38–54) have shown that the styles and tactics of group strategies are significantly conditioned by the goals sought. For our purposes, these goals can be categorized at three levels: conflict-relevant resources, the structural conditions of satisfaction, and some set of specific satisfactions. Thus powered and guided, conflict groups enter into the business of strategy production.

The social strategy of instrumental conflict itself is an inclusive plan of action composed of at least four related parts. First is a step-by-step design of collective action leading the group from the launching of the program to the final success. Intrinsic to the inclusive plan are choices of strategic style and selection of specific tactical instruments. We have seen above how these vary in response to the influence of a wide range of intervening conditions. The third component of strategy is a set of contingency plans for unforeseen as well as anticipated eventualities. The basic step-by-step plan seldom unfolds as perfectly as it is set out. Alternative steps must be foreseen and laid by in case of need. Further, while the attacking group seeks and expects success, it must be prepared to receive and utilize success once it comes. This calls for plans to consolidate and exploit the victories won. At the same time, while defeat is neither planned for nor expected, it must be foreseen as a real possibility. Contingency plans are made to answer the question brought on by defeat: What do we do now?

We have observed that the precise character of a strategic design will be affected by a large number of factors. In Figure 8-1 these conditioning factors have been classified as characteristics of the conflict participants, potential third-party intervention, relevant information, environing social organization and culture, and internal organization and psychological state of the challenging group itself. Most of these factors are self-evident. It may be useful, though, to mention that for strategic purposes, the conflict actors will acquire information about themselves, their surrounding social and physical situations, and future possibilities, to mention only a few. If challenge groups make rational use of such information, they enhance their chances of constructing realistic and functional strategies.

Gamson has made it clear that strategy formation must take account of the opposition in the struggle, the antagonist. These groups are likely to control the resources that are required to prosecute conflict. They must be dealt with in a way that permits access to the necessary resources of power, status, and the like. Because they possess or control required conflict resources and the cherished values that are the objects of struggle, they have to be taken into account when planning and organizing. And, finally, therefore, for both reasons, such groups can be expected to engage in counter-conflict. It seems likely that the strategies of all conflict groups will reveal some variation of this tripartite strategic model. As indicated, though, the precise form and content will be uniquely determined by numerous preconditioning and intervening variables.

In this chapter we have recognized that many groups resort to social conflict through collective decision as the instrument for the attainment of cherished social goals. At the same time these and many other groups also oppose the expression of social conflict. Sometimes they oppose it because they are challenged directly as antagonists. More often, though, they oppose social conflict because it violates norms they support and appears as nonlegitimate. These groups act collectively to contain conflict. The remaining four chapters of this book will examine the strategies that groups use when they oppose social conflict.

Prevention: Eliminating Causes

In this chapter we will examine the management strategy called prevention by the elimination of causes. In this strategy, groups act in advance of the eruption of nonlegitimate struggle to obviate it by mitigating or eliminating its causes. The nature of prevention is illuminated by showing its relation to the theory of conflict as developed earlier. Several cases are reviewed to set the stage for formulating a general strategy of conflict prevention.

THE NATURE OF CONFLICT PREVENTION

Boulding (1962: 2) conceptualizes prevention as a social process and identified two salient components. First he says that in speaking of conflict prevention we imply that there is an ongoing dynamic social system which is developing in the direction of nonlegitimate struggle. If nothing is done to interrupt the ongoing process, then nonlegitimate conflict is a predictable outcome. Second, Boulding argues that we also imply that it is possible to change the situation by substituting a different dynamic social system for the existing conflict-bound one. The substitute system will be programmed to produce socially legitimate outcomes instead of conflict. Essentially, Boulding is discussing the prevention of nonlegitimate conflict, specifically World War III, by eliminating its probable causes. This perspective permits us to define the term *conflict prevention* as a series of calculated actions taken by an individual or collective actor to mitigate or remove the causal factors and processes that are leading a social system toward the transformation of an existing pattern of legitimate struggle into a form of nonlegitimate conflict. That is, prevention will replace one set of social relations by another. If the preventive action is successful, the buildup of conflict causation will be terminated temporarily, at least until the buildup begins again under altered conditions.

The theoretical system that serves to explain the transformation of legitimate struggle into nonlegitimate conflict also provides a frame of reference for analyzing the process of conflict prevention. The theoretical model of conflict explanation that was developed in chapter 2 included three major components: societal preconditions, collective motivation, and a catalyzing process. It was argued that the societal preconditions—structural maladjustments, cultural inconsistencies, interactional unreciprocities, and alienation—consist of aspects of the inclusive social structure which collectively produce a built-in potential for social conflict. The orientation toward nonlegitimate struggle can be mitigated or even prevented by manipulating or eliminating any or all of these factors. For example, the United Nations has prevented many potential wars by assisting economic, political, or communications systems to operate successfully in various developing or beleaguered societies. The "series of calculated actions" mentioned above may also apply to the motivational phase or the catalyzing process of the conflict buildup. Serious conflicts can be put off, temporarily at least, by providing ego satisfaction or public recognition for hard-pressed groups without any substantive modifications of societal structures.

It was said that the agent of conflict prevention may be "an individual or collective actor." The most obvious preventive collective agent is governments. By virtue of their unique power situation, governments are usually most able to alter basic institutional conditions by formulating and executing broad programs of reform and improvement. Thus, the United States government initiated the New Deal in the 1930s and launched civil rights and anti-poverty programs in the 1960s. Supernational polities like the United Nations and the oas (Organization of American States) perform similar preventive functions between the various American nations. Units of local governments, e.g., good neighbor commissions or state mediation services, also act as conflict-preventive agencies. However, as suggested, both nongovernmental collective actors and individuals acting alone can execute the preventive function as well. For example, religious bodies, civic associations, and multinational corporations sometimes act to prevent conflicts; and influential individuals often serve as conflict-preventers or peacemakers.

It might seem self-evident that the practice of conflict prevention is a wholly desirable matter. The orientation against nonlegitimate conflict is grounded in the consensus of the dominant values of the social system. The practice therefore enjoys substantial inherent legitimacy. However, the actual practice of conflict prevention is challenged by several subheritages in the inclusive culture. Marx (1932) crystallized an influential revolutionary tradition in the Western heritage that challenges the general opposition to all nonlegitimate dissent and struggle. Sorel (1950) fabricated a moral justification for violence as a strategic tactic of protest and rebellion. A so-called universal antiestablishment orientation has been identified and variously called "utopia" by Mannheim (1936), "antithesis" by Lenski (1966: 1–23), and "subversion" by Fals-Borda (1969: 1–9). Such subtraditions tend to surround the practice of conflict prevention with a number of unsettled issues which can be categorized by the two questions: Who should, or may, manage conflict prevention? And which (i.e., whose) conflicts should be prevented? No altogether satisfactory answers have ever been found to these questions. As a consequence, there is a continuous controversy between conflict groups and preventive agents regarding both issues. This state of affairs permits us to observe that although continuous effort is made in every society to prevent certain conflicts, the endeavor always takes place within a field of clashing values and unsettled questions.

SOME CONDITIONS OF CONFLICT PREVENTION

Many conditions affect the resort to conflict prevention. In the present discussion, the following six are considered: value orientations, system openness, cost-benefit estimations, the possibility of intervention, legitimacy of the managing agent, and availability of resources. First, it is evident that leading value orientations direct people to be kind and considerate in relation to others. Their values teach them to oppose coercion and violence and other nonlegitimate forms of struggle. For example, the Society of Friends lays great store by peace and nonharmful human relations. The Quakers work at devising ways to compromise differences of interests and manage disagreements. Tomasson (1970: 271–94) reports that the "abhorrence of violence" is a major theme in Swedish value orientations. He asserts that Swedish culture contains strong sanctions against violence and aggression. In the United States, the ladies garment industry has a long history of industrial peace and labor-management accord. The International Ladies Garment Workers Union has developed and enforced low-level, legitimate mechanisms for managing relations with the diffuse industry.

Pacific value orientations provide a hospitable climate for the anticipatory management strategies of prevention. Conflict management agents are encouraged to anticipate the trend of group relations and social conflict and to initiate operations that will forestall the resort to nonlegitimate tactics. When combined with other factors, such value orientations constitute a significant facilitating force for conflict prevention.

Second, open social systems provide opportunities for disadvantaged groups to realize their important goals. The ordinary methods of striving and competition may function to produce expected rewards. There is a recognized balance in the effort-reward system. Groups are not severely harassed by the sense of relative deprivation and unrelieved discontent. They are free of the intense pressure to resort to nonlegitimate means to obtain socially approved ends. In his discussion of the conditions of intensity and violence in conflict, Dahrendorf (1959: 239) makes the same point. He asserts that violence in class conflict tends to decline when absolute deprivations of rewards and facilities are replaced by relative deprivations. Later he makes the same point in two propositions about the intensity of conflict.

Rapidly expanding socioeconomic systems, like western Canada or New Zealand, often constitute open systems with many opportunities for all and few restrictions on social movement. The support for anticipatory conflict management is enhanced if at the same time the culture contains pacific value orientations and limited ideological commitments. Steinbeck (1939) described the fluid open systems of the migratory communities of "Okies" and "Arkies" which emphasized prevention of nonlegitimate conflict. Disagreements and clashes could, in most instances, be resolved by the rules and patterns of communal leadership and sanction. In socialist and quasi-socialist systems of the "middle way," like those in the Scandinavian countries, the socioeconomic structure is kept open by formal rules. In this way, important causes of nonlegitimate conflict are mitigated or removed.

In situations like these, the effort-reward system is kept flexible and working. The sense of deprivation does not become intolerable and people are not burdened by feelings of unrelieved discontent. If preferred avenues of effort are blocked or uninviting, acceptable alternatives are available. As Ryan (1969: 118) has observed, the ordinary conflicts of social life can be managed by the ordinary methods of conflict settlement. In such circumstances, when governments or other authoritative organizations consider anticipatory strategies for managing conflict, they find a congenial environment and atmosphere ready at hand.

Estimating the cost of conflict in relation to possible gains may also encourage efforts to avoid struggle. Often it can be seen that activities designed to prevent or mitigate open strife are cheaper in many respects than coercion and violence. Yet estimating cost in reference to social conflict may be a sophisticated collective activity. In some situations it may be perceived as an available alternative. In others it may seem to be a task that is impossible or too difficult to undertake. However, wherever this perspective exists as a viable option, it functions as one condition facilitating conflict prevention. Calculating the costs and benefits of conflict has become realistic in recent years with advances in the field of peace research. In this connection, Finsterbusch and Greisman (1974) observe that the advances of recent history have made it possible for societies to view the use of force in war as a dangerous and expensive form of collective action. They go on to declare that the results of international force seldom benefit any group.

Communities and societies may gain the poise and sophistication required to calculate the costs of nonlegitimate conflict in several ways. After an unfortunate experience, some groups may be motivated to take precautionary action. For example, following the urban riots of the mid-1960s, many American cities established agencies and programs to monitor intergroup relations and to judge the relative costs of preventive action against the risks of further rioting. In other instances, one social unit learns from the experiences of others. This line of precautionary action is illustrated in the experience of Greensboro, whose civic and governmental leaders studied the experiences, in terms of both their price and their desirability, of a number of other comparable urban places. International bodies like the United Nations or the Organization of American States make such cost-benefit estimating of international war one of their major operations.

Fourth, people come round in various ways to perceive that conflict can indeed be prevented. Skolnick (1969: 8–9) has argued that many people believe that the American tradition provides legitimate ways for disadvantaged groups to advance without resort to aggressive conflict. Other people, however, take the opposite view. They believe that coercive and violent struggle is inevitable. They come only slowly to recognize that conflicts can be managed. They have first to outgrow the lingering vestiges of fatalism and ignorance. Smith (1971: xv) described this trend toward rationality and control in a study of conflict resolution. He asserted that, by contrast to earlier generations, the traditional ideas of pessimism and powerlessness regarding our destiny are slowly being replaced by attitudes of ambivalence and even, in some circumstances, of hope. The change of attitude is stimulated by the knowledge explosion and by the increasing recognition of the costs of unrestrained conflict. This development is focused in part on studies of conflict management and peace research taking place in a growing number of research centers.

At the same time, increasing numbers of individuals and communities are recognizing that within limits conflict management is possible. This recognition comes about in various ways. Some groups may stumble upon this insight through their own experience. Faced with a crisis situation for which they are not prepared, they may experiment with various alternatives to avoid or prevent the outbreak of serious conflict. Upon reflection and through a kind of trial-and-error process, they perceive that certain actions "worked," i.e., achieved desirable results. They then "see," i.e., reason, that if these things had been "done" in the first place, the crisis might have been prevented. Understanding may come in other ways. The people in one society or community may learn from observing or reading about the experiences of other groups. In some other situations, the academics and other intellectuals who are engaged in peace research and the study of conflict management may be able to counsel leaders. Social policy thus is grounded directly in the results of research activity; both are instructive to the enterprise of conflict prevention. Once this insight is gained, the chances of acting to prevent conflict are enhanced. The restraints of superstition, ethnocentrism, ignorance, lethargy, and the like, may be swept away. The possibility of acting becomes the invitation to act. People perceive the various operations of investigation, prediction, planning, and implementation as reasonable, sensible, and efficacious behavior.

Evidence of the growing conviction that it is possible to manage conflict comes not only from the theory and knowledge that constitute the intellectual corpus of peace research, but also from the deliberate activities of organizations, nations, and even international bodies. Since the end of World War II, the central theme of American foreign policy has been the continuing effort to manage the Cold War with the Soviet Union. Administrations of both political parties have dedicated great time, talent, and energy to discovering and implementing relationships that lessen the causes of struggle between the two world giants. The United Nations has operated on the conviction that it is possible to manage the endless disputes and controversies between modern nations and so to prevent serious and destructive international strife. Theoretical formulations, empirical research, talented staffs, implementing organizations, and vast human and social resources have been dedicated to this continuing work. The fact that World War III has not erupted and that international disputes have so far been limited in both scope and duration functions to bolster the growing conviction that nonlegitimate, morally reprehensible conflicts can be prevented at least temporarily. This conviction has also manifested itself at the international level and local level in all parts of the world. The growth of this point of view constitutes a significant condition facilitating the effort to manage social conflicts.

Further action in anticipating and managing conflict may also be enhanced by widespread belief in the legitimacy of the managing agent, i.e., the government or some other organization. Such an agent is perceived as legitimate when it is thought of as honest, fair, and competent. If people agree that such an agent is a justifiable and proper representative they may respond favorably to its preventive efforts. Gurr (1969: 605) stated that citizens are likely to trust political leaders and to desist from coercive or violent action if they have a positive regard for the managerial system, governmental or otherwise. The authority of the controlling agent is not contested and its commands or requirements are complied with.

The organizations that manage conflict acquire the aura of legitimacy in two major ways. First, people come to recognize them as legitimate through direct personal experience. For example, a certain group protested to its city council about a neglected service or an abuse of treatment. It was heard with attention and respect. Its protests were found to be valid and the city council did something about them. That is, the group was convinced that the community, as represented by its city council, acted in honesty, fairness, and with competence to rectify the situation. Hoselitz and Moore (1965) note that in modernizing societies, leaders can acquire and maintain legitimacy by working for the "utopian" aims of the people. Often, though, the authoritative organization has already acquired a reputation, be it of legitimacy or the opposite. People learn from each other and act as though what they have heard is true, whether it is or not. In this case people recognize the organization as legitimate through hearsay. They trust it and comply with its rules and meet its demands upon them. The organization's reputation may be composed of a mixture of reported empirical experiences and good public relations.

The International Court has played the role of conflict preventer in disputes between contending nations. If the dispute cannot be reconciled by direct negotiation and the controversy is moving toward open conflict, the parties may agree to accept the judgment of the Court. This is possible because the Court enjoys legitimacy in the international community and because both parties to the dispute trust its honesty, fairness, and competence. The settlement worked out may constitute not only a formula for the present dispute, but also a plan for relieving international tension by mitigating or removing conflict-causal conditions. While labor mediation and conciliation services approach and manage conflict in other ways, sometimes they can act to prevent oncoming labor-management clashes by manipulating causal factors. In this way they establish or permit the emergence of patterns of intergroup relations that inhibit the development of conflict-causing processes for some time in the future. These agencies can perform such conflict-preventive service because they enjoy high legitimacy in the industrial relations community.

Finally, leaders, information, previous experience, collective power, organization, equipment, and the like constitute resources that are important in preventing social conflict. The groups that opt for this approach use such resources in facilitating the prevention of social conflict. The significance of leadership is augmented if the leaders are supported by other resources. Of particular importance are technical persons who can bring special knowledge and skills to the collective task. Researchers, planners, and managers of various kinds are particularly important. If such personnel are available, the initiation of anticipatory intervention may be facilitated. Adequate and appropriate organization is essential to conflict management. Communities and other groups must have ways to reach members and participants and to bring them under the discipline of management. For this purpose, an existing organization is mandatory. Wernette (1972: 531–38) argues that successful conflict prevention may also require the creation of new institutions and organizations specifically for that purpose.

Another key resource is adequate social power. The resort to non-legitimate conflict can be impeded if causal factors are removed and remedial changes are initiated. But the management agent must have access to adequate social power in order to take these actions. The management agent that does not have the authority or finances to initiate and carry through fundamental changes runs the risk of aggravating the conflict situation. In the next chapter it will be pointed out that management agencies like labor relations and human relations boards are likely to be handicapped if they lack the authority to execute their decisions and judgments. And finally, such organizations must have access to certain kinds of material resources. This may mean land at one time, or equipment at another, or funds at still another. In any case, at times the management of conflict requires the use of dispersal of material resources. Sometimes also, organizations that exist for other purposes undertake the sponsorship of conflict-prevention enterprises. For example, the Chamber of Commerce of Greensboro took the lead in forestalling the possibility of open conflict over forced school busing. It was shown earlier that accommodative mechanisms like recreational programs, established opportunities and occasions for self- and group expression, and frustration sublimation function to prevent the buildup of conflict causation. These mechanisms ventilate feelings, channel drives, meet needs, and in other ways reduce or mitigate the motivations toward extreme or nonlegitimate modes of struggle.

CONFLICT PREVENTION: SOME ILLUSTRATIONS

In this section of the chapter we summarize three different illustrations of conflict prevention. All focus upon prevention by eliminating, or at least manipulating, conflict-causal factors. The cases have been selected because they approach the task of conflict prevention in different ways and at quite different levels of sophistication and rationality. These materials can assist us to move on in the following section of the chapter to formulate a general strategy for conflict prevention by the elimination of causes.

Preventing a Riot in New Brunswick

The first case describes a community that felt its way in a crisis situation to forestalling an imminent race riot. The processes of calculation and planning emerged in the course of taking immediate necessary action. Yet in retrospect it can be seen that functionally efficacious actions were taken that prevented the eruption of violence.

The National Advisory Commission on Civil Disorders (1968: 82–84) described how people of New Brunswick, New Jersey, avoided serious conflict in the summer of 1967. New Brunswick is a county seat, site of Rutgers University, and a local center of commerce. In the summer of 1967 it was populated by a mixture of native whites, immigrants, blacks, and Puerto Ricans. Although none of these groups was confined to a clearly defined ghetto, they managed to live together with little tension and avoided open violence. However, according to Mayor Patricia Sheehan and antipoverty worker James Amos, by mid-July the town was "haunted by reports of the riots in Newark and Plainfield," and a "tenseness in the air that got thicker and thicker." Dissatisfaction in the black community increased and revolved around several issues: closing by the police of a teenage coffee house, lack of a swimming pool and other public recreation facilities, and the release of a white couple on very low bond after being arrested for allegedly shooting at three black teenagers.

Responding to these conditions, leaders in the black community decided that something must be done right away. As a result, early in the week staff members of the antipoverty agency met with the mayor and city commissioners to plan preventive action to reduce tension and avert a possible riot. The mayor appointed a black policeman as community liaison officer and authorized him to report directly to her. Other black policemen were sent into the streets in plain clothes to fight rumors and act as counter-rioters. Uniformed policemen were advised to act with restraint to avoid the possibility of escalating the controversy. The radio station played down news of rumors and disturbances. The antipoverty agency named a task force of workers to go into all neighborhoods— white, black, and Puerto Rican—to check on rumors, to report official information and to cool the situation. The chief of police met with the chiefs of surrounding communities to plan cooperation in case disorder broke out.

In spite of these precautions, just after nine P.M. on Monday the police began to receive scattered reports of windows being broken. At 10:30 about 100 youngsters were observed marching in a column of twos. A tall black minister attempted unsuccessfully to stop them. Local police were reinforced by 100 men from surrounding communities. Road blocks were set up on all principal thoroughfares. Wild rumors of armed black and white gangs, shootings, burnings, beatings, and deaths swept the city. What actually happened was minor vandalism and much random activity, "much like Halloween," according to Mayor Sheehan.

On Tuesday morning further actions were taken. The mayor imposed a curfew, and recorded a tape that was played over the local radio station calling on the people to be calm. Most of the persons who had been arrested the previous night were released on their own recognizance or low bail. The antipoverty agency hired a double shift of teenagers as recreation aids.

The black teenagers got into the act. Thirty-five of them met with the mayor and city commissioners, pouring out their souls to the city officials, who listened with respect and understanding. The city officials and the youths drew up a statement attacking discrimination, inferior educational and employment opportunities, police harassment, and poor housing. The youngsters began broadcasting their achievement, by radio and in the streets, urging the people to "cool it" because the mayor had promised to act.

Despite these measures, a confrontation between the police and a crowd of blacks occurred near a housing project that Tuesday evening. The crowd was angry over a concentration of police in riot dress. After some harsh negotiation, the police were withdrawn. A short time later, older and rougher elements of the crowd appeared in front of the police station demanding to see the mayor. Mayor Sheehan came out on the station steps and talked to the people, asking to be given time to correct conditions. After a slight further altercation, the crowd was allowed to satisfy itself that all persons arrested the previous night had been released. In the end, the people agreed to give the mayor time and opportunity to make improvements. As the commission report concluded, "the New Brunswick riot had failed to materialize."

In New Brunswick, preventive action was initiated only hours before a riot erupted. There was no time to eliminate nor even to manipulate the societal causes—inadequate schooling, poor housing, unemployment, general disrespect. The leaders decided correctly in this situation to focus on the motivational and catalyzing factors in the causal process. By lowering the immediate motivational pressure, time was gained, an eruption was postponed, and promises of substantive changes were given and accepted. Open violent conflict was thus postponed. Long-term conflict prevention would depend upon fulfillment of the promises made by the mayor and city council.

Preventing "Trouble" in the Wake of School Busing

The conflict-preventing situation in Greensboro differed from that in New Brunswick. For several years, the community had faced the possibility of a court order to initiate large-scale busing of school children to dismantle a racially dual school system and to achieve "racial balance." This lead time offered the community two options. It could be used as an organization-action vacuum in which to stew, become increasingly alarmed, grow resentful, and prepare for resistance and open disorder. Or, alternatively, it could be used to decide on a course of action and then to prepare and plan what should be done when the time came. The community opted for the second alternative and developed an effective strategy of conflict prevention by reducing certain causes.

Greensboro is a city of some 175,000 people in the upper-Appalachian piedmont. It has a mixed economic base dominated by tobacco and textiles. Two branches of the state university system and three private liberal arts colleges make education an important aspect of community life. Blacks, constituting about two-fifths of the population, are concentrated in the northeast quadrant. There are very few foreign-born persons. A number of protest activities, disturbances, and riots in the 1960s functioned to relax race relations to some extent.

Following the Supreme Court decision of 17 May 1954, mandating desegregation of public schools with "all deliberate speed," Greensboro resisted and resorted to subterfuges and in other ways dragged its feet. In the early 1960s, impatient with this delay, a group of black families

sued the board of education in the federal district court to enforce immediate compliance with the Supreme Court decision. The case dragged on
in court for years, never being terminated, yet never coming to a definitive decision. In the early spring of 1971, the court ordered Greensboro
to dismantle its dual school system and to achieve "racial balance" in all
schools by busing students.

The community felt itself faced with a crisis. It could no longer escape
definitive action. To defy the court would bring certain and extreme
sanction. To comply with the order, it was believed, would stir up strong
reactions and possibly ugly and open confrontations, disturbances, and
violence. At this juncture, a number of thoughtful and responsible citizens were drawn together by the situation that confronted and threatened
the community in an effort to decide what should be done. They organized as Concerned Citizens for the Schools and led the community-
wide discussion. In time, the decision (with lingering dissent and
misgiving) was made to comply, but to prevent the "trouble," i.e., open
noncompliance, public disturbances, and riot behavior that had plagued
Charlotte, Louisville, Richmond, and other communities. Operationally,
this meant changing the educational and racial structures abruptly and
on a large scale, while taking definitive action to allay collective fears,
perceptions of mistreatment and deprivation, feelings of discontent and
resentment, and the intensification of the conflict-catalyzing process.
Leadership, in concert with the black community, was taken on behalf of
the businesses and the school system by the Chamber of Commerce and
by the Board of Education. Together the black and white leaders, working with the Concerned Citizens for the Schools, formulated a strategy
for conflict prevention tailored to the specific needs of Greensboro.

The strategy included the following components and related steps:

1—Clear, firm, but compassionate stand of the leadership—to facilitate the busing order without resistance and conflict.

2—Information gathering: possible citizen reactions, social science
findings, experiences of other communities in similar circumstances, advantages and benefits of busing for racial balance, possible costs and
disadvantages, how the system would actually work, etc.

3—Massive public education program, including the following steps:
total support of the media—newspapers, television, radio; mass public
meetings led by outstanding white and black leaders; presentations and
discussions before all kinds of organized groups; small, informal coffee
klatsch discussion meetings in all neighborhoods; discussion meetings of
junior and senior high school students led by student leaders.

All this community activity was intended to involve the total community in the policy and resolve taken by its leaders and to allay the fears of people and to dampen the processes of motivation and catalysis. This program developed and intensified through the summer holiday.

The community faced the opening of school with hope, uncertainty, and high resolve. Active involvement of a large proportion of all citizens in the discussions and action of the summer allayed their fears and led them to perceive the policy and resolve as their own. They would make it work and earn a good reputation for their city. There were some centers of opposition. An organization calling itself the National Association for the Advancement of White People offered acrimonious opposition, but seemed to have little solid support in the community. Many families faced the fall with reservations and reluctance. Some parents moved outside the city into surrounding districts where schools were still largely segregated. Some families enrolled their children in private segregated schools. Most, however, decided to comply. At last the schools opened and the first buses rolled. Various precautions were taken to obviate the risks of "trouble," and the first day passed uneventfully. Greensboro got through the first week without any significant racial outburst. By the end of the first month, most opposition had evaporated and the system was working successfully. Conflict had been prevented by eliminating or reducing the force of motivation and by dampening the catalyzing process.

System Substitution

Likert and Likert (1976: 16–17 and passim) examined administrative policies and organizational structure in a series of industries and from this study constructed an organizational model that would prevent internal conflict. "System 4," as the Likerts called their preventive model, is applicable to strife between components of "micro" and "macro" organizations. This system aims to facilitate cooperation among integral working parts of the organization and thus to make conflict both nonfunctional and irrelevant. Under "System 4" the organization is comprised of "interlocking work groups" that reveal high-level collective loyalty along with trust and positive attitudes among superiors, subordinates, and peers. The Likerts stressed that under "System 4," relations within the organization are characterized by considerateness, humanistic skills, and group problem solving. These human relations skills and achievements are essential since they permit and facilitate "effective participation in decisions on common problems." Collective formulation of organizational objectives which satisfactorily integrate the needs and desires of members and related other persons functionally operate to encourage cooperation and thus to block the development of tension and strife. At the same time, the Likerts argue, "System 4" organization enhances the fulfillment of basic manifest and latent functions of the organization, e.g., high motivation, reciprocal positive influence, coordination of member actions, efficient and effective communication, and skilled leadership. The Likerts conclude (34) that the organizational system produces an "interaction-influence network" that functions to cope with conflict while facilitating the work of the organization. Central processes of the system include, among others, leadership, communication, motivation, control, decision making, coordination, role setting, and evaluation.

Under "System 4" conflict prevention is anticipatory organizational action. The structure of the organization is patterned in a way that functions to forestall the buildup of conflict motivations. The essence of prevention is structural change and coordination. Conflict prevention is postulated on the proposition that group relations are composed of a mix of cooperation and conflict. Thus the way to prevent conflict is to replace a conflict-maximizing system by one that maximizes cooperation.

A STRATEGY FOR CONFLICT PREVENTION

Sometimes social systems wait, like New Brunswick and Greensboro, until they are faced with the danger of extreme or nonlegitimate conflict before taking preventive action. If they opt to act in this critical situation, they can take a series of steps to deal with the problems and to mitigate or eliminate the basic causes. These steps form a preventive paradigm including the following components:

A—Preliminary actions: reading and interpreting the warning signals.

B—Investigation, covering minimally: (1) the build-up of conflict causation; (2) experiences of comparable groups in similar circumstances; (3) resources that can be utilized.

C—Program of preventive action: (1) cause mitigation (short-run actions); (2) cause removal (long-run actions).

Preliminary Actions

A community or society that sets out to prevent unwelcome social conflict will have recognized that the danger of such conflict exists and is imminent. Leaders cannot be caught off guard, like Mayor Sheehan in New Brunswick, by a sudden escalation of tension and the threat of riot behavior. A state of vigilance and informed anticipation constitutes the

prelude to preventive action. This preliminary phase of conflict prevention exists as readiness to recognize the warning signals of oncoming conflict and the ability to interpret these signals. For example, the business,
civic, and educational leaders of Greensboro were sensitive to the pulse
of intergroup relations in the community and so could recognize the
premonitory signals of the possibility of "trouble" following the inception of large-scale busing of school children. Thus, they were able to read
and interpret the indicators of uneasiness and anxiety, the complaints
and threats of alarmed or hostile parents, the low rumblings of discontent
that flew on the wings of gossip and rumor. They recognized and interpreted these warning signals, and so were prepared to launch a program
of conflict prevention. Four categories of warning signals of oncoming
conflict can be identified. They are restlessness, tension, disturbances,
and limited violence.

The basic motivations of social conflict are relative deprivation and
collective discontent. People respond to these cognitive-affective states by
milling randomly. Smelser (1959: 32–40) described this response as
"dissatisfaction" and "manifest unrest." People signal their uncertainty,
ambivalence, and anxiety by fidgety gestures and movements, and by
spreading rumors. They give the collective appearance of being jumpy
and jittery. Faced with the threat of an unknown situation, they become
restless. Experienced leaders or researchers recognize these behaviors as
indicators of trouble. They begin looking for other clues and try to determine the causes for the restlessness in precise and relevant terms.

Restlessness is accompanied by tension as a second warning signal. In
practical use, tension refers to strains or unreciprocities in relations
among people who are accustomed to interact. The relaxation accompanying customary reciprocation is replaced by increased social distance,
brittleness, and edginess. One feels the tension in relationships and situations which used to be easygoing and rewarding. The sensation of social
tension is like the feeling one has just before a severe thunderstorm. If
the wind doesn't change, something is likely to break loose. Seasoned
leaders sense the tension and recognize it as a warning signal of possible
trouble. They can make rough readings by devices like straws in the wind
or alerting their psycho-affective sensors. Trained researchers have access
to various tension indicators, i.e., measurable, correlated variables. Recognition of heightened and heightening tension again prompts leaders to
seek out the causes.

When disturbances and violence occur, the conflict has already begun.
Yet as Coser (1967: 82–87) has observed, if such collective expressions

are perceived as "danger signals" rather than definitive conflict action, prevention may still be possible. Disturbances and minor violences may erupt in institutional settings—university campuses, school grounds and buildings, work places, recreational areas—when people gather and interact. Students, workers, or players may separate into ethnic, racial, religious, economic or other groups and eye each other with suspicion or hostility. Necessary contacts may be punctuated by abusive verbalizations —disparagements and epithets—leading to sporadic fights in corridors, lunch rooms, recreation areas, or on the access routes from home to gathering place. Parents may keep their children home from school, complaining that it isn't safe for them to go. Workers and players may boycott the unpleasant and threatening places. Community meetings proliferate as people gather to express their dissatisfactions, protest, threaten, and organize "to take action." Committees are sent to the board of education, city hall, or "front management" to lay out the grievances, press demands for action and make proposals of perceived solutions. Such an ordinarily routine activity may expand into a noisy, aggressive crowd. The National Advisory Commission on Civil Disorders (1968: 51) described such a crowd in Cincinnati in the summer of 1967: "The City Council held an open session. The chamber was jammed with Negro residents, many of whom gave vociferous support as their spokesmen criticized the city administration. When the audience became unruly, a detail of National Guardsmen was stationed outside the council chamber. Their presence resulted in a misunderstanding, causing many of the Negroes to walk out, and the meeting to end." The mass rally, city-hall crowd or other adventitious gathering may turn into a march or other public demonstration that obstructs pedestrian or auto traffic. Davison (1974) has shown that such premonitory warnings of oncoming international strife can be read in the content and thrust of mass communication.

If caught in time and correctly interpreted, such actions can be perceived as warning signals indicating the buildup of conflict causation and the danger of more serious trouble in the future. Persons in positions to control or significantly affect collective decisions must ask whether such events are symptomatic of deeper conditions and forces, or whether they constitute the definitive conflict. Do these developments give us time to plan and prevent the serious outburst, or are we now in the midst of a serious and destructive struggle? What conditions, motivations and social forces are causing the onrushing outburst? What action should be taken? Reading the warning signals means giving correct answers to these and similar questions. In Greensboro leaders asked the right questions and found the right answers. In New Brunswick, on the other hand, the leaders were caught off guard and were slow to ask the right questions. They acted just before the disturbances escalated into a serious riot.

Investigation

In the strategy of conflict prevention by mitigating or removing causes, investigation is an essential element. As suggested, investigation is going on during the preliminary warning-signal stage. The questions raised and answered are an act of inquiry. But effective, relevant, preventive action requires access to more information. The activity of investigation can produce information on the following issues: What does conflict and peace research tell us about the causation, etiology, and prevention of conflict? Are we given reliable guides of a general nature that can be used in our specific situation? Second, drawing upon this theoretical knowledge as a guide, what are the salient causes of the conflict that we confront at this point in our situation? Specifically, what causal conditions and forces do we have to face and manage? Third, what have other comparable groups done in similar situations? Which tactics worked; which ones failed? What lessons are there for us in their experiences? And fourth, what resources do we have for fashioning a program of preventive action—leadership, organizations, social power, social integration and collective morale, funds and material equipment, and so on? Have we got enough of the proper kinds of resources to do the job? Will they be available when needed?

The formulations and findings of conflict studies and peace research can have several uses in the practical task of conflict prevention. They can demolish myths the layman might believe about the causes and nature of social conflict. For example, the fruits of research can lead to questioning the common tendency to attribute local disturbances and violence to "out-of-town agitators" or to "Communists." Such basic knowledge suggests that the agitators who seem to be making trouble may be local people, employees, fellow citizens, and neighbors who must be confronted and dealt with in the course of preventing more serious trouble. The problem cannot be solved merely by driving the unwanted agitators out of town or by cracking down on the Communists. Some acquaintance with this systematic research material may also question the comfortable notion that absence of agitation and protest indicates that all is well in the local community or the society at large. Such quiet may be a false sign, masking the seething dissatisfaction that is rampant in the community. Some years ago, after a study of the fluoridation controversy in eighteen

New England communities, Gamson (1966: 81) reported, "the absence of rancorous conflict is no . . . sign of an 'ideal' community." On the other hand, rancorous conflict made communities "vital" and brought the "advantages of stimulation and growth." Many years ago Gunnar Myrdal (1944: 40–42) drew our attention to the same fallacy in his apt phrase, "the convenience of ignorance" that characterized the attitude of many southern whites toward the blacks in their midst. There is also much research that shows that "law and order" is far from the solution to the problems of conflict in many instances. Cracking down on law violators and insisting on the maintenance of order at any cost has been shown to have a sharp escalating effect in many situations.

Practical leaders in social systems of any size or type are not likely to be social scientists. They cannot engage in extensive "searches of the related literature." What is required is a good grasp of the general theory of conflict causation. For this purpose, lay leaders in government and other organizations can consult knowledgeable scholars in sociology, political science, or social planning. As indicated in chapter 2, the scientific studies will reveal that background, structural, and personal factors function to generate collective motivations that, when properly catalyzed, result in the conflicts that disturb all kinds of social systems. Lay leaders need this basic perspective, and an indication of the categories of structural, personal, and motivational factors that are likely to be at work in any social situation. In a significant collection of essays, Nettleship et al. (1975) indicate some ways in which the findings of social science can be put to practical use in preventing social conflicts.

The search for conflict causes need not be a formidable technical enterprise. In most instances, the information required to define the general situation and point to prime causes is already at hand, awaiting assembly and evaluation. Such information exists in census, economic, and social data in the files of the Chamber of Commerce, crime data at the juvenile court or the police department, demographic information and statistics on housing assembled by the housing authority and the local government planning agencies, economic figures and facts collected regularly by the employment service, welfare department, and so on, through a list of other public and private agencies. The United Nations and other international bodies also collect systematic information that has relevance for the prevention of international conflicts. With such relevant information in hand, it is possible for leaders to determine the principal short-run causes and long-run determinants of the current disturbances and the potential greater outbreak that is anticipated, things continuing as they are. The National Advisory Commission on Civil Disorders has shown how this kind of investigation leads to definitions of situations and determinations of causes. Speaking of the riot in Houston in the summer of 1967, their report (1968: 118) asserted that "these earlier or prior incidents were linked in the minds of many Negroes to the pre-existing reservoir of underlying grievances." Working backward from numerous specific triggering events like that in Houston, the Commission research staff identified a series of structural and personal causal factors that operated everywhere. In some communities, economic disadvantage and discrimination had been significantly reduced, but lack of general recognition was still deeply disturbing. In others, inadequate housing and unemployment were felt acutely and kept the black community continuously deprived and discontent. The search through the assembled information enables the leaders to identify and evaluate the specific conditions that are operating in the locale in question. These long-run causal factors may appear as the basic conditions of social organization that Smelser (1963: 12–21) called "structural conduciveness." That is, in certain aspects the community or society is structured in such a way as to deprive, penalize, or frustrate certain groups or sectors. In relation to other groups or sectors whom they believe to be comparable in characteristics and deserts, the deprived groups see themselves as unusually disadvantaged. Used in this way, the investigation and evaluation of data can help define the nature and size of the prevention job that lies ahead, orient the group toward fruitful preventive actions, and enhance the efficiency and facility with which they carry out the task. This factfinding and fact-analyzing tactic can also aid the group in the search for ways of tackling the task of preventing the oncoming nonlegitimate conflict.

Groups can also get help in the task of deciding what to do and how to do it by examining the experiences that comparable groups encountered in similar circumstances. This is an extension of the investigation, factfinding operation. It is desirable to look at the experiences of groups that failed as well as those that succeeded. For example, it was important for Greensboro to look at the experience of Charlotte, North Carolina, where violence was not averted following enforced busing, as well as at other places which did carry the change through without serious strife and violence. Such activity provides additional information and useful insights. More than this, such inquiry brings together a wide range of alternative techniques for executing the work of conflict prevention. This broadens the field of options of action and improves the community's chances of designing a scheme to fit its unique conditions and needs.

The inventory of resources is another aspect of the investigation. The group will wish to ask itself whether it has all the materials required to carry out a successful preventive program. This can be known only after available resources have been inventoried. The strategy for conflict prevention can then be fitted to this reserve of resources as well as to the size and nature of the task to be accomplished. Although almost any phenomenon may be perceived and utilized as a resource, the following are some obvious categories: leadership, organization, social skills, social power, *esprit de corps,* and material objects. Most of these categories are self-evident; however, it may be instructive to illustrate the variety and meaning of a few. As Wernett (1972: 531–38) has mentioned, it may be necessary to create specialized institutions and organizations to do the job of conflict prevention. For example, the people of Greensboro established the Concerned Citizens for the Schools. On the other hand, existing organizations can be drafted into this effort. Thus, for example, in Greensboro, the Chamber of Commerce, student athletic associations, and women's garden clubs became important parts of the organizational apparatus of conflict prevention. In New Brunswick, extensive use was made of local radio stations and the antipoverty organization. Although blacks, the white poor, and various immigrant ethnic groups may feel alienated and severely deprived and discontent, the affluent sectors of the community may be enjoying a temporary sense of *esprit de corps* and euphoria over the completion of a favorite community project, say, erection of a War Memorial Auditorium or passing a bond issue to improve and expand the local airport. Faced by the crisis of court-enforced, massive busing to achieve racial balance in the schools, leaders may draw on this high community spirit and achievement-produced morale to help prevent violence. Planning for conflict prevention in these situations permits these organizational and integrative factors to be defined as resources and used to carry out the preventive strategy.

Preventive Actions

A preventive strategy consists of a series of systematized and integrated action-steps designed to mitigate current irritants and to remove long-range causes of conflict. A series of definitive actions intended to produce specific accomplishments are fitted together in a schedule and supported by relevant resources. For example, Boulding (1962: 2–12) constructed a strategy for preventing World War III that includes five sequential stages, each with numerous specific tactics. An adjunct to such a program is a series of contingency plans to meet possible unanticipated developments. The whole is tailored to the social situation and to the goal of preventing possible conflict. As suggested, this plan is designed to meet two related problems. First, in the short run, it is expected to mitigate the irritating conditions that produced the immediate tension, disturbance, or limited violence. For example, a series of events and actions in New Brunswick led to a tense, threatening confrontation with the police that almost ended in bloodshed. Something had to be done immediately to avert the eruption of serious violence. The strategy includes two immediate steps to meet this kind of problem: communication and concrete action. Some kind of meeting is arranged immediately between "authorities" and "protesters." In this meeting protesters are encouraged to air their grievances, state their demands and offer proposals for remedy. Authorities hear these statements carefully and sympathetically, express concern, support, and reassurances, and agree on specific and concrete actions to be taken immediately to ameliorate the present irritating conditions. Suppose, for example, that the complaint is about police brutality. Then the meeting should result in agreements that are reflected the following day in restrained police behavior. If the complaint is about housing shortage, a condition that cannot be fully altered in a single day, the protesters should *see* tangible overt actions that indicate the promise of relief is being carried out. Such action mitigates the immediate irritants in two ways. First, it actually reduces the frequency with which they occur, or appears to give concrete evidence of such reduction in the foreseeable future. And second, it is social earnest of the good faith and serious intentions of the authorities.

The main aspect of the strategic plan, as Rapoport (1974) has suggested, is designed to remove or alter the underlying structural causes of the deprivations and discontents. Thus, for example, if, as in Rhodesia, the underlying problem is political exclusion and economic exploitation of the Africans, then prevention will require basic reconstruction of the political and economic structures of the inclusive society. Such changes may require a long time to carry out, yet the protesting group needs an earnest of good faith, evidence of serious intentions, and demonstration of actual work on the part of the government. If the immediate issue is substandard housing, city officials can take steps to see to it that housing regulations are enforced in the poor and protesting neighborhoods. Results can begin to be evident within the week, and news will spread rapidly by the "bush radio." It takes much longer to provide adequate housing, i.e., enough housing of an acceptable quality. Yet city council can immediately begin to make motions and generate news as a demonstration that they are acting in good faith.

Such strategic actions may forestall the outbreak of serious and destructive social conflict. If carried out, these actions can abort the causal buildup and avert the outcome of serious conflict. Yet it is evident that the changes produced and the arrangements developed can be only transitory at best. As Himes (1968: 446) has pointed out, the preventive process seeks to manage the flow of change in order to produce the social structure required to achieve "a predetermined series of substantive and qualitative experiences" as its manifest function. In the specific case of conflict prevention, the predetermined substantive and qualitative experiences consist of social relations free of destructive or disruptive conflict. In Greensboro, the aim of conflict prevention was to facilitate change of the racial and educational structures while maintaining desirable community relations. Likert and Likert developed "System 4" to implement substantive structural changes without any loss of good intraorganizational relations. Boulding, in the article mentioned above, proposed fundamental changes of world structure in order to avoid war while retaining positive international relations. Yet even though conflicts may have been prevented, the process of social change will not have been terminated and the force of social change will not have been permanently neutralized. In time, change will again dislocate the remedial structures and conditions and produce new instances of ill-fitting structures, social stress, and collective deprivation and discontent. A new buildup of the causes of conflict may threaten the group and require it to do the job of conflict prevention over again. In the following chapter, we will examine that strategy of long-range conflict prevention that establishes more or less durable institutions to provide for the expression of conflict while keeping its manifestations within the bounds of social legitimacy. We call this strategy "institutionalization."

Prevention: Institutionalizing Struggle

Aberle and associates (1950: 108) showed that the "regulation of affective expression" is one prerequisite of a society. The untrammeled manifestation of hostility can be so disruptive as to lead to the breakdown of a social system. Lofchie (1965: 257) revealed how lack of regularizing mechanisms permitted Zanzibar to drift into violence during the transfer of power from the Arab oligarchy to the African majority. Collective feelings were not disciplined and intergroup relations drifted into violence. Ordinarily, societies develop mechanisms and processes for regularizing emotional expression and social relations. These mechanisms and processes are called *institutionalization*. In this chapter, we will examine institutionalization as a conflict-preventive strategy. The discussion begins by defining institutionalization in two ways. First, the concept is defined by specifying and examining its distinguishing characteristics. From another perspective, the meaning of conflict institutionalization is revealed by demonstration, by specifying the referent of the concept. For this purpose, two typical cases are presented. We then turn to a consideration of conditions under which collective actors resort to this approach to regulating struggle. The major task of the chapter is the formulation of a general strategy of conflict institutionalization. The chapter ends with a consideration of some unsettled issues inherent in the process of institutionalizing legitimate conflict.

THE NATURE OF CONFLICT INSTITUTIONALIZATION

Institutionalization Defined

In the present context, the term *institutionalization* is understood to refer to a set of binding social norms and a pattern of collective action that endorse, regularize, and reward legitimate social struggle as one way of preventing the resort to nonlegitimate conflict. The concept denotes the process of bringing conflict under the control of binding rules, the cluster of those rules in effect at any given time, and the pattern of collective action required by those rules. In the course of preventing the resort to nonlegitimate conflict, the strategy of institutionalization seeks to accomplish three ends. First, by endorsing legitimate conflict, it aims to encourage and support groups to seek legitimate ends and cherished values by socially approved means. At the same time, institutionalization seeks to pattern and regularize their struggles, thus making them both comprehensible and predictable. And third, the practice of institutionalization undertakes to give some assurance that conflict conducted in this approved and regular fashion will lead to success. That is, the conflict actor can expect to achieve part, at least, of his manifest goals, and the social system can expect to be protected from nonlegitimate and possibly harmful conflict.

In authoritarian social systems such as feudalism or the present structure of South Africa or the Soviet Union, conflict is institutionalized by legitimating extreme deprivation of subordinate social categories and by prohibiting them from engaging in dissent or rebellion. In this situation nonstruggle by the inferior categories is made normative. For example, under feudalism the normative system legitimated the lot of the serfs and defined dissent or rebellion as improper and impermissible. Conflict between serfs and nobles was, therefore, limited and ritualized. After an exhaustive study, *Conflict and Decision Making in Soviet Russia,* Ploss (1965) concluded that dissent and rebellion on the part of the suppressed classes were virtually nonexistent. Schermerhorn (1976: 47–50) reported that, following severe rioting in Gujarat State (India) in 1969, the use of repressive police and paramilitary force prior to threatening situations was recommended as a strategy for preventing future riots. On the other hand, in open social systems such as Canada, the United States, or the United Kingdom, social institutions are employed to prevent the resort to nonlegitimate conflict by facilitating and rewarding the expression of legitimate struggle. Galtung (1965: 348–98) stresses this point in his analysis of the strategy of "institutionalized conflict resolutions." He catalogues the familiar systems of the institutionalization of conflict that typify western political societies.

Sumner (1960: 62) pointed out that institutional arrangements for collective action may be either "crescive," i.e., growing gradually out of the mores; or "enacted," i.e., produced by "rational invention and intention." The crescive process produces traditional rules and patterns. In an earlier chapter we referred to these traditional patterns as adjustive or accommodative mechanisms. For example, in some American Indian tribes the peace pipe ceremony functioned to maximize accord and limit conflict. Passing the pipe while engaged in discussion facilitated the ventilation of feelings and the maintenance of relations within the confines of custom. In large urban settings, athletic matches, political contests, fund-raising competitions, policy debates, and similar legitimate competitive and conflict activities are used to generate collective satisfaction and reduce discontent, tension, and the inclination to nonlegitimate struggle. Public gatherings, like parades, receptions, and concerts permit members of separated and opposed categories to associate and thereby maximize sentiments of mutual acceptance and social integration while ventilating hostile feelings. However, in advanced industrial societies there is an increasing tendency to rely on enacted or instrumental preventive mechanisms. This tendency results not only from the growing prevalence and destructiveness of nonlegitimate conflict, but also because the fund of preventive knowledge and technology is great and continues to increase. The result is a growing number of organizations, courts, commissions, boards, and the like at every level of political organization, from global to neighborhood, engaged in the business of containing conflict. Familiar examples include the United Nations and the World Court, NATO and the OAS, the National Labor Relations Board, and the various state and local human relations commissions. Licklider (1976–77: 619–24) observed that American participation in NATO results in part at least from an interest in preventing thermonuclear war.

Institutionalization Illustrated

The following two cases are instances of conflict institutionalization. In the first, it is shown how the United States regularized political behavior and thereby reduced political violence and corruption. The normative controls and collective patterns grew crescively over the whole life of the republic. In the aggregate, these devices compose a conflict-accommodative mechanism. The second case, the national labor relations system, is an enacted apparatus. In time it too has grown and altered by crescive additions to the original structure. Both approaches serve to prevent nonlegitimate conflict to a significant degree.

The nation was born in intense and ultimately revolutionary political struggle against the parent power. Skolnick (1969: 11–12) reported that this "international" struggle "pitted Americans against Americans," in a pattern of increasing internal political strife. The writers of the Constitution faced and managed to institutionalize this pervasive political rivalry and contention. However, Skolnick (10–16) went on to show that following this first success in conflict institutionalization, political strife has characterized every period of national history and engaged most sectors of the population at one time or another. Over the years, leading contenders included many Indian tribes, Allegheny and Appalachian farmers, the Confederate South, white "nativists," labor and management, blacks and whites, rebellious women, the old, the young, the poor, and all the racial and ethnic minorities.

This succession of abrasive and violent conflicts combined to set in motion a series of remedial actions. One evidence was passage, both in the Congress and in the several states, of laws designed to regulate the competitive political process. At the same time, moral revulsion and adverse publicity operated to force the political parties to impose practices of self-regulation. Illustrating these developments at the local level, Cressey (1949: 389–94) described the early pattern of political conflict and corruption in the Harlan County, Kentucky, coal mining community. He went on to show how these competitions and rivalries were regularized and cleaned up in later practice.

At the federal level, one device for the regulating and regularizing of political conflict was the establishment of a series of regulatory agencies. Among the better known are the Federal Utilities Commission, the Federal Trade Commission, the Federal Communications Commission, the Federal Aviation Administration, and the National Labor Relations Board. The manifest function of these agencies is to promote and facilitate "competition" within important sectors of the economy and society while preventing and limiting conflict, especially nonlegitimate struggle. The latest federal political regulatory agency is the Federal Elections Commission. Established in 1974, this agency is charged with monitoring financial activities in national elections and preventing impermissible conflict and corruption.

In the 1950s and 1960s, the nation was faced with a new series of political and politicized conflicts. They have emerged from the new conditions of life in the society and from the politicization of collective activity. As a consequence, the disadvantaged groups and sectors of the society—the poor, the minorities, the young and the old, women, and the ideologically deviant—have transformed their struggles for "liberation" and "equality" into political and quasi-political contests. The society was unprepared to absorb and manage this new type of political struggle. Only slight progress has as yet been made toward devising and implementing mechanisms for institutionalizing these conflicts.

Stimulated by the ideas of Karl Marx and the experiences of European workers, American workers began to rebel against the conditions of their work and lives, and against the capitalist order as a whole. Here and there during the course of the nineteenth century, workers began to organize. In 1886 some of these local organizations were fused into the Knights of Labor. The efforts of organized workers to improve their lot were met by fierce resistance from the owner-managers. The last quarter of the nineteenth century and the first third of the twentieth centuries were characterized by ferocious battles between workers and managers. Taft and Ross (1969: 281–396) summarized this remarkable record of uncontrolled violence and coercion.

This appalling demonstration was one of the factors that stimulated the national revulsion that was expressed in part in the "muckraking" movement of the late 1890s and early 1900s. Pressure for federal legislation to clean up this national mess and establish order in the relations of workers and industries grew rapidly. The Congress sought ways to regulate the jungle of labor relations and experimented with various remedies. Many states began to enact industry-regulating legislation, often based on the models established in England and Germany. In a number of places, industrial and labor leadership began experimenting with voluntary schemes of accord and reconciliation. Timidly at first and later with more certainty, the federal government entered the field of labor-management regulation under terms of the "general welfare" clause of the Constitution.

Taylor (1949) discusses the actions and programs of the government during the first half of this century to regulate and order these relations. At first, the laws prohibited violence on the part of labor unions and restrained the actions of workers. Later, legislation and court action were directed to protecting some rights of workers, e.g., the right to strike and the outlawing of "yellow dog" contracts. In the 1930s, under the New Deal, forthright steps were taken by the federal government to protect workers from powerful management and to regularize relations between these sectors. The essential elements of an institutionalizing system were gradually accumulated by legislation and volunteer action. These developments climaxed in passage of the Wagner National Labor Relations Act in 1935 during the Great Depression. By this step, the Congress enacted a model for institutionalizing conflict. It enunciated as national policy the right of workers to organize into unions of their own choice and to struggle for legitimate ends of their own selection. The act laid down the basic rules of labor-management relations, recognizing the divergence of interests and regulating the consequent conflict. The Wagner Act established a national agency, the National Labor Relations Board, to administer the rules, adjudicate disputes, and enforce the regulation of conflict. In the conduct of this business it was recognized that the guiding principle should be compromise of divergent and clashing claims.

The operation of the system is conditioned by the nature of the potential conflict situation. For example, when two unions compete for members in an unorganized industry or factory, both may claim to have a majority and therefore the right to represent all the workers, thus creating an institutionalizable potential conflict situation. The Labor Relations Board is authorized to step into such a situation, take control of the organizing campaign, arrange and conduct an election among the workers and declare and certify the winner and sole representative. Breakdown of contract negotiations may require somewhat different operations. If the strike that has already been set is in a crucial industry, e.g., railroads, steel, or petroleum, the Board may ask the president to impose a stay of action for a "cooling off" period while negotiations continue. The mediation staff of the Board enters the process, seeking to facilitate communication and compromise. If these actions are successful, as is often but not always the case, a harmful and wasteful strike can be avoided. In other situations, if requested, the Board can activate institutionalized procedures to settle specific grievances, and prevent their escalation into serious collective conflict. Typically, a single complainant or union on behalf of a group of complainants files a petition with the Board. The field staff investigates the allegations and the hearing staff reviews their report and takes evidence from the parties to the issue. On the basis of this evidence and with the interests of the opposing parties and the general community in mind, the Board renders a decision which it has the authority to enforce. Commenting upon the inclusive labor-management system, Taft and Ross (1970: 378–80) showed how it utilized institutional patterns to prevent nonlegitimate strife and to facilitate and regularize industrial struggle. They write as follows about the general operations of the system:

> A fundamental purpose of the national labor policy, first enunciated by the Wagner Act and confirmed by its subsequent amendments in the Taft-Hartley and Landrum-Griffin Acts was the substitution of orderly procedures for trials of combat. But in balancing the public interest in the peaceful settlement of industrial disputes with the freedom of labor and management to work out their problems in light of their needs and experience, the law did not outlaw the exercise of economic force. Indeed, by endorsing collective bargaining, the NLRA explicitly acknowledged that tests of strength, i.e., the infliction of economic harm, with all its costs and hardships, is superior to such alternatives as compulsory arbitration.

In the same passage, Taft and Ross go on to indicate the consequences of the institutionalization of labor-management conflict. They stress that struggle between these two giants of the American economic system was not terminated, nor as a matter of fact substantially reduced. However, violence in the labor-management field was dramatically curtailed and the possibility of its recurrence was prevented in significant degree. Speaking of these accomplishments, Taft and Ross (385–86) report:

> Because employer refusal to meet and deal with unions was the major cause of past violent labor strikes, the effective enforcement of the Wagner Act reduced sharply the number of such encounters. This diminution of labor violence was not a temporary phenomenon but endured the strains of major and minor wars, a number of business cycles, and substantial changes in national and local political administrations. The reconversion of American industry after World War II brought on the greatest strike wave in our history. Yet, these mammoth strikes were accompanied by virtually no violence, completely at variance with the experience after 1918. The diminution of violence on labor's side has correspondingly lowered the propensity of employers to resort to force as either a defensive or aggressive tactic. The McClellan Committee's 1956–59 investigation of improper union and employer activities found no evidence of large-scale violence except in a few instances such as the Kohler and Perfect Circle cases.

SOME CONDITIONS OF CONFLICT INSTITUTIONALIZATION

In every social system, some conflicts have been brought under management by social institutions. Some others have been neglected and tend to flare up from time to time into disruptive nonlegitimate episodes. In Northern Ireland, for example, competition and rivalry in the marketplace have been regulated by long established economic institutions and agencies. However, the animosities and struggles between the deprived Roman Catholic minority and the advantaged Protestant majority have been left to follow their own internecine course. In Rhodesia, the struggle of the whites' under-classes against the white elites is managed and proceeds in an orderly fashion. From the time of first contact in the 1880s, however, the struggles of alien whites and native Africans have been bloody, fierce, and unrelenting. Situations like these lead us to ask why certain conflicts are brought under regulation by social norms and organizations while others are not. A number of the conditions that support the resort to strategies of prevention were discussed in the foregoing chapter. They include value orientations, system openness, cost-benefit estimation, the possibility of intervention, legitimacy of the managing agent, and availability of resources. Three additional conditions tend to prompt the resort to the strategy of institutionalization. They are established willingness to submit to institutional constraint, the trauma of a previous destructive conflict, and access to appropriate technical knowledge.

First, as Deutsch (1973: 377–78) pointed out, actors may be willing to turn to conflict institutionalization if they can accept the outcome even when "it is considered to be unfavorable to their interests," and if they believe the opposition is legitimate. This means that the institutionalization strategy requires considerable investment of discipline and commitment on the part of the participants. For example, the American labor relations system was able to work because both industrial management and organized labor perceived each other as legitimate and could accept the program and live with its outcome. On the other hand, it has been difficult to regularize conflict in the Middle East in this way because neither participant has come to regard the opposition as fully legitimate and been able to accept the process of institutionalization and its possible outcomes.

Second, a particularly destructive conflict or telling series of violent episodes may drive a collective actor to determine to do something about its situation. The conviction spreads that people "have had it," and relief must be found in some way. Institutionalization is one of the options of action that are still available. For example, many large American cities reacted to the extremities of the riots of the 1960s by setting in motion various schemes for institutionalizing intergroup conflict. Sometimes these efforts took the form of human relations systems. In a few instances, more elaborate programs were designed to bring intergroup relations under the discipline of legal and community norms. The classic illustration of this facilitating condition and the enactment of an institutionalization program was the establishment of the United Nations in 1945. Eggleston (1957: 323) noted that the determination to establish a United Nations Organization issued from the shocking experiences of the Second World War, the disappointing failures of the League of Nations and the disastrous holocaust of World War I.

Third, advances in social knowledge and changing social orientations may lead people to believe that something indeed can be done about their situation. In this connection, Smith (1971: xv) observed that "in contrast to previous generations, traditional attitudes of pessimism and powerlessness over our destiny are being replaced by those of ambivalence and even hope." In addition, there is available a growing fund of technical knowledge of how to proceed to institutionalize social conflict. There are relevant precedents of arrangements that worked and schemes that failed. Much has been learned about how to organize and act collectively to prevent war and maintain international peace. As a result, when the United Nations was established idealism was tempered with realism. For example, although by then it had been recognized that there was little chance of abolishing war entirely, it was known that it could be prevented for a time and mitigated in both scope and violence. It was shown in an earlier chapter that research and publication on the issues of conflict and peace burgeoned dramatically after World War II. In the United States, research in this field gained further impetus from the damaging city riots of the 1960s. Meanwhile, experimentation had been going on in many places with strategies and tactics for the institutionalization of conflict.

A STRATEGY FOR INSTRUMENTAL CONFLICT INSTITUTIONALIZATION

The prevention of conflict by institutionalization of legitimate struggle differs from prevention by removing causes as discussed in the foregoing chapter. Both seek to forestall the resort to nonlegitimate means by reducing or removing the causal pressures issuing from heightened deprivation and discontent. However, they differ in the strategy employed to accomplish this reduction of pressure. In the first case, the manifest aim of strategy is to facilitate legitimate struggle and the accomplishment of collective goals and thus reduce the inclination to resort to nonlegitimate tactics. In the latter case, strategy is controlled and focused in order to remove the causes of nonlegitimate conflict.

In this section we identify and examine the central components of an instrumental preventive strategy that focuses on facilitating legitimate forms and levels of struggle. Attention is centered on using the normative system to this end. The image created by this strategy is that of a social system which operates in such a way that discontented groups harboring divergent and clashing goals can achieve reasonable satisfaction without feeling constrained to resort to coercion, violence, terrorism, war, or the other forms of nonlegitimate struggle. A governing body or other authoritative organization that undertakes to institutionalize social conflicts will take minimally four kinds of instrumental actions, which in the aggregate constitute a strategy for conflict institutionalization. The four types of collective action can be stated in the following way:

1—Recognition as a matter of policy that various groups and sectors of the community or society are likely to have divergent, incompatible, or clashing interests.

2—Guarantees to the several groups and sectors of the right to pursue their interests, with the understanding that this right is limited by the rights of other groups and sectors and by the requirements of the inclusive social system.

3—Establishment and enforcement of binding institutions to regularize and regulate the resultant struggles in order to ensure satisfaction to the adversaries and with a view to the reciprocal rights of participants and the welfare of the society or community.

4—Establishment and support of an agency to supervise and enforce the institutional rules, and to work for solutions of disputes and conflicts that issue from the pursuit of divergent and clashing interests.

Legitimacy of Divergent Interests

Lenski (1966: 24–42) has argued that divergence and clash of interests is a universal fact of human social life. He goes on to assert that, since people always seek to maximize rewards and to limit penalties, the divergence of interests and the inequality of opportunities to fulfill them make social conflict virtually universal and inevitable. The diversity of collective interests and resulting controversies are reported in the histories of all known societies. From the beginning, the diversity of cultures and races in the young American society were seen as a problem. George Washington, John Adams, and Thomas Jefferson deplored the deviations of the newcomers from the English normative standard that they had established. Throughout the eighteenth and nineteenth centuries, the reaction of the dominant culture to growing diversity was expressed in a series of nativistic movements and violent outbursts. Gordon (1964: 84–131) reported that the strategies of managing diversities and conflict were formulated in three main ways. At first the strategy was defined as expectation or requirement of conformity of newcomers to the Anglo-American norm. In this way conflict would be minimized and harmony would be stabilized. Later on, it was believed that controversies and conflicts would be institutionalized through the process of reciprocal cultural fusion in a societal melting pot. Beginning early in the 1900s the mechanism and process of conflict management was envisaged as coexistence of diverse people within an inclusive pluralistic social system.

As a strategy of conflict management, the aims of institutionalization intersect the conflict activities of collective actors who are pursuing their divergent and "legitimate" interests. Facilitating the realization of such

collective interests (within reasonable limits) while restraining the ensuing conflicts constitutes the basic aim of the institutionalization strategy. The preventive strategy is formulated in different ways to fit
different actual situations. For example, an institutionalization strategy
for a global situation would differ in significant ways from the strategy
designed for a small tribal village. The strategy used to regularize and
regulate conflict around a school desegregation issue would not fit a
major labor-management controversy, even though both would be
grounded in similar principles. It was shown in an earlier section that
institutionalizing labor-management strife in the United States differs
from the arrangements needed to manage political conflict.

Recognition and acceptance of the fact of the diversity and clash of
collective interests and the resultant predisposition toward social conflict is the prelude to institutionalization. This recognition and acceptance must be *instituted*, i.e., established institutionally as the collective
policy of some social unit or societal system. What is required thus is a
policy statement by the institutionalizing agency, e.g., the government,
the school board, the assembled nations of the free world. For example,
Eggleston (1957: 223) observed that, when the representatives of many
nations met in San Francisco in 1945, one of the first actions they took
was to affirm this basic conflict-institutionalizing policy. He noted that
they affirmed the fact that the cooperating nations were independent,
sovereign bodies and that they brought with them divergent and often
clashing interests. The problem they faced was to work forward from this
fact to arrangements that would facilitate efforts to fulfill these interests
and at the same time restrain the disputes and controversies that were
sure to flow from these efforts. The Wagner Labor Relations Act of
1935 promulgated this same principle. It was noted that employers and
workers had divergent and sometimes clashing "legitimate" interests.
The right of each sector to work on behalf of these interests was affirmed and the legitimate means of these efforts were noted. Taft and
Ross (1970: 381) reported that, although violence declined sharply in
labor-management struggle after the Wagner Act went into effect, the
volume of conflict increased. Both sides found that they could achieve
many of their legitimate goals by legitimate means. Violence became
unnecessary and dysfunctional. The importance of recognition of di-
vergency of interests and the risk of nonlegitimate conflict is demonstrated in the embattled sphere of school desegregation in the United
States. When school boards issued firm, clear policy statements on the
matter, recognizing the divergent interests of the two sides but defining
violence and social disruption as impermissible, changes in the school

systems proceeded with a minimum of disruption. Such school boards could proceed with establishing the rules of conduct and facilitating the efforts and interests of all parties concerned. Failure to make these principles of policy clear tends to create a control vacuum within which conflict escalates. For example, Edleman (1973: 32–42) pointed out that failure of American presidents to take a firm, clear policy stand on school desegregation following the Brown decision of 1954 seriously impeded control and institutionalization of the racial conflicts that flared up in the ensuing years. The policy statement should stress at least three salient points. First, authorities should make the empirical observation that different groups are likely to possess and advocate different and sometimes clashing values and interests. Second, all participating groups have the basic right to pursue their interests, provided they do not interfere with other groups, and provided the pursuit of these interests does not damage or threaten the general welfare. And third, the actions designed to achieve the various collective interests may sometimes produce forms and levels of conflict that the society or community will not tolerate. In this event, the society or community must intervene on behalf of the collective welfare and the well-being of the individuals concerned.

Rules of Conflict

The institutionalization of social conflict requires establishment of a system of binding rules for the participating collective actors. These regulations lay out the patterns and set boundaries to action in the pursuit of collective interests. Baumgartner (1975: 417–37) speaks of "relational control" or institutionalization as the means of managing international conflicts. He describes relational control as the means to structuring long-term social processes and outcomes. The rules that produce relational control can be used both to encourage cooperation and to regulate competition and conflict. The relational control or conflict-regulating institutions can be illustrated in many ways. The various national labor relations acts in the United States require parties to a dispute to "negotiate in good faith," and to avoid certain traditional practices, e.g., blacklisting offending workers or obstructing the access by picketing workers to struck factories. Falk (1970: 33–40) pointed out that international law permitted traditional armed conflict in Vietnam, but prohibited the massacre of civilian populations as occurred in Songmy village. The rules in any institutionalization system should cover at least the following four issues:

1—Differentiation of legitimate and nonlegitimate tactics. For example, stipulation that in a strike a boycott is legitimate but that a secondary boycott is not.

2—Approval of legitimate modes of struggle for legitimate goals. For example, workers may organize into unions to bargain for wages, hours, and working conditions, but may not damage the property of employers in the course of the strike.

3—Procedures for the redress of grievances, for example, hearing procedures to right an alleged wrong against an aggrieved actor. This procedure includes the right to appeal to a higher authority if the aggrieved party is not satisfied with the first decision.

4—Procedures or ways to revise or amend these rules. Circumstances change and existing rules must be revised or replaced. There should be clear directions on how to make these changes.

A crucial task of rule-making for conflict institutionalization is differentiating in concrete terms between those forms and levels of conflict that the social system will tolerate and those that it will not. This is the issue of legitimacy that was examined in the first chapter of this book and that has been a central referent in all the subsequent discussions. Such distinctions eliminate ambiguity and confusion in the business of conflict executing and management. Yet, as noted several times, the definitions of legitimate and nonlegitimate change from time to time and vary from place to place. Nevertheless, such distinctions need to be recognized and specified for the time and place of the institutionalizing operation. This aspect of institutionalization tactic can be illustrated. In Northern Ireland, the IRA regards terrorism as a legitimate conflict tactic under the circumstances of its struggle against the dominant Protestants and the British government. However, in the larger world society, as well as among much of the Protestant and Roman Catholic communities of Northern Ireland, terrorism is defined as nonlegitimate. To institutionalize this conflict would require some consensus on the moral definition of this tactic. The rules of labor-management relations under the present American system contain many normative prescriptions that define legitimate and nonlegitimate modes of action and struggle. The system works because both parties have accepted these normative definitions.

Definitions of legitimacy are conditioned both by changes of conflict tactics and weapons, and by alterations of social values. Arendt (1963: 3) observed that following World War I moral values of the Western world distinguished between "aggressive" and "defensive" wars. Therefore a basis existed for institutionalizing war in the modern world. In World War I the introduction of techniques of chemical and germ warfare and the invention of such weapons as the military plane and the tank raised unprecedented issues of legitimacy. In World War II, new tactics and weapons raised other unsettled issues of conflict legitimacy. These included, among others, the treatment of refugee populations, the practice of psychological warfare, the bombing of populated areas, and the management of nuclear weapons. There were no institutions to deal with tactics like the sit-in, massive demonstrations that blocked streets and sidewalks, confrontations where the operations of universities or business firms were interrupted, or the widespread instrumental use of limited violence. In the United States, the riots of the 1960s raised other issues of legitimacy. Institutionalization of conflict in such situations requires the development of appropriate rules for the conduct of conflict and their acceptance by contending parties and enforcement by institutionalizing organizations. In time also, as Turner (1969: 815–31) has shown, new tactics acquire legitimacy and thus become increasingly amenable to regularization by social institutions. The history of such noteworthy institutionalization systems as the United Nations and the American labor relations system shows that it took much experimentation over a long time to develop the existing institutional complexes.

As noted, a second obligation of the rules of conduct is to guarantee to the various groups and sectors of a social system the right to protest abuses and to struggle for advantages. These rules are a major indicator of the openness of the system. The foregoing discussion has suggested that the rules of conduct must not only differentiate legitimate forms and levels of struggle from those that are defined as nonlegitimate and therefore prohibited; they must also support and facilitate striving in legitimate ways for legitimate ends. For example, the Wagner Labor Relations Act of 1935 stipulated that workers enjoyed the right to organize into unions of their own choice and through these unions to bargain collectively for improvements in wages, working hours, and the conditions of work. As the labor relations system has evolved since its inception, this right has been extended and redefined to cover other "legitimate" ends, such as paid vacations, job security, retirement benefits, and limited participation of workers in company management. The system now ensures workers the right to struggle by legitimate means for these and other goals.

In addition, the rules stipulate appropriate ways to fight. That is, potential contenders in situations of dispute are directed into the appropriate channels for acting out their opposition. For example, when the students of a university wish certain rules or arrangements changed to their advantage, the institutionalizing system spells out in greater or lesser detail and clarity how they should go about attaining this end. The procedures may suggest that an appropriate proposal be sent to a certain university official or committee. This originating proposal may be supported by direct representations to the university official or committee. If the students believe they are not getting a serious hearing or that their proposal is being unreasonably resisted, there may be procedures or at least traditions that indicate further steps to putting pressure on the decision makers. Ultimately, the affair that started as a routine petition for change may escalate into a major controversy between organized students and the university administration. If institutionalized rules exist, this inclusive struggle may be conducted in legitimate ways that minimize disruptions, damage of property, or the risk of personal injury. If such rules exist and if the students as well as the administration know and accept them, then the struggle of the students will be made easier, and substantive accomplishments and collective satisfactions may result. There would then be little occasion for the students to consider resorting to nonlegitimate means to gain their ends.

Further, the rules of conflict also establish procedures for the redress of grievances. An individual or a group contends that it has been abused, exploited or in some way mistreated. An applicant for a job claims he was rejected because of sex or race. The Catholics in Northern Ireland, the French-speaking people of Quebec, the Moslems in Lebanon, the Africans in South Africa, complain that as a category they are segregated, discriminated against, exploited, abused, and in other ways mistreated. The accumulated mistreatment constitutes a grievance that they protest or complain about. The handling of such grievances and complaints may initiate a process of controversy and conflict which, as has often happened, escalates into rebellion, civil war, or revolution. The rules of institutionalization can provide clear and workable procedures for handling such grievances and complaints if nonlegitimate conflict is to be prevented.

These procedures can include clear step-by-step actions for presenting grievances, for petitioning for their redress, for the collection and review of evidence, and for the rendering and enforcement of decisions. These functions are the clear responsibility of an agency that has the appropriate competence and authority. The nature and functions of such an agency are discussed below. Typically, this aspect of the institutionalization process is assigned to a specialized agency, e.g., the United Nations, the Arab League, the National Labor Relations Board, or the state or local human relations commission. Such a practice is a matter of structural convenience. Governmental bodies are the most universal and inclusive authoritative units of general social organization. In open social systems, the use of government in such a role seems reasonable and customary. However, such managerial agencies may be established under private auspices. For example, vast religious bodies like the Roman Catholic Church, the Moslem faith, the Methodist Church, or the Anglican Church have institutional systems and managerial agencies for the regulation of internal conflicts. In the management of religious strife in the United States, attention may be directed to the institutionalizing functions of ecumenical organizations like the National Council of Churches and the National Council of Christians and Jews. Large private universities also maintain conflict-institutionalization systems with conflict-managing agencies, boards, or committees. Such investigatory, judicial, and adjudicatory agencies function to drain off much of the tension and pressure in dispute situations. Thus, while they may not abort the buildup of deprivations and discontents, they may reduce the risk of resort to nonlegitimate means. Widespread experience indicates that the mere existence and knowledge of such adjudicatory processes and agencies often serve to head off the buildup of resentment and hostility.

Sometimes the issues in dispute can be settled by the process of compromise. The contending parties may be brought together to discuss the disputed matter. The United Nations, the OAS, the National Labor Relations Board, and the various human relations commissions perform this service, sometimes serving as convener and mediator. Such processes of negotiation may lead to a compromise in which the two contending parties find common ground by reducing their opposing demands. Thus, typically, the striking labor union demands a 45 percent pay raise over a three-year period. Management offers only 15 percent over the same time period. After much haggling, they agree, i.e., compromise, on a figure of 27 percent over a four-year period. The struggle has been confined to the patterns of legitimacy set out in the conflict institutions, and settlement has been achieved by injecting flexibility into the opposing demand structures. However, some situations of dispute cannot be compromised. Either the claimant is awarded the decision or he is not. Then satisfaction may be achieved by the use of collateral concessions and arrangements. For example, if Puerto Secreto and Costa Pobre are locked in a dispute over claims to a single village, it may not be possible to find an acceptable compromise. It is ridiculous to suggest drawing a line through the middle of the village, giving half to each country. The division of Berlin and Jerusalem has demonstrated that such mechanical arrangements are awkward and unsatisfactory. Negotiation, with or without a mediator, may lead to an acceptable arrangement. Puerto Secreto gets the village, and Costa Pobre is granted certain important water rights which it long desired to a river flowing through the other nation's territory. Whatever the settlement, rules of legitimate struggle have been followed and the resort to warfare has been rendered unnecessary.

In addition, the rules of conflict will provide opportunities for disappointed actors to appeal settlements of their grievances or complaints. The conditions and procedures for this appeal should be made clear and accessible to all. The rule will suggest that defeat in one skirmish or on one day is not the end of the battle. The disappointed actor may fight his battle another day at a higher level of authority. Under the American system, the appeals procedures permit actors to take their cases ultimately to the Supreme Court. This procedure works and maintains openness and flexibility in the system if all parties have agreed to the set of rules. In other words, this is the system's way of assuring disappointed contenders that they have had full and fair chances to win their struggles. Various legitimate procedures are linked into a multilevel system as a way of obviating resort to nonlegitimate means to gain satisfaction.

Finally, the institutionalization system builds in ways for amending and revising the rules of conflict. Circumstances alter from time to time and the rules of legitimacy that were acceptable at one time may be unacceptable later. For example, the Northern Irish Catholics and the French-speaking Canadians lived under a set of norms that had become traditional. In recent years, however, both groups have made new demands and are restive under the old institutions. In Rhodesia, demands and tactics of the Africans emerged that were not envisaged and covered by traditional rules of intergroup struggle. Since no new rules were developed, the struggle between Africans and whites drifted into violence. Thus it is clear that institutional arrangements that at one time seemed to represent dramatic breakthrough may seem to oppress a little later. The system must contain procedures for making the necessary revisions and amendments of the rules of conflict.

Agency

Wernette (1972: 531–38) has observed that in order to apply the findings of research and to prevent conflict, it may be necessary to create new institutions and organizations specifically for conflict prevention. Such an established specialized agency constitutes one essential component of the institutionalization strategy. There is ample precedent for this step, e.g., the World Court, the United Nations, the National Labor Relations Board. Speaking of the roles of such regulatory agencies, Leone

(1972: 46–58) called them the main advocates of the public interest. He asserts that they watch the watchdogs. Although the best known such agencies are governmentally sponsored, this is a matter of convenience and tradition. Some of these agencies are private instrumentalities. Figure 10-1 illustrates the range and nature of such administrative and operating agencies by listing some familiar examples. Such administrative agencies ideally are composed of well-known persons with a demonstrated reputation for competence, fairness and high principles. If established by federal or state governments, they should be insulated from political pressure and control. Though technically answerable to the government, such agencies are basically accountable only to the people, since they are in a significant sense the agent and voice of the people.

It is crucial that the laws that make the basic rules and establish such agencies should also give them the authority to enforce the rules. Experience has shown that, without such power, such agencies tend to be little more than discussion groups. They are hampered in managing routine conflicts and often cannot prevent collective actors from resorting to nonlegitimate tactics. But established and armed, such institutionalizing agencies can perform at least four basic services. First, they can officially and publicly represent the conflicting interests of attacker and defender as well as that of the general community. In theory, and we hope in fact as well, they would stand outside the competing interests, holding them in mind, and examining issues with due regard for them all. The genius of these agencies is their ability to be directly concerned with the struggling and competing interests while keeping the common good in mind. But it is also evident that competing interests are also common interests and these could be well-served by such administrative and regulatory agencies. Speaking of the crucial role of such agencies and their hearings representatives, Zwerdling (1972: 27–35) concluded that the decisions made regulate competing private and public interests in areas that are economically and socially sensitive, and often politically explosive.

A second function of the agency is to administer the rules of conflict. It would interpret definitions and distinctions made by the law and, when needed, make additional definitions and distinctions. It would differentiate legitimate from prohibited conflict tactics and take steps to terminate nonlegitimate actions. At the same time, it would provide ways for legitimate disagreements to work themselves out to satisfactory settlements. In the case of grievances and complaints, the agency (or its representatives) could receive evidence, investigate allegations, clarify disagreements, and render and enforce decisions. In this respect, the agency is the servant and guardian of the public interest.

FIGURE 10-1

SOME CONFLICT-INSTITUTIONALIZING AGENCIES

INTERNATIONAL AGENCIES

The United Nations and its constituent agencies:
UNESCO, United Nations Educational,
    Scientific and Cultural Organization
UNICEF, United Nations Children's Fund
WHO, World Health Organization
WFAO, World Food and Agriculture Organization
Trustee Commission

World Court

Specialized worldwide conferences:
On food
On population
On religion, ecumenical conferences
On aviation
On use of the seas

REGIONAL AGENCIES

NATO, North Atlantic Treaty Organization
EEC, European Economic Community
Pan African Council
OAS, Organization of American States
Arab League
Warsaw Pact

NATIONAL AGENCIES

National Labor Relations Board
National Council of Churches
AFL-CIO
FTC, Federal Trade Commission
FAA, Federal Aviation Administration
FDA, Food and Drug Administration
American Arbitration Association
FCC, Federal Communications Commission
Federal Utilities Commission
FEC, Federal Elections Commission

STATE/LOCAL AGENCIES

Human Relations Councils
Councils of Churches
State mediation services
Ad hoc committees and commissions

Third, a residual function of the agency is to keep social conflict from taking nonlegitimate expression. In this connection, the agency can clarify the distinctions between legitimate and nonlegitimate modes of action. For example, the charter of the United Nations and the Labor Relations Act stipulate these distinctions and rights for participating groups. That is, these documents say to the public that one mode of struggle is permissible but another will not be tolerated. In this way, the agency could work to facilitate expressions of struggle and complaint that are legitimate while deterring by example and action the resort to nonlegitimate methods.

And finally, the agency could act in many ways to anticipate the build-up of tensions or the drift toward nonlegitimate struggle. It could conduct investigations, take positions, issue statements, recommend needed legislation and the like. In this connection such an agency should play an active educational role, explaining and interpreting trends and changes in the society that might affect the posture of conflict. In this role, the agency functions as a guardian of the general welfare.

ISSUES IN THE INSTITUTIONALIZATION OF CONFLICT

It has been said above that the aims, the manifest functions, of the conflict institutionalization strategy are to facilitate the realization of important collective interests through legitimate means and to manage the struggles that issue from the conflict of these efforts. An important residual or latent function of this structure of action is prevention, or at least the limitation of nonlegitimate conflict. These results are to be achieved by subjecting conflict actions to a set of binding rules, i.e., social institutions. However, the critics of the leading conflict institutionalization systems—the United Nations, the World Court, the national labor relations program, human relations commissions and so on—have argued that these schemes and mechanisms not only fail to accomplish their intended purposes, but also produce a number of dysfunctional consequences. As a result, this approach to conflict prevention as well as the existing agencies and programs are the center of a continuing debate. We can conclude this chapter by summarizing the arguments for and against this approach to conflict prevention.

The main criticisms of conflict institutionalization can be gathered up under four points. First, it is claimed that they tend to be inefficient. Inefficiency is said to result from ritualization of procedures, structural rigidity, preoccupation with self-maintenance, waste of social resources, and the like. Because of its inefficiency it is often argued that relatively little nonlegitimate conflict is prevented in relation to the investment of resources and energy. For example, critics point out that in spite of the efforts of the United Nations, there are serious international wars on every continent. Second, many people point out that matters are made worse, not better, by the fact that schemes of conflict institutionalization tend to increase the volume of social conflict. This criticism is often true. However, advocates of conflict institutionalization do not claim that this strategy will reduce the volume of social conflict; the aim is the prevention of nonlegitimate struggle. Gamson (1966: 71–81) pointed this out after a study of political conflicts in community situations. Third, the critics of conflict institutionalization contend also that such schemes tend to regiment, inhibit, and exploit conflict actors even though the intention may be to help them. Baran and Sweezy (1966: 155) argued that regulatory agencies, labor boards, consumer advocates, and human relations bodies actually serve to reinforce the conflict. At the same time, they tend to establish and intensify individual alienation. From the perspective of the radicals, conflict institutionalization is regarded as a hoax. As a consequence, monotony and rigidity are introduced into the social system under the pretense of achieving regularity and order. And finally, some of the critics claim that institutionalization provides a cloak under which bureaucratic officials can paralyze or coopt the conflict process. Thus, pompous little people and rigid, insecure officials gain control of the institutionalizing apparatus and paralyze it. Worse yet, it is feared that wicked, selfish people can coopt the machinery and process, turning them to their own advantage.

These are serious criticisms that have a strong enough basis in fact to command thoughtful attention. Moreover, recognition of such criticisms can serve two useful ends. First, they argue for balanced judgment in evaluating the institutionalization strategy. The efficacy of this strategic option of conflict management must be judged in the light of its disadvantages as well as its strengths. And second, these and other faults of the institutionalization strategy constitute problems or shortcomings that must be taken into account when establishing and operating such programs. But actions to remedy faults should be taken only after consideration of the possible dysfunctions of the remedies themselves.

Part of the response to these criticisms is an accounting of the latent functions of conflict institutionalization. The functions of conflict examined by Coser (1956) and discussed in chapter 6 have relevance for the institutionalization operation. For example, institutionalization operates to enhance the realistic character of social conflict, to increase social solidarity and strengthen internal group cohesion. Further, institutionalization gains for the business of conflict execution and management some of the advantages of bureaucracy. Merton (1957: 195–206) cities efficiency, economy, and expedition of operations as being among these advantages. That is, when managed under formal organization by competent officials and when controlled by specific rules, conflict is likely to consume fewer resources to produce desired ends than when otherwise managed. These advantages are evident when one considers the settlement of a threatening interracial dispute by a human relations council, or the regulation of an international controversy by the United Nations. The alternative to such management is likely to be wasteful and destructive. These considerations suggest that when the latent functions of conflict institutionalization are taken into account, the criticism of inefficiency reveals less validity than when taken at face value.

Moreover, the institutionalization strategy contributes to the integration of social systems. Enhanced social integration from regularized conflict manifests itself in several ways. The diverse interests of struggling social actors are brought into increased agreement with one another. Moreover, as Himes (1966: 6–7) has argued, the contending parties often seek the same basic value when struggling against one another. When their struggle is regulated by social institutions, they may maximize common basic values and move toward recognition of their common interests. Means for the attainment of these diverse and common interests become more congruent with the approaches and values of the inclusive social system. As a consequence, groups that at one time were on a collision course, once put under the control of the social institutions, discover new ways to realize their various goals while participating cooperatively within the inclusive social system and common interest. In the end, these criss-crossing institutionalized conflicts function to "sew" society together more securely.

At the same time, institutionalized conflict feeds a stream of adaptive changes into the social system that serves to keep it open and flexible. This occurs as groups realize their common interests through the facilitation of legitimate modes of struggle. The adversary groups adapt their patterns of struggle to the requirements of the control institutions, thus injecting further adaptive changes into the system. In this way the social system is kept vital and adaptable. Thus the argument of the critics that the institutionalization mechanism fosters structural rigidity is countered, in part at least, by the fact of latent change and adaptation. The vitality of the social system is also sustained by facilitating legitimate struggle for legitimate ends. Groups and sectors of the system enjoy the freedom and encouragement to work for the interests that are important to them. This effort keeps them alert and vital, while anti-social feelings—hostility, animosity, jealousy—are regularly ventilated. In short, institutionalized conflict performs a therapeutic service for the social system.

One hopes that social systems will confront the problems of conflict before they arise. In that event, they will make use of some of the numerous management tactics that fall under the aegis of the two preventive strategies discussed in this and the preceding chapter. Sometimes, however, conflict has exceeded the bonds of legitimacy before control action is initiated or after preventive techniques have been tried and proved unsuccessful. In such an event, steps are likely to be taken to terminate the process of nonlegitimate conflict and to reduce the intensity and/or violence of struggle to acceptable levels. For these purposes, social systems make use of two management strategies. One of these, called *resolution*, seeks to achieve agreement of the contending parties to the termination of nonlegitimate strife through processes of communication and exchange. The other, called *suppression*, seeks the same ends by the use of counterforce against one or both of the conflicting parties. In the following chapter we explore the strategy of conflict resolution.

The Resolution of Social Conflict

The subject of this chapter is the resolution of social conflict. As used here, that term refers to a process of change through which nonlegitimate conflict is replaced by a normative pattern of legitimate struggle. The precise meaning of *conflict resolution* is specified in a definition and clarified both in an analysis of the definition and the presentation of a concrete case. Long-standing, intense, and violent struggles like those in Northern Ireland and the Middle East suggest that some nonlegitimate conflicts are difficult or impossible to resolve. This thought turns our attention to the conditions that facilitate conflict resolution. The main part of the chapter is occupied by an anaysis of the resolution process. At this point, we construct a paradigm of conflict resolution.

THE NATURE OF CONFLICT RESOLUTION

Resolution Defined

In common usage the phrase *conflict resolution* has been applied to all types of collective efforts and approaches designed to lessen the danger of war, to mitigate intergroup strife, to expand the possibility of amity and peace, and the like. Galtung (1965: 357–60) identified twelve resolution mechanisms ranging from ordeals to mediation, from court processes to voting. However, some of these are preventive tactics and others are suppressive actions. LaTaur and others (1967: 319–55) listed "autocratic solution," "arbitration," "moot," and "bargaining" as conflict resolution strategies. In the present context, the term *conflict resolution* is used in a more restricted sense.

When we speak of conflict resolution, we understand that a fully developed nonlegitimate conflict is in existence. Resolution means terminating such a nonlegitimate conflict by techniques of social interaction and restoring relations between the contending actors to a level of legitimacy. From this perspective, the concept *conflict resolution* can be defined as processes of communication and exchange between collective actors engaged in nonlegitimate conflict, which are initiated with or without an intermediator, and which seek to terminate nonlegitimate conflict and to restore social relations between the actors to some level of legitimacy under specific normative terms.

The act of resolution is a shift in the mode of interaction between contending parties. The conflict is terminated and legitimacy is restored when conflict actors cease using force as attacker or defender to gain or control scarce values and, instead, begin to employ substitutions and tradeoffs to defend or gain these values. Once this happens, the context of social relations is altered. Nonlegitimate conflict is terminated and social struggle is confined by the institutions to the realm of legitimacy. For example, a labor union goes on strike to enforce its demand for higher wages. Management refuses, arguing it cannot afford higher wages. Instead, the managers demand that worker productivity should be increased. This conflict is resolved when it is perceived that each can get what it wants by an exchange: higher wages for increased productivity. The Israelis demand ironclad guarantees of national integrity and boundaries and the Arabs insist upon return of conquered territory and decent settlement of the problems of Palestinian refugees. Each side controls the value desired by the other. The conflict can be resolved when the antagonists cease to use force to gain their ends and agree to a tradeoff, i.e., national integrity for the Jews and territorial and refugee concessions for the Arabs.

Conflict resolution involves the manipulation of social relations. By the very nature of the case the shift from intense and/or violent struggle to negotiation and exchange will require conscious and often prolonged effort. In a later section of this chapter, the main techniques of managing this shift of social relations are examined. It should also be recognized that resolution does not necessarily mean a change of a social pattern nor a permanent termination of nonlegitimate struggle. Resolution produces an arrangement that may continue for a limited time only. Factors and forces emanating from other sources may alter the temporary adjustment and introduce new conditions of tension, discontent, and nonlegitimate conflict.

Resolving the Middle East Conflicts

The circumstances surrounding the settlement of Jews in the Middle East and the establishment of the State of Israel ensured endless strife between Jews and Arabs. As is typical in these cases, this strife has flared up into violence and subsided into barely tolerable legitimacy from time to time over a period of thirty years. The resolution of each "war" or violent episode helped to prepare the stage for the outbreak of the next. The Israeli war to defend her independence in 1947 was terminated by the intervention of the United Nations. With the assistance of intermediators, a cease-fire was established; communication between the combatants was facilitated, and after long, hard negotiations, a settlement of sorts was forged. Both sides made substantial gains. However, many crucial issues remained unsettled—the problem of Arab refugees and displaced persons, clashing claims to territory, rights to resources and transportation lines, etc.

This resolution maintained a fragile state of nonwar for nearly twenty years. However, hostility continued high between Arabs and Jews. The Arabs harassed the Jews endlessly. The Jews struck back in violent raids and by oppressing subject and displaced Arabs. Sporadic border violence increased dramatically in the mid-1960s. Davidson (1974: 119–34) reported that absent or faulty communication between the two peoples exacerbated the situation. He pointed out that in 1956 the Israelis terminated talks in the Egyptian Mixed Armistice Commission. Thereafter, for almost ten years there was no official communication between Israel and her Arab neighbors. The two parties communicated by propaganda, which further exacerbated their relations. At the same time, individuals and groups that favored negotiation and compromise were isolated and rendered powerless by the media.

In 1967 this brittle nonwar broke into violence with the Israeli "defensive" attack against Jordan and Egypt. The fighting was brief, savage, destructive, and decisive. Within six days the Israeli forces had destroyed the vaunted Jordan air force, immobilized her ground legions, and soundly defeated the Egyptian armies in the field. Having attained her limited objectives, Israel was ready to resolve the fight. Again with the help of the United Nations, a cease-fire was implemented, negotiations were carried through, and agreements were worked out and accepted.

The resolution of this attack created an even more fragile and brittle nonwar than had emerged two decades earlier. Suspicion, hostility, and conflict between Jews and Arabs continued at a higher and less tolerable level of intensity than prior to the outbreak of the Six Day War. Each side devoted itself to arming or rearming in preparation for the next episode. The level and intensity of propaganda increased. A steady stream of violent incidents along Israel's borders kept tension at an almost intolerable level. The inevitable attack came by surprise. Without notice, Egypt and Syria attacked 17 September 1973, while the Jews were celebrating their high holy days of Yom Kippur. Again the fighting was ferocious. With the advantage of surprise and better arms than before, the Arabs at first made quick gains on all fronts. In a short time, though, the Israelis recovered and went on the offensive. When they began winning, forcing the Arabs back into their own territory, concerned third parties—the United Nations, the United States, and others—intervened to arrange a cease-fire and some settlement of the war. The American secretary of state, Henry Kissinger, became the intermediator and carried through the resolution process by means of "shuttle diplomacy." First, he persuaded both sides to enter into a cease-fire that resembled a stalemate. The field armies were induced to pull back from the fighting lines and maintain these new positions. Later, arrangements were made to guard these temporary battle-line boundaries by United Nations peacekeeping forces. Under pressure from all quarters, both sides curtailed their propaganda and expressed interest in making permanent settlements. Little by little, by employing all the tactics of resolution, the intermediator enabled the contending parties to narrow differences and widen areas of agreement until a minimally workable arrangement could be forged and written. This interim settlement dealt with armed forces in the field, temporary boundaries, questions of arms and their disposition, rights of the warring nations, and plans for a multinational conference to meet later in Geneva to hammer out a permanent peace treaty. Little further progress toward permanent settlement could be made beyond these initial arrangements.

The fragile "resolution" and indeterminate "war" ground on, punctuated from time to time by terrorist attacks against Israeli border communities and unsuspecting citizens in the cities. In December of 1977 the pattern was interrupted by President Anwar Sadat's dramatic visit to Jerusalem to discuss peace and a permanent agreement with Israeli officials. This spectacular event set in motion a series of meetings and activities that slowly petered out over the succeeding months. In April 1978 Israel rocked the region by a large-scale military attack against the Palestinian guerrilla bases in southern Lebanon. Again the United Nations intervened and assisted with maintaining order in the area as the Israeli troops withdrew. In the summer of 1978 the situation remains indecisive, unclear and continuously threatening to explode into another ferocious little war.

SOME CONDITIONS OF CONFLICT RESOLUTION

It is not possible to resolve every episode of nonlegitimate conflict. The requirements of an ideology, the state of the conflict itself, the participants' estimates of their chances of winning, pressures from the inside or outside—these and other conditions may prevent the combatants from considering resolution as a viable option. On the other hand, certain conditions increase the possibility of a conflict's being resolved.

First, a collective conflict actor that is characterized by homogeneity of members, stability of organization and competence of leaders may feel self-assured and willing to risk the effort to resolve an ongoing struggle. Leaders can explore the possibility of negotiating an end to the conflict without fear of losing face or undermining their legitimacy. In his "Proposition 17" Williams (1977: 335) notes that the absence of these internal characteristics tends to limit the chances of conflict resolution. Thus he asserts that when leaders have limited control over heterogeneous memberships, they cannot guarantee compliance with agreements when made. For example, in some societies a national election may trigger a rash of disturbances during the campaign and a full-scale revolution after the returns are in. This reaction was illustrated in the March 1977 Pakistani elections and in the May 1978 elections in the Dominican Republic. In other societies, the conditions are present to facilitate popular elections as a way of resolving political contests. Second, certain aspects of the preconflict relations between the contending parties tend to facilitate the resolution of their controversy. If in the past they had experienced a pattern of harmonious relations, a commitment to reasonable settlement of disputes, and a substantial area of shared values, then a present conflict has a good chance of being resolved peaceably. Such conditions as these make it possible for collective actors to live together for a long time within the same social system and yet experience periodic disagreements, controversies, and open conflicts. They are held together by solid bonds of social relations, mutual orientations, and shared values. In all modern societies, big labor and big industry coexist permanently as essential antagonistic allies. From time to time their relations flare up into strident, sometimes violent strife. Nevertheless, they neither destroy the system nor permanently withdraw from it. They resolve their struggles in ways that benefit the inclusive social system, the total economy, and the well-being of both participants. Third, if moderates can operate and speak out within their group of collective actors in a conflict, they can sustain and enhance the chances of resolution.

These elements help to maintain a rational perspective and calm climate within which options other than the resort to conflict can be presented and considered. They constitute a rallying point around which individuals and groups who disagree with the struggle and long for peace can gather and reinforce each other. The articulate moderates can bring pressures to bear upon leaders and generate a public opinion that pushes for extrication from the conflict. One of the important factors that moved the United States toward resolution of the Vietnam War was the continuous and urgent voices of moderates calling for exploration of ways of getting out of the increasingly unpopular and destructive conflict. In his analysis of the communication problems of the Middle East, Davidson (1974: 124–28) discusses these functions of the moderates in the resolution of a long and difficult struggle.

Again, stalemate, the danger of defeat, and the achievement of limited goals function to influence the recourse to the alternative of resolution. The chances that contending parties may turn to resolution are enhanced when their conflict has reached a stalemate. In this situation, either combatant is making significant gains. Each may estimate that his chances of winning, or indeed of gaining a significant advantage from the struggle, have been exhausted. Coser (1961: 348) observed that it is important to both contenders to note and mark the point beyond which no further gains can be anticipated from the struggle. At this juncture, termination of the conflict becomes an important problem for both the parties. Recognition of the existence of stalemate permits latent opposition to the conflict to surface and the willingness to withdraw from the conflict to gain popular support. Mueller (1971: 358–75) used a public opinion poll to reveal the declining popular support for the Vietnam War. He showed that citizen support declined as the casualty lists lengthened and people came to see the endless war as a stalemate. This changing public opinion pressed the Nixon administration to abandon the war and sue for peace.

An actor who finds himself facing almost certain defeat, or who has accomplished limited ends, may come around to the decision that withdrawal is the best option. Since the contender estimates that he cannot win, the best choice may appear to be termination of the conflict on the best terms he can get. This aim characterized the American action in terminating the Vietnam War. The aim was to extricate the nation from the unpopular and pointless struggle without the opprobrium of defeat. If on the other hand this action has sought objectives short of absolute victory, the contender may be willing to quit the fight as soon as these goals have been attained. For example, in the Six Day War, after the Israelis had achieved their specific objectives, they were willing to initiate a conflict-resolution process.

Another condition that facilitates conflict resolution is loss of legitimacy by the government or leadership cadre in the eyes of citizens, members, or constituents. This happens when they begin to lose faith in the organization and its leaders and to reject its policies as unworthy of support. Wolf (1972: 927–37) observes that recognition of failure on the part of the government or leadership cadre in this situation can have salutary consequences, since the leaders may find that resolution can be viewed as an acceptable and face-saving escape from an untenable course of action. This development was illustrated in the erosion of the sense of legitimacy of the federal government during the second Nixon administration. Schuman (1972: 513–36) reported a study of adults and students in the Detroit area on the growing disenchantment with the Vietnam War. He found that both moral and pragmatic considerations figured in the collective change of opinion and erosion of the sense of the legitimacy of the government and the war. The shift in the focus of public opinion and moral judgment meant that the people had come to regard the conflict as no longer legitimate. The erosion of legitimacy derives from two related developments. First, if the fight drags on for a long time, people may develop new interests that challenge the old struggle for their attention and loyalty. Second, they may grow weary of the fighting and long for peace, for a termination of the endless struggle. Faced with these conditions, the government or leadership agency may find resolution a desirable line of action.

A final condition that may facilitate the resort to conflict resolution is access to an appropriate intermediator. Sometimes, conflict actors are able themselves to initiate negotiations to resolve the conflict that may lead to settlement of differences and termination of a conflict. Often, however, as in Northern Ireland, the struggle may be so bitter and the hostility so implacable that the contending parties cannot communicate directly. Deutsch (1973: 376) wrote that the work of the intermediator is easier if he is well known, readily accessible to the relevant parties, prestigeful in the community, and skilled, impartial, and discreet in his actions. This cluster of characteristics may appear as the residual wisdom of persons who are heads of prestigious organizations, e.g., heads of states, great religious leaders, managers of industries and business firms, etc. However, Taft and Ross (1970: 385–86) note that, following passage of the Wagner Labor Relations Act in 1935, conflict mediation in the labor-management field became increasingly professionalized. This type of mediator brings great skill to the task of resolving conflict, but does not rely heavily on social visibility and prestige as resources. The chances of success of the resolution process are likely to be further enhanced if the intermediator enjoys the support of the leadership and public opinion of both contending groups. It seems evident that Mr. Kissinger's efforts in the Yom Kippur War and in settling the American

war with Vietnam succeeded because he had wide support from both
contending parties in both cases. On the other hand, the efforts of the
United Kingdom (and later the United States as well) to intermediate
in the Rhodesian civil war have failed to date because the attempt has
little support from either belligerent.

A STRATEGY FOR CONFLICT RESOLUTION

The conflict resolution process unfolds in a time sequence. Theoretically
separable operations develop one after another in a series. Yet these
analytically separable actions are not altogether neatly separated in either
operation or time. We therefore speak of them as components rather
than stages of the resolution process. The strategy of conflict resolution
includes five functionally linked operations which may or may not appear in the sequence indicated here. First is a series of preliminary contacts and arrangements. These enable the combatants to enter into a
"cease-fire," or cessation of violent, hostile actions and aggressive
communication. The other three operations include resolution-communication, exchange, and formalization of agreements. The result of
these operations is to restore the ongoing struggle to some level of legitimacy.

Preliminaries

Before the parties to a conflict launch a serious resolution effort, they
will have taken certain preliminary actions. The creative talk that is
part of resolution is a long way socially from the process of active conflict. At least four major preliminary steps can be identified: (1) a
firm decision to terminate the struggle in some manner, (2) establishment of nonbelligerent contacts through some kind of communication
channel, (3) facilitation of the processes of communication and agreement, often by means of an intermediator, (4) a set of ground rules to
control and pattern the substantive negotiations and agreements to follow.

The process of conflict resolution can begin only after both parties to
the conflict have decided that they want the struggle resolved. This is a
policy decision of the first order. It represents a reversal of the policies
that have sustained and guided the conflict. Sometimes such a policy
change can be made only with difficulty. For example, it required several

years for the dissenting groups and movements in the United States to swing public opinion around to forcing the Nixon administration to seek a termination of the Vietnam War. It took the ruling white regime in Rhodesia many years to come around to the decision for resolution in the civil strife with the African rebels. Writing in 1974 Alroy (56–61) contended that no serious progress had been made in resolving the Arab-Israeli strife because the Arabs did not really "want peace." Nevertheless, in 1973 Egypt and Syria agreed to Dr. Kissinger's resolution efforts, partly because that was a way out of their untenable military situation and partly because they did indeed want peace, but only on their terms.

Sometimes, as in the United States' decision on Vietnam, public opinion presses the government to make the policy change. At other times a tottering government, such as Rhodesia's, can prevent the civil society from expressing and implementing the decision to seek conflict resolution. Once the policy decision is taken, the government must seek the agreement of all major factions. It needs substantial social and political consensus to support the actions that follow. The collective effort to agree on conflict resolution may have significant consequences for the systems of one or both the contending parties. An extremist or fanatical group may reject the proposed decision, creating prolonged internal dissension. The result may be a serious split in the basic social system. In extreme cases, such an internal split may lead to defeat in the main conflict or to breakup of the social system.

A second preliminary action of the party that has decided to seek resolution is to ascertain whether the adversary is willing to enter the discussions. This step presents some initial difficulties, since, being adversaries locked in an overt conflict, they may not have regular channels of contact and communication. Yet it is essential to signal to the other party, "we are ready to quit; are you?" Ladner (1973: 175–84) has suggested that such messages can sometimes be transmitted by "strategic interaction." That is, the party that is ready to stop the fight can take strategic conflict actions that are intended to signal to the enemy that it is time to quit the struggle. For example, the leader of the conflict party wishing to terminate the struggle can send up a "trial balloon," say, a comment in a news conference or a significant sentence in a public speech. Or again, he can have his diplomats in friendly capitals drop the hint of his willingness to terminate the fighting and work out agreeable terms. Each of these actions could be reinforced by some gesture on the battlefield, e.g., deliberate failure to follow up a tactical advantage, actual termination of hostilities on one or more fronts, or unsolicited release of prisoners. If such "strategic" actions are correctly read, and if the enemy too is ready to quit the fight, then ways can be found for more substantive communication.

Davidson (1974: 124–28) has suggested that third parties can provide channels for diplomatic and conciliatory communication between the conflict actors, who have no official means of communication. Such third parties may include the foreign office of a mutually friendly nation, the field staff of private service agencies such as the Red Cross or the American Friends Service Committee, or private citizens who serve quietly as unofficial representatives of a government. These individuals and groups can communicate the initiating desire to terminate the struggle, and seek peace and the agreement of the opposition. As will be mentioned below, through third parties the belligerents in war, labor strife, intergroup hostility, or the like, can settle various preliminary details: the place and time of a formal meeting, the intermediator, and the preliminary ground rules. These and other preliminary actions precede the formal resolution process. Meanwhile, lacking a formal cease-fire or treaty, the fighting goes on. As a matter of fact, all these preliminaries are likely to take place informally. For the general population or membership, the conflict continues unchanged.

Often the contending parties, or at least one of them, may feel that an intermediator is necessary or at least desirable. Part of the preliminaries, therefore, is the search for such a person or group. Sometimes, a leader or group voluntarily offers its good offices to serve as intermediator. An intermediator is not only a special party; he is also acceptable to both contending parties. Deutsch (1973: 376) has identified the distinguishing characteristics of the intermediator type. They include, among other things, high public visibility, unquestioned integrity and trustworthiness, and special skills in diplomacy and human relations. This sort of person is required because he must serve as catalyst and communicator in a delicate and volatile situation. In actual experience, persons have been proposed and selected as intermediators because of known skills, outstanding reputation, high visibility as heads of well-known and respected organizations, or the presumption of great power.

Sometimes the resolution process is initiated by an intermediator. For example, Dr. Kissinger launched the resolution effort that ended the Yom Kippur War. David Owens of the United Kingdom and Andrew Young of the United States continued working for some time in an effort to resolve the guerrilla war in Rhodesia. In such a case, the intermediator must start seeking agreement of both parties to enter into the resolution process under his supervision and guarantee. In addition to facilitating communication and conciliating disagreements, Boulding (1962: 317–18) notes that intermediators can also propose options of action and bring public opinion and pressure to bear upon the contending parties. Sometimes, one party to the conflict has proposed an intermediator to move in and terminate the fighting. This is likely to happen when that party has achieved his limited goals or when he believes he faces certain defeat. In some other situation, intermediation is built into an official conflict institutionalization system. The United States Labor Mediation Service is a case in point. When, in the judgment of the proper federal officials, a strike threatens the "general welfare," the Mediation Service is authorized to step in and seek to resolve the dispute. Although the Service cannot impose a settlement on the contending parties—labor union and industrial management—they must join the intermediator in negotiation sessions, and failure to achieve a speedy settlement may bring certain legally prescribed penalties. If resolution results from binding arbitration, then the arbitrator can enforce the resolution.

With a preliminary communication system in operation and an intermediator chosen and in place, the contending parties can move forward toward substantive conflict resolution. The final preliminary step is a series of operating agreements and rules. These arrangements are preliminary, required only to get the formal resolution process started. Such temporary arrangements can be developed in various ways. For example, in the 1973 Yom Kippur War in the Middle East, Dr. Kissinger engaged in his famous shuttle diplomacy to work out these preliminary agreements. The final resolution of the long-standing Arab-Israeli conflict was to be developed in the Geneva Conference which convened some months later. Less dramatically, these preliminary agreements are often worked out by low-level foreign-service personnel. They may work in the embassies of friendly nations, never setting foot in the territory of either contending party. If the intermediator is working with a local dispute, say between racial or ethnic groups, the preliminary settlements may be developed by separate conferences with leaders of both parties. The process is formally informal. Sometimes, as with the national labor relations program, the ground rules are part of a formally established system.

As suggested, before official representatives can sit down to forge an official resolution agreement, there must be understandings and agreements regarding a number of preliminary matters. What are the issues that will appear on the agenda of negotiation, and in what order? What kind of conference or meeting should be held? Who will be expected or permitted to be present and in what roles? What goals will be sought in the negotiations, at what level, and with what scope? At what place, at what time will the representatives convene to discuss these and other issues? What about the press, visitors, secrecy, news releases, and so on and on, often in great detail? These are not final decisions. They are only the preliminary ground rules of the official resolution convention to be held.

If the dispute to be resolved is something less than an international war, the process of preliminary agreement is nevertheless essential. Leaders of a student group that has occupied the administration building and interrupted the operation of the university must come to some understandings with the university administration regarding how they go about resolving the issues in contest. Arriving at these understandings may take place as the initial sparring part of the basic meeting of leaders from both camps. Work on the basic issues cannot really make much progress until such understandings have been worked out and the negotiators comprehend the nature of their task and the constraints under which they operate. As noted, all these actions, taking the resolution decision, initiating contact and communication between contending parties, finding an acceptable intermediator, and working out the ground rules of negotiation can be carried out while the fight is still going on. In actual situations these preliminaries come about in different ways. Sometimes the contending parties come to resolution from a strong desire for long-time peace, i.e., the institutionalization of their struggles at the level of legitimacy. Sometimes, however, a collective actor may turn to resolution to escape an untenable position and a hopeless conflict, and in another situation a contender may see resolution as the way to institutionalize limited gains won in the fight. There are instances when the intermediator enters an active nonlegitimate struggle and persuades the parties to initiate resolution. He helps them to perceive residual motives and desires that support this policy decision. Usually, the intermediator facilitates communication and decision making by the contending parties. In arbitration, though, the process begins with an agreement to terminate nonlegitimate struggle. The intermediator acts as judge, deciding the terms of the resolution. However, movement forward from these preliminaries to substantive work on resolving the conflict is impossible so long as the adversaries continue to fight openly and aggressively.

The Cease-Fire

It is manifestly difficult if not impossible to settle down to serious talk about terminating a conflict while it rages. The first act of resolution, therefore, is to arrange a cease-fire. As a matter of fact, a cease-fire may have been called for, and indeed even arranged, while the preliminary activities are taking place. Henry Kissinger contrived a stalemate-like cease-fire in the Yom Kippur War as one initial preliminary action. In an onrushing labor dispute that may tie up a critical national industry, the president can impose a "cooling-off period."

A cease-fire is more than a preliminary action. It means termination of coercive or violent, i.e., nonlegitimate conflict. While it does not terminate the main struggle, it does take the heat off of it, or cool it. The cooler heads are permitted to proceed with calmer business. In the case of war, the meaning of a cease-fire is clear. The field forces stop shooting at one another. In the case of community strife or intergroup struggle, the image is less clear. If the civil strife is a violent disturbance or riot, then *cease fire* means stop and desist from further physical attack. If the struggle is nonviolent, then *cease-fire* refers to termination of the conflict tactics that are being used, e.g., obstructing streets, occupying buildings, inflammatory rhetoric, or the like. In all cases, the cease-fire means that combatants halt all coercive, violent or aggressive actions at once.

The military cease-fire demonstrates another feature of this component of conflict resolution. Under this decision, the forces in the field disengage and pull back to new neutral positions. They are frozen in position. It is understood that the cease-fire means both no more actual overt combat (for the time) and no change in the position or situation specified in the cease-fire agreement. Replacements and reinforcements may not be brought up. The force in the field cannot be reequipped or regrouped. Everybody simply holds his position. In the case of civil strife, essentially the same requirement applies. Rioters, demonstrators, pickets, and participants in civil disobedience cannot remain indefinitely in the streets. They must go home at night at least. But for the purposes of the conflict they retain their tactical positions.

It is evident that the cease-fire has several conflict-resolving functions. First, it acts out a no-win situation. It indicates, whether actually or only in simulation, that neither side can win, or that limited objectives have already been achieved. Thus it creates a condition in which an effort can be made to resolve the conflict. Second, it produces a cooling-off period when emotions can be slowed down and calmed. This is also a time when the intermediator and other responsible persons on both sides can move forward toward definitive action in resolving the conflict. With emotions calmed down, it is possible for people to recognize the advantages and tasks of conflict resolution. The cease-fire constitutes a time for people to reflect on the struggle. They can recognize its folly and wasteful character. As Davidson (1974: 124–28) pointed out, the moderates can gain a hearing and influence the trend of public opinion. The intermediator and heads of the contending parties can get along without interruption in the business of resolving the conflict. This is a welcome time, a breather, and an opportunity for some useful work.

Resolution Communication

Conflict resolution refers to a series of reciprocal and complementary actions on the part of conflict actors. It is thus both interaction and joint action. The cease-fire is an enterprise in joint action. Initiation of the resolution is an instance of social collaboration. Conflict can be resolved only when and as the contending parties manage their communication in such a way as to generate substantial areas of agreement and joint action. Speaking of the possible role of communication in a solution of the Arab-Israeli conflict, Davidson (1974: 128) listed the mobilization of public opinion on both sides in favor of peace, the preparation of the ground for formal negotiations, an effort to generate a climate of opinion, and the emotional mood in which peace could be accepted.

First the adversaries must minimize combative communication. This means deliberate management of the sources of propaganda and systems of communication in order to reduce the content of provocative and incendiary material. Each actor must refrain from issuing threats and challenges to the other side. Such threats are often couched as defensive actions, e.g., if the enemy continues to do so and so, then we shall have no recourse except to retaliate in such and such fashion. This kind of communication functions to continue or escalate conflict. In other words, as Yalen (1971: 263–72) and Mitchell (1973: 123–32) have argued, communication between belligerents must be controlled to make it work for conflict resolution and peace instead of serving to exacerbate conflict.

The crucial aspect of combative communication is the charges and accusations leveled against the enemy. It is a commonplace item of conflict tactics to charge the opposition with many kinds of unfair, unjust, and inhuman actions. Such charges and accusations justify the conflict tactics of the group that hurls them. For example, a striking labor union regularly accuses management of being unfair, unjust, or exploitative. In the black protest struggles, whites were accused of being prejudiced, heartless, and discriminating. The Afrikaaners of South Africa justify oppressing and abusing the black Africans by claiming that they are inferior, uncivilized, and given to violent behavior. Pugh (1975: 310–28) showed how the media were used in the Arab countries to fan anti-Israeli hostility and thus to support the running conflict. Sometimes such charges are so extreme that the only way to make them seem credible is to claim that the enemy is nonhuman, subhuman, or bestial. If the enemy is indeed this way, then one cannot expect civilized behavior from him. The implication of such ethnocentric accusations is that the group making them is, of course, quite civilized. This group naturally abides by the requirements of international law or the rules of fair play.

Often, also, this propaganda of conflict is accompanied by extreme demands against the enemy which may be called "legitimate" or "nonnegotiable." At first blush, such demands may seem to be ludicrous. But if repeated, pressed with vigor, and presented in a serious manner, they tend to be provocative. This kind of extreme demand was typical of Hitler's attacks against Poland and the other nations he crushed. The propaganda-laden communication of Arabs and Jews is also of this kind.

Since such communication functions to continue or escalate the conflict, it must be terminated or reduced immediately. The actions required to achieve this end are part of one component of the resolution strategy. Since much of this provocative communication emanates from the government or other official source, it can be managed with some ease and expedition. The process of resolution cannot proceed far until the combatants cease to fight one another with their words. Numerous strategies can be employed to achieve this end. Davidson (1974: 124–28) advocates the use of third parties to support and implement "accurate" conflict-resolving communication. He also believes that some progress can be made with the official communications of the belligerents to achieve increased objectivity and accuracy of content. Intermediators and their staffs can help by feeding conflict-resolving materials into the channels of communication. The United Nations is strategically situated to assist in this respect. Graber (1970: 339–78), from a study of United Nations General Assembly debates on the Middle East, reported that conflict-moderating predominated over conflict-stimulating traits in the speeches of the delegates. Doob and Foltz (1974: 237–55) reported a workshop of young Catholic and Protestant leaders of Northern Ireland held to stimulate the increase of positive images and conflict-moderating communication. Although it was impossible to measure results with accuracy, they believed this device had positive effects.

Second, the process of conflict resolution is advanced when simultaneously with the minimization of combative communication, both sides act to maximize the communication of conciliation. That is, the conflict actors begin to discover and talk about the fact that they share important characteristics and have grounds for agreement and cooperation. This is in fact true and has been true throughout the conflict. Now they may begin to recognize this fact and to talk about it. For example, one value that they possess in common is the desire for peace. The yearning for peace and security is one important thread in the basic fabric of opinion and normative attitudes on both sides. The universal desire for peace needs to be recognized, articulated, and introduced into the channels of communication. Hearing it stressed, each side can begin to see the other as essentially nonhostile, really wanting peace, and therefore like itself. Perceived in this perspective, the two sides, former enemies, have something to talk about and to cooperate over. President Sadat of Egypt exploited this theme in his dramatic approach to Israel in December of 1977.

With encouragement, each side can begin to discover that it shares other interests, values, and goals with the opposition. For example, a boundary river not only separates them; it also binds them together. It waters the land of both countries. It is a resource that they share. They can get greater use of it if they cooperate in its preservation and utilization. Minorities and majorities struggle for justice, freedom, dignity, jobs, wages, houses, and the like. With the shift in the emphasis of communication, as Himes (1966: 7) has shown, they can come to recognize that these are common possessions, to be enjoyed and kept only if they cooperate. In the bitterness of the Afrikaaner-African struggle in South Africa, there are glimmers of insight here and there that each group needs the other and neither can have what it wants without the other. Little by little, a piece at a time, the areas of shared interests may appear to widen and the spheres of controversy and strife shrink. A main task of the intermediator is to help each side to perceive these areas of common interest and to see them as important objects of communication and cooperation.

As a consequence, the contending parties may begin to understand their demands better and to clarify and modify them. They will discover, that some of these demands can be achieved only, or at least best, through discussion, sharing, and cooperation. For example, if the fight is over a boundary river or small strip of territory, the parties to the struggle may come to perceive that there is only one river and that the territory is limited. Each can have a piece of the territory or partial use of the river if they cooperate. If they continue to fight, one is likely to lose, and have nothing; or together they may destroy the river or territory as a useable resource. Some Afrikaaners are beginning to see that they enslave and degrade themselves in the effort to control and exploit the African people. In free communication, mutual aid, and cooperation, both can be freer than they are now. In the end, each party may come to be able to do business with the other because each recognizes that the other has something of value for which he is willing to pay. In this event, resolution-communication has been the prelude to exchange. The transitory vacuum of communication produced by minimizing provocative pronouncements and accusations is now being filled with positive communication. Deutsch (1973: 376) and others have observed that skill in promoting this kind of communication is one salient characteristic of the intermediator role.

Exchange and Sharing

It was said in chapter 1 that social conflict is a struggle between collective actors for scarce or incompatible values of which power, status, and resources were said to be the most important categories. Ongoing conflicts can be resolved when contending parties alter their relations with reference to these values. For example, as Himes (1966: 7) has observed, if the struggle is for such abstract values as justice, freedom, security, or dignity, they can be possessed only when shared. The adversaries can resolve their fight only when they collaborate in protecting and advancing such ends. If, however, the conflict is over territory, natural resources, status, or other values that are presumed to be limited, the contending parties can terminate their struggle by arrangements for sharing, trading off, substituting, or compromising such values. For example, it is conceivable that Israel may be willing to relinquish some of the territory acquired in the Six Day War for firm guarantees by the Arabs of her right to exist as a nation. The United States and Canada have learned over the years to share the Great Lakes and the St. Lawrence River as an indivisible value. Labor unions and industries settle strikes by compromising their wage demands and offers. Communist, socialist, and democratic nations minimize conflict and coexist by learning to tolerate ,and respect each others' incompatible economic and political philosophies and systems. An essential task in conflict resolution is to bring contending actors around to recognize that scarce or incompatible values can be managed in ways that are advantageous to both parties.

The prelude to sharing and exchange is the shift of communication discussed above. Through positive communication, conflict actors can perceive that satisfactory tradeoffs and joint usage are possible. In the change from the rhetoric of conflict to a communication of conciliation, and in the reduction of demands to negotiable levels, each contending party places itself in the position of recognizing that the other has possessions and resources that are worth having. A basic step in the sharing process is the identification and display of exchangeable values. For example, one party may have more agricultural products than it needs, while the opposition has a surplus of minerals or manufactured items. In the Middle East, Israel produces a surplus of manufactured goods which it could exchange with the Arab nations which have oil and raw materials to export. In many American cities, poor whites and poor blacks are victimized by the community's elites and encouraged to compensate by engaging in nonrealistic racial strife. However, in realistic struggles with the political and economic machines, each group needs the resources of the other—it may need numbers of individuals as voters, or customers from the ranks of a particular ethnic group. Blacks could support the whites in one situation, e.g., a close political race, in exchange for help later from the whites in a fight with industries for jobs or promotions. Kaliadin (1972: 236–45) has suggested that the Cold War could be resolved and the balance of terror reduced by tradeoffs in disarmament between the great powers of East and West.

The intermediator can be a crucial figure in the exchange-sharing process of conflict resolution. He can seek to persuade each side to make an offer to the other. He transmits these offers between the contending parties, trying to extract from each side a better counter-offer. More than that, as noted above, he can introduce exchanges and sharing arrangements that may not have occurred to the conflict actors. In this way, he enriches the exchange process by increasing the number of available options. Boulding (1962: 317–18) points out also that a competent intermediator can bring public pressures to bear upon recalcitrant conflict actors. He can be particularly effective if he can mobilize supporting opinion in the closest and strongest reference group of one of the parties to the conflict. Thus, for example, national labor-management conflict mediators often take actions to mobilize public opinion for or against one of the conflicting parties, or in favor of a reasonable settlement.

The values bargained in a tradeoff will vary with the situation. In a military situation, geographic territory may be an important exchangeable value. When there is talk about pulling back from the frozen battle lines of a stalemate, the question is how far back, to what earlier position. Such territory is a tradeable value. But in some military circumstances, one side may have little tradeable territory to offer. If one party has been invaded and has lost important territory, it may look for other values to present in a possible tradeoff. In such an event, other natural resources, industrial products, or cultural symbols may be perceived as tradeable. Often, as in labor-management or interracial strife, recognition, status, and respect are important tradeable values. The intermediator must help the contending parties to perceive these conditions as tradeable values. This principle is illustrated in relations between American labor unions and big industries. In the 1930s and 1940s, the new industrial unions struggled for recognition and the right to represent large numbers of workers. In response, the industries demanded "responsible unionism." Lipset (83ff.) pointed out in 1954 that big industry had learned to resolve disputes with big labor by acceding to demands for recognition, higher wages, shorter working hours, and fringe benefits by insisting upon "responsible unionism," i.e., control of union locals, suppression of wildcat strikes, and uninterrupted production. Hilmy (1972: 133–35) argued that the only way to settle the dispute in the Middle East between Jews and Arabs is to compromise the maximum demands of both sides in return for a relatively balanced solution. In other words, he envisages step-by-step reduction of opposing demands in a process of compromise which then would be traded for a balanced solution.

Formalizing the Resolution

In time, if the communication, exchange, and sharing processes are successful, the contending parties will reach agreement on all (or at least on the important) issues under contest. These agreements comprise the state of resolution. Relations between the former nonlegitimate conflict opponents can now continue at a level of competition and struggle that is mutually regarded as permissible. Agreement or resolution occurs because, as Coser (1961: 348) argued, both parties to the conflict made some contribution to the termination of the struggle. He goes on to note that the end of the conflict arrives when the parties agree on rules and norms which allow them to assess their respective altered power positions and move forward into a new pattern of relationship.

A time arrives when the parties to an attempt at resolution can review and summarize the specific agreements that have issued from communication and exchange. The parties have concluded that an inclusive settlement has been produced. All that remains is to tidy it up and write it down. These concluding activities take two forms. First, the participants must be assured by reviewing their discussions that each of the specific agreements and understandings is stipulated in a form and couched in a language that can be accepted. And second, all these specific agreements are usually arranged and codified into an inclusive document or instrument of agreement. The contending parties can then know clearly what they have agreed to. At this time, the conflict actors are ready to formalize their agreements by official signatures and publication. Such resolution-formalizing documents may take various forms. If the conflict has been between a striking union and industrial management, the written document will be called a labor contract. If the belligerents are nation-states, then the conflict-resolving document will be called a treaty or convention. The document may be less ritualistic or lengthy than a labor contract or international treaty. It may be a resolution passed by an official or quasi-official body, or a letter exchanged between leading participants in the resolution negotiations. If the adversaries are entrenched Indians, street-fighting blacks, or embattled students, the conflict-resolving document (if indeed there is one) may be titled an agreement. Sometimes, however, the termination of such conflicts is not celebrated by a document.

The preamble of the conflict-resolving agreement will make general statements of policy. These statements will deal with such matters as the intentions of both parties, their agreed judgments about relations between them, goals they hope to achieve, and the place of nonlegitimate conflict—especially war—in their continuing relations. The preamble is intended to set the tone of the inclusive agreement and to establish the atmosphere of public relations for the termination of hostilities and subsequent relations. In later paragraphs, the document may be meticulous and long.

In the resolution of military conflict, there will be a declaration that the cease-fire has been made permanent. The pullback and relocation of field forces must be specified. Such military operations will have to be keyed into territorial exchanges. As a consequence, new maps must be drawn to designate the new boundaries that have been agreed to in the resolution process. At the same time, the agreeing parties will wish to state in the document what kind of forces and equipment can be kept by each party and at what locations. These and other arrangements will express the termination of the military aspect of the struggle.

The tradeoff of territory, resources, population, economic advantages, social conditions, and the like that conclude a war will have to be stipulated in the formal document. If one nation agrees to give up a piece of territory, it will wish to know exactly what it is getting in return. A union contract will specify what management expects to gain from the union in exchange for recognition, higher wage rates, and fringe benefits. Usually, one value involved in the negotiations is the status of the two parties *vis à vis* one another. Most scholars agree that one social object of conflict is status. The settlement of this issue will be of crucial importance to both combatants. For example, many strikes turn on the issue of recognition of the union as the bargaining agent of the workers. In her struggles with the Arab nations, Israel has insisted on confirmation of the status of the country as a permanent nation. These recognitions of status will be written into the resolution documents as one aspect and condition of terminating the conflict.

The conflict-resolution document will also specify actions permitted and forbidden to the two adversaries. These stipulations are essential in order to avoid dangerous misunderstandings. For example, the agreement may specify that the embattled Indians may not enter a certain community, assemble in a certain way, or infringe on the rights of non-involved people. On the other hand, the document may grant the belligerent Indian group the right to use certain properties, or entitlement to certain payments. A labor contract is replete with such stipulations of permitted and prohibited actions. At the same time, the document sets out the expectations that each group entertains regarding the other, first and foremost being adherence to the terms of the agreement. They may also refer to certain actions that were peripheral to the issues in the conflict. If they are seen as important, and if they can be agreed to, such expectations may be written into the agreement document. For example, one party may insist that the document must state that the other party is expected to avoid certain kinds of propaganda, or entering into any political and economic arrangements with third parties which can be interpreted as unfriendly or threatening.

The document may also designate or create an agency to supervise and enforce the agreements. Such an agency may be the United Nations or a multinational commission in the case of an international war. In the case of a domestic dispute within a large nation, the agency may be one of many public or nonpublic organizations already in existence. Such arrangements make it clear that both parties understand that the agreements set out in the document are not self-enforcing. Clarifications, supervision, intermediation, and enforcement from time to time may be necessary. For example, a multinational commission was established to supervise the termination of the Korean War, and a convention of participating nations was called in Geneva to extend and formalize the Kissinger truce of the Yom Kippur War in the Middle East. Ethnic strife in the United States often ends with a public commission charged with managing group relations and social change for some time to come.

The conflict-resolving document is a term agreement, that is, it is relevant and applicable for a limited span of time only. This fact is often recognized in the language of union contracts. Sometimes, for propaganda purposes, politicians and diplomats seek to create the illusion that the arrangements are timeless. In reality, all arrangements are term arrangements. This is so because no matter what the hopes and illusions of the leaders may be, social, economic, and political circumstances change with the passage of time. Often the adversary nations or groups have formal planning agencies to stimulate and manage the course of their change. The arrangement that seemed possible or desirable at one time may, therefore, be inappropriate at a later period. The agreements that terminated a conflict in one era may serve as a condition tending to facilitate misunderstanding, tension, and conflict at a later time. For example, the Versailles Treaty that formalized the termination of the First World War proved to be a major, festering condition of the Second World War. However, the terms and agreements of a conflict-resolving document can be understood to describe the social conditions under which the two parties hope to move forward through change into a positive and dynamic pattern of peaceful relationship. The document that terminates a nonlegitimate conflict thus sets out the conditions and norms that underlie a pattern of legitimate relationships. The nature and management of that process of change and development lie outside the scope of this book. But the process is the sequel to the conflict in the relationship between former belligerents.

The Suppression of Social Conflict

The subject of this chapter is the interruption and termination of episodes of nonlegitimate conflict by the application of force. This method of conflict management is called *suppression* and constitutes an alternative to resolution as discussed in the preceding chapter. The first task is to delineate the characteristics and conditions of this approach to management. Conflict suppression is shown to be counter-conflict and as such different from conflict resolution. The resort to suppression suggests the failure or neglect of conflict resolution tactics. Although conflict suppression is almost as widespread as social conflict itself, and though it is an alternative to resolution, it is not a strategy of conflict management in the strict sense. This approach is expressed in a series of well-known tactical devices. It is shown that the consequences of conflict suppression are mixed, and deeply involved with the issue of legitimacy. Even though conflict suppression is practiced in all known societies, it is nowhere fully supported by the dominant value system. As a consequence, this approach to dealing with conflict continues to be an issue in the study of social conflict.

The Nature of Conflict Suppression

Wolfe (1973: 5–6) has identified a powerful authoritative group and a challenging conflict actor as the major protagonists in conflict suppression. When those in charge in a society or community believe that the norms have been violated and their security has been threatened by an outside group or class, they may take action to suppress the offending group and terminate the threat. Wilson (1977: 469–81) points out that although this usually means governmental activity, that is not necessarily the case. For example, a labor union may go out on strike if its contract with management is not renewed on time. This is a common labor tactic in many societies. The community is not likely to think that the union has violated an important norm and there may be no general sense of danger. If, however, as in the case of the United Mine Workers in 1977 and

1978, the strike is prolonged and coal reserves dwindle seriously, some conservative newspapers and television stations may attack the union with propaganda in an effort to discredit it and hasten an end to the strike. If at the same time the strike becomes bitter and striking miners attack nonstriking men on their way to work, treating them roughly and even injuring some of them, the police, the national guard, or federal troops may be sent in to break up, i.e., to suppress, the rioting. Later, if the strike continues and worsens, until it is believed to endanger the health and welfare of the community, the president may go into the courts to invoke the penalties of the Taft-Hartley Act to suppress the strike.

Conflict suppression takes place within a pluralistic public where interests are clashing and values are diverse. The suppression actor and its supporters believe that the use of force is legitimate, justified, and in the public interest. However, other members of the public, particularly the challenging conflict actor, disagree with this judgment. The suppressor believes that his action is legitimate; the challenger regards the suppressing actor and his action as nonlegitimate. At the same time, the nonparticipating "neutrals" have a stake in the suppression action. Some organized sectors of the public may join the action through coalitions with the two primary actors. Turner and Killian (1972: 224) observe that some individuals form a "mediating public" that stands "between the event and the community," defining the event and identifying the issues raised by it. Other neutrals constitute a "bystander public" (Turner and Killian, 1972: 294) which, though not directly involved in the action, nevertheless "reacts to the disruptions and inconveniences" of the struggle. The authors go on to note that still other members of the community form a "humanitarian public" in sympathy with the defending actor which is being punished. In these ways, most members of the inclusive public are identified with the suppression action. They may be thought of as constituencies.

This normative aspect of conflict suppression has two significant consequences. First, it defines conflict suppression as a leading issue of legitimacy for both the members of the community where it occurs and for the social scientists who investigate this phenomenon. This topic is discussed in the last section of the present chapter. Second, it reveals that the whole community becomes drawn into the action and that the nature of their participation is defined by the resulting conflicting value judgments. This aspect of the matter can be illustrated in any suppression event. When the conservative media attacked the striking coal miners in

1978 with hostile and adverse propaganda, sympathizers sprang up in many quarters. At the same time, conservatives far from the scene of the strike arose to applaud the media and urge the needs and rights of the suffering public. This dichotomy of constituencies was expanded when the police entered the fray to quell the riots and discipline the aroused striking workers. As time passed and as the suppression action expanded and intensified, more and more nonparticipants were drawn into the action by normative identifications and resultant actions.

A number of scholars, e.g., Hook (1933: 265), Ploss (1965), and Wilson (1973: 47), have observed that when an authority commands overwhelming power, deprived and discontented groups are unable or loath to challenge or attack. In such societal situations, there is no need to practice conflict suppression since virtually no dissident conflict occurs. On the other hand, suppression is a commonplace management action in open, pluralistic societies where groups are permitted to use power in conflict as instruments of collective effort to gain scarce values and generate desired social change. When such legitimate conflict efforts traverse the bounds of legitimacy, authoritative organizations and groups have the option to act with "legitimate" force to quell such conflict and restore "law and order." For example, dissatisfied miners without a confirmed contract are permitted to go out on strike against the mine operators. However, when their strike produces violence, it is defined as nonlegitimate and suppression may be initiated. Since conflict suppression is characteristic of open, pluralistic social systems, it becomes embroiled in normative disagreements over legitimacy. This fact serves to define the goal of suppression as the termination of specific episodes of nonlegitimate conflict. Once this end is achieved, suppressive action can find no legitimate justification, since legitimate forms of instrumental struggle are permitted. Operationally speaking, suppression is counter-conflict. It is an instance of instrumental conflict as discussed in chapter 8. An authoritative organization of the established social order applies power through conflict tactics to limit or neutralize another conflict group and thus to terminate an episode of "nonlegitimate" struggle. For example, when the Soviets felt that insurgency in Hungary had gone far enough in 1956, they sent in and mobilized massive military forces to put the rioting and rebellion down. When protesting blacks, rebelling university students, or dissident young people violated the norms and transgressed the limits of legitimacy, the police, state troopers, or United States army forces were mobilized and sent in to quell, put down, or in other ways fight against the conflict.

CONDITIONS OF CONFLICT SUPPRESSION

An established authority is more likely to resort to conflict suppression under certain conditions than under others. These facilitating conditions tend to vary from one place to another and from one time to another within the same society. For example, in the mid-1960s, student activism on American university campuses was rather regularly met with suppressive tactics by university administrations. Local and state police were often called in to break up strikes, disturbances, and rioting, and disorderly and unruly students were arrested and hauled off to jail. A decade later, the same kind of student activity on university campuses was less often suppressed. University administrations tended to avoid this management option, preferring to prevent or resolve their problems. The research on social conflict has identified some of the variable conditions that influence the resort to conflict suppression. Here the factors are presented as conditions that tend to facilitate the resort to suppression. It is understood that their absence or opposites are likely to function to impede this choice on the part of authorities. The factors discussed here are called relative strength and self-confidence, perception of an undeserving attacker, only or best way, and conditions of overreaction.

When an established authority feels strong and self confident *vis-à-vis* an attacker, it may be prone to meet the challenge of conflict with suppressive tactics. The effort to resolve the controversy may be rejected as time-consuming and likely to suggest weakness or timidity. In such circumstances, considerations of legitimacy, efficiency, or consequences may be subordinated or ignored. The authority preserving law and order believes it can crush the opposition and terminate the nonlegitimate struggle.

In the early days of student protest, university administrations would sit down to talk with students. They felt confident they could outtalk the students, and negotiation was regarded as a suppressive tactic. Regularly, the students left such negotiating sessions empty handed. For the administration, the student disturbance had ended. Later on, when the students recognized that, under such conditions, negotiation was a device of suppression, they began to confront administrations with "nonnegotiable demands." However, feeling confident of their greater power, the administrations opted to meet the students with disciplinary treatment, police action, and even national guard intervention.

The use of superior strength to suppress conflict is manifested in another way. Authoritative actors may wish to use their power to give a premonitory example to would-be challengers by making a show of strength. It is assumed that one conflict publicly and soundly suppressed will serve as a warning to other dissident groups who may be tempted to try their luck at opposing the establishment. Dahrendorf (1958: 182–83) showed how the Soviets used their overwhelming military strength to cow their East European subjects. In 1953 in East Berlin and later in Hungary, the Russians opted for suppressive violence to teach the restless and challenging people a lesson. The National Advisory Commission on Civil Disorders (1968: 50) reported that "a judge of the Cincinnati Municipal Court, before whom most of the persons charged were to be brought, said he intended to mete out the maximum sentence to anyone found guilty of a riot-connected offense . . . because the 'city was in a stage of siege,' and he intended it to act as a deterrent against further violence."

The correctness of the suppression alternative may be maximized by defining the challenging opponent as undeserving of consideration. If past experience and current propaganda portray the opponent as nonlegitimate, immoral, or in some fashion inhuman, he would seem to deserve only the swiftest and most severe punishment. An authoritative organization may utilize the mass media and other communication channels to present the enemy in these terms. It makes the resort to suppression seem justified and obligatory. The sympathetic consideration in efforts to prevent or resolve disagreements are too good for this kind of adversary.

In an interesting study, Turner and Surace (1956: 14–20) showed how newspapers and people in authority in Los Angeles during World War II operated to define the young Mexican Americans as such an undeserving group. To be a Chicano was to be a "zoot suiter," and to be a zoot suiter was to be guilty of disloyal or suspicious actions, sly and conniving behavior, an oversexed threat to young white American women. They were painted as a thoroughly evil and sinister group. As a consequence, the police harassed them and stood by while white vigilante gangs attacked any youth whom they caught in the street. Turner (1969: 815–31) concluded that the mode of conceptualizing conflict groups conditioned the reaction of the community to them. He reported that communities perceive group conflict in three different ways: as crime, as rebellion, or as protest. He goes on to argue that social conflict defined as protest is legitimate and permits the authorities to negotiate a settlement of outstanding disputes and dissatisfaction. However, if the group struggle is called "crime" or "rebellion," it requires some suppressive management action. Josephy (1973: 18–19) reported on conflict actions of the American Indians in the early 1970s—the Mount Rushmore Memorial, the Bureau of Indian Affairs, Alcatraz, and finally, Wounded Knee—to which the national public responded. The conflict episodes, especially the one at Wounded Knee, were variously defined as crime, rebellion, and protest. Defined as crime, the required response was arrest, trial, and punishment. Rebellion, however, must be suppressed by military attack.

There are times when an authoritative organization may believe that suppression is the only, or at least the best, way to confront and terminate a disapproved episode of conflict. Talk of alternatives may appear unrealistic, and seems to amount to giving away the advantage. The resort to suppressive tactics tends to become almost automatic. In some instances, attacking conflict actors may leave an authoritative organization no alternative save suppression. Turner and Killian (1972: 291–97) observed that, committed to a radical ideology, some groups can tolerate only coercive tactics of struggle. Under such circumstances the struggle has been called "absolute conflict," i.e., a fight to the death. This is the situation in the case of ideological revolution of the kind that Marx envisaged. As he saw it, the workers were bound by the Communist ideology to inevitable revolution and destruction of the bourgeoisie. In such a situation, the government may feel that it has no alternative save to react with overwhelming force, not only to protect the community but to preserve the state itself.

Habitual reliance on suppression may blind institutionalized authorities to alternative ways of managing challenge and dissent. Over time, they develop a trained incapacity to recognize other ways to respond to protest and confrontation. These other ways are regarded as unthinkable, risky, and manifestations of weakness. Autocratic political leaders like General Salazar of Portugal and President Park of Korea exhibited this trained fixation on suppression and coercion. Torrence (1977: 473–96) reported that, for many years, Canadian governments have reacted to violence in this manner. In every case, the government regarded the incident as a grave threat, requiring strong suppressive action. In addition, Torrence noted, the resort to suppressive tactics was supported by the "tendency to see the violent as strangers and aliens," unworthy of more considerate treatment.

Sometimes the tendency to resort to suppressive tactics may result from ignorance of alternative management approaches. It can be assumed that if such leaders knew of preventive approaches to conflict resolution, they would employ them. Often practical leaders of authoritative organizations lack the depth and breadth of social background and perspective to perceive the vast possibilities of social action that are inherent in situations of challenge and confrontation. If educated in the physical sciences or engineering, they may find human relations and collective protest baffling, especially if they have little expertise in the processes of social management. This situation is illustrated in the policies and actions of corporation presidents, city managers, or military officers who are accustomed to operate within authoritarian bureaucracies that emphasize command and compliance. If command fails to bring compliance, and if discontent foments dissidence, then force is the only remedy.

Often the resort to conflict suppression constitutes overreaction to a social situation. The convergence of various factors—repeated incidents and disturbance, inflammatory propaganda and rhetoric, unresponsiveness of the dissident organization, and the like—may generate a state of tension. Tension is revealed in heightened sensitivity, a sense of threat, and unusual suspiciousness. In this psychoemotional state, every act of a dissenting group may be read as a major challenge. The jittery authority tends to respond almost automatically with coercive defensiveness that exceeds the requirements of the situation. Research on crowd behavior by Turner and Killian (1972: 96–111) indicates that this type of situation facilitates the resort to suppression. Such overreaction functions to generate conflict escalation, which in turn constitutes a further stimulus to coercion and/or violence on the part of the managing actor. Walker (1968: 129–61) presented a graphic description of police overreaction in Lincoln Park, Chicago, during the 1968 Democratic National Convention. This source of suppressive violence is illustrated in the following excerpt from the account of the Newark riot of 1966 as presented in the Report of the National Advisory Commission on Civil Disorders (1968: 65):

> At 3:30 P.M. that afternoon [*sic*], the family of Mrs. D. J. was standing near the upstairs windows of their apartment, watching looters run in and out of a furniture store on Springfield Avenue. Three carloads of police rounded the corner. As the police yelled at the looters, they began running. The police officers opened fire. . . . About 60 persons had been on the street watching the looting. As the police arrived, three of the looters cut directly in front of the group of spectators. The police fired at the looters. Bullets plowed into the spectators. . . . Bullets continued to spatter against the walls of the buildings. Finally, as the firing died down, Morris . . . yelled to a sergeant that innocent people were being shot. "Tell the black bastards to stop shooting at us," the sergeant, according to Morris, replied. "They don't have guns; no one is shooting at you," Morris said.

As suppression, overreaction loses much of its effectiveness as a tactic for dealing with conflict. This type of suppressive action is one instance of what Coser (1956: 48–55) has called "unrealistic conflict." Over-reactive action patterns are directed more toward release of tension and self-expression than toward the solution of external problems and the achievement of collective goals. In this situation, overreaction may be as counterproductive as the conflict it is intended to manage. And, as noted above, overreaction to nonlegitimate behavior and disapproved conflict action often stimulates escalation, thus worsening the total situation.

CONFLICT SUPPRESSION TACTICS

In any nonlegitimate conflict situation, the authorities have access to a variety of suppression tactics. This fact provides the management agent some choice in selecting the manner of suppressing the conflict episode at hand. Many different circumstances may operate to influence the decisions made and the tactics chosen. Some of the factors that influence the decision to suppress nonlegitimate conflict may also function to help decide which tactic or tactics should be used to achieve this end. Some of the common types of suppression tactics in use today, together with some of the specific tactics in each type, are listed in Figure 12-1. It is immediately evident that all these tactics are instruments of control on the part of governmental authorities, except for group vigilantism. This is not surprising, for it was pointed out in discussing the nature of conflict suppression that governments are prime suppressing agents. The prevalence and importance of vigilantism reminds us that nongovernmental groups and organizations may also act to suppress nonlegitimate conflict by taking the side of the establishment.

In terms of their consequences, the most extreme tactics available to authorities are attacks with lethal weapons. These weapons include all the devices available to police forces and military personnel from the night stick to field artillery and fragmentation bombs. In 1971 in a cele-brated siege attack the police of New Orleans used light artillery pieces to corner and capture an allegedly desperate member of the Black Pan-thers on top of the Holiday Inn. Bayley (1976: 160–63) recounted a sensational action of the Japanese police to capture a violent gang where extreme weapons and instruments were employed. All such weapons can injure and/or kill people. When used in the suppression of nonlegitimate conflict, injuring or killing individuals is an incidental objective.

In many localities, the police nowadays have access to a range of non-lethal weapons. The worst these weapons can do is to injure the victim.

FIGURE 12-1

TYPES OF CONFLICT SUPPRESSION TACTICS

I. Physical Violence
    A. Attacks with lethal weapons
    B. Attacks with nonlethal deterrents
    C. Breaking and entering premises
    D. Destruction and/or seizure of property

II. Coercive Interference
    A. Threats and harassment
    B. Arrest and detention
    C. Police and court abuse
    D. Denial of use of streets, parks, meeting halls, other facilities
    E. Blockage of access to the mass media

III. Infiltration and Cooptation
    A. Infiltration of organization by agents
    B. Cooptation of leaders and members
    C. Taking of ideas, programs, and plans
    D. Exposure of organizational secrets
    E. Neutralization and/or takeover of organizations

IV. Propaganda
    A. Support for sagging legitimacy of authoritative institutions
    B. Discrediting leaders, goals, and tactics of conflict organizations
    C. Undermining of morale of conflict organizations
    D. Fomenting opposition or hostility to conflicting groups

V. Crowd Control Tactics
    A. Isolation and subdivision of the crowd
    B. Removal of crowd leaders and unruly individuals
    C. Distraction of crowd attention and lowering of crowd excitement
    D. Making a show of strength

VI. Group Vigilantism:
    Suppressive actions, both nonviolent and violent, of private organizations on behalf of a challenged or threatened authoritative organization, most often directed against communal, political and economic conflict groups, designed to terminate nonlegitimate conflict and support the status quo.

Ordinarily, they make them ill or uncomfortable. This category of nonlethal weapons includes such devices as tear gas, Mace, fire hoses, police dogs, night sticks, truncheons, and electric cattle prods. Use of these weapons is intended to neutralize or intimidate the opposition and thus cause him to withdraw from the struggle or give it up.

    Other tactics of the police are designed to damage or destroy the property of an offending group. These tactics include breaking and entering private premises, destroying property, confiscating weapons and records. Such actions are intended to intimidate the group and to lessen its capability to carry on the disapproved struggle. This tactic is also used to search for "contraband" of various kinds, e.g., unauthorized weapons, important documents, fugitives from justice, or the like. Although the search for these objects could be legitimized by a search warrant, the act of breaking and entering (with or without such a warrant) is itself a conflict suppression tactic. It is thus often not an alternative to legal search, but a conflict tactic in its own right. Sometimes, in connection with breaking and entering, police officers may destroy or seize property. Contraband or illegal weapons, organizational records, and printed matter may be seized as material evidence against the conflict organization. Sometimes, some of these and other properties may be destroyed. Both destruction and seizure of property may be important ends of police activity. They can also have tactical significance in the process of conflict suppression, since they may be perpetrated to communicate certain messages to the conflict attacker.

Figure 12-1 listed several actions that can interfere coercively with a conflict episode. In some cases, the force of government is used against a dissident conflict opponent, a revolutionary party, or a protest reform movement. At other times, the government acts as conflict manager in the case of struggle between rival groups. In this latter case, Wolfe (1973: 44) asserts that the government will likely support the favored antagonist and suppress the challenging and threatening group. In all such cases, however, the government uses some form of coercive, non-destructive force against a conflict group. In some instances, the authority may use its legitimate power to threaten or harass members of the offending organization. Tax returns of leading members may be meticulously scrutinized, requiring the production of detailed records and successive visits to the tax collector's office. The community may be lax or tardy in providing adequate police, fire, and garbage collection services. Traffic officers may stop leaders or members of conflict organizations for repeated (although most courteous) inspections of driver's licenses, other papers, and conditions of their automobiles. The wives, children, and relatives of the offending conflict actors may encounter significantly increased difficulty in performing quite ordinary and routine activities. For example, wives may encounter unaccustomed difficulty in cashing checks, or be required to give identifications where none had been required before. Children of prominent movement leaders may find themselves harassed and shunned by former friends and classmates. Children in high school may not make the varsity team even though they are admittedly excellent athletes.

In many places it is common practice to arrest and detain leaders and activists in conflict enterprises. They are picked up for "questioning," on "suspicion," for "vagrancy," and one or another of the standard covers that all police systems maintain. The arresting officer need not have a warrant, no charge need be lodged against the individual, and he may be held in detention for two or three days, long enough to make it uncomfortable and clear to him that his conflict activities are regarded as threatening and improper. In some countries, e.g., South Africa and Rhodesia, leaders of disapproved parties and movements are regularly arrested without warrant and placed in "detention," imprisoned, or "banned" for indefinite periods without any public explanation or accounting. In the Communist dictatorships, such political prisoners sometimes simply disappear, never to be heard of again. The aim is to break or weaken the conflict action by removing or intimidating leaders and front-running activists. Such action is expected to injure the morale of the conflict organization.

The courts act in various ways to aid the suppression of antiauthoritarian conflict. Sometimes, such court action is quite legal. For example, the president may go into the courts to secure an injunction under terms of the Taft-Hartley Act to break a damaging labor strike, impose an eighty-day "cooling off period," and permit collective bargaining to proceed to a mutually acceptable end. On the other hand, participants in many kinds of conflict episodes may find it difficult or impossible at times to get judicial relief from police harassment and abuse. Once hailed into court on valid or trumped-up charges, these individuals often face the prospect of nearly sure conviction and stiff sentences. For example, it now seems clear that the celebrated "Wilmington ten" were given maximum prison terms for their part in a controversial incident. When laws permit judicial discretion in handing out sentences, conflict offenders often get the heavy sentences rather than the alternatives of probation or a small fine. Judges sometimes take advantage of their position and authority to attempt to deter participants in a conflict by imposing a severe sentence on a prominent participant. Unable to raise bail and facing crowded court dockets, conflict activists sometimes spend weeks in jail awaiting trial.

Other officials of local governments also lend a helping hand in the suppression of conflict. Often, for flimsy and questionable reasons, they deny the conflict group the right to parade or demonstrate on the streets. The Veterans get a permit with ease to parade down Main Street on the Fourth of July, but the Poor People's Association is denied a permit to march down the same street on the following Sunday. In the same way, city or county officials may deny conflict groups the right to hold rallies in a park or to stage a mass meeting in the Veterans Memorial Auditorium. Each denial is supported by a "good" reason, a "legal" limitation, or a "valid" justification. The effect, nevertheless, is to interfere with the conflict activities of the attacking group.

At the same time, authoritative organizations, e.g., newspapers and television stations as well as city governments, impede conflict groups' access to established communication channels and the mass media. For instance, when demonstrations, rallies, or mass meetings are staged, they may be ignored, inadequately covered, or reported on the back pages. News releases sent to press or television and radio are shortened, given a minor position, or not used at all. Information about such conflict groups and their activities is sometimes garbled, distorted, and otherwise misrepresented. Afterwards, it is virtually impossible to get adequate corrections. The conflict groups find it difficult, if not impossible, to get a serious hearing when they protest these abuses. Very little is done by public agencies and communication media to correct these discriminatory practices.

Another set of suppression tactics (see Figure 12-1) is called infiltration and cooptation. Agents of the government and private authoritative organizations work their way into the ranks of disapproved groups and associations. Generally this is not difficult, since such organizations are characteristically open. Once inside, such agents work their way into positions of knowledge and power where they can be effective counteragents. Infiltrating agents steal and reveal secrets and plans of the threatening organizations.

Information gained in this manner can be used in two ways by the authoritative conflict actor. First, he can move to checkmate the conflict attacker, thus blunting or frustrating his efforts. Not knowing how its secrets and plans came into the hands of the opposition, leaders and participants of the dissident group may be dismayed by the new opposition confronting them. Conflict-managing organizations also use such stolen information to mount adverse propaganda against the dissident group. Such control actions have an adverse effect upon the morale and program of disapproved organizations.

Wolfe (1973: 192–93) points out that private organizations join with governments in infiltration activities to foil revolutionary movements and actions in many countries. Used in this way, he argues, infiltration replaces international law and the United Nations. Wolfe states that corporations, universities, foundations, and labor unions have acted in the past on behalf of the United States "in subverting revolutionary consciousness abroad." Much of this kind of infiltration for subversion is directed to the training and support of a political elite that is responsive to American interests and ideologies. Wolfe (193) also reports that the American Federation of Labor "has a full-scale espionage program" that works throughout Latin America "engaging in violence against some labor leaders and encouraging the success of others."

The infiltrating agents can work themselves into sensitive and controlling positions of organizations where they can take over the whole operation. By opposing existing policies and by installing new policies, such agents can defeat existing conflict programs and turn the organizations around to conform with interests of the establishment. The infiltrating authoritative organization can also coopt enemy organizations by taking critical resources. Sometimes the effort may be to coopt leaders and members. Being poor and insecure, leaders are vulnerable and can sometimes be won away from the conflict organization by offers of lucrative, prestigious positions in the establishment. If the leader is crucial and momentarily irreplaceable, his loss may severely handicap the organization. Sometimes it may be members, program ideas, and material resources that are taken by cooptation. In every case, such losses hamper and limit the dissenting organization.

Some years ago, the author witnessed this cooptation tactic in a northern city. An organization of young blacks was pressing the board of education to desegregate schools and increase the number of opportunities for prospective black teachers. As time passed, they increased the pressure and drew a number of allied organizations into coalition with them. The city establishment replied with various coercive tactics. Suddenly the board of education restaffed with blacks an entire elementary school (a principal and some twenty teachers) in a racially changing neighborhood. As was hoped, the young blacks deserted the fight and joined the scramble for the new jobs.

Hard-pressed authorities sometimes fight back by taking the ideas, plans, proposals, or programs advanced by attacking organizations and installing them as operating policy. The conflict group or movement is not given credit for the ideas and the authoritative institution takes full credit. The attacking group is thus left organized to fight for a goal which is already achieved in toto or at least in part. In this situation, the enthusiasm and vigor of struggle tend to diminish abruptly. The classic illustration of this suppression tactic was President Franklin D. Roosevelt's cooptation of the old-age pension idea of the Townsend Movement, and its installation as a crucial component of the Social Security System. While the "old age and survivors insurance" plan as enacted by the Congress differed in significant ways from the Townsend Plan, it nevertheless contained the principal features of the plan. Messinger (1955: 3–10) reports that the Townsend Movement underwent rapid and drastic reorientation and organizational transformation. Struggle against the government for old-age pensions was abandoned.

The authoritative establishment, whether public or private, is singularly situated to utilize propaganda as an instrument in the suppression of conflict. For example, Leone (1972: 46–58) claims that the public interest advocates, such as Ralph Nader's groups, complain that regulatory agencies of government (the Federal Communication Commission) are most responsive to the regulated industry (the press, radio, and television). This special relationship of establishment to media enables officials to pour persuasive materials into the communication streams. The result is always limiting, sometimes even disastrous for the challenging and dissenting groups. Propaganda is used by the establishment in several ways to limit or suppress challenge and conflict. A challenged authoritative institution may use propaganda to support its sagging legitimacy. It may need to regain the confidence and support of those individuals and categories who are inclined to question its validity and to press for change. Material that is calculated to demonstrate the concern of the institution, the adaptability of its programs and actions, and the moral justice and rightness of its approaches to issues is fed into the communication channels of press, radio, and television. Leaders of government, industry, education, and other institutions are praised for their forward orientation, their selflessness, and their genuine concern for the needs and wishes of the people. Since the movements and conflict groups are effectively shut off from the media, they cannot challenge this propaganda line. If it is repeated often enough, and if it is occasionally validated by public actions, institutional legitimacy may be shored up.

The institutional authorities also use propaganda to discredit their opposition. Propaganda material is fed into the mass communication streams questioning or criticizing the conflict leaders. Unanswered questions are raised about their honesty, their trustworthiness, their reasonableness, their effectiveness and so on. The aim is to induce conflict participants to lose confidence in their leaders and to grow lukewarm about the struggle. It is now reliably reported, for example, that under J. Edgar Hoover's direction, the FBI mounted a massive character assassination campaign against Martin Luther King, Jr. At the same time, propaganda questions the goals and tactics of the movement and struggle. An effort may be made to show that announced goals are unreasonable and unattainable, and so tend to lead unsuspecting conflict followers down a primrose path to certain failure. The tactics espoused by leaders and organizations are said to be radical, extremist, and un-American, that is, nonlegitimate. The people are warned darkly that such tactics will surely generate backlash and lead to rejection of their goals and efforts. Skolnick (1969: 9) argued that the basis of such propaganda often rests in racial and ethnic myths and prejudice. Thus he wrote regarding the big-city riots of the 1960s that many people believed that "community violence is a uniquely Negro phenomenon—for clearly the only way to explain what happened in Watts, Newark, or Detroit without challenging anyone's belief in the essential workability of established machinery for peaceful group advancement, was to assume that black people were the great exception to the law of peaceful progress." And since this was so, their demands for equality and their tactics of violence would surely fail.

Much of the conflict activity of social movements and conflict groups takes place in the form and under the auspices of crowd action: the protest, the antiauthoritarian people's march, the demonstration, the boycott, the sit-in, the bloc vote, and so on. Each of these conflict activity tactics may generate crowd behavior. To manage the conflict action of such movements and collectivities, it would seem to become necessary to control, i.e., to suppress, crowd behavior. Over the years, a substantial literature and important body of experience on the control of crowd behavior have been accumulated. Crowd control tactics constitute a further type of the actions that are taken by institutional authorities to suppress conflict.

Lohman (1947: 83) and Turner and Killian (1972: 160–67) report that the first principle of crowd control is to isolate the crowd and attempt to subdivide it. It is essential to separate the crowd from its supporting audience. This act not only interrupts the interaction between crowd performers and bystanding audience, it also dries up the source of new crowd recruits. It therefore has a dampening effect upon the crowd and its activities.

If, at the same time, the crowd can be subdivided into a series of smaller units, the power of the crowd as a conflict agent can be further reduced. Lacking an audience and reduced in size by subdivision, each of the subcrowds finds it difficult to maintain itself and retain action momentum. A significant step has been taken toward controlling the crowd and suppressing conflict. Simultaneously, the police or other crowd control agent should seek to remove the crowd leaders and unruly individuals. However, all writers on the subject warn that care must be taken not to incite the crowd to anger because this will intensify the excitement and turn it against the control agents. Lacking leaders and agitators, the crowd is likely to weaken still further. Participants lose enthusiasm for the action and excitement subsides.

A third tactic in controlling crowds is to distract their attention. Sometimes this may occur naturally after the crowd has been isolated and divided. An incidental event may capture the attention of the crowd and divert it from its original purpose. Sometimes, however, the control agent must create the distracting event. For example, in 1962 when angry whites were protesting the desegregation of New Orleans' public schools, a disorderly, angry mob of whites bearing down on a central city high school was distracted by sending a dixieland jazz band marching down a parallel street. Once distracted, the crowd loses excitement and the individuals tend to become a different kind of collectivity. Under such circumstances, they can be managed and fed back into the stream of ordinary citizens doing everyday kinds of things.

Finally, if it seems indicated, the police can make a show of strength. The isolated crowd can be surrounded by a cordon of officers. In other ways the control agents may show their numbers, their equipment, and their discipline. Shellow and Roemer (1966: 12–19) described how the show of strength of police functioned to suppress a potentially nasty crowd episode. One summer the Hell's Angels planned to rendezvous in Prince Georges County, Maryland, a suburb of Washington, for drag racing and general festivities. A group of short-haired, neatly dressed locals tried to impose some order over the drag racing. One young man tried to flag each pair of racers to the starting line. For several hours, things worked well. Finally, though, the prodigious quantity of beer, hard liquor, and green wine they drank undermined the discipline of the racers. A fight broke out between a wobbling Angel and a helmeted local. The local slugged the Angel into unconsciousness. He was defended as the other Hell's Angels rushed forward to assault him. The short-haired victor made the mistake of sitting astride the hood of a truck, waving his beer can in a challenging manner. At this, all the rowdy groups joined in a mass charge against the short-haired locals. Just at that moment, a drunken cyclist was jolted off his machine and fell in the rutty track. His mishap was noted by the police who were patrolling the highway. Immediately they dispatched an ambulance and five cruisers to handle the situation. The police vehicles poured onto the rutty field, fanning out into a half circle around the injured man. By this action they presented the rowdy crowd with a row of red flashing lights and police cars. The unexpected show of power was so sudden and apparently overwhelming that the would-be warriors broke rank and fled back to their own staging area. In this way the police put a stop to what might have been a bloody fight.

Private groups often engage in vigilante actions, assisting governments or acting alone, to execute the conflict-suppression tactics discussed above. For example, the conservative media in a community may launch a propaganda attack against a labor union on strike or a minority protest effort. In the case sketched above, the police acted to quell the near riot among the Hell's Angels. In many places, private citizen groups have performed this function. Private, nongovernmental groups and organizations, with or without government sanction, engage in vigilante counter-conflict against other organizations and movements whose ideologies and tactics are regarded as inimical or threatening to the establishment. For example, in the early 1960s white vigilante gangs regularly set upon and harassed protesting blacks when they marched or demonstrated in southern cities. Rosenbaum and Sederberg (1976: 12–17) note that group vigilantism is regularly directed against organized efforts for communal, economic, and political change. The tactics employed have ranged from propaganda and law suits to physical harassment and massive riots.

In many places, vigilante groups have initiated conflict against subordinate castes or caste-like categories to keep them in their place and to break up organized efforts for social change. For example, Mandelbaum (1970: 477–78) told how a low caste of earth workers of Senapur Village and its surroundings decided to claim that they belonged to a higher caste by putting on the "sacred thread." When the land owners saw this, they beat them, pulled the thread off and laid a fine on the whole group. In multi-religious societies, the dominant sect has often engaged in vigilantism when the religious establishment seemed threatened by secularism, heresy, or sectarian competition. Coogan (1970) reported that in Northern Ireland the Roman Catholic community has been periodically subjected to group vigilantism by the dominant Protestant category. In the mid- and late-nineteenth century, the Irish Catholic minority in New England and the Northeast was often subjected to violent attacks by Protestant groups. In the early 1960s, racial protest in the United States was often marred by white group vigilantism. Two celebrated illustrations are the marches from Selma to Montgomery led by Martin Luther King, Jr., and from Memphis to Jackson led by James Meredith.

In the United States, the history of labor-management relations is marked by extravagant manifestations of group vigilantism. Taft and Ross (1970: 281–395) describe many of these encounters in which armed gangs, company police, private detectives, and state militia have attacked protesting and striking workers in savage onslaughts. The efforts of organized and organizing workers were regarded as a nonlegitimate threat to the economic establishment and industrial companies. As Rosenbaum and Sederberg (1976: 15–16) pointed out, organized struggle for political change has also stimulated vigilante reprisals. In the South at the time of the Reconstruction, the Ku Klux Klan and similar secret organizations functioned for decades as vigilante groups. Sometimes these groups have the open or tacit endorsement of government. Always they operated in the interests of various establishments.

CONSEQUENCES OF CONFLICT SUPPRESSION

It cannot be assumed that conflict suppression is always successful. Sometimes the use of force in counterconflict does in fact terminate episodes of nonlegitimate struggle. More often, though, it has a contrary effect. Succeed or fail, conflict suppression always has consequences for the social system within which it is practiced. By making somewhat arbitrary definitions of success and failure, it is possible to identify and classify some of the social consequences of conflict suppression. For the purposes of the present discussion, these consequences are called success, failure, and institutionalization.

If lateral social consequences are ignored and if attention is focused exclusively on the nonlegitimate conflict in question, conflict suppression can be said to succeed if it leads to the termination of the relevant episode of nonlegitimate struggle. That is, if police intervention is followed by termination of the riot action, then the suppressive tactic is said to have succeeded. From this narrow perspective, it can be said that one consequence of conflict suppression is success. Success of this type was illustrated by the Soviet Union's intervening with overwhelming military force in the radical uprising in Budapest and other Hungarian centers in 1956. Open protest and rebellion were crushed although the spirit of dissidence continues. In the ensuing twenty years, there has been no further overt insurgence in Hungary. With strict reference to the suppression of nonlegitimate conflict, this suppression enterprise was successful. Obviously, of course, the massive Soviet intervention in Hungary had other important consequences for the Hungarian social system.

Sometimes suppression of the overt action of nonlegitimate conflict is accompanied by tactics designed to assuage feelings and harmonize other aspects of human relations. Success is more complete since in the same action overt strife is terminated and some measure of harmony of social relations is restored. This mode of conflict suppression is illustrated in the work of police officers who have had modern "community relations" training in the skills discussed above in connection with crowd control tactics. From this training background, police move into a disturbance or riot situation under the constraint of a series of skills that are designed to terminate the violence and move the participants back into ordinary social relations. This mode of conflict suppression is illustrated in the case of the Hell's Angels described above, where, by a show of strength, the police prevented a bloody fight and returned the crowd situation to its former nonaggressive state. In this situation the success of suppression does not entail dysfunctions that may continue or intensify the conflict later in another location.

When defined by limited external criteria, crowd control can be said to fail when the overt nonlegitimate conflict is not terminated but escalates instead. Such a definition again ignores ancillary social consequences and focuses solely on the overt nonlegitimate struggle. Escalation, or failure, is revealed in two ways. First, the conflict may become more intense or violent. In both these respects, its nonlegitimacy is increased. The escalation of nonlegitimate conflicts is a familiar fact for most people. The National Advisory Commission on Civil Disorders (1968: 35–108) recorded the histories of many big-city riots in the summers of 1965 to 1968 which were the product of escalation processes triggered by inept suppression efforts.

Failure of suppression is revealed in another development. Efforts to suppress a limited nonlegitimate overt conflict may cause it to spread and engulf many more individuals than at first. Bystanders may be drawn into the active fight. Others, either in direct contact with the acting crowd or in touch with it only by mass communication may join in a "humanitarian public" that supports the offending conflict actor. In this way a whole community or society may be drawn into the fray. Such a struggle may in time produce a deep permanent rift in the inclusive social structure. In such an event it can be said that the initial suppression had failed.

Sometimes the effort to suppress an episode of nonlegitimate conflict may actually serve to institutionalize a conflict group. As Coser (1956: 87–110) has shown, opposition stimulates increased internal integration and stabilization of the organization. The rioting crowd tends to become a social movement. Hopper (1950: 270–79) formulated the process of institutionalization in a four-stage model of the "revolutionary process." Under pressure, an inchoate crowd is transformed into an issue-oriented public which in time becomes a social movement. Continued suppressive pressure may push the organization to the ideological left, thus institutionalizing it as a revolutionary party.

On the other hand, the effort to suppress a nonlegitimate conflict action may drive the conflict organization out of sight, either underground or abroad in exile. In the security of invisibility the group can formalize its ideology, structure, and program, and continue the fight which it could not carry on when operating in public. In many countries the underground or exiled political organization eventually emerged from secrecy or returned home to continue the struggle for national independence and majority rule. Typical cases in point are the Russian Communists under Lenin, the French government in exile under de Gaulle, the Mau Mau of Kenya, the Ghanaian revolutionary party under Nkrumah's leadership just after World War II and the Moslem movement in Iran under the Ayatullah Khomeini in 1979.

CONTINUING ISSUES IN CONFLICT SUPPRESSION

In democratic social systems, established authorities have the responsibility of exercising social control and of maintaining basic order while at the same time encouraging wide participation in decision-making and managing social change. The discharge of this paradoxical responsibility tends to involve the authority in controversy. Actors who espouse a boundary-extending orientation chafe at the restraints of social control and public order. At the same time, the defenders of existing boundaries wish the authority to resist the efforts for change and expansion. Thus the putative obligation to suppress some conflicts constitutes the center of a clash of opposing views and the focus of several continuing social issues.

We have noted that physical violence attracts wide response in mass communication. As a matter of fact, the rather general opposition to conflict is aimed at a limited number of aspects that are still moot in terms of the moral and legal norms of modern societies. Many, perhaps even most, of the tactics of suppression are controversial, i.e., still debatable in moral and legal terms. The areas, nature, and sources of these controversies constitute continuing issues in the study of conflict suppression. These continuing issues form one of the active frontiers of the research and interpretation of social conflict. In the present discussion three such issues will be examined briefly. They are the issues of legitimacy, efficiency, and escalation.

Until challenged, the established authorities go about the business of "social control" and the maintenance of "law and order" under the assumption that their actions enjoy universally accepted legitimacy. They believe that their right and duty to act as they do are grounded in prescriptions of the law, customary usage, and the need to protect the public interest. The means of maintaining order and exercising social control are said to be justified by the moral norms and the ends sought. In this way, it is asserted, all members of the community are guaranteed freedom, justice, and well-being. The means used are seen as economical, time-saving and efficient, and justified by the ends sought. In the end, it is argued, the suppression of antiauthoritarian conflicts and challenges maintains the image of a strong social system, acts as a deterrent against further threats, and reduces the prevalence of conflict by terminating current nonlegitimate episodes.

However, many individuals dissent from this view of the matter. Even though many of these people would admit the right, or at least the necessity of established authorities to exercise control, they would nevertheless disagree with the manner of this control. Many critics of the established authority point to occasions where, it is argued, the means of control exceed the limits of legitimacy as established in the legal and moral codes and the needs of practical situations. This kind of objectionable control practice is found in the use of terrorism, torture, and needless violence in the course of routine social control actions. The celebrated massacre at My Lai (Hersch, 1970: 49–75) was so named because it was reported that American soldiers perpetrated needless killings of noncombatant women, old people, and children in the course of military duty. Another classic case of excessive violence in the course of social control is the killing of four students on Kent State University campus in 1970. It was claimed that police and soldiers had neither the authority nor the need to kill defenseless students in managing a protest action. Some people argue that even when constitutional law has been suspended and martial law is in effect, the social control agents are not authorized to kill or injure unarmed, defenseless citizens in the act of protesting abuses and petitioning for the redress of wrongs. The objection to the so-called legitimacy of suppression tactics rests on the fact that often the force used and tactics practiced exceed the authority of the control agent and the requirements of the situation to be controlled.

It is also argued that suppression is resorted to in lieu of or in spite of the availability of other nonextreme and constructive tactics. It is contended that use of suppression tactics and the application of force under such circumstances is patently nonlegitimate. In many such cases, it is asserted, the conflicts could have been managed by making concessions, devising compromises, negotiating planned changes, admitting the dissenters to a share of decision making, and so on. From this perspective it is argued that resort to suppression is justified, i.e., legitimate, only when all the other approaches and tactics have been tried and have failed. Part of the issue from this point of view rests on the disagreement between contending parties as to when all the other alternatives have in fact been exhausted.

In further opposition to the resort to suppression it is argued that such tactics tend to destroy or violate basic human rights and values. Even if legitimated by law or tradition, the excesses have the same effect. Justice, freedom, security, the sense of dignity, and respect are damaged or destroyed by such conflict experiences. Even after the conflict is terminated, the damage to these values is a nonlegitimate net loss. The attack upon these rights and values is illustrated in the mass arrest and jailing of participants and innocent bystanders; the attacks against participants with water hoses, electric cattle prods, or police dogs; and the breaking and entering of the premises of a suspected person or conflict group.

It is also argued that the social ends mentioned do not justify the suppressive means utilized. Social control and public order cannot be maintained securely by suppressing the efforts of people to express their discontent and to initiate desired social changes. It is argued that freedom, justice, respect, opportunity, and the other values are not sustained and realized by resort to violence and coercion. In fact, it is contended, the means employed in conflict suppression are the very ones that are guaranteed to damage, lessen, or destroy these important social ends.

The established authority contends that resort to suppression of challenges and conflicts is efficient. It saves resources and time and it achieves a maximum of control with a minimum investment of effort. And more than this, it functions to terminate conflict in several ways by giving a show of the strength of the existing system, by deterring future conflict ventures, and by terminating present conflict episodes.

The question of the efficiency of conflict suppression is an issue because opponents do not accept these arguments as definitive and valid. For them the matter is open, unsettled. The resort to conflict suppression is said not to be efficient, because it often reflects a nonrational, noninstrumental choice of means. The inclination to suppressive means is tropistic, revealing the force of habit and the restriction of reflection. Little (certainly inadequate) attention has been given to the possible relevance of other methods of conflict management.

Efficiency in this action requires some assessment of the nature of the conflict and the character of the attacking group. The goals sought and the means of meeting them should be examined. With this kind of information in hand, the authoritative institution can then ask which management strategies give the greatest promise of handling the present situation and of producing the most desirable consequences. It is argued that in many cases judicious or diplomatic public officials might be more likely to arrange a mutually satisfactory settlement than the police armed with their weapons of suppression.

Finally, opponents to conflict suppression perceive that this strategy tends to generate social dysfunctions. Often the coercive or violent tactics of local police or state troopers create emotional scars, a sense of anguish, and intense hostilities that linger long after the conflict episode has terminated. Some of these emotionally injured individuals later join dissident groups and oppose suppressive actions. Thus Adamek and Lewis (1973: 342–47) learned by interviewing Kent State University students who witnessed the 1970 killings that many were radicalized by the experience and were more willing to join radical and extremist groups than before the riot action. Such persons are drawn into the fray because they are appalled or incensed by the clumsy tactics employed. The result of this dialectical process is to escalate the conflict. This effect of conflict suppression has been manifested in many places where suppressive tactics have been resorted to in the effort to manage struggle by students, urban youths, dissident workers, disenchanted farmers, women, and so on. Thus the claim that suppression is an efficient and economical way to manage social conflict is in fact one focus of controversy. The issue remains open, abrasive, and infectious, generating controversy and misunderstanding. Although serious effort has been made in the last decade to face and meet this problem, the two sides of this controversy are still unreconciled.

The established authority claims that strong-arm methods of suppression operate to terminate conflict. The old saying is repeated solemnly: "You must fight fire with fire." There is the uneasy feeling that the establishment dare not tamper with the conflict by trying alternative management methods. The conflict must be crushed and the opposition must be held up as a deterring example to other would-be challengers. In this way the present conflict is ended and future uprisings may be prevented.

The evidence of empirical observation as well as the arguments of the opponents of suppression indicate that this judgment is often incorrect. It was stated above that suppression often operates to trigger escalation of the struggle. The crucial problem in these situations is that leaders and decision-makers did not ask what the consequences of their acts might be. They assumed that force would lead to compliance. Numerous situations illustrate the escalating effect of coercive conflict control methods. For Americans the most dramatic is the sad and disastrous Vietnam War. The step-by-step increase of American involvement and level of fire power did not, as expected, result in weakening the enemy's attack and termination of the conflict. As a matter of fact, this escalation of the suppressive attack seemed to increase the Viet Cong's determination not to give in under terms dictated by the United States. As a consequence the war dragged on for years. In the end, by the strategic use of time, the North Vietnamese were able to foil the Americans and conquer South Vietnam.

On the other hand, suppressive tactics may drive the attacker underground rather than out of business. There he survives, maintaining a struggle of irritation and attrition, to emerge some day in the future into open battle once more. This effect of suppression has been illustrated again and again in the experience of developing colonial societies. A political movement of the indigenous people arises to press for liberation and national independence. It is attacked by the colonial authority with overwhelming force. To avoid heavy losses and utter defeat, the party and its leaders go into hiding within the colonial territory. From there they continue the fight in secret and surprising ways. With the passage of time, the colonial power tends to lose legitimacy, both at home and abroad. When the time seems propitious, or when the party is granted amnesty, the leaders emerge from hiding and reassemble the followers for a frontal attack.

Although controversy over the legitimacy of conflict suppression may be more outspoken and intense at present, at least in the United States, it is also true that there is a renewed collective and conscious effort to enervate and replace this approach to conflict management. The tumultuous years of protest and riots raised the level of public awareness and concern has been generated to manage the national tendency toward authoritarianism, control, and violence. The experience of the big-city riots produced a nationwide drive for training police officials and for increased emphasis on the human relations dimension of official control. The Watergate era tended to stiffen the opposition to authoritarianism and raise the level of moral awareness among the American public. President Carter's preoccupation with and emphasis on human rights has raised this whole issue and its correlates to a high position on the national agenda of concerns. All these developments augur well for the national orientation toward social conflict and its management. Indeed, the very fact that conflict suppression continues to be an issue is one hopeful and helpful indicator of the trend toward national consciousness and conscience.

Conflict Management in Perspective

If one looks at the world around one through the news headlines and mass media reports, one is likely to be pessimistic. Terrorism, violence, war, and lesser forms of conflict are rampant and seem to be increasing. The human race appears to stand in daily peril of destroying both itself and human civilization. If, however, one steps back and views the current scene from the perspective of the history even of the twentieth century, one may be less pessimistic, and indeed may experience a slight sensation of optimism. The forms of conflict seem to have changed for the better, and perhaps there is even proportionately less strife now than at an earlier time.

The slight optimism produced by this historical view of conflict results from three principal recent developments. First, as Arendt (1963: 3) observed, World War I was followed by a wave of moral revulsion that led to the rejection of aggressive struggle as a proper instrument of national policy. Second, World War II intensified the deliberate search for peace and accelerated the emergence of the peace research movement. In many advanced societies the techniques of science were brought to the problems of conflict and ways were sought to apply increased knowledge to the reduction and control of social strife. And third, as a consequence of these developments, the conviction emerged and spread that something could in fact be done about war and conflict.

The approach to conflict management is related to the level of development in various societies. In the advanced societies, where scientific effort and knowledge are greatest, there is a great flurry of conflict-management activity. Problems are attacked with all the managerial strategies—prevention, resolution, and suppression. The tendency, or at least the effort, is to maximize preventive action and to limit suppressive tactics. Typically, for example, urban police departments develop and implement community relations programs to prevent crime and stress humane nonviolent tactics in dealing with offenders. Or again, world opinion decries violence in the Middle East and supports the great effort invested in the complicated task of conflict resolution.

On the other hand, in emerging societies effort is still largely focused on building the moral infrastructure of opposition to war and conflict as instruments of national and social policy. Thus for example, the local, so-called brush wars that constantly threaten world peace occur typically in developing societies—Ethiopia and Somalia, Angola and Mozambique, Nicaragua, and Rhodesia, for example. In many of these societies the struggle forward toward effective conflict management and the prevention of war is also hampered by Communist intervention. Nevertheless, as societies develop in the long run, the orientation toward conflict management will become more pronounced and sophisticated.

References
and
Index

References

Books

Adams, Richard N. 1975. *Energy and Structure: A Theory of Social Power*. Austin: University of Texas Press.

Aiken, Michael, and Paul E. Mott, eds. 1970. *The Structure of Community Power*. New York: Random House.

Akindele, R. A. 1976. *The Organization and Promotion of World Peace: A Study of Universal Regional Relationships*. Toronto: University of Toronto Press.

Alpert, Harry. 1939. *Emile Durkheim and His Sociology*. New York: Columbia University Press.

Appelbaum, Richard P. 1970. *Theories of Social Change*. Chicago: Markham.

Ardrey, Robert. 1966. *The Territorial Imperative*. New York: Atheneum.

Arendt, Hannah. 1963. *On Revolution*. New York: Viking.

Bailey, Robert. 1974. *Radicals in Urban Politics*. Chicago: University of Chicago Press.

Balbus, I. D. 1973. *The Dialectics of Legal Repression: Black Rebels Before the American Criminal Courts*. New York: Russell Sage Foundation.

Banner, Mae Guyer. 1975. *Black Power and Community Decision-Making*. Ph.D. dissertation, University of Tennessee.

Baran, Paul A. 1973. *Monopoly Capital*. Lexington, Mass.: Lexington Books.

Baran, Paul A., and Paul M. Sweezy. 1966. *Monopoly Capital: Essays on the American Economic Social Order*. New York: Monthly Review Press.

Barber, Bernard. 1957. *Social Stratification*. New York: Harcourt, Brace.

Barbour, Floyd B., ed. 1968. *The Black Power Revolt*. Boston: Porter Sargent Publisher.

Bateson, Gregory. 1958. *Naven: A Survey of the Problems Suggested by a Composite Picture of the Culture of a New Guinea Tribe Drawn from Three Points of View*. Stanford: Stanford University Press.

Bayley, David H. 1976. *Forces of Order: Police Behavior in Japan and the United States*. Berkeley: University of California Press.

Bazelon, David T. 1967. *Power in America: The Politics of the New Class*. Bergenfield, N.J.: New American Library.

Bell, Daniel. 1960. *The End of Ideology*. New York: Free Press.

Bell, Daniel, and Irving Kristol, eds. 1969. *The Student Rebellion and the Universities*. New York: Basic Books.

Bensman, Joseph, and Bernard Rosenberg. 1963. *Mass Class and Bureaucracy: The Evolution of Contemporary Society*. Englewood Cliffs, N.J.: Prentice-Hall.

Berger, Elena L. 1974. *Labour, Race and Colonial Rule: The Copperbelt from 1924 to Independence*. Oxford, England: Clarendon Press.

Bernard, Jessie. 1957. "The Sociological Study of Conflict." In International Sociological Association, *The Nature of Conflict*. Paris: UNESCO, pp. 33–117.

Bernard, Luther. 1924. *Instincts*. New York: Holt and Co.

Biderman, Albert D. 1967. "What is Military?" In Sol Tax, ed., *The Draft: A Handbook of Facts and Alternatives*. Chicago: University of Chicago Press, pp. 122–37.

Bienan, Henry. 1974. *The Politics of Participation and Control*. Princeton: Princeton University Press.

Blackey, Robert, and Clifford Paynton. 1976. *Revolution and the Revolutionary Ideal*. Cambridge: Schenkman.

Blake, Robert R., and Jane S. Mouton. 1964. *The Managerial Grid*. Houston: Gulf Publisher.

Blake, Robert R., and Jane S. Mouton. 1969. *Building a Dynamic Corporation through Grid Organizational Developments*. Reading, Mass.: Addison-Wesley.

Blau, Peter M. 1975. *Approaches to the Study of Social Structure*. New York: Free Press.

Blumenthall, Monica, Robert L. Kahn, Frank M. Andrews, and Kendra B. Head. 1972. *Justifying Violence: Attitudes of American Men*. Ann Arbor: University of Michigan.

Blumer, Herbert. 1969. "Social Movements." In A. M. Lee, ed., *Principles of Sociology*. New York: Barnes and Noble, pp. 67–121.

Bokhari, Ahned S. 1955. *Aims of the United Nations*. New York: Dutton.

Bonilla, Frank. 1970. *Student Politics in Chile*. New York: Basic Books.

Boulding, Kenneth E. 1962. *Conflict and Defense: A General Theory*, New York: Harper.

Bozeman, Adda B. 1976. *Conflict in Africa: Concepts and Realities*. Princeton: Princeton University Press.

Brinton, Clarence Crane. 1965. *The Anatomy of Revolution*. New York: Vintage Books.

Broom, Leonard, and Phillip Selznick. 1968. *Sociology*. New York: Harper and Row.

Brown, Richard Maxwell. 1970. "The American Vigilante Tradition." In Hugh Davis Graham and Ted Robert Gurr, eds., *The History of Violence in America*. New York: Bantam, pp. 154–226.

Brown, Richard Maxwell. 1970. "Historical Patterns of Violence in America." In Hugh Davis Graham and Ted Robert Gurr, eds., *The History of Violence in America*. New York: Bantam, pp. 45–100.

Burgess, Ernest W. 1925. "Growth of the City." In Robert E. Park and Ernest W. Burgess, eds., *The City*. Chicago: University of Chicago Press, pp. 47–62.

Burns, Tom R. and Walter Buckley, eds. 1976. *Power and Control: Social Structures and Their Transformation*. London: Sage.

Burton, John W. 1962. *Peace Theory: Preconditions of Disarmament*. New York: Knopf.

Burton, John W. 1969. *Conflict and Communication: The Use of Controlled Communication in International Relations*. New York: Free Press.

Campbell, Ernest Q., ed. 1972. *Racial Tensions and National Identity*. Nashville: Vanderbilt University Press.

Carstairs, George M. 1969. "Overcrowding and Human Aggression." In Hugh Davis Graham and Ted Robert Gurr, eds., *The History of Violence in America*. New York: Bantam.

Cartwright, Dorwin. 1965. "Influence, Leadership, Control." In J. G. March, ed., *Handbook of Organizations*. Chicago: Rand McNally.

Chalmers, David M. 1965. *Hooded Americanism: The First Century of the Ku Klux Klan, 1865–1965*. Garden City, N.Y.: Doubleday.

Chapman, Dwight W. 1939. "Industrial Conflict in Detroit." In G. W. Hartman and Theodore Newcomb, eds., *Industrial Conflict*. New York: Cordon, pp. 51–71.

Chason, Gerald, and Barbara Chason. 1974. *Power and Ideology*. New York: General Learning Press.

Chicago Commission on Race Relations. 1922. *The Negro in Chicago*. Chicago: University of Chicago Press.

Cloward, Richard, and Lloyd E. Ohlin. 1960. *Delinquency and Opportunity*. Glencoe, Ill.: Free Press.

Cohen, Ronald. 1964. "Conflict and Change in a Northern Nigerian Emirate." In George K. Zollschan and Walter Hirsh, eds., *Explorations in Social Change*. Boston: Houghton Mifflin, pp. 495–521.

Coleman, James S. 1957. *Community Conflict*. Glencoe, Ill.: Free Press.

Collins, Randall. 1975. *Conflict Sociology*. New York: Academic Press.

Conroy, Patrick. 1972. *The Water Is Wide*. Boston: Houghton Mifflin.

Coogan, Tim. 1970. *The I.R.A.* New York: Praeger.

Cooley, Charles Horton. 1909. *Social Organization*. New York: Scribner.

Cooley, Charles Horton. 1918. *Social Process*. New York: Scribner.

Coser, Lewis A. 1956. *The Functions of Social Conflict*. New York: Free Press of Glencoe.

Coser, Lewis A. 1967. *Continuities in the Study of Social Conflict*. New York: Free Press.

Coser, Lewis A. 1968. "Conflict: Social Aspects." In David Sills, ed., *International Encyclopedia of the Social Sciences*. New York: Macmillan, pp. 232–36.

Coser, Lewis A. 1971. *Masters of Sociological Thought*. New York: Harcourt Brace Jovanovich.

Covington, Robert N., and James E. Jones. 1971. *Labor Relations and Social Problems*. Washington: Bureau of National Affairs.

Cummings, Elaine, and William E. Henry. 1961. *Growing Old: The Process of Disengagement*. New York: Basic Books.

Dahl, Robert A. 1963. *Modern Political Analysis*. Englewood Cliffs, N.J.: Prentice-Hall.

Dahrendorf, Ralf. 1959. *Class and Class Conflict in Industrial Society*. Stanford: Stanford University Press.

D'Antonio, William V., and William H. Form. 1965. *Influentials in Two Border Cities*. Notre Dame: University of Notre Dame Press.

Davidson, Chandler. 1972. *Biracial Politics: Conflict and Coalition in the Metropolitan South*. Baton Rouge: Louisiana State University Press.

Davies, Dorothy Keyworth. 1975. *Race Relations in Rhodesia*. London: Rex Collings.

Davison, W. Phillips. 1974. *Mass Communication and Conflict Resolution: The Role of the Information Media in the Advancement of International Understanding*. New York: Praeger.

Dawson, Carl A., and Warner E. Gettys. 1929. *An Introduction to Sociology*. New York: Ronald.

Demisoff, R. S. 1974. *The Sociology of Dissent*. New York: Harcourt Brace Jovanovich.

Deutsch, Morton. 1973. *The Resolution of Conflict: Constructive and Destructive Processes*. New Haven: Yale University Press.

Dollard, John, et al. 1939. *Frustration and Aggression*. New Haven: Yale University Press.

Domhoff, G. William. 1974. *The Bohemian Grove and Other Retreats*. New York: Harper and Row.

Domhoff, G. William. 1978. *Who Really Rules? New Haven and Community Power Reexamined*. New Brunswick, N.J.: Transaction Books.

Durkheim, Emile. 1938. *The Rules of Sociological Method*. Edited by George E. G. Catlin. Chicago: University of Chicago Press.

Durkheim, Emile. 1947. *The Division of Labor in Society*. Translated by George Simpson, Glencoe, Ill.: Free Press.

Eckstein, Harry, and Ted Robert Gurr. 1975. *Patterns of Authority: A Structural Basis for Political Inquiry*. New York: John Wiley.

Edwards, Lyford P. 1927. *The Natural History of Revolution*. Chicago: University of Chicago Press.

Eggleston, Sir Frederic. 1957. "The United Nations as an Instrument for Preserving Peace." In V. H. Wallace, ed., *Paths to Peace*. Carlton, Victoria: Melbourne University Press, pp. 317–35.

Eisenstadt, Schmuel Noah. 1963. *The Political Systems of Empires*. New York: Free Press.

Eisenstadt, Schmuel Noah. 1964. "Processes of Change and Institutionalization of the Political Systems of Centralized Empires." In George K. Zollschan and Walter Hirsch, eds., *Explorations in Social Change*. Boston:
Houghton Mifflin.

Eisinger, Peter. 1976. *Patterns of Interracial Politics*. New York: Academic
Press.

Elliott, Mabel A. 1952. *Crime in Modern Society*. New York: Harper.

Etzioni, Amitai. 1966. *Studies in Social Change*. New York: Holt, Rinehart
and Winston.

Etzioni, Amitai. 1968. *The Active Society*. New York: Free Press of Glencoe.

Fainstein, Norman, and Susan Fainstein. 1974. *Urban Political Movements:
The Search for Power by Minority Groups in American Cities*. Englewood
Cliffs, N.J.: Prentice-Hall.

Falk, Richard A. 1971. *The International Law of Civil War*. Baltimore:
Johns Hopkins University Press.

Fals-Borda, Orlando. 1969. *Subversion and Social Change in Colombia*. New
York: Columbia University Press.

Fanon, Frantz. 1963. *The Wretched of the Earth*. New York: Grove Press.

Feagin, Joe R., and Harlan Hahn. 1973. Ghetto Revolts: *The Politics of
Violence in American Cities*. New York: Macmillan.

Feierabend, Ivo K., et al. 1969. "Social Change and Political Violence:
Cross-National Patterns." In Hugh Davis Graham and Ted Robert Gurr,
eds., *The History of Violence in America*. New York: Bantam, pp. 632–
87.

Fidel, Kenneth. 1975. *Militarism in Developing Countries*. New Brunswick,
N.J.: Transaction Books.

Fields, Rona M. 1976. *The Portuguese Revolution and the Armed Forces
Movement*. New York: Praeger.

Fish, John Hall. 1973. *Black Power / White Control: Struggle of Woodlawn
Organization in Chicago*. Princeton: Princeton University Press.

Flacks, Richard. 1974. *Youth and Social Change*. Chicago: Markham Publishing Co.

Foster, John. 1974. *Class Struggle and the Industrial Revolution: Early Industrial Capitalism in Three English Towns*. New York: St. Martin's.

Franklin, John Hope. 1956. *The Militant South*. Cambridge: Belknap.

Freire, Paulo. 1979. *Pedagogy of the Oppressed*. New York: Herder and
Herder.

Fromm, Erich. 1941. *Escape From Freedom*. New York: Farrar and Rinehart.

Galbraith, John Kenneth. 1952. *American Capitalism: The Concept of
Countervailing Power*. Boston: Houghton Mifflin.

Gamson, William A. 1968. *Power and Discontent*. Homewood, Ill.: Dorsey.

Gamson, William A. 1975. *The Strategy of Social Protest*. Homewood, Ill.:
Dorsey.

Garner, Roberta Ash. 1977. *Social Movements in America.* Chicago: Rand McNally.

Geertz, Clifford. 1963. *The Integrity of Revolution.* New York: Free Press.

Gelfand, Donald E., and Russell D. Lee. 1973. *Ethnic Conflicts and Power: A Cross-National Perspective.* New York: Wiley.

Gerlach, Luther P., and Virginia H. Hine. 1970. *People, Power, Change: Movements of Social Transformation.* Indianapolis: Bobbs-Merrill.

Gerth, H. H., and C. Wright Mills. 1946. *From Max Weber: Essays in Sociology.* New York: Oxford.

Giddings, Franklin H. 1896. *The Principles of Sociology.* New York: Macmillan Co.

Girdner, Audrie, and Anne Goftis. 1969. *The Great Betrayal.* New York: Macmillan.

Givens, R. Dale, and Martin A. Nettleship, eds. 1976. *Discussions of War and Human Aggression.* The Hague: Mouton.

Gluckman, Max. 1956. *Custom and Conflict in Africa.* New York: Free Press of Glencoe.

Gordon, Milton M. 1964. *Assimilation in American Life.* New York: Oxford.

Graham, Hugh Davis, and Ted Robert Gurr. 1969. *The History of Violence in America.* New York: Bantam Books.

Green, Arnold. 1975. *Social Problems: Arena of Conflict.* New York: McGraw-Hill.

Grier, William H., and Price M. Cobbs. 1968. *Black Rage.* New York: Basic Books.

Grimshaw, Allen D. 1969. *Racial Violence in the United States.* Chicago: Aldine.

Grundy, Kenneth W. 1971. *Guerrilla Struggle in Africa: An Analysis and Preview.* New York: Grossman.

Grundy, Kenneth W. 1973. *Confrontation and Accommodation in Southern Africa: The Limits of Independence.* Berkeley: University of California Press.

Gumplowicz, Ludwig. 1883. *Der Rassenkampf.* Innsbruck: Maguerische Universitäts-Buchhandlung.

Gurr, Ted Robert. 1969. "A Comparative Study of Civil Strife." In Hugh Davis Graham and Ted Robert Gurr, eds., *The History of Violence in America.* New York: Bantam, pp. 572–626.

Gurr, Ted Robert. 1970. *Why Men Rebel.* Princeton: Princeton University Press.

Gurr, Ted Robert. 1976. *Rogues, Rebels, and Reformers: A Political History of Urban Crime and Conflict.* Beverly Hills: Sage.

Halebsky, Sandor. 1976. *Mass Society and Political Conflict: Toward a Reconstruction of Theory.* Cambridge: Cambridge University Press.

Hamilton, Richard F., and James Wright. 1975. *New Directions in Political Sociology.* Indianapolis: Bobbs-Merrill.

Hamilton, Walton. 1933. "Institution." *Encyclopedia of the Social Sciences.* New York: Macmillan, pp. 84–89.

Hawley, Willis D., and Frederic Wirt, eds. 1968. *The Search for Community Power.* Englewood Cliffs, N.J.: Prentice-Hall.

Heberle, Rudolf. 1951. *Social Movements.* New York: Appleton-Century-Crofts.

Heirich, Max. 1970. *The Beginning: Berkeley, 1964.* New York: Columbia University Press.

Heirich, Max. 1973. *The Spiral of Conflict: Berkeley, 1964.* New York: Columbia University Press.

Hendin, Herbert. 1969. *Black Suicide.* New York: Basic Books.

Henshel, R. L. 1976. *On the Future of Social Prediction.* Indianapolis: Bobbs-Merrill.

Herberg, Will. 1955. *Protestant, Catholic, Jew.* Garden City, N.Y.: Doubleday.

Hersch, Seymour M. 1970. *My Lai Four: A Report on the Massacre and Its Aftermath.* New York: Vintage.

Hersey, John. 1968. *The Algiers Motel Incident.* New York: Knopf.

Himes, Joseph S. 1964. "Prediction." *A Dictionary of the Social Sciences.* New York: Free Press, pp. 525–27.

Himes, Joseph S. 1968. *The Study of Sociology.* Glenview, Ill.: Scott, Foresman.

Himes, Joseph S. 1973. *Racial Conflict in American Society.* Columbus, Ohio: Merrill.

Himes, Joseph S. 1974. *Racial and Ethnic Relations.* Dubuque, Iowa: Brown.

Hobsbawm, Eric J. 1959. *Primitive Rebels: Studies in Archaic Forms of Social Movement in the Nineteenth and Twentieth Centuries.* New York: Praeger.

Hobsbawn, Eric J. 1959. *Social Bandits and Primitive Rebels.* New York: Free Press.

Hoglund, Bengt, and Jorgen William Ulrich, eds. 1972. *Conflict Control and Conflict Resolution.* Copenhagen: Munksgaard.

Hook, Sidney. 1933. "Violence." *Encyclopedia of the Social Sciences.* New York: Macmillan, pp. 264–67.

Hoyt, Homer, 1939. *Structure and Growth of Residential Neighborhoods in American Cities.* Washington: U.S. Government Printing Office.

Hunter, Floyd. 1953. *Community Power Structure: A Study of Decision Makers.* Chapel Hill: University of North Carolina Press.

Hunter, Floyd. 1959. *Top Leadership, U.S.A.* Chapel Hill: University of North Carolina Press.

Jablow, Joseph. 1966. *The Cheyenne in Plains Indian Trade Relations: 1795–1840.* Seattle: University of Washington Press.

Janowitz, Morris R. 1968. *The Social Control of Escalated Riots.* Chicago: University of Chicago Center for Policy Study.

Janowitz, Morris R. 1970. *Political Conflict.* Chicago: Quadrangle Books.

Janowitz, Morris R. 1975. *Military Conflict*. Beverly Hills: Sage.

Jenkins, Gwyn Harries, and Jacques Van Doorn, eds. 1976. *The Military and the Problem of Legitimacy*. Beverly Hills: Sage.

Johnson, Harry M. 1960. *Sociology: A Systematic Introduction*. New York: Harcourt, Brace and World.

Kahn, Si. 1970. *How People Get Power*. New York: McGraw-Hill.

Keller, Suzanne I. 1963. *Beyond the Ruling Class*. New York: Random House.

Killian, Lewis M. 1975. *The Impossible Revolution Phase II: Black Power and the American Dream*. New York: Random House.

King, Martin Luther, Jr. 1963. *Strength to Love*. New York: Harper and Row.

King, Martin Luther, Jr. 1964. *Why We Can't Wait*. New York: Harper and Row.

King, Martin Luther, Jr. 1967. *Where Do We Go from Here?* New York: Harper and Row.

Kornhauser, Arthur, Robert Dubin and Arthur M. Ross, eds. 1954. *Industrial Conflict*. New York: McGraw-Hill.

Kornhauser, William. 1959. *The Politics of Mass Society*. Glencoe, Ill.: Free Press.

Kriesberg, Louis. 1973. *The Sociology of Social Conflicts*. Englewood Cliffs, N.J.: Prentice-Hall.

Kruger, Marlis, and Frueda Silvert. 1975. *Dissent Denied: The Technocratic Response to Protest*. New York: Elsevier.

Ladd, Everett, with Charles D. Hadley. 1975. *Transformation of the American Party System: Political Coalitions from the New Deal to the 1970s*. New York: Norton.

Lamb, Curt. 1975. *Political Power in Poor Neighborhoods*. New York: Halstead.

Landsberger, Henry A. 1961. "Parsons' Theory of Organizations." In Max Black, ed., *The Social Theories of Talcott Parsons*. Englewood Cliffs, N.J.: Prentice-Hall.

Lang, Kurt, and Gladys Engel Lang. 1961. *Collective Dynamics*. New York: Crowell.

Lasswell, Harold D., and Abraham Kaplan. 1950. *Power and Society: A Framework for Political Inquiry*. New Haven: Yale University Press.

Latham, Earl. 1966. *The Communist Controversy in Washington*. Cambridge: Harvard University Press.

Lauer, Robert H. 1973. *Perspectives on Social Change*. Boston: Allyn and Bacon.

Lee, Alfred M. 1969. *Principles of Sociology*. New York: Barnes and Noble.

Lenski, Gerhard E. 1966. *Power and Privilege*. New York: McGraw-Hill.

Levin, Murray. 1971. *Political Hysteria in America*. New York: Basic Books.

Levy, Marion. 1952. *The Structures of Society*. Princeton: Princeton University Press.

Levy, Sheldon, G. 1970. "A 150-Year Study of Political Violence in the United States." In Hugh Davis Graham and Ted Robert Gurr, eds., *The History of Violence in America*. New York: Bantam, pp. 84–100.

Lewy, Guenter. 1974. *Religion and Revolution*. New York: Oxford.

Likert, Rensis, and Jane Likert. 1976. *New Ways of Managing Conflict*. New York: McGraw-Hill.

Linton, Ralph. 1936. *The Study of Man*. New York: Appleton-Century.

Lipset, Seymour Martin. 1954. "The Political Process in Trade Unions: A Theoretical Statement." In Morroe Berger and Theodore Abel and Charles H. Page, eds., *Freedom and Control in Modern Society*. New York: Van Nostrand, pp. 88ff.

Lipset, Seymour Martin. 1960. *Political Man*. New York: Doubleday.

Lipset, Seymour Martin. 1976. *Rebellion in the University*. Chicago: University of Chicago Press.

Lofchie, Michael F. 1965. *Zanzibar: Background to Revolution*. Princeton: Princeton University Press.

Lohman, Joseph D. 1947. *The Police and Minority Groups*. Chicago: Chicago Park District.

Lorenz, Konrad. 1966. *On Aggression*. New York: Harcourt, Brace and World.

Lowi, T. J. 1971. *The Politics of Disorder*. New York: Basic Books.

Lowie, Robert H. 1940. *Introduction to Cultural Anthropology*. New York: Farrar and Rinehart.

Luard, D. Evan. 1972. *The International Regulation of Civil War*. New York: New York University Press.

MacIver, Robert M. 1942. *Social Causation*. Boston: Ginn and Co.

MacIver, Robert M., and Charles H. Page. 1949. *Society*. New York: Rinehart.

MacRae, Donald. 1961. *Ideology and Society*. New York: Free Press of Glencoe.

McDougall, William. 1908. *Introduction to Social Psychology*. London: Methuen.

McLuhan, H. Marshall. 1968. *War and Peace in the Global Village*. New York: McGraw-Hill.

Mandelbaum, David G. 1970. *Society in India, Continuity and Change*. Berkeley: University of California Press.

Mannheim, Karl. 1936. *Ideology and Utopia*. London: K. Paul, Trench, Trubner.

Marx, Karl. 1906. *Capital*. Edited by Friederick Engels. New York: Modern Library.

Marx, Karl. 1932. *Capital*. New York: Modern Library.

Mason, Phillip. 1958. *The Birth of a Dilemma: The Conquest and Settlement of Rhodesia*. London: Oxford.

Mead, George Herbert. 1934. *Mind, Self, and Society*. Chicago: University of Chicago Press.

Merton, Robert K. 1957. *Social Theory and Social Structure*. Glencoe, Ill.: Free Press of Glencoe.

Michelman, Cherry. 1975. *Black Sash of South Africa*. New York: Oxford.

Michels, Robert. 1959. *Political Parties*. New York: Dover.

Miller, Delbert C. 1961. "Democracy and Decision-Making in the Community Power Structure." In William V. D'Antonio and Howard H. Erlich, eds., *Power and Democracy in America*. Notre Dame: University of Notre Dame Press.

Miller, Delbert C. 1970. *International Community Power Structures*. Bloomington: Indiana University Press.

Miller, G. R., and H. W. Simons. 1974. *Perspectives on Communication in Social Conflict*. Englewood Cliffs, N.J.: Prentice-Hall.

Mills, C. Wright. 1956. *The Power Elite*. New York: Oxford.

Mishkin, Bernard. 1966. *Rank and Warfare among the Plains Indians*. Seattle: University of Washington Press.

Montgomery, D., and L. Johnson. 1976. *Forecasting and Time Series Analysis*. Hightstown, N.J.: McGraw-Hill.

Moore, Barrington, Jr. 1950. *Soviet Politics: The Dilemma of Power*. Cambridge: Harvard University Press.

Moore, Wilbert E. 1965. *The Impact of Industry*. Englewood Cliffs, N.J.: Prentice-Hall.

Mosca, Gaetano. 1939. *The Ruling Class*. New York: McGraw-Hill.

Mumford, L. 1973. *Interpretations and Forecasts: 1922–1972*. New York: Harcourt Brace Jovanovich.

Murphree, Marshall W., and Donald G. Baker. 1976. "Racial Discrimination in Rhodesia." In Willen Veenhaven, ed., *Case Studies in Human Rights and Fundamental Freedoms*. The Hague: Martinus Nijhoff.

Murray, Robert K. 1955. *Red Scare*. Minneapolis: University of Minneapolis Press.

Musarurwa, E. D. 1977. "African Nationalism in Rhodesia." In Robert Cary and Diana Mitchell, eds., *African Nationalist Leaders in Rhodesia Who's Who*. Johannesburg: African Book Society.

Myrdal, Gunnar. 1944. *An American Dilemma*. New York: Harper and Row.

Nellis, John R. 1972. *A Theory of Ideology: The Tanzanian Example*. London: Oxford University Press.

Nelson, Harold D., et al. 1975. *Area Handbook for Southern Rhodesia*. Washington, D.C.: U.S. Government Printing Office.

Nettleship, Martin A., et al. 1975. *War: Its Causes and Correlates*. The Hague: Mouton.

Newman, William M. 1973. *American Pluralism: A Study of Minority Groups and Social Theory*. New York: Harper and Row.

Nieburg, H. L. 1969. *Political Violence: The Behavioral Process*. New York: St. Martin's.

Oberschall, Anthony. 1973. *Social Conflict and Social Movements.* Englewood Cliffs, N.J.: Prentice-Hall.

Odegard, Peter. 1928. *Pressure Politics: The Story of the Anti-Saloon League.* New York: Columbia University Press.

Ogburn, William F. 1922. *Social Change.* New York: B. W. Heubsch, Inc.

Olsen, Marvin E. 1970. *Power in Societies.* London: Macmillan.

Olson, Mancur. 1965. *The Logic of Collective Action.* Cambridge: Harvard University Press.

O'Meara, Patrick. 1975. *Rhodesia: Racial Conflict or Coexistence?* Ithaca: Cornell University Press.

Orum, Anthony M. 1972. *Black Students in Protest: A Study of the Origins of the Black Student Movement.* Washington, D.C.: American Sociological Association.

Palmer, Stuart. 1970. *Deviance and Conformity.* New Haven: College and University Press.

Pareto, Vilfredo. 1963. *The Mind and Society: A Treatise on General Sociology.* Translated by Andrew Bongiorno and Arthur Livingston; edited by Arthur Livingston. New York: Dover.

Park, Robert E., and Ernest W. Burgess. 1921. *Introduction to the Science of Sociology.* Chicago: University of Chicago Press.

Parkin, Frank. 1971. *Class Inequality and Political Order.* New York: Praeger.

Parsons, Talcott. 1949. *The Structure of Social Action.* New York: Free Press of Glencoe.

Parsons, Talcott. 1951. *The Social System.* Glencoe, Ill.: Free Press of Glencoe.

Pettee, George S. 1938. *The Process of Revolution.* New York: Harper and Row.

Pinkney, Alphonso. 1976. *Red, Black, and Green: Black Nationalism in the United States.* New York: Cambridge University Press.

Piven, Frances, and Richard A. Cloward. 1974. *The Politics of Turmoil.* New York: Pantheon.

Ploss, Sidney. 1965. *Conflict and Decision Making in Soviet Russia.* Princeton: Princeton University Press.

Preston, William, Jr. 1963. *Aliens and Dissenters.* Cambridge: Harvard University Press.

Rapoport, Anatol. 1974. *Man-Made Environments.* Baltimore: Penguin.

Ratzenhofer, Gustav. 1898. *Die sociologische Erkenntnis.* Leipzig: F. A. Bockhaus.

Record, Wilson. 1964. *Race and Radicalism.* Ithaca, N.Y.: Cornell University Press.

Report of the National Advisory Commission on Civil Disorders. 1968. New York: Bantam.

Riesman, David, et al. 1950. *The Lonely Crowd.* New Haven: Yale University Press.

Rose, Arnold M. 1967. *The Power Structure: Political Process in American Society.* New York: Oxford University Press.

Rosenbaum, H. Jon, and Peter C. Sederberg. 1976. *Vigilante Politics.* Philadelphia: University of Pennsylvania Press.

Ross, Arthur M., and Paul T. Hartman. 1960. *Changing Patterns of Industrial Conflict.* New York: Wiley.

Ross, Edward Alsworth. 1920. *The Principles of Sociology.* New York: Century.

Rossi, Peter H. 1970. *Ghetto Revolts.* Chicago: Aldine.

Rostow, W. W. 1962. *The Process of Economic Growth.* New York: Norton.

Rubin, Lillian. 1972. *Busing and Backlash.* Berkeley: University of California Press.

Rude, George F. 1964. *The Crowd in History.* New York: Wiley.

Rummel, Rudolph J. 1975. *Understanding Conflict and War. 2 vols.* New York: Halsted Press.

Runciman, Walter. 1966. *Relative Deprivation and Social Justice.* Berkeley: University of California Press.

Russell, D. E. H. 1974. *Rebellion, Revolution, and Armed Forces: A Comparative Study of Fifteen Countries with Special Emphasis on Cuba and South Africa.* New York: Academic Press.

Ryan, Bryce F. 1969. *Social and Cultural Change.* New York: Ronald.

Salert, Barbara. 1976. *Revolutions and Revolutionaries: Four Theories.* New York: Elsevier.

Schecter, Betty. 1963. *The Peaceable Revolution: The Story of Non-Violent Resistance.* Boston: Houghton Mifflin.

Schermerhorn, Richard A. 1976. *Communal Violence in India.* Kalamazoo, Mich.: Consultative Committee of Indian Muslims, Western Michigan University.

Schiffrin, Harold Z. 1976. *Military and State in Modern Asia.* Jerusalem: Academic Press for Hebrew University.

Scott, Joseph W. 1976. *The Black Revolts: Racial Stratification in the U.S.A.* Cambridge: Schenkman.

Scott, Marvin, and Stanford Lyman. 1970. *The Revolt of the Students.* Columbus, Ohio: Merrill.

Seliger, Martin. 1976. *Ideology and Politics.* New York: Free Press.

Shamuyarira, Nathan M. 1965. *Crisis in Rhodesia.* London: A. Deutsch.

Sharp, Gene. 1970. *Exploring Nonviolent Alternatives.* Boston: Porter Sargent.

Sharp, Gene. 1974. *Power and Struggle.* Boston: Porter Sargent.

Shatland, R. Lance. 1976. "Spontaneous Vigilantism: A Bystander Response to Criminal Behavior." In H. Jon Rosenbaum and Peter C. Sederberg,

Vigilante Politics. Philadelphia: University of Pennsylvania Press, pp. 130–44.

Simmel, George. 1955. *Conflict*. Translated by Kurt H. Wolff. Glencoe, Ill.: Free Press of Glencoe.

Simpson, Richard L. 1972. *Theories of Social Exchange*. Norristown, N.J.: General Learning Press.

Singer, Jerome L. 1971. *The Control of Aggression and Violence*, New York: Academic Press.

Skolnick, Jerome. 1969. *The Politics of Protest*. New York: Simon and Schuster.

Small, Albion W., and George E. Vincent. 1894. *An Introduction to the Study of Society*. New York: American Book Co.

Smelser, Neil J. 1959. *Social Change in the Industrial Revolution: An Application of Theory to the British Cotton Industry*. Chicago: University of Chicago Press.

Smelser, Neil J. 1963. *Theory of Collective Behavior*. New York: Free Press of Glencoe.

Smith, Clagett. 1971. *Conflict Resolution: Contributions of the Behavioral Sciences*. Notre Dame: University of Notre Dame Press.

Sorel, Georges. 1941. *Reflections of Violence*. Translated by T. E. Hulme. New York: Peter Smith.

Sowell, Thomas. 1975. *Race and Economics*. New York: David McKay.

Steinbeck, John. 1939. *The Grapes of Wrath*. New York: Viking Press.

Sterba, Richard. 1947. "Some Psychological Factors in Negro Race Hatred and in Anti-Negro Riots." In Gezarohein, ed., *Psychoanalysis and the Social Sciences*. Vol. 1. New York: International Universities Press, pp. 411–27.

Stohl, Michael. 1976. *War and Political Violence: The American Capacity for Repression and Reaction*. Beverly Hills: Sage.

Stouffer, Samuel A., et al. 1949. *The American Soldier: Adjustment during Army Life*. Princeton University Press.

Sumner, William G. 1940. *Folkways*. New York: Ginn.

Supplement to the Monthly Digest of Statistics. July 1977. Compiled and issued by the Central Statistical Office, Salisbury, Rhodesia.

Taft, Phillip, and Phillip Ross. 1969. "American Labor Violence: Its Cause, Character, and Outcome." In Hugh Davis Graham and Ted Robert Gurr, eds., *The History of Violence in America*. New York: Bantam, pp. 281–396.

Tandon, Yashpal. 1970. "The Organization of African Unity as an Instrument and Forum of Protest." In Robert I. Rotberg and Ali A. Mazrui, eds., *Protest and Power in Black Africa*. New York: Oxford, pp. 1153–83.

Tax, Sol, ed. 1967. *The Draft: A Handbook of Facts and Alternatives*. Chicago: University of Chicago Press.

Taylor, George W. 1948. *Government Regulation of Industrial Relations*. New York: Prentice-Hall.

Terrill, Ross. 1972. *Eight Hundred Million: The Real China*. Boston: Little, Brown.

Tilly, Charles. 1969. "Collective Violence in European Perspective." In Hugh Davis Graham and Ted Robert Gurr, eds., *The History of Violence in America*. New York: Bantam, pp. 4–44.

Tomasson, Richard F. 1969. "The Value System of the Most Developed Society: Sweden." Paper presented to the American Sociological Association, 1969. Unpublished.

Tomasson, Richard F. 1970. *Sweden: Prototype of Modern Society*. New York: Random House.

Tomlinson, T. M. 1968. "The Development of Riot Ideology Among Urban Negroes." In Louis H. Masotti and Don R. Bowen, eds., *Riots and Rebellion: Civil Violence in an Urban Community*. Beverly Hills: Sage, pp. 17–428.

Townsend, Sara Bertha. 1958. *The American Soldier*. Raleigh: Edwards and Broughton.

Turner, Ralph H. 1970. "Determinants of Social Movement Strategies." In Tamotsu Shibutani, ed., *Human Nature and Collective Behavior: Papers in Honor of Herbert Blumer*. Englewood Cliffs, N.J.: Prentice-Hall, pp. 145–64.

Turner, Ralph H., and Lewis M. Killian. 1972. *Collective Behavior*. Englewood Cliffs, N.J.: Prentice-Hall.

Useem, Michael. 1973. *Conscription, Protest and Social Conflict: The Life and Death of the Draft Resistance Movement*. New York: Wiley.

Useem, Michael. 1975. *Protest Movements in America*. Indianapolis: Bobbs-Merrill.

Vayda, Andrew P. 1976. *War in Sociological Perspective*. New York: Plenum.

Vittachi, T. 1958. *Emergency '58: The Story of the Ceylon Race Riots*. London: Andre Deutsch.

Walker, Daniel. 1968. *The Walker Report: Rights in Conflict*. New York: Bantam.

Walker, Eugene Victor. 1969. *Terror and Resistance: A Study of Political Violence, with Case Studies of Some Primitive African Communities*. New York: Oxford.

Wallace, Victor H., ed. 1957. *Paths to Peace: A Study of War, Its Causes and Prevention*. Carlton, Victoria: Melbourne University Press.

Ward, Lester F. 1913. *Dynamic Sociology*. New York: Appleton.

Wilkerson, David. 1976. *Cohesion and Conflict: Lessons from the Study of Three Party Interaction*. New York: St. Martin's.

Williams, Robin M., Jr. 1976. *Mutual Accommodation: Ethnic Conflict and Cooperation*. Minneapolis: University of Minnesota Press.

Wills, A. J. 1973. *An Introduction to the History of Central Africa*. London: Oxford.

Wilson, Godfrey, and Monica Wilson. 1945. *The Analysis of Social Change:*

Based on Observations in Central Africa. Cambridge, England: Cambridge University Press.

Wilson, John. 1968. *Varieties of Police Behavior.* Cambridge: Harvard University Press.

Wilson, John. 1973. *Introduction to Social Movements.* New York: Basic Books.

Wilson, William J. 1973. *Power, Racism and Privilege.* New York: Macmillan.

Wolfe, Alan. 1973. *The Seamy Side of Democracy: Repression in America.* New York: David McKay.

Yarmolinsky, Adam. 1971. *The Military Establishment.* New York: Harper and Row.

ARTICLES

Aberle, D. F., et al. 1950. "The Functional Prerequisites of a Society." *Ethics* 60 (January): 100–111.

Aberbach, J. D., and J. L. Walker. 1970. "The Meanings of Black Power: Comparison of White and Black Interpretations of a Political Slogan." *American Political Science Review* 64 (June): 367–88.

Acker, Joan. 1973. "Women and Social Stratification: A Case of Intellectual Sexism." *American Journal of Sociology* 78 (January): 936–44.

Adamek, Raymond J., and Jerry M. Lewis. 1973. "Social Control, Violence and Radicalization: The Kent State Case." *Social Forces* 51 (March): 342–47.

Adelman, Kenneth Lee. 1975. "The Church-State Conflict in Zaire: 1969–1974." *African Studies Review* 13 (April): 102–15.

Afheldt, Horst. 1973. "The Consequences of War and the Prevention of War." *Journal of Peace Research* 10: 259–63.

Afheldt, Horst, and Philipp Sonntag. 1973. "Stability and Deterrence through Strategic Nuclear Arms." *Journal of Peace Research* 10: 245–50.

Agger, Robert E., and Daniel Goldrich. 1958. "Community Power Structures and Partisanship." *American Sociological Review* 23 (August): 383–92.

Akzin, B. 1966. "On Conjecture in Political Science." *Political Studies* 14 (February): 1–15.

Albed, Wil. 1977. "Between Harmony and Conflict: Industrial Democracy in the Netherlands." *The Annals* 431 (May): 74–82.

Albrecht, Ulrich. 1973. "The Costs of Armamentism." *Journal of Peace Research* 10: 265–83.

Albrecht, Ulrich. 1975. "Militarization, Arms Transfer, and Arms Production in Peripheral Countries." *Journal of Peace Research* 12: 195–212.

Alcock, Norman, and Alan G. Newcombe. 1970. "The Perception of National Power." *Journal of Conflict Resolution* 14 (September): 335–43.

Aldrich, Howard E. 1973. "Employment Opportunities for Blacks in the

Black Ghetto: The Role of White-Owned Businesses." *American Journal of Sociology* 78 (May): 1403–25.

Almy, Timothy A. 1973. "Residential Location and Electoral Cohesion: The Pattern of Urban Political Conflict." *American Political Science Review* 67 (September): 914–23.

AlRoy, Gil Carl. 1966. "Insurgency in the Countryside of Underdeveloped Societies." *Antioch Review* 26 (Summer): 149–57.

AlRoy, Gil Carl. 1974. "Do the Arabs Want Peace?" *Commentary* 57 (February): 56–61.

Amin, Samir. 1972. "Underdevelopment and Dependence in Africa: Historical Origin." *Journal of Peace Research* 9: 105–19.

Anderson, Clifford W., and Betty A. Nesvold. 1972. "A Skinnerian Analysis of Conflict Behavior: Walden II Goes Cross-National." *American Behavioral Scientist* 15 (July–August): 883–910.

Anderson, William A. 1973. "Organizational and Political Transformation of a Social Movement: A Study of Thirtieth of May Movement in Curacao." *Social Forces* 51 (March): 330–41.

Archibald, Drew. 1969. "The Africaners as an Emergent Minority." *British Journal of Sociology* 20 (December): 416–26.

Aron, William S. 1974. "Student Activism of the 1960's Revisited: A Multivariant Analysis Research Note." *Social Forces* 52 (March): 408–14.

Ashworth, A. E. 1968. "The Sociology of Trench Warfare, 1914–1918." *British Journal of Sociology* 19 (December): 407–23.

Atkinson, Carylon A. 1968. "Coalition Building in Mobilization against Poverty." *American Behavioral Scientist* 12 (November–December): 48–52.

Bachrach, Peter, and Morton Baratz. 1962. "Two Faces of Power." *American Political Science Review* 56 (December): 947–52.

Bachrach, Peter, and Morton Baratz. 1963. "Decisions and Nondecisions: An Analytical Framework." *American Political Science Review* 57 (September): 632–42.

Bahr, Hans-Eckehard. 1973. "The Politicising of Everyday Life: Social Conditions of Peace." *Journal of Peace Research* 10: 37–49.

Baldassare, Mark. 1975. "The Effects of Density on Social Behavior and Attitudes." *American Behavioral Scientist* 18 (July–August): 815–25.

Baldwin, David A. 1971. "Money and Power." *Journal of Politics* 33 (August): 578–614.

Baldwin, David A. 1971. "Thinking about Threats." *The Journal of Conflict Resolution* 15 (March): 71–77.

Baldwin, David A. 1971. "The Costs of Power." *Journal of Conflict Resolution* 15 (June): 145–55.

Ball-Rokeach, Sandra M. 1973. "Values and Violence: A Test of the Subculture of Violence Thesis." *American Sociological Review* 38 (December): 736–49.

Banks, Arthur S. 1972. "Patterns of Domestic Conflict, 1919–1939 and 1946–1966." *Journal of Conflict Resolution* 16: 41–50.

Baron, Harold M., et al. 1968. "Black Powerlessness in Chicago." *Trans-Action.* 6 (November): 27–33.

Barsegov, Yuri, and Rusten Khairov. 1973. "A Study of the Problems of Peace." *Journal of Peace Research* 10: 71–80.

Barth, Ernest A. T., and Donald L. Noel. 1972. "Conceptual Framework for the Analysis of Race Relations: An Evaluation." *Social Forces* 50 (March): 333–48.

Baumgartner, T., et al. 1975. "Relational Control: The Human Structuring of Cooperation and Conflict." *Journal of Conflict Resolution* 19 (September): 417–37.

Bechtal, Robert B. 1971. "The Discovery of Areas of Potential Social Disturbance in the City." *Sociological Quarterly* 12 (Winter): 114–21.

Beck, E. M. 1974. "Conflict, Change and Stability: A Reciprocal Interaction in Schools." *Social Forces* 52 (June): 517–31.

Beit-Hallahmi, Benjamin. 1972. "National Character and National Behavior in the Middle East Conflict: The Case of the 'Arab Personality.' " *International Journal of Group Tensions* 2: 19–26.

Bell, Daniel. 1964. "Twelve Modes of Prediction: A Preliminary Sorting of Approaches in the Social Sciences." *Daedalus* 93: 845–80.

Bell, Daniel, and Virginia Held. 1969. "The Community Revolution." *Public Interest* 16 (Summer): 142–77.

Bendix, Rheinhard. 1976. "The Mandate to Rule: An Introduction." *Social Forces* 55 (December): 242–56.

Benjamin, Roger W. 1975. "Images of Conflict Resolution and Social Control." *Journal of Conflict Resolution* 19 (March): 123–37.

Benjamin, Roger W., and Lewis J. Edinger. 1971. "Conditions for Military Control over Foreign Policy Decisions in Major States." *Journal of Conflict Resolution* 15 (March): 5–31.

Benson, J. Kenneth. 1971. "Militant Ideologies and Organizational Context: The War on Poverty and the Ideology of Black Power." *Sociological Quarterly* 12 (Summer): 328–39.

Benson, J. Kenneth. 1973. "The Analysis of Bureaucratic Professional Conflict: Functional versus Dialectical Approaches." *Sociological Quarterly* 14 (Summer): 376–94.

Bernard, Jessie. 1950. "Where is the Modern Sociology of Conflict?" *American Journal of Sociology* 56: 11–16.

Bernstein, B. J. 1975. "Roosevelt, Truman and the Atomic Bomb, 1941–1945: A Reinterpretation." *Political Science Quarterly* 90 (Spring): 23–69.

Bierstedt, Robert. 1950. "An Analysis of Social Power." *American Sociological Review* 15 (December): 730–38.

Black, Donald, and Albert Reiss. 1970. "Police Control of Juveniles." *American Sociological Review* 34 (February): 63–77.

Black, Gordon S. 1974. "Conflict in the Community: A Theory of the Effects of Community Size." *American Political Science Review* 68 (September): 1245–61.

Blake, Joseph. 1970. "The Organization as Instrument of Violence: The Military Case." *Sociological Quarterly* 11 (Summer): 331–50.

Blake, R. R., and Jane Mouton. 1961. "Comprehension of Own and Outgroup Positions Under Intergroup Competition." *Journal of Conflict Resolution* 5: 304–10.

Blalock, Hubert M., Jr. 1960. "A Power Analysis of Racial Discrimination." *Social Forces* 39 (October): 53–59.

Blau, Kim, and James T. Richardson. 1973. "Contract Formation and Overt Power: A Reexamination." *Social Forces* 51 (June): 440–47.

Blau, Peter M., and Ellen L. Slaughter. 1971. "Institutional Conditions and Student Demonstrations." *Social Problems* 18 (Spring): 475–87.

Boehringer, G. H., et al. 1974. "Stirling: The Destructive Application of Group Techniques to a Conflict." *Journal of Conflict Resolution* 18 (June): 257–84.

Bolton, Charles D. 1972. "Alienation and Action: A Study of Peace Group Members." *American Journal of Sociology* 78 (November): 537–61.

Bonnemaison, Antonine. 1975. "The Social Conflict in France." *Conflict Studies* 55 (March): 1–15.

Boserup, Anders. 1970. "The Politics of Protracted Conflict." *Trans-Action* 7 (March): 22–31.

Boulding, Kenneth E. 1962. "The Prevention of World War III." *Virginia Quarterly Review* 38 (Winter): 2–12.

Boulding, Kenneth E. 1973. "Equality and Conflict." *The Annals* 409 (September): 1–8.

Brady, David W. and Kathleen Kemp. 1976. "The Supreme Court's Abortion Rulings and Social Change." *Social Science Quarterly*. 57 (December): 535–45.

Brand, C. 1976. "Race and Politics in Rhodesian Trade Unions." Centre for Interracial Studies, University of Rhodesia. Unpublished.

Brenner, Phillip. 1974. "Committee Conflict in the Congressional Arena." *The Annals* 411 (January): 87–101.

Britt, David, and Omer R. Galle. 1972. "Industrial Conflict and Unionization." *American Sociological Review*. 37 (February): 46–57.

Brown, Judson S. 1957. "Principles of Intra-personal Conflict." *Journal of Conflict Resolution* 1 (June): 135–54.

Brucan, Silviu. 1975. "The Systematic Power." *Journal of Peace Research*. 12: 63–70.

Brundenius, Claes. 1972. "The Anatomy of Imperialism: The Case of the Multinational Mining Corporations in Peru." *Journal of Peace Research* 9: 189–207.

Burki, Shahid Javed. 1971. "Social and Economic Determinants of Political

Violence: A Case Study of the Punjab." *Middle East Journal* 25 (Autumn): 465–80.

Burnstein, Paul, and William Freudenburg. 1978. "Changing Public Policy: The Impact of Public Opinion, Antiwar Demonstrations, and War Costs on Senate Voting in Vietnam War Motions." *American Journal of Sociology* 84 (July): 99–122.

Burrowes, Robert, and Douglas Muzzio. 1972. "The Road to the Six Day War: Aspects of an Enumerative History of Four Arab States and Israel, 1965–1967." *Journal of Conflict Resolution* 16 (June): 211–26.

Campbell, John C. 1972. "The Soviet Union and the United States in the Middle East." *The Annals* 401 (May): 126–35.

Cantril, Hadley. 1942. "Public Opinion in Flux." *The Annals* 220 (March): 136–50.

Carroll, Bernice A. 1970. "War Termination and Conflict Theory: Value Premises, Theories, and Policies." *The Annals* 392 (November): 14–29.

Carroll, Bernice A. 1972. "Peace Research: The Cult of Power." *Journal of Conflict Resolution* 16 (December). 585–616.

Casey, Thomas J. 1967. "The Compatibility of Free Choice with the Prediction of Human Behavior." *Rocky Mountain Social Science Journal* 4 (October): 151–59.

Cefkin, J. Leo. 1968. "The Rhodesian Question at the United Nations." *International Organization* 22 (Summer): 649–69.

Chamberlain, Neil W. 1971. "Stabilization of Labor Relations?" *The Annals* 396 (July): 79–89.

Chatterjee, Bishwa B., and Shyam S. Bhattacharjee. 1971. "Meanings of Nonviolence: Type of Dimensions?" *Journal of Peace Research* 8: 155–61.

Chen, K. C. 1975. "Hanoi's Three Decisions and the Escalation of the Vietnam War." *Political Science Quarterly.* 90 (Summer): 239–59.

Chen, K. C. 1975. "Reviewing Forecasting Techniques." *Power* 119 (August): 48–49.

Clark, Dennis. 1970. "The Passion of Protected Conflict." *Trans-Action* 7 (March): 15–21.

Clark, Kenneth B. 1944. "Group Violence: A Preliminary Study of the Attitudinal Pattern of Its Acceptance and Rejection: A Study of the 1943 Harlem Riot." *Journal of Social Psychology* 19: 319–37.

Clark, Kenneth B., and James Barker. 1945. "The Zoot Effect in Personality: A Race Riot Participant." *Journal of Abnormal and Social Psychology* 40: 143–48.

Clarke, James W., and Joseph Egan. 1972. "Social and Political Dimensions of Protest Activity." *Journal of Politics* 34 (May): 499–523.

Clifford-Vaughan, Michalina, and Margaret Scotford-Norton. 1967. "Legal Norms and Social Order: Petrazycki, Pareto, Durkheim." *British Journal of Sociology* 18 (September): 269–77.

Coates, Joseph F. 1973. "Urban Violence: The Pattern of Disorder." *The Annals* 405 (January): 25–40.

Cochran, Peggy. 1971. "A Situational Approach to the Study of Police-Negro Relations." *Sociological Quarterly* 12 (Spring) : 232–37.

Cohen, Nathan E. 1967. "The Los Angeles Riot Study." *Social Work Journal* 12 (October) : 14–21.

Cole, David. 1973. "Perceptions of War and Participants in Warfare: A Ten-Year Replication." *Journal of Peace Research* 10–11: 115–59.

Cole, Stephen. 1969. "Teacher's Strike: A Study of the Conversion of Predisposition into Action." *American Journal of Sociology* 74 (March) : 506–20.

Cole, Stephen, and Hannelore Adamsons. 1970. "Professional Status and Faculty Support of Student Demonstrations." *Public Opinion Quarterly* 34 (Fall) : 389–94.

Coleman, A. L. 1960. "Social Scientists' Predictions about Desegregation, 1950–1955." *Social Forces* 38 (March) : 258–62.

Coleman, James S. 1973. "Loss of Power." *American Sociological Review* 38 (February) : 1–17.

Collins, Randall. 1971. "A Conflict Theory of Sexual Stratification." *Social Problems* 19 (Summer) : 3–21.

Conant, Ralph W. 1968. "Rioting, Insurrection, and Civil Disobedience." *American Scholar* 37 (Summer) : 420–33.

Conforti, Joseph N. 1974. "Racial Conflict in Central Cities." *Society* 12 (November–December) : 22–34.

Coser, Lewis A. 1957. "Social Conflict and the Theory of Social Change." *British Journal of Sociology* 8: 197–207.

Coser, Lewis A. 1961. "The Termination of Conflict." *Journal of Conflict Resolution* 5: 347–53.

Cox, Oliver Cromwell. 1974. "Jewish Self-Interest in 'Black Pluralism.'" *Sociological Quarterly* 15 (Spring) : 183–98.

Cressey, Paul F. 1949. "Social Disorganization and Reorganization in Harlan County, Kentucky." *American Sociological Review* 14 (June) : 389–94.

Cross, Malcom. 1971. "On Conflict, Race Relations, and the Theory of the Plural Society." *Race* 12 (April) : 477–94.

Crotty, William J. 1972. "Violence in America." *Society* 9 (May) : 26–27.

Crouch, Colin. 1968. "New Military vs. Old Liberalism." *Manchester Guardian Weekly* (June 20) : 7.

Culbert, Samuel A., and James M. Elden. 1970. "An Anatomy of Activism for Executives." *Harvard Business Review* (November–December) : 131–42.

Curtis, Russel A., Jr., and Louis A. Zurcher, Jr. 1973. "Stable Resources of Protest Movements: The Multi-Organization Field." *Social Forces* 52 (September) : 53–61.

Dahl, Robert A. 1958. "A Critique of the Ruling Elite Model." *American Political Science Review* 52 (June) : 463–69.

Dahrendorf, Ralf. 1958. "Toward a Theory of Social Conflict." *Journal of Conflict Resolution* 2: 170–83.

Danigelis, Nicholas. 1977. "A Theory of Black Political Participation in the United States." *Social Forces* 56 (September): 31–47.

Danzger, M. Herbert. 1964. "Community Power Structure: Problems and Continuities." *American Sociological Review* 29 (October): 707–17.

Danzger, M. Herbert. 1975. "Validating Conflict Data." *American Sociological Review* 40 (October): 570–84.

Davies, James C. 1962. "Toward a Theory of Revolution." *American Sociological Review* 27 (February): 5–18.

Davies, James C. 1970. "Violence and Aggression: Innate or Not?" *Western Political Quarterly* 23 (September): 611–23.

Davis, Kingsley. 1959. "The Myth of Functional Analysis as a Special Method in Sociology and Anthropology." *American Sociological Review* 24 (December): 757–72.

Debnam, Geoffrey. 1975. "Nondecisions and Power: The Two Faces of Bachrach and Baratz." *American Political Science Review* 69 (September): 889–99.

Degler, Carl N. 1972. "Indians and Other Americans." *Commentary* 54 (November): 68–72.

DeJouvenel, B. 1966. "A Letter on Predicting." *American Behavioral Scientist* 9 (June): 51.

Dekmejian, R. Hrair. 1976. "Marx, Weber, and the Egyptian Revolution." *Middle East Journal* 30 (Spring): 158–72.

Dodson, Don. 1974. "The Four Modes of *Drum*: Popular Fiction and Social Control in South Africa." *African Studies Review* 17 (September): 317–44.

Doob, Leonard W., and William J. Foltz. 1974. "The Impact of a Workshop on Grass Roots Leaders in Belfast." *Journal of Conflict Resolution* 18 (June): 237–55.

Dornbusch, Sanford M. 1955. "The Military Academy as an Assimilating Institution." *Social Forces* 33 (May): 316–21.

Dowdall, George W. 1974. "White Gains from Black Subordination in 1960 and 1970." *Social Problems* 22 (December): 162–83.

Downes, Bryant T. 1970. "A Critical Examination of the Social and Political Characteristics of Riot Cities." *Social Science Quarterly* 51 (September): 349–80.

Dowty, Allen. 1971. "Foreign-Linked Factionalisms as a Historical Pattern." *Journal of Conflict Resolution* 15 (December): 429–41.

Draper, Theodore. 1973. "From 1967 to 1973: The Arab-Israeli Wars." *Commentary* 56 (December): 31–45.

Dubey, Sumati N. 1971. "Powerlessness and Mobility Orientations among Disadvantaged Blacks." *Public Opinion Quarterly* 35 (Summer): 183–88.

Dubin, Robert. 1965. "Industrial Conflict: The Power of Prediction." *Industrial and Labor Relations Review* 18 (April): 352–63.

Duncanson, Dennis. 1973. "Indo-China: The Conflict Analyzed." *Conflict Studies* 39 (October): 1–19.

Dunlap, Riley. 1970. "A Comment on Multiversity, University Size, University Quality and Student Protest: An Empirical Study." *American Sociological Review* 35 (June): 525–28.

Duster, Troy. 1968. "Student Interests, Student Power, and the Swedish Experience." *American Behavioral Scientist* 11 (May–June): 21–27.

Dye, Thomas. 1978. "Oligarchic Tendencies in National Policy Making: The Role of the Private Claim Organizations." *Journal of Politics* 40 (May): 309–32.

Eckhardt, William. 1974. "A Conformity Theory of Aggression." *Journal of Peace Research* 11: 31–39.

Eckhardt, William. 1975. "Primitive Militarism." *Journal of Peace Research* 12: 55–61.

Edelman, Marian Wright. 1973. "Southern School Desegregation, 1954–73: A Judicial-Political Overview." *The Annals* 407 (May): 32–42.

Ehrlich, Howard. 1971. "Social Conflict in America: The 1960s. *Sociological Quarterly* 12 (Summer): 295–307.

Eide, Asbjørn. 1972. "Dialogue and Confrontation in Europe." *Journal of Conflict Resolution* 16 (December): 511–22.

Eide, Asbjørn. 1974. "International Law, Dominance, and the Use of Force." *Journal of Peace Research* 11: 1–20.

Eide, Asbjørn. 1975. "Global or Parochial Perspectives in International Studies and Peace Research." *Journal of Peace Research* 12: 79–86.

Eisinger, Peter K. 1971. "Protest Behavior and the Integration of Urban Political Systems." *Journal of Politics* 33 (November): 980–1007.

Eisinger, Peter K. 1973. "The Conditions of Protest Behavior in American Cities." *American Political Science Review* 67 (March): 11–28.

Eisinger, Peter K. 1974. "Racial Differences in Protest Participation." *American Political Science Review* 68 (June): 592–606.

Elder, Glenn H., Jr. 1970. "Group Orientations and Strategies in Racial Change." *Social Forces* 48 (June): 445–61.

Eldridge, J. T., and G. C. Cameron. 1964. "Unofficial Strikes." *British Journal of Sociology* 15 (March): 19–37.

Emery, F. E. 1974. "Methodological Premises of Social Forecasting." *The Annals* 412 (March): 97–115.

Etzioni-Halevy, Eva. 1975. "Patterns of Conflict Generation and Conflict 'Absorption.' " *Journal of Conflict Resolution* 19 (June): 286–309.

Etzioni-Halevy, Eva, and Moshe Livne. 1977. "The Response of the Israeli Establishment to the Yom Kippur War Protest." *Middle East Journal* 31: 281–96.

Ewing, David W. 1964. "Tension Can Be an Asset." *Harvard Business Review* 42 (September–October): 71–78.

Fahlund, G. Gregory. 1973. "Retroactivity and the Warren Court: The Strategy of a Revolution." *Journal of Politics* 35 (August): 570–93.

Falk, Richard A. 1970. " 'Songmy' War Crimes and Individual Responsibility." *Trans-Action* 7 (January): 33–40.

Feagin, Joe R. 1971. "White Separatists and Black Separatists: A Comparative Analysis." *Social Problems* 19 (Fall): 167–80.

Fendrich, James M., and Ailson Tarleau. 1973. "Marching to a Different Drummer: Occupational and Political Correlates of Former Student Activists." *Social Forces* 52 (December): 245–53.

Feuer, Lewis S. 1972. "Student Unrest in the United States." *The Annals* 404 (November): 170–82.

Feierabend, Ivo, and Rosalynd L. Feierabend. 1972. "Coerciveness and Change." *American Behavioral Scientist* 15 (July–August): 911–28.

Fink, Clinton F. 1972. "Conflict Management Strategies by Expected Utility Models of Behavior." *American Behavioral Scientist.* 15 (July–August): 837–58.

Finsterbusch, Kurt, and H. C. Greisman. 1974. "The Unprofitability of Warfare: An Historical-Quantitative Approach." Paper prepared for the American Sociological Association annual meeting, 29 August, Montreal, Canada. Mimeograph.

Firestone, Joseph M. 1972. "Theory of the Riot Process." *American Behavioral Scientist* 15 (July–August): 859–82.

Firestone, Joseph M. 1974. "Continuities in the Theory of Violence." *Journal of Conflict Resolution* 18 (March): 117–42.

Fischer, Claude S. 1971. "A Research Note on Urbanism and Tolerance." *American Journal of Sociology* 76 (March): 847–56.

Fischer, Claude S. 1975. "The City and Political Psychology." *American Political Science Review* 69 (June): 559–71.

Fitzgerald, Bruce D. 1975. "Self-Interest or Altruism." *Journal of Conflict Resolution* 19 (September): 462–79.

Flacks, Richard. 1970. "Social and Cultural Meanings of Student Revolt: Some Informal Comparative Observations. *Social Problems* 17 (Winter): 340–57.

Flacks, Richard. 1970. "Young Intelligentsia in Revolt." *Trans-Action.* 7 (June): 47–55.

Flanner, Philip. 1976. "Conflicting Loyalties and the American Military Ethic." *American Behavioral Scientist* 19 (May–June): 589–603.

Foltz, William J. 1977. "U.S. Policy toward Southern Africa: Economic and Strategic Constraints." *Political Science Quarterly* 92 (Spring): 47–64.

Ford, William F., and John H. Moore. 1970. "Additional Evidence on the Social Characteristics of Riot Cities." *Social Science Quarterly* 51 (September): 339–48.

Ford, William Scott. 1973. "Interracial Public Housing in a Border City: Another Look at the Contact Hypothesis." *American Journal of Sociology* 78 (May): 1426–47.

Form, Eric M. 1972. "Civil War as a Source of International Violence." *Journal of Politics.* 34 (November): 1111–34.

Form, William H., and Joan Rytina. 1969. "Ideological Beliefs on the Distribution of Power in the United States." *American Sociological Review* 34 (February): 19–31.

Forward, J., and J. Williams. 1970. "Internal-External Control and Black Militancy." *Journal of Social Issues* 26 (Winter): 75–95.

Fox, William, et al. 1977. "Authority Position, Legitimacy and Authority Structure, and Acquiescence to Authority." *Social Forces* 55 (June): 966–72.

Frauenglass, Elliott. 1973. "Assessing the Paths to Peace." *The Futurist* 7 (February): 22–25.

Frazier, Thomas R. 1968. "An Analysis of Nonviolent Coercion as Used by the Sit-in Movement." *Phylon* 29 (Spring): 27–40.

Frei, Daniel. 1974. "The Regulation of Warfare." *Journal of Conflict Resolution* 18 (December): 620–33.

Friedlander, Dov, and Calvin Goldscheider. 1974. "Peace and the Demographic Future of Israel." *Journal of Conflict Resolution* 18 (September): 486–501.

Gales, Kathleen. 1966. "A Campus Revolution." *British Journal of Sociology* 17 (March): 1–19.

Gall, Norman. 1970. "Latin America: The Church Militant." *Commentary* 49 (April): 25–35.

Galliher, John. 1971. "Explanations of Police Behavior: A Critical Review and Analysis." *Sociological Quarterly* 12 (Summer): 308–18.

Galtung, Johan. 1965. "Institutionalized Conflict Resolution: A Theoretical Paradigm." *Journal of Peace Research* 2: 348–97.

Galtung, Johan. 1971. "The Middle East and the Theory of Conflict." *Journal of Peace Research* 8: 173–206.

Galtung, Johan. 1972. "Europe: Bicentric or Cooperative?" *Journal of Peace Research* 9: 1–26.

Galtung, Johan. 1973. "Japan and Future World Politics." *Journal of Peace Research* 10: 355–85.

Gamson, William A. 1966. "Rancorous Conflict in Community Politics." *American Sociological Review* 31 (February): 71–81.

Gamson, William A., and James McEvoy. 1970. "Police Violence and Its Public Support." *The Annals* 391 (September): 97–110.

Gans, Herbert J. 1968. "The Ghetto Rebellions and Urban Class Conflict." *Proceedings of the Academy of Political Science* 29 (July): 42–51.

Gantzel, Klaus Jurgen. 1973. "Dependency Structure as the Dominant Pattern in World Society." *Journal of Peace Research* 10: 203–15.

Garcés, Joan E. 1974. "World Equilibrium, Crisis and Militarization of Chile." *Journal of Peace Research* 11: 81–93.

Gareau, Frederick H. 1970. "Cold-War Cleavages as Seen from the United National General Assembly: 1947–1967." *The Journal of Politics* 32 (November): 929–68.

Garner, Katherine, and Morton Deutsch. 1974. "Cooperative Behavior in Dyads." *Journal of Conflict Resolution* 18 (December): 634–44.

Garnham, David. 1976. "Diadic International War 1816–1965: The Role of Power Parity and Geographical Proximity." *Western Political Quarterly* 29 (June): 231–41.

Garrett, Marcia, and James F. Short, Jr. 1975. "Social Class and Delinquency: Prediction and Outcomes of Police-Juvenile Encounters." *Social Problems* 22 (February): 368–83.

Gecas, Viktor. 1972. "Motives and Aggressive Acts in Popular Fiction: Sex and Class Differences." *American Journal of Sociology.* 77 (January): 680–96.

Gelb, Joyce, and Alice Sardell. 1974. "Strategies for the Powerless: The Welfare Rights Movement in New York City." *American Behavioral Scientist* 17 (March–April): 507–31.

Geschwender, Barbara N., and James A. Geschwender. 1973. "Relative Deprivation and Participation in the Civil Rights Movement." *Social Science Quarterly* 54 (September): 403–11.

Geschwender, James. 1964. "Social Structure and the Negro Revolt: An Exploration of Some Hypotheses." *Social Forces.* 43 (December): 248–56.

Geschwender, James A. 1968. "Explorations in the Theory of Social Movements and Revolutions." *Social Forces* 47 (December): 127–35.

Geschwender, James A., et al. 1970. "Deprivation and the Detroit Riot." *Social Problems* 17 (Spring): 457–63.

Gilbert, Claire W. 1967. "Some Trends in Community Politics: A Secondary Analysis of Power Structure Data from 166 Communities." *Southwest Social Science Quarterly* 48 (December): 373–83.

Glenn, Edmond S., et al. 1970. "A Cognitive Interaction Model to Analyze Culture Conflict in International Situations." *Journal of Conflict Resolution* 14 (March): 35–48.

Golan, Schmuel. 1957. "Collective Education in the Kibbutz." *Psychiatry* 22 (May): 167–77.

Goldstein, Joel W. 1970. "The Psychology of Conflict and International Relations." *Journal of Conflict Resolution* 14 (March): 113–20.

Goode, William J. 1972. "Presidential Address, The Place of Force in Human Society." *American Sociological Review* 37 (October): 507–19.

Gordon, T. J. 1974. "Anticipating World Crises: Five Overarching Crises in Prospect." *Current* 168 (December): 48–60.

Gould, William B. 1973. "Black Workers Inside the House of Labor." *The Annals* 407 (May): 78–90.

Graber, Doris A. 1970. "Conflict Images: An Assessment of the Middle East Debates in the United Nations." *Journal of Politics* 32 (March): 339–78.

Grady, Robert C. 1976. "Obligation, Consent, and Locke's Right to Revolution: Who is to Judge?" *Canadian Journal of Political Science* 9 (June): 277–92.

Graham, Hugh Davis. 1970. "The Paradox of American Violence: An Historical Appraisal." *The Annals* 391 (September): 74–82.

Gray, Louis N., and Bruce H. Mayhew. 1970. "The Stability of Power Structures in Small Groups." *Pacific Sociological Review* 13 (April): 110–20.

Green, Charles S. III. 1975. "Modernization, Cultural Heterogeneity, and Civil Strife." *Human Organization* 34 (Spring): 69–77.

Green, Jack P. 1973. "The Social Origins of the American Revolution: An Evaluation and an Interpretation." *Political Science Quarterly* 88 (March): 1–22.

Greenberg, Edward S. 1970. "Black Children and the Political System." *Public Opinion Quarterly* 34 (Fall): 333–45.

Grimshaw, Allen D. 1963. "Police Agencies and the Prevention of Violence." *Journal of Criminal Law* 54 (March): 110–13.

Grimshaw, Allen D. 1970. "Interpreting Collective Violence: An Argument for the Importance of Social Structure." *The Annals* 391 (September): 9–20.

Grofman, Bernard, and Edward N. Muller. 1973. "The Strange Case of Relative Gratification and Potential for Political Violence: The V-Curve Hypothesis." *American Political Science Review* 67 (June): 514–39.

Gruder, Charles L. 1974. "Cost and Dependency as Determinants of Helping and Exploitation." *Journal of Conflict Resolution* 18 (September): 473–84.

Grupp, Fred W., Jr., and Alan R. Richards. 1975. "Variations in Elite Perceptions of American States as Referents for Public Policy Making." *American Political Science Review* 69 (September): 850–58.

Guenther, Roth. 1976. "Religion and Revolutionary Beliefs: Sociological and Historical Dimensions in Max Weber's Work." *Social Forces* 55 (December): 257–72.

Guetzkow, H., and J. Gyr. 1954. "An Analysis of Conflict in Decision-Making Groups." *Human Relations* 7: 367–82.

Gurr, Ted Robert. 1968. "A Causal Model of Civil Strife: A Comparative Analysis Using New Indices." *American Political Science Review* 62 (December): 1104–24.

Gurr, Ted Robert. 1972. "The Calculus of Civil Conflict." *Journal of Social Issues* 28: 27–48.

Gurr, Ted Robert, and Vaughn F. Bishop. 1976. "Violent Nations and Others." *Journal of Conflict Resolution* 20 (March): 79–109.

Gurr, Ted Robert, et al. 1973. "Internal vs. External Sources of Anti-Americanism." *Journal of Conflict Resolution* 17 (September): 455–88.

Haavelsrud, Magnus. 1970. "Views on War and Peace among Students in West Berlin Public Schools." *Journal of Peace Research* 7: 99–120.

Hahn, Harlan. 1970. "Civic Responses to Riots: A Reappraisal of Kerner Commission Data." *Public Opinion Quarterly* 34 (Spring): 101–7.

Hahn, Harlan. 1970. "Cops and Rioters: Ghetto Perceptions of Social Conflict and Control." *American Behavioral Scientist* 13 (May–August): 761–79.

Hahn, Harlan. 1970. "Correlates of Public Sentiments about War: Local Referenda on the Vietnam Issue." *American Political Science Review*. 64 (December): 1186–98.

Hahn, Harlan, and Joe R. Feagin. 1970. "Rank and File vs. Congressional Perceptions of Ghetto Riots." *Social Science Quarterly* 51 (September): 361–73.

Hahn, Harlan, David Klingman, and Harry Pachon. 1976. "Cleavages, Co-alitions, and the Black Candidate: The Los Angeles Mayoralty Elections of 1969 and 1973." *Western Political Quarterly* 29 (December): 507–19.

Haines, Nicholas. 1971. "Politics and Protest: Hegel and Social Criticism." *Political Science Quarterly* 86 (September): 406–28.

Hall, Peter H., et al. 1970. "The Quasi-Theory of Communication and Management of Dissent." *Social Problems* 18 (Summer): 17–26.

Hansen, Robert C. 1959. "Predicting a Community Decision: Test of the Miller-Form Theory." *American Sociological Review*. 24 (October): 662–71.

Harding, Harry. 1972. "Political Trends in China since the Cultural Revolution." *The Annals* 402 (July): 67–82.

Harf, James E. 1973. "A Model of Inter-Nation Conflict Resolution." *International Journal of Group Tensions* 3 (April): 91–121.

Harris, C. D., and E. L. Ullman. 1945. "The Nature of Cities." *The Annals* 242 (November): 7–17.

Harris, George S. 1970. "The Causes of the 1970 Revolution in Turkey." *Middle East Journal* 24 (Autumn): 438–54.

Hart, Parker T. 1970. "An American Policy toward the Middle East." *The Annals* 390 (July): 98–113.

Hazelrigg, Lawrence E. 1972. "Class, Property and Authority: Dahrendorf's Critique of Marx's Theory of Class." *Social Forces* 50 (June): 473–86.

Henderson, Bruce D. 1967. "Brinkmanship in Business." *Harvard Business Review* 45 (March–April): 49–55.

Henderson, Hazel. 1971. "Toward Managing Social Conflict." *Harvard Business Review* 49 (May–June): 82–90.

Herbst, Robert L. 1973. "The Legal Struggles to Integrate Schools in the North." *The Annals* 407 (May): 43–62.

Hermann, Charles, Margaret Hermann, and Robert Cantor. 1974. "Counter-attack or Delay." *Journal of Conflict Resolution* 18 (March): 75–106.

Hess, Gary R. 1974. "The Iranian Crisis of 1945–46 and the Cold War." *Political Science Quarterly* 89 (March): 117–46.

Hicks, Alexander, et al. 1978. "Class, Power and State Policy: The Case of Large Business Corporations, Labor Unions and Government Redistribution in the American States." *American Sociological Review* 43 (June): 302–15.

Hilmy, Hany. 1972. "Re-Partition of Palestine: Toward a Peaceful Solution in the Middle East." *Journal of Peace Research* 9: 133–45.

Hilton, Gordon. 1971. "A Closed and Open Model: Analysis of Expressions of Hostility in Crisis." *Journal of Peace Research* 8: 249–62.

Himes, Joseph S. 1961. "Negro Teen-Age Culture." *The Annals* 338 (November): 91–101.

Himes, Joseph S. 1966. "The Functions of Racial Conflict." *Social Forces* 45 (September): 1–10.

Himes, Joseph S. 1971. "A Theory of Racial Conflict." *Social Forces* 50 (September): 53–60.

Hippler, Arthur E. 1970. "The Game of Black and White at Hunter's Point." *Trans-Action* 7 (April): 56–63.

Hoerning, Karl. 1971. "Power and Social Stratification." *Sociological Quarterly* 12 (Winter): 3–14.

Hoge, Dean R., and Jeffery L. Faue. 1973. "Sources of Conflict over Priorities of the Protestant Church." *Social Forces* 52 (December): 178–94.

Holsti, K. J. 1975. "Underdevelopment and the 'Gap' Theory of International Conflict." *American Political Science Review* 69 (September): 827–39.

Holsti, Ole R. 1970. "Individual Differences in Definition of the Situation." *Journal of Conflict Resolution* 14 (September): 303–11.

Hopkins, Keith. 1966. "Civil-Military Relations in Developing Countries." *British Journal of Sociology* 17 (June): 165–82.

Hopper, Rex D. 1950. "The Revolutionary Process: A Frame of Reference for the Study of Revolutionary Movements." *Social Forces* 28 (March): 270–79.

Horn, Klaus. 1973. "Approaches to Social Psychology Relevant to Peace Research as Developed in the F.R.G." *Journal of Peace Research* 10: 305–18.

Horowitz, Irving L. 1970. "Separate but Equal: Revolution and Counter-Revolution in the American City." *Social Problems* 17 (Winter): 294–312.

Horowitz, Ruth, and Gary Schwartz. 1974. "Honor, Normative Ambiguity and Gang Violence." *American Sociological Review* 39 (April): 238–51.

Horst, Afheldt, and Philipp Sonntag. 1973. "Stability and Deterrence through Strategic Nuclear Arms." *Journal of Peace Research* 10: 245–50.

Houghton, N. C. 1964. "Historical Bases for Prediction in International Relations: Some Implications for American Foreign Policy." *Western Political Quarterly* 17 (December): 632–58.

Hövik, Tord. 1971. "Social Inequality: The Main Issues." *Journal of Peace Research* 8: 119–42.

Hövik, Tord. 1972. "Three Approaches to Exploitation: Markets, Products and Communities." *Journal of Peace Research* 9: 259–69.

Huizer, Gerritt. 1972. "Land Invasion as a Non-Violent Strategy of Pleasant Rebellion." *Journal of Peace Research* 9: 121–32.

Hunter, Douglas E. 1972. "Some Aspects of a Decision-Making Model in Nuclear Deterrence Theory." *Journal of Peace Research* 9: 209–22.

Huntington, Samuel P. 1973. "After Containment: The Functions of the Military Establishment." *The Annals* 406 (March): 1–16.

Hveem, Helge. 1973. "The Global Dominance System: Notes on a Theory of Global Political Economy." *Journal of Peace Research* 10: 319–40.

Iklé, Fred Charles. 1967. "Can Social Predictions Be Evaluated?" *Daedalus* 96 (Summer): 733–58.

Imrie, John. 1976. "Wrab's Problem: Little Money, No Structures, Lots of Red Tape." *Rand Daily Mail*, May 12.

Ismael, Tareq Y. 1969. "The United Arab Republic and the Sudan." *Middle East Journal* 23 (Winter): 14ff.

Jabber, Fuad. 1974. "Not by War Alone: Curbing the Arab-Israeli Arms Race." *Middle East Journal* 28 (Summer): 233–47.

Jahn, Egbert. 1973. "Civilian Defense and Civilian Offense." *Journal of Peace Research* 10: 286–94.

Janke, Peter. 1974. "Ulster: Consensus and Coercion." *Conflict Studies* 50 (October): 1–6.

Janowitz, Morris. 1975. "Sociological Theory and Social Control." *American Journal of Sociology* 81 (July): 82–106.

Jo, Yung-Hwan, and Stephen Walker. 1972. "Divided Nations and Reunification Strategies." *Journal of Peace Research* 9: 247–58.

Johnson, Chalmers. 1976. "Political Alienation among Vietnam Veterans." *Western Political Quarterly* 29 (September): 398–409.

Johnson, Norris. 1973. "Collective Behavior as Group-Induced Shift." Paper presented to the Southern Sociological Society, 13 April 1973, Atlanta, Georgia. Unpublished.

Johnson, Paula. 1976. "Women and Power: Toward a Theory of Effectiveness." *Journal of Social Issues* 32: 99–110.

Josephy, Alvin M., Jr. 1973. "Wounded Knee and All That: What the Indians Want." *The New York Times Magazine* (18 March): 18 and passim.

Kabwegyere, Tarsis B. 1972. "The Dynamics of Colonial Violence: The Inductive System in Uganda." *Journal of Peace Research* 9: 303–24.

de Kadt, Emanuel J. 1965. "Conflict and Power in Society." *International Social Science Journal* 17: 454–71.

Kahan, Jerome H., and Anne K. Long. 1972. "The Cuban Missile Crisis: A Study of Its Strategic Context." *Political Science Quarterly* 87 (December): 564–90.

Kahn, Robert L. 1972. "The Justification of Violence: Social Problems and Social Solutions." *Journal of Social Issues* 28: 155–76.

Kaliadin, A. M. 1972. "Problems of Disarmamnent Research." *Journal of Peace Research* 9: 237–46.

Katz, Daniel. 1967. "Group Process and Social Integration: A System Analysis of Two Movements of Social Protest." *Journal of Social Issues* 23 (January): 3–22.

Kee, Herbert W., and Robert E. Knox. 1970. "Conceptual and Methodological Consideration in the Study of Trust and Suspicion." *Journal of Conflict Resolution* 14 (September): 357–65.

Keim, Willard D. 1971. "Nations and Conflict Individuality." *Journal of Peace Research* 8: 287–92.

Kelidar, Abbas. 1975. "Iraq: The Search for Stability." *Conflict Studies* 59 (July): 1–22.

Kelly, Joe. 1970. "Making Conflict Work for You." *Harvard Business Review* 48 (July–August): 103–13.

Kende, Istvan. 1971. "Twenty-Five Years of Local Wars." *Journal of Peace Research* 8: 5–22.

Kerbo, Harold B. 1978. "Foreign Involvement and the Preconditions for Political Violence: The World System and the Case of Chile." *Journal of Conflict Resolution* 29 (September): 363–78.

Kewenig, Wilhelm. 1973. "The Contribution of International Law to Peace Research." *Journal of Peace Research* 10: 227–33.

Killian, Lewis M. 1972. "The Significance of Extremism in the Black Revolution." *Social Problem* 20 (Summer): 41–49.

Kim, Samuel S. 1976. "The Lorenzian Theory of Aggression and Peace Research: A Critique." *Journal of Paece Research* 13: 254–76.

Kirkpatrick, Jeane. 1973. "The Revolt of the Masses." *Commentary* 55 (February): 58–62.

Kirlin, John J. 1975. "Electoral Conflict and Democracy in Cities." *Journal of Politics* 37 (February): 262–69.

Klein, Rudolf. 1973. "The Stalemate Society." *Commentary* 56 (November): 42–47.

Klingberg, Frank L. 1966. "Predicting the Termination of War: Battle Casualties and Population Losses." *Journal of Conflict Resolution* 10: 129–71.

Klitgaard, Robert E. 1971. "Gandhi's Non-Violence as a Tactic." *Journal of Peace Research* 8: 143–53.

Klitgaard, Robert E. 1972. "Institutionalized Racism: An Analytic Approach." *Journal of Peace Research* 9: 41–49.

Kochan, Thomas A., and Todd Jick. 1978. "The Public Sector Mediation Process." *Journal of Conflict Resolution* 22 (June): 209–41.

Kohler, Gernot, and Norman Alcock. 1976. "An Empirical Table of Structural Violence." *Journal of Peace Research* 13: 343–56.

Kolodziej, Edward A. 1971. "Revolt and Revisionism in the Gaullist Global Vision: An Analysis of French Strategic Policy." *Journal of Politics* 33 (May): 448–77.

Komorita, S. S. 1973. "Concession-Making and Conflict Resolution." *Journal of Conflict Resolution* 17 (December): 745–62.

Kornberg, Allan, and Mary L. Brehm. 1971. "Ideology, Institutional Identification and Campus Activism." *Social Forces* 49 (March): 445–59.

Kramer, Helmut, and Helfried Bauer. 1972. "Imperialism, Intervention Capacity, and Foreign Policy Making." *Journal of Peace Research* 9: 285–302.

Kreps, Gary, and Dennis Wenger. 1973. "Toward a Theory of Community Conflict: Factors Influencing the Initiation and Scope of Conflict." *Sociological Quarterly* 14 (Spring): 158–74.

Krieger, David. 1977. "What Happens If . . .? Terrorists, Revolutionaries, and Nuclear Weapons." *The Annals* 430 (March): 44–57.

Krippendorff, Ekkehart. 1973. "Peace and the Industrial Revolution." *Journal of Peace* 10: 185–201.

Kritzer, Herbert M. 1977. "Political Protest and Political Violence: A Nonrecursive Causal Model." *Social Forces* 55 (March): 630–40.

Krohn, R. G. 1971. "Conflict and Function: Some Basic Issues in Bureaucratic Theory." *British Journal of Sociology* 22 (June): 115–32.

Krugman, Herbert E., and Eugene L. Hartley. 1970. "Passive Learning from Television." *Public Opinion Quarterly* 34 (Summer): 184–90.

Kuper, Leo. 1971. "Theories of Revolution and Race Relations." *Comparative Studies in Society and History* 13 (January): 87–107.

Labovitz, Sanford, and Jon Miller. 1974. "Implications of Power, Conflict and Change in an Organizational Setting." *Pacific Sociological Review* 17 (April): 214–39.

Ladner, Robert. 1973. "Strategic Interraction in Conflict." *Journal of Conflict Resolution* 17 (March): 175–84.

Lambelet, John C. 1975. "Do Arms Races Lead to War?" *Journal of Peace Research* 12: 123–28.

Lang, Gladys Engel, and Kurt Lang. 1972. "Some Pertinent Questions on Collective Violence and the News Media." *Journal of Social Issues* 28: 93–110.

Langton, Kenneth P. 1966. "Political Partisanship and Political Socialization in Jamaica." *British Journal of Sociology* 17 (December): 419–29.

Lapchick, Richard E. 1976. "Apartheid Sport: South Africa's Use of Sport in Its Foreign Policy." *Journal of Sport and Social Issues* 1: 52–79.

Laqueur, Walter, and Edward Luttwak. 1973. "Oil." *Commentary* 56 (October): 37–43.

LaTour, Stephen, et al. 1976. "Some Determinants of Performance for Modes of Conflict Resolution." *Journal of Conflict Resolution* 20 (June): 319–55.

Lawler, Edward. 1975. "The Impact of Status Differences on Coalitional Agreements." *Journal of Conflict Resolution* 19 (June): 271–85.

Lenski, Gerhard. 1954. "Status Crystallization: A Non-Vertical Dimension of Social Status." *American Sociological Review* 19 (August): 405–13.

Leone, Richard C. 1972. "Public Interest Advocacy and the Regulatory Process." *The Annals* 400 (March): 46–58.

Lever, H. 1972. "Changes in Ethnic Attitudes in South Africa." *Sociology and Social Research* 56 (January): 202–9.

LeVine, Robert. 1959. "Anti-European Violence in Africa: A Comparative Analysis." *Journal of Conflict Resolution* 3 (December): 420–29.

Lewis, Jerry, and Raymond Adamek. 1974. "Anti-R.O.T.C. Sit-In: A Sociological Analysis." *Sociological Quarterly* 15 (Autumn): 542–47.

Lewis, Robert A. 1971. "Socialization into National Violence: Familial Correlates of Hawkish Attitudes toward the War." *Journal of Marriage and the Family* 33 (November): 699–708.

Li, Richard P. Y., and William R. Thompson. 1975. "The 'Coup Contagion' Hypothesis." *Journal of Conflict Resolution* 19 (March): 63–88.

Licklider, Roy. 1976–77. "Soviet Control of Eastern Europe: Morality versus American National Interest." *Political Science Quarterly* 91 (Winter): 619–24.

Lieberson, Stanley. 1966. "The Meaning of Race Riots." *Race* 7 (April): 317–78.

Lincoln, James R. 1976. "Power and Mobilization in the Urban Community: Reconsidering the Ecological Approach." *American Sociological Review* 41 (February): 1–15.

Lipsitz, Lewis, and Herbert M. Kritzer. 1975. "Unconventional Approaches to Conflict Resolution." *Journal of Conflict Resolution* 19 (December): 713–33.

Lodgaard, Sverre. 1973. "Industrial Cooperation, Consumption Patterns and Division of Labor in the East-West Setting." *Journal of Peace Research* 10: 387–99.

Lodgaard, Sverre. 1977. "The Functions of SALT." *Journal of Peace Research* 14: 2–22.

Lodhi, Abdul, and Charles Tilly. 1973. "Urbanization, Crime and Collective Violence in Nineteenth-Century France." *American Journal of Sociology* 79 (September): 296–318.

Lonsdale, Richard C. 1975. "Futures Research, Policy Research, and the Policy Sciences." *Education and Urban Society* 7 (May): 246–302.

Luschen, Gunther. 1970. "Cooperation, Association and Contest." *Journal of Conflict Resolution* 14 (March): 21–34.

Luterbacher, Urs. 1975. "Bipolarity and Generational Factors in Major Power Military Activity, 1900–1965." *Journal of Peace Research* 12: 129–38.

McCarthy, John D., and Mayer N. Zald. 1976. Resource Mobilization and Social Movements: A Partial Theory." *American Journal of Sociology* 82 (May): 1212–41.

McClintock, David W. 1970. "The Southern Sudan Problem: Evolution of an Arab-African Confrontation." *Middle East Journal* 24 (Autumn): 466–78.

McCormack, Donald J. 1973. "Stokely Carmichael and Pan-Africanism: Back to Black Power." *Journal of Politics* 35 (May): 386–409.

McDowell, Sophia F., et al. 1970. "Howard University's Student Protest Movement." *Public Opinion Quarterly* 34 (Fall): 383–88.

McGowan, Patrick J., and Robert M. Rood. 1975. "Alliance Behavior in Balance of Power Systems: Applying a Poisson Model to Nineteenth-Century Europe." *American Political Science Review* 69 (September): 859–70.

Mack, Raymond, and Richard C. Snyder. 1957. "The Analysis of Social Conflict: Toward an Overview and Synthesis." *Journal of Conflict Resolution* 1: 212–48.

McPhail, Clark. 1971. "Civil Disorder Participation: A Critical Examination of Recent Research." *American Sociological Review* 36 (December): 1058–73.

Madron, Thomas, Hart Nelson, and Raytha Yokley. 1974. "Religion as a Determinant of Militancy and Political Participation among Black Americans." *American Behavioral Scientist* 17 (August): 783–98.

Malecki, Edward S. 1973. "Theories of Revolution and Industrialized Societies." *Journal of Politics* 35 (November): 948–85.

Mandle, Joan D. 1971. Women's Liberation: Humanizing Rather Than Polarizing." *The Annals* 397 (September): 118–28.

Marks, Stephen R. 1974. "Durkheim's Theory of Anomie." *American Journal of Sociology* 80 (September): 329–63.

Markus, Gregory B., and Raymond Tanter. 1972. "A Conflict Model for Strategists and Managers." *American Behavioral Scientist* 15 (July–August): 809–36.

Marsh, Judith. 1973. "Patterns of Conflict in American· Society, 1952–1968." *Sociology and Social Research* 57 (April): 315–34.

Martin, William C., Vern L. Bengston, and Alan C. Acock. 1974. "Alienation and Age: A Context-Specific Approach." *Social Forces* 53 (December): 266–74.

Marty, William R. 1971. "Nonviolence, Violence and Reason." *Journal of Politics* 33 (February): 3–21.

Marx, Gary T. 1970. "Issueless Riots." *The Annals* 391 (September): 21–24.

Marx, Gary T. 1974. "Thoughts on a Neglected Category of Social Movement Participant: The Agent Provocateur and the Informant." *American Journal of Sociology* 80 (September): 402–40.

Marx, John H., and Burkhart Holzner. 1977. "The Social Constitution of Strain and Ideological Models of Grievance in Contemporary Movements." *Pacific Sociological Review* 20 (June): 411–38.

Mathobi, Don. 1976. "The Dynamics of Technical Training for African Workers in Rhodesian Industry: A Case Study of the Apprenticeship System." Paper written for the Centre for Interracial Studies, University of Rhodesia. Mimeograph.

Mazur, Allan. 1972. "The Causes of Black Riots." *American Sociological Review* 37 (August): 490–93.

Meier, August, and Elliott Rudwick. 1970. "Organizational Structure and Goal Succession: A Comparative Analysis of NAACP and CORE, 1964–1968." *Social Science Quarterly* 51 (June): 9–24.

Melady, Thomas Patrick. 1964. "The Sweep of Nationalism in Africa." *The Annals* 354 (July): 91–96.

Melish, Ilone. 1970. "Attitudes toward the White Minority on a Black Campus 1966–1968." *Sociological Quarterly* 11 (Spring): 321–30.

Melson, Robert, and Howard Wolpe. 1970. "Modernization and Politics of Communalism: A Theoretical Perspective." *American Political Science Review* 64 (December): 1112–30.

Merriam, Alan P. 1974. "Social and Cultural Change in a Rural Zairian Village." *African Studies Review* 17 (September): 345–61.

Milburn, Thomas W. 1977. "The Nature of Threat." *Journal of Social Issues* 33 (Winter): 126–239.

Miller, A. J. 1971. "Consensus and Conflict in Functionalism: Implications for the Study of International Integration." *Canadian Journal of Political Science* 4 (June): 178–90.

Miller, Delbert C. 1957. "The Predictions of Issue Outcome in Community Decision Making." *Proceedings of the Pacific Sociological Society* 25 (June): 137–47.

Miller, Jon P. 1970. "Social-Psychological Implications of Weber's Model of Bureaucracy: Relations among Expertise, Control, Authority, and Legitimacy." *Social Forces* 49 (September): 91–102.

Misra, K. P. 1972. "Intra-State Imperialism, the Case of Pakistan." *Journal of Peace Research* 9: 27–39.

Mitchell, C. R. 1973. "Conflict Resolution and Controlled Communication: Some Further Comments." *Journal of Peace Research* 10: 123–32.

Modigliani, Andre. 1972. "Hawks and Doves, Isolationism and Political Distrust: An Analysis of Public Opinion on Military Policy." *American Political Science Review* 66 (September): 960–78.

Moore, Charles H. 1970. "The Politics of Urban Violence: Policy Outcomes in Winston-Salem." *Social Science Quarterly* 51 (September): 374–88.

Moore, Wilbert E. 1964. "Predicting Discontinuities in Social Change." *Proceedings of the Southwest Sociological Association* 14 (March): 59–69.

Morgan, William R., and Terry N. Clark. 1973. "The Causes of Racial Disorders: A Grievance-Level Explanation." *American Sociological Review* 38 (October): 611–24.

Morley, David. 1976. "Industrial Conflict and the Mass Media." *Sociological Review* 24 (May): 245–68.

Morrison, Donald G., and Hugh M. Stevenson. 1971. "Political Instability in Independent Black Africa: More Dimensions of Conflict Behavior within Nations." *Journal of Conflict Resolution* 15 (September): 347–68.

Morrison, Donald G., and Hugh M. Stevenson. 1972. "Cultural Pluralism, Modernization and Conflict: Empirical Analysis of Sources of Political Instability in African Nations." *Canadian Journal of Political Science* 5: 82–103.

Morrison, Donald G., and Hugh M. Stevenson. 1972. "Integration and Instability: Patterns of African Political Development." *American Political Science Review* 66 (September): 902–27.

Morrison, Donald G., and Hugh M. Stevenson. 1974. "Social Complexity, Economic Development and Military Coups d'Etat: Convergence and Divergence of Empirical Tests of Theory in Latin America, Asia and Africa." *Journal of Peace Research* 11: 345–47.

Morse, N., et al. 1951. "Regulation and Control in Hierarchical Organizations." *Journal of Social Issues* 7: 41–48.

Moskos, Charles C. 1973. "The American Dilemma in Uniform: Race in the Armed Forces." *The Annals* 496 (March): 94–106.

Mueller, Ernest F. 1970. "Attitudes toward West-Bound Refugees in the East German Press." *Journal of Conflict Resolution* 14 (September): 311–33.

Mueller, John E. 1971. "Trends in Popular Support for the Wars in Korea and Vietnam." *American Political Science Review* 65 (June): 358–75.

Murphy, James T. 1974. "Political Parties and the Porkbarrel: Party Conflict and Cooperation in House Public Works Committee Decision." *American Political Science Review* 68 (March): 169–86.

Muslih, Muhammed Y. 1976. "Moderates and Rejectionists within the Palestine Liberation Organization." *Middle East Journal* 30 (Spring): 127ff.

Myers, Frank E. 1971. "Civil Disobedience and Organizational Change: The British Committee of One Hundred." *Political Science Quarterly* 86 (March): 92–112.

Myers, Frank E. 1973. "Dilemmas in the British Peace Movement Since World War II." *Journal of Peace Research* 10: 81–90.

Nachmias, David. 1973. "Status Inconsistency and Political Opposition: A Case Study of an Israeli Minority Group." *Middle East Journal* 27 (Autumn): 456–70.

Nakhleb, Emile A. 1971. "The Anatomy of Violence: Theoretical Reflections on Palestinian Resistance." *Middle East Journal* 25 (Spring): 180–200.

Nakhre, Amrut. 1976. "Meanings of Nonviolence: A Study of Satyagrahi Attitudes." *Journal of Peace Research* 13: 185–96.

Nathan, James A., and James K. Oliver. 1974. "Diplomacy of Violence." *Society* 11 (September–October): 32–40.

Nelson, Harold A. 1971. "Leadership and Change in an Evolutionary Movement: An Analysis of Change in the Leadership Structure of the Southern Civil Rights Movement." *Social Forces* 49 (March): 353–71.

Nieburg, H. L. 1970. "Agonistics: Rituals of Conflict." *The Annals* 391 (September): 56–73.

O'Brien, Conor Cruise. 1973. "On the Rights of Minorities." *Commentary* 55 (June): 46–50.

Oleszek, Walter J. 1974. "House-Senate Relationships: Comity and Conflict." *The Annals* 411 (January): 75–87.

Olsen, Marvin E. 1968. "Perceived Legitimacy of Social Protest Actions." *Social Problems* 15 (Winter): 297–310.

Onate, Andes D. 1974. "The Conflict Interactions of the People's Republic of China." *Journal of Conflict Resolution* 18 (December): 578–93.

Onuf, N. G. 1975. "Peace Research Parochialism." *Journal of Peace Research* 12: 71–77.

Orbell, John M., and Geoffrey Fougere. 1973. "Intra-Party Conflict and the Decay of Ideology." *Journal of Politics* 35 (May): 439–53.

Overholt, William H. 1977. "An Organizational Conflict Theory of Revolution." *American Behavioral Scientist* 20 (March–April): 493–518.

Owen, Raymond E. 1975. "On Rubbing Raw the Sores of Discontent: Competing Theories and Data on the Effects of Participation in a Black Protest Group." *Sociological Focus* 8 (April): 143–59.

Page, Charles H. 1952. "Bureaucracy in the Liberal Church." *The Review of Religion* 16 (March): 137–50.

Paige, Jeffery. 1971. "Political Orientation and Riot Participation." *American Sociological Review* 36 (October): 810–20.

Parsons, Talcott. 1961. "Some Considerations on the Theory of Social Change." *Rural Sociology* 26 (September): 219–39.

Parvin, Manoucher. 1973. "Economic Determinants of Political Unrest: An Econometric Approach." *Journal of Conflict Resolution* 17 (June): 271–96.

Paton, Alan. 1976. "Must Everything Be Destroyed?" *New York Times Magazine* (19 September 1976).

Pearce, W. Barnett, et al. 1971. "Communication and Polarization during a Campus Strike." *Public Opinion Quarterly* 35 (Summer): 228–34.

Pearson, Frederic. 1974. "Geographic Proximity and Foreign Military Intervention." *Journal of Conflict Resolution* 18 (September): 432–60.

Pelligrin, Roland J. 1967. "A Selected Bibliography on Community Power Structure." *Southwest Social Science Quarterly* 48 (December): 451–66.

Peres, Yochanan. 1971. "Ethnic Relations in Israel." *American Journal of Sociology* 76 (May): 1021–47.

Perlmutter, Amos. 1970. "Assessing the Six-Day War." *Commentary* 49 (January): 71–75.

Perrucci, Robert, and Marc Pilisuk. 1970. "Leaders and Ruling Elites: The Interorganizational Bases of Community Power." *American Sociological Review* 35 (December): 1040–57.

Petras, James, and Maurice Zeitlin. 1968. "Agrarian Radicalism in Chile." *British Journal of Sociology* 19 (September): 254–69.

Pfaltzgraff, Robert L., Jr. 1971. "Should the United States Retain a Military Presence in Europe and Asia?" *The Annals* 397 (September): 1–10.

Pfautz, Harold W., Harry C. Huguley, and John W. McClain. 1975. "Changes in Reputed Black Community Leadership, 1962–1972: A Case Study." *Social Forces* 53 (March): 460–67.

Pitcher, Brian L., et al. 1978. "The Diffusion of Collective Violence." *American Sociological Review* 43 (February): 23–35.

Platt, J. 1975. The Future of Social Crises." *Futurist* 9 (October): 266–68.

Polsby, Nelson W. 1959. "The Sociology of Community Power: A Reassessment." *Social Forces* 37 (March): 232–36.

Porsholt, Lars. 1971. "A Quantitative Conflict Model." *Journal of Peace Research* 8: 55–66.

Portes, Alejandro, and Adreain Ross. 1974. "Model for the Prediction of Leftist Radicalism." *Journal of Political and Military Sociology* 2 (Spring): 33–56.

Posvar, Wesley W. 1971. "Reshaping Our Foreign Policy." *The Annals* 396 (July): 105–14.

Power, Paul F. 1970. "On Civil Disobedience in Recent American Democratic Thought." *American Political Science Review* 64 (March): 35–47.

Power, Paul F. 1972. "Civil Disobedience as Functional Opposition." *Journal of Politics* 34 (February): 37–55.

Power, Paul F. 1972. "Civil Protest in Northern Ireland." *Journal of Peace Research* 9: 223–36.

Pressman, Jeffrey L. 1972. "Preconditions of Mayoral Leadership." *American Political Science Review* 66 (June): 511–24.

Price, D. L. 1975. "Oman: Insurgency and Development." *Conflict Studies* 53 (January): 1–19.

Pugh, M. D., Joseph Perry, et al. 1972. "Faculty Support of Student Dissent." *Sociological Quarterly* 13 (Fall): 525–32.

Pugh, William A. 1975. "Arab Media and Politics during the October War." *Middle East Journal* 29 (Summer): 310–28.

Quester, George H. 1972. "Some Conceptual Problems in Nuclear Proliferation." *American Political Science Review* 66 (June): 490–97.

Quinley, Harold E. 1970. "The Protestant Clergy and the War in Vietnam." *Public Opinion Quarterly* 34 (Spring): 43–52.

Raab, Earl. 1974. "Is There a New Anti-Semitism?" *Commentary* 57 (May): 53–55.

Raack, R. C. 1970. "When Plans Fail: Small Group Behavior and Decision-Making in the Conspiracy of 1808 in Germany." *Journal of Conflict Resolution* 14 (March): 3–16.

Rake, Alan. 1968. "Black Guerrillas in Rhodesia." *Africa Report* 13 (December): 23–25.

Ransford, H. Edward. 1968. "Isolation, Powerlessness and Violence: A Study of Attitudes and Participation in the Watts Riot." *American Journal of Sociology* 73 (March): 581–91.

Rapoport, Anatol. 1970. "Can Peace Research Be Applied?" *Journal of Conflict Resolution* 14 (June): 277–86.

Rapoport, Anatol. 1974. "War and Peace." *The Annals* 412 (March): 152–62.

Record, C. Wilson. 1974. "White Sociologists and Black Students in Predominantly White Universities." *Sociological Quarterly* 15 (Spring): 164–82.

Reed, John Shelton. 1971. "To Live and Die in Dixie: Contribution to the Study of Southern Violence." *Political Science Quarterly* 86 (September): 429–43.

Rittberger, Volker. 1973. "International Organization and Violence with Special Reference to the Performance of the UN System." *Journal of Peace Research* 10: 217–25.

Ritterband, Paul, and Richard Silberstein. 1973. "Group Disorders in the Public Schools." *American Sociological Review* 38 (August): 461–67.

Rivera, Deodato. 1974. "Let Us Face Chile, Yes, but: Which Chile?" *Journal of Peace Research* 11: 105–13.

Robinson, J. P. 1970. "Public Reaction to Political Protest: Chicago, 1968." *Public Opinion Quarterly* 34 (Spring): 1–9.

Robinson, Thomas W. 1972. "The Sino-Soviet Border Dispute: Background, Development, and the March 1969 Clashes." *American Political Science Review* 66 (December): 1175–1203.

Rodgers, Harrell R. 1975. "Prelude to Conflict: The Evaluation of Censorship Campaigns." *Pacific Sociological Review* 18 (April): 194–205.

Rogin, Michael. 1969. "Politics, Emotion, and the Wallace Vote." *British Journal of Sociology* 20 (March): 27–49.

Rosenthal, Marilynn. 1971. "Where Rumor Raged." *Trans-Action* 8 (February): 34–43.

Rossi, Peter H. 1957. "Community Decision Making." *Administrative Science Quarterly* 1 (March): 415–43.

Rossi, Peter H., and Richard A. Berk. 1970. "Local Political Leadership and Popular Discontent in the Ghetto." *The Annals* 391 (September): 111–27.

Rothman, Stanley. 1970. "Barrington Moore and the Dialectics of Revolution." *American Political Science Review* 64 (March): 61–82.

Rowe, Edward T. 1970. "Human Rights Issues in the UN General Assembly 1946–1966." *Journal of Conflict Resolution* 14 (December): 425–37.

Ruf, Werner Klaus. 1971. "The Bizerta Crisis: A Bourguibist Attempt to Resolve Tunisia's Border Problems." *Middle East Journal* 25 (Spring): 201–11.

Runkle, Gerald. 1976. "Is Violence Always Wrong?" Journal of Politics 38: 367–88.

Rushing, William A. 1971. "Class, Culture, and 'Social Structure and Anomie.'" *American Journal of Sociology* 76 (March): 857–71.

Russett, B., and M. Nincic. 1976. "American Opinion on the Use of Military Force Abroad." *Political Science Quarterly* 91 (Fall): 411–31.

Rustin, Bayard. 1966. "The Watts 'Manifesto' and the McCone Report." *Commentary* 41 (March): 29–35.

Sandbrook, Richard. 1972. "Patrons, Clients, and Factions: New Dimensions of Conflict Analysis in Africa." *Canadian Journal of Political Science* 5 (March): 104–19.

Schellenberg, James A. 1970. "County Seat Wars: A Preliminary Analysis." *Journal of Conflict Resolution* 14 (September): 345–52.

Schlemmer, Lawrence. 1972. "City or Rural 'Homeland': A Study of Patterns of Identification among Africans in Southern Africa's Divided Society." *Social Forces* 51 (December): 154–64.

Schlenker, Barry and Bonoma Thomas. 1978. "Fun and Games: The Validity of Games for the Study of Conflict." *Journal of Conflict Resolution* 22 (March): 7–33.

Schnall, David J. 1977. "Native Anti-Zionism: Ideologies of Radical Dissent in Israel." *Middle East Journal* 31 (Spring): 157–74.

Schumaker, Paul D. 1975. "Policy Responsiveness to Protest-Group Demands." *Journal of Politics* 37 (May): 488–521.

Schuman, Howard. 1972. "Two Sources of Antiwar Sentiment in America." *American Journal of Sociology* 78 (November): 513–36.

Schuman, Howard, and Barry Gruenberg. 1970. "The Impact of City on Racial Attitudes." *American Journal of Sociology* 76 (September): 213–61.

Schuman, Howard, and Jean M. Converse. 1971. "The Effects of Black and White Interviewers on Black Responses in 1968." *Public Opinion Quarterly* 35 (Spring): 44–68.

Schwartz, Barry. 1974. "Waiting, Exchange, and Power: The Distribution of Time in Social Systems." *American Journal of Sociology* 79 (January): 841–70.

Scoble, Harry M., and Laurie S. Wiseberg. 1974. "Human Rights and Amnesty International." *The Annals* 413 (May): 11–26.

Scott, J. P. 1977. "Agonistic Behavior: Function and Dysfunction in Social Conflict." *Journal of Social Issues* 33 (Winter): 9–21.

Sebald, Hans, and Rudolfo N. Gallegos. 1971. "Voices of War and Peace: What Do They Know?" *Pacific Sociological Review* 14 (October): 487–510.

Seeman, Melvin. 1959. "On the Meaning of Alienation." *American Sociological Review* 24 (December): 783–91.

Seeman, Melvin. 1972. "The Signals of '68: Alienation in Pre-Crisis France." *American Sociological Review* 37 (August): 385–402.

Seligson, Mitchell A. 1972. "The 'Dual Society' Thesis in Latin America: A Reexamination of the Costa Rican Case." *Social Forces* 51 (September): 91–98.

Senghaas, Dieter. 1973. "Conflict Formations in Contemporary International Society." *Journal of Peace Research* 10: 163–84.

Sennett, Richard. 1970. "Genteel Backlash: Chicago 1886." *Trans-Action* 7 (January): 40–50.

Shellow, Robert, and Derek V. Roemer. 1966. "No Heaven for Hell's Angels." *Trans-Action* 3 (July–August): 12–19.

Shields, James, and Leonard Weinberg. 1976. "Reactive Violence and the American Frontier: A Contemporary Evaluation." *Western Political Quarterly* 29 (March): 87–101.

Siegel, Bernard J. 1970. "Defensive Structuring and Environmental Stress." *American Journal of Sociology* 76 (July): 11–31.

Sigal, Leon V. 1975. "Official Secrecy and Informal Communication in Congressional-Bureaucratic Relations." *Political Science Quarterly* 90 (Spring): 71–92.

Sigelman, Lee. 1972. "Do Modern Bureaucracies Dominate Underdeveloped Politics? A Test of the Imbalance Thesis." *American Political Science Review* 66 (June): 525–28.

Sigelman, Lee, and Miles Simpson. 1977. "A Cross-National Test of the Linkage between Economic Inequality and Political Violence." *Journal of Conflict Resolution* 21 (March): 105–27.

Simon, Herbert A. 1953. "Notes on the Observation and Measurement of Political Power." *Journal of Politics* 15 (November): 500–516.

Simpson, Richard L. 1972. "Beyond Rational Bureaucracy: Changing Values and Social Integration in Post-Industrial Society." *Social Forces* 51 (September): 1–6.

Singer, Benjamin D. 1970. "Mass Media and Communication Processes in the Detroit Riot of 1967." *Public Opinion Quarterly* 34 (Summer): 236–45.

Singer, Benjamin D. 1970. "Violence, Protest, and War in Television News: The U.S. and Canada Compared." *Public Opinion Quarterly* 34 (Winter): 611–16.

Siverson, Randolph. 1972. "The Evaluation of Self, Allies and Enemies in the 1956 Suez Crisis." *Journal of Conflict Resolution* 16 (June): 203–10.

Skjelsbaek, Kjell. 1973. "A Study of the Problems of Peace: A Rejoinder." *Journal of Peace Research* 10: 121–22.

Skjelsbaek, Kjell. 1973. "Value Incompatibilities in the Global System." *Journal of Peace Research* 10: 341–53.

Skocpol, Theda. 1976. "Old Regime Legacies and Communist Revolutions in Russia and China." *Social Forces* 55 (December): 284–315.

Skoler, Daniel L. 1971. "There's More to Crime Control Than the 'Get Tough' Approach." *The Annals* 397 (September): 28–39.

Skolnick, Jerome H. 1970. "Violence Commission Violence." *Trans-Action* 7 (October): 32–38.

Small, Melvin, and J. David Singer. 1970. "Patterns in International Warfare, 1816–1965." *The Annals* 391 (September): 145–55.

Smoker, Paul. 1969. "Social Research for Social Anticipation." *American Behavioral Scientist* 12 (July): 7–13.

Smolensky, Eugene. 1973. "Poverty, Propinquity, and Policy." *The Annals* 409 (September): 120–24.

Snyder, David. 1975. "Institutional Setting and Industrial Conflict: Comparative Analysis of France, Italy, and the United States." *American Sociological Review* 40 (June): 259–78.

Snyder, David. 1978. "Collective Violence: Research Agenda and Some Strategic Considerations." *Journal of Conflict Resolution* 22 (September): 499–529.

Snyder, David, and Charles Tilley. 1972. "Hardship and Collective Violence in France, 1830–1960." *American Sociological Review* 37 (October): 520–32.

Snyder, David, and William R. Kelly. 1976. "Industrial Violence in Italy, 1878–1903." *American Journal of Sociology* 82 (July): 131–62.

Somjee, A. H. 1973. "Caste and the Decline of Political Homogeneity." *American Political Science Review* 67 (September): 799–816.

Soule, John W., and James W. Clarke. 1971. "Issue Conflict and Consensus:

A Comparative Study of Democratic and Republican Delegates to the 1968 National Conventions." *The Journal of Politics* 33 (February): 72–91.

South African Institute of Race Relations. *RR. 118/76. RR. 119/76. RR. 120/76.*

Spencer, Martin E. 1971. "Conflict and the Neutrals." *Sociological Quarterly* 12 (Spring): 219–31.

Spillerman, Seymour. 1970. "The Causes of Racial Disturbances: A Comparison of Alternative Explanations." *American Sociological Review* 35 (August): 627–49.

Spillerman, Seymour. 1970. "Comments on Wanderer's Article on Riot Severity and Its Correlates." *American Journal of Sociology* 75 (January): 556–60.

Spillerman, Seymour. 1971. "The Causes of Racial Disturbances: Tests of an Explanation." *American Sociological Review* 36 (June): 427–42.

Stallings, Robert. 1973. "Patterns of Belief in Social Movements: Classifications from an Analysis of Environmental Groups." *Sociological Quarterly* 14 (Autumn): 465–80.

Stark, Margaret J., et al. 1974. "Some Empirical Patterns in a Riot Process." *American Sociological Review* 39 (December): 865–76.

Stern, Louis W., Robert A. Schulz, Jr., and John R. Grabner. 1973. "The Power Base-Conflict Relationship: Preliminary Findings." *Social Science Quarterly* 54 (September): 412–19.

Stohl, Michael, and Mary Chamberlain. 1972. "Alternative Futures for Peace Research." *Journal of Conflict Resolution* 16 (December): 523–30.

Suber, Malcolm. 1975. "Police Shooting Sparks Mass Protests." *The Southern Patriot* (Louisville, Kentucky), April 1975.

Sugimoto, Yoshio. 1975. "Surplus Value, Unemployment and Industrial Turbulence." *Journal of Conflict Resolution* 19 (March): 25–47.

Suleiman, Michael. 1972. "Crisis and Revolution in Lebanon." *Middle East Journal* 26 (Winter): 11–24.

Suleiman, Michael. 1973. "Attitudes of the Arab Elite toward Palestine and Israel." *American Political Science Review* 67 (June): 482–89.

Sullivan, Michael P. 1972. "Commitment and the Escalation of Conflicts." *Western Political Quarterly* 25 (March): 28–38.

Talikka, Annikki. 1970. "Economic and Power Frustrations as Predictors of Industrial and Political Conflict Strategies." *Journal of Peace Research* 7: 267–87.

Tanaka, Yasumasa. 1970. "Japanese Attitudes toward Nuclear Arms." *Public Opinion Quarterly* 34 (Spring): 26–42.

Taylor, Michael, and V. M. Herman. 1971. "Party Systems and Government Stability." *American Political Science Review* 65 (March): 28–37.

Tedeschi, James T. et al. 1977. "Aggression and the Use of Coercive Power." *Journal of Social Issues* 33 (Winter): 101–23.

Terrell, Louis M. 1971. "Societal Stress, Political Instability and Levels of Military Effort." *Journal of Conflict Resolution* 15 (September): 329–46.

Thee, Marek. 1972. "U.S.–Chinese Rapprochement and Vietnam." *Journal of Peace Research* 9: 63–67.

Thee, Marek. 1977. "Arms Control: The Retreat from Disarmament—The Record to Date and the Search for Alternatives." *Journal of Peace Research* 13: 95–114.

Theoharis, Athan. 1972. "Roosevelt and Truman on Yalta: The Origins of the Cold War." *Political Science Quarterly* 87 (June): 210–41.

Thompson, William R., and George Modelski. 1977. "Global Conflict Intensity and Great Power Summitry Behavior." *Journal of Conflict Resolution* 21 (June): 339–69.

Til, Jon Van. 1970. "Citizen Participation in Social Policy: The End of the Cycle?" *Social Problems* 17 (Winter): 313–23.

Tinker, Jerry M. 1971. "The Political Power of Non-Violent Resistance: The Gandhian Technique." *Western Political Quarterly* 24 (December): 775–88.

Tittle, Charles R. 1977. "Sanction Fear and the Maintenance of Social Order." *Social Forces* 55 (March): 579–96.

Torrance, Judy. 1977. "The Response of Canadian Governments to the Violence." *Canadian Journal of Political Science* 10 (September): 473–96.

Tropper, Richard. 1972. "The Consequences of Divestment in the Process of Conflict." *Journal of Conflict Resolution* 16 (March): 97–98.

Turner, Jonathan H. 1973. "From Utopia to Where?: A Strategy for Reformulating the Dahrendorf Conflict Model." *Social Forces* 52 (December): 236–44.

Turner, Jonathan H. 1975. "Marx and Simmel Revisited: Reassessing the Foundations of Conflict Theory." *Social Forces* 53 (June): 618–27.

Turner, Jonathan H. 1975. "A Strategy for Reformulating the Dialectical and Functional Theories of Conflict." *Social Forces* 53 (March): 433–44.

Turner, Ralph H. 1969. "The Public Perception of Protest." *American Sociological Review* 34 (December): 815–31.

Turner, Ralph H. 1972. "Campus Peace: Harmony or Uneasy Truce?" *Sociology and Social Research* 57 (October): 5–21.

Turner, Ralph H. 1972. "Integrative Belief in Group Crises." *Journal of Conflict Resolution* 16 (March): 25–40.

Turner, Ralph H., and Samuel J. Surace. 1956. "Zoot Suiters and Mexicans: Symbols in Crowd Behavior." *American Journal of Sociology* 62: 14–20.

Tygart, Clarence E., and Norman Holt. 1972. "Examining the Weinberg and Walker Typology of Student Activists." *American Journal of Sociology* 77 (March): 957–67.

Vander Zanden, James W. 1963. "The Non-Violent Resistance Movement against Segregation." *American Journal of Sociology* 68 (March): 544.

Vasquez, John A. 1076. "A Learning Theory of the American Anti-Vietnam War Movement." *Journal of Peace Research* 13: 299–314.

Verba, Sidney, and Richard A. Brody. 1970. "Participation, Policy Preferences and the War in Vietnam." *Public Opinion Quarterly* 34 (Fall): 325–32.

Vilmar, Fritz. 1973. "The Military-Industrial Complex in West Germany and the Consequences for Peace Policy." *Journal of Peace Research* 10: 251ff.

Vincent, Jack E. 1977. "Analyzing International Conflict and Corporation Flows: An Application of Attribute Theory." *Social Science Quarterly* 58 (June): 111–19.

Vinogradov, Amal, and John Waterbury. 1971. "Situations of Contested Legitimacy in Morocco: An Alternative Framework." *Comparative Studies in Society and History* 13 (January): 32–59.

Vital, David. 1974. "Israel after the War: The Need for Political Change." *Commentary* 57 (March): 46–50.

Vromen, Suzanne Donner. 1977. "Pareto on the Inevitability of Revolutions." *American Behavioral Scientist* 20 (March–April): 521–28.

Wadoski, Kenneth W. 1977. "Nonviolent Action and Social Change in Contemporary Society." *American Behavioral Scientist* 20 (March–April): 529–34.

Wallensteen, Peter. 1976. "Scarce Goods as Political Weapons: The Case of Food." *Journal of Peace Research* 13: 277–98.

Wallerstein, Immanuel. 1976. "From Feudalism to Capitalism: Transition or Transitions?" *Social Forces* 55 (December): 273–83.

Walton, John. 1970. "Development Decision Making: A Comparative Study in Latin America." *American Journal of Sociology* 75 (March): 828–51.

Walzer, Michael. 1970. "The Obligations of Oppressed Minorities." *Commentary* 49 (May): 71–80.

Wanderer, Jules J. 1970. "Reply to Spillerman's Commentary and Critique." *American Journal of Sociology* 75 (January): 560–61.

Wattenberg, Ben J., and Richard M. Scannon. 1973. "Black Progress and Liberal Rhetoric." *Commentary* 55 (April): 35–44.

Weede, Erich. 1970. "Conflict Behavior of Nation-States." *Journal of Peace Research* 7: 229–35.

Weiss, Thomas G. 1975. "The Tradition of Philosophical Anarchism in Future Directions in World Policy." *Journal of Peace Research* 12: 1–17.

Welch, William. 1971. "Soviet Expansionism and Its Assessment." *Journal of Conflict Resolution* 15 (September): 317–27.

Welfling, Mary B. 1975. "Models, Measurements and Sources of Error: Civil Conflict in Black Africa." *American Political Science Review* 69 (September): 871–88.

Welfling, Mary, and Raymond Duvall. 1973. "Social Mobilization, Political Institutionalization, and Conflict in Black Africa: A Simple Dynamic Model." *Journal of Conflict Resolution* 17 (December): 673–702.

Wells, Alan. 1974. "The Coup d'Etat in Theory and Practice: Independent Black Africa in the 1960s." *American Journal of Sociology* 79 (January): 871–87.

Wences, Rosalio, et al. 1970. "Faculty Opinion on the Issues of Job Placement and Dissent in the University." *Social Problems* 18 (Summer): 27–37.

Wernette, Dee R. 1972. "Creating Institutions for Applying Peace Research." *Journal of Conflict Resolution* 16 (December): 531–38.

Westermeyer, Joseph J. 1973. "Indian Powerlessness in Minnesota." *Society* 10 (March–April): 45–52.

Westhues, Kenneth. 1972. "Hippiedom 1970: Some Tentative Hypotheses." *Sociological Quarterly* 13 (Winter): 81–90.

White, Ralph K. 1971. "Propaganda: Morally Questionable and Morally Unquestionable Techniques." *The Annals* 398 (November): 26–35.

Wilensky, Harold L. 1970. "Intelligence in Industry: The Uses and Abuses of Experts." *The Annals* 388 (March): 46–58.

Wiles, Peter. 1971. "Crisis Prediction." *The Annals* 393 (January): 32–39.

Wilkenfeld, Jonathan, et al. 1972. "Conflict Interaction in the Middle East, 1949–1967." *Journal of Conflict Resolution* 16 (June): 135–54.

Williams, Robin M., Jr. 1972. "Conflict and Social Order: A Research Strategy for Complex Propositions." *Journal of Social Issues* 28: 11–27.

Wilson, John. 1977. "Social Protest and Social Control." *Social Problems* 24 (April): 469–81.

Wilson, Robert. 1971. "Anomie and Militancy among Urban Negroes: A Study of Neighborhood and Individual Effects." *Sociological Quarterly* 12 (Summer): 369–86.

Wilson, William J. 1976. "Class Conflict and Jim Crow Segregation in the Post-Bellum South." *Pacific Sociological Review* 19 (October): 431–46.

Winter, J. Alan. 1970. "On the Mixing of Morality and Politics: A Test of a Weberian Hypothesis." *Social Forces* 49 (September): 36–41.

Wolf, Charles, Jr. 1972. "The Logic of Failure: Vietnam Lesson." *American Behavioral Scientist* 15 (July–August): 927–37.

Wood, James R. 1970. "Authority and Controversial Policy: The Churches and Civil Rights." *American Sociological Review* 35 (December): 1057–69.

Wood, James R. 1972. "Unanticipated Consequences of Organizational Coalitions: Ecumenical Cooperation and Civil Rights Policy." *Social Forces* 50 (June): 512–21.

Worchel, Philip, Philip G. Hester, and Philip S. Kopala. 1974. "Collective Protest and Legitimacy of Authority." *Journal of Conflict Resolution* 18 (March): 37–54.

Worchel, Stephen et al. 1978. "Determinants of the Effect of Intergroup Cooperation on Intergroup Attraction." *Journal of Conflict Resolution* 22 (September): 429–39.

Xydis, Stephen. 1974. "Coups and Counter-Coups in Greece, 1967–1973." *Political Science Quarterly* 89 (Fall): 507–38.

Yalem, Ronald J. 1971. "Controlled Communication and Conflict Resolution." *Journal of Peace Research* 8: 263–72.

Zagorin, Perez. 1973. "Theories of Revolution in Contemporary Historiography." *Political Science Quarterly* 88 (March): 23–52.
Zellentin, Gerda. 1973. "Intersystemic Regionalism and Peace in Europe." *Journal of Peace Research* 10: 235–43.
Zurcher, Louis, and Russell Curtis. 1973. "A Comparative Analysis of Propositions Describing Social Movement Organizations." *Sociological Quarterly* 14 (Spring): 175–87.
Zwerdling, Joseph. 1972. "The Role and Functions of Federal Hearing Examiners." *The Annals* 400 (March): 27–35.

BIBLIOGRAPHIES

Aggarlwal, G. 1977. *Bibliography on War, Peace, and Conflict.* Philadelphia: Peace Science Department, University of Pennsylvania. Unpublished.
Boulding, Elise, ed. 1974. *Bibliography on World Conflict and Peace.* Boulder: Institute of Behavioral Science, University of Colorado. Mimeograph.
Carter, April, et al. 1970. *Nonviolent Action: A Selected Bibliography.* London: Housemans.
Gurr, Ted Robert. 1970. *Why Men Rebel.* Princeton: Princeton University Press, pp. 360–407.
Sharp, Gene. 1971. *Exploring Nonviolent Alternatives.* Boston: Porter Sargent, pp. 133–61.
Wehr, Paul. 1978. *Conflict Regulation.* Boulder, Colo.: Westview Press.

Index

Accommodation mechanisms, 40, 133, 212
Adaptation, 123
Alienation, 42, 47, 54, 56–58, 109–10, 117, 142; components of, 56–57
Anomie, 47, 117, 142

Categories, 37, 53, 58
Cease-fire, 237–38, 246–48
Change, 55, 66, 69–70, 78, 117–18, 132–33, 273
Coalition, 71, 86
Communication, 89–90, 110, 235–39, 242–51, 268–70, 276
Conflict: nature of, 3–26; history of, 3–4; sociology of, 4–5; typology of, 6–11; definition of, 11–17; tactics of, 15–17; legitimacy of, 17–22; in contemporary sociology, 22–26; in the public, 58–60. *See also* Legitimacy
Conflict analysis, 2
Confrontation, 61–62, 90
Consensus, 18, 20, 37, 167–68, 251–56; as dissensus, p. 41
Conspiracy, 8. *See also* Violence, Revolution
Crowd. *See* Riot
Culture. *See* Norms, Values
Custom. *See* Norms

Dysfunctions, 121, 139–43, 279. *See also* Function

Ecology, 134–35
Ethnocentrism, 64–65
Exchange, 235–36, 251–53
Explanation of conflict, 155–56, 190, 196; problem of, 21–22; theories of, 27–37; explanatory model, 37–50; alternative outcomes, 48–50

Force, 236
Frustration-Aggression theory, 33–34, 44; alternative formulations, 34. *See also* Relative deprivation
Functions, 123–43, 279; definition of, 122–23; manifest, 124–27; latent, 127–39; search for, 129; inventories of, 129–32; social change as, 132–33

Ideology, 45, 52, 54, 114, 125, 175–77
Ingroup-Outgroup, 39, 47, 62, 64–65
Instincts, theory of, 28–29
Institution, 40, 138, 212, 218, 228–31, 270
Instrumental conflict, 14, 167–89; and realistic conflict, 167; components of, 167–70; conditions of, 171–77; strategy of, 177–89; strategic models, 179–89
Integration, 41, 55, 136–39
Interaction, 12–13, 17, 35–38, 42–43, 45–47, 51, 63, 77, 236, 238, 248–51
Intermediator, 236–37, 241, 244, 252

Legitimacy, 17–22, 168, 171–77, 221–23, 236, 240–41, 274–76, 280

Management, 22, 166, 281; of power, 83–85; possibility of, 195
Military, 69, 114
Moderates, 239–40
Motivation, 43–45, 117–204

Negotiation, 236–42
Neutrals, 58–60
Nonlegitimacy. *See* Legitimacy
Nonviolence. *See* Violence
Norms, 18, 21, 52–53, 63–66, 110, 113, 117–18, 122, 138–39, 212–13, 223–28; and legitimacy, 18; malintegration of, 41–42

Orientation. *See* Social Policy

Peace, viii, 4–5, 166, 206
Power, 13–16, 21, 36, 38–39, 65, 76–99; perspectives on, 77–79; two faces of, 77; characteristics of, 78; types of, 78–79; resources of, 81–84; implementation, 84–85; Black Power, 85–92; organization of, 91–99; inequitable distribution of, 91–92, 113, 137–39, 173, 197, 260, 272. *See also* Violence
Preconditions of conflict, 39–43, 46
Prediction, 144–66; in social science, 145; definition of, 146–49; alternative definitions of, 146–47; elements of, 148; in the literature, 149–54; predictive strategy, 154–58; in Soweto, 158–64
Prevention: removing causes, 190–211, 275–76; definition, 190–92; agents of, 191–92; illustrations of, 198–202; strategy of, 202–11; investigation of, 206–9; action forms, 209–11; by institutionalization, 212–34; conditions of, 218–20; strategy for, 220–31; issues in, 231–34
Private conflict, 7
Public, the, 58–60
Public opinion, 4, 240, 243

Red Brigades, vii, 85, 145, 173–74
Relative deprivation, 33–36, 43–45, 143, 204
Research, 4–5, 22–23, 47–50, 154–58, 206–9, 228–31, 243–44, 251–53
Resolution, 235–56; variable meanings, 235; definition of, 235–36; as temporary state, 236; of Middle East conflict, 236–38, 242–56; conditions of, 238–42; strategy of, 242–56; formalizing of, 253–56
Resources, 67–68, 80–82, 87, 140–41; of prevention, 197
Revolution, 9, 40, 69, 268
Riots, 6–7, 40, 55, 106, 112–13, 158–64, 171–74, 198–202, 263, 271. *See also* Violence
Roles, 12–13, 53; conflict roles, 61–66, 71; reversal of, 66–68

Scale, 42
Social control, 9–10, 43, 106, 114–15, 121, 173–74, 278
Social movements, 7, 47, 62, 68–71, 137–39
Social organization, 60–61, 68–71, 86, 260, 268; conflict theories of, 133–37. *See also* Structure
Social policy, 21, 43, 52, 115–16, 176–79, 219–20, 242–43, 269, 281–82
Soweto, 158–64
Stalemate, 238, 240, 247
Status, 36, 39, 65, 254–55
Strategy. *See* Instrumental conflict, Prevention, Conflict resolution
Stratification, 53–54, 65, 86, 91–99, 111–19, 273
Strike, 8. *See also* Violence
Structure, 6–11, 14, 37–43, 45–46, 51–75; meanings of, 51; conditions of, 51–58; rigidity of, 54–55; impersonality of, 56–58; complexity of, 57; as publics, 58–60 (*see also* Public opinion); neutrals in, 58–60; implementation, 60–75; conflict structure, 61–66; clustering mechanisms, 71–75, 86–87
Suppression, 257–82; definition of, 257–59; by authoritative groups, 257–58; open pluralistic setting of, 258–59; as counter-conflict, 259; conditions of, 260–64; tactics of, 264–74; success of, 274–75; failure of, 275–76; issues of, 276–82
System, 18, 41, 57, 58, 92, 141, 192–93, 213, 215–18, 233

Tactics, 15–17, 89–90, 178, 224–25, 262–74, 277–80
Tension, 29–30, 45–47, 146–49, 158–64
Termination, 240–47, 274, 279
Tradition. *See* Norm, Culture
Turmoil, 7. *See also* Violence

Values, 13–16, 18–19, 39, 41–42, 53–54, 62–63, 80, 111, 117–18, 139, 145, 174, 192, 239–40, 250–51, 224–25, 261, 278, 281
Violence, 6–19, 21, 45–47, 90, 140, 204–5, 212, 219, 264–66, 273–76;

prevalence, 100–101; perspectives on, 101–2; definition of, 103–4; varieties of, 104–6; legitimacy issues, 106–9; theories of, 109–13; conditions of, 113–18; functions, 118–21; in Middle East, 236–38. *See also* Riot

War, vii, 3–4; civil war, 9; international war, 10–11, 69